PEOPLE AND SOCIETY
IN SCOTLAND

PEOPLE AND SOCIETY IN SCOTLAND

1830–1914

Edited by
W. HAMISH FRASER
and
R. J. MORRIS

A Social History of Modern Scotland

JOHN DONALD
AN IMPRINT OF BIRLINN LTD
EDINBURGH
IN ASSOCIATION WITH
THE ECONOMIC AND SOCIAL HISTORY SOCIETY OF SCOTLAND

Published by
John Donald
an imprint of Birlinn Ltd
8 Canongate Venture
5 New Street
Edinburgh EH8 8BH

ISBN 0 85976 211 4

Reprinted 2000

British Library Cataloguing-in-Publication Data
A catalogue record for this book is available from the British Library

Also in this series:

People and Society in Scotland, I: 1760–1830
edited by T. M. Devine and Rosalind Mitchison

People and Society in Scotland, III: 1914–1990
edited by Tony Dickson and D. H. Treble

Typeset by Quorn selective Repro, Loughborough
Printed and bound by J. W. Arrowsmith Ltd., Bristol

General Introduction

Modern Scottish historical studies have experienced a vigorous phase of unprecedented growth over the last quarter of a century. Scholars are addressing a novel range of issues and themes, fresh perspectives on established topics are common and innovative methods are helping to transform the nature of research investigation. The subject has, in consequence, a new intellectual vitality. Of course, much remains to be done. Indeed, one of the fascinations for the professional historian is that so many key areas still remain unexplored. This contributes both to the challenge and the excitement of ongoing research in the archives and libraries. But substantial advances have already been made in the serious study of Scottish society since the eighteenth century and have produced results which warrant exposure to a wider audience than the readership of learned journals and scholarly monographs.

In 1985 the Economic and Social History Society of Scotland and John Donald Publishers agreed to publish a three-volume social history of Scotland from the middle decades of the eighteenth century to the present day. It is intended that the series should appear over a cycle of three years from 1988. Each volume has two editors and all contributors are recognised authorities in their respective fields. The project as a whole was supervised by an editorial committee appointed by the Society, consisting of T.M. Devine, Chairman (Strathclyde University), Anne Crowther (Glasgow University), T. Dickson (Glasgow College of Technology), W. Hamish Fraser (Strathclyde University), Rosalind Mitchison (Edinburgh University), R.J. Morris (Edinburgh University) and J.H. Treble (Strathclyde University).

The series is intended to appeal to undergraduate and postgraduate students, lecturers, teachers, archivists, museum staff, local historians and others with an interest in the social history of modern Scotland. Each author attempts to convey the results of recent published research while at the same time introducing insights, interpretations and evidence from their own personal investigations. None of the various themes are analysed in an exhaustive fashion but contributors provide in the notes at the end of each chapter references to the most important published work in the relevant field as a guide to further reading. Individual chapters convey something of the vitality of the subject at its present stage of development. Historical analysis inevitably produces variations in opinion, method and conclusion and these are honestly revealed in the different approaches adopted by different contributors. The editors made no attempt to iron out contrasting interpretations of key issues. The resulting volumes are therefore not so much bland textbooks as studies which reveal the 'state of the art' in modern Scottish history.

T.M. Devine
Chairman
Editorial Advisory Committee

The Economic and Social History Society of Scotland

Over the last few years there has been a remarkable increase in both popular interest and serious research in Scottish historical studies. A series of major books has appeared; local history societies are flourishing: museums continue to improve in both quality and quantity; in television and press there is a new fascination with Scotland's history.

The subject is now taught in seven of the eight Scottish universities and curricular changes in school examinations ensure that more attention is devoted than ever before to the study of Scottish historical development. The Economic and Social History Society of Scotland was formed in 1983 to provide a national focus for much of the current research which is being undertaken in this expanding field. Its current membership of around 500 includes professional historians from universities and colleges, schoolteachers, undergraduate and postgraduate students, representatives from local history societies and museums, and members of the public with an interest in Scottish history. Most come from the United Kingdom but there are several also from Australasia, Canada, Europe, Ireland, Japan and the U.S.A. Members automatically receive a copy of the Society's journal, *Scottish Economic and Social History*. The first issue was published in 1981 and annual volumes of approximately 150 pages in length have appeared since then. The journal always includes the following items.

★ Three to four main articles. These are either based on original research or contain critical evaluations of recent work on major themes. In the last four years essays have been published on the Highland Clearances; the Union of 1707; Early Modern Towns; Urban Elites; the Clyde Tobacco Fleet; the Twentieth-Century Economy; Literacy and Education in Scotland.

★ A comprehensive book review section with essays on new publications of general interest and specialised reviews of recent work.

★ An annual *Register of Research* which lists the interests of individuals engaged in serious research in this field.

★ A list of annual publications of both books and articles.

The Society also publishes an annual *Newsletter* with a diary of forthcoming events, conferences and seminars of interest to members. The *Newsletter* in addition provides a focus for correspondence relating to the Society's activities and development.

Among ESHSS's most successful activities are its conferences which are normally held twice a year in different centres throughout Scotland. At each meeting a particular topic is explored in depth with formal lectures combining with panel discussions and workshop sessions. Recent conferences have focused on Women in Scottish Society, Business Elites, Urban History and Unemployment in the Twentieth Century.

In September, 1987, the Society organised its first Residential Conference at the University of Aberdeen on the Society and Economy of the North of Scotland, 1700 to the Present, with sessions on Government and Crofting; Famine; Migration and Emigration; Landlords.

If you are interested in Scottish history or economic and social history and want to keep abreast of developments in the field your modest membership fee will be a worthwhile investment. Applications for membership and further information should be addressed to ESHSS, Department of History, University of Strathclyde, McCance Building, 16 Richmond Street, Glasgow G1 1XQ, Scotland.

Contributors

M. Anderson
Professor in Economic History, University of Edinburgh

Callum G. Brown
Lecturer in History, University of Strathclyde

R.H. Campbell
Professor Emeritus in Economic History, University of Stirling

Helen Corr
Research Fellow in Sociology, University of Edinburgh

M.A. Crowther
Lecturer in Economic History, University of Glasgow

T.M. Devine
Professor in History, University of Strathclyde

W. Hamish Fraser
Senior Lecturer in History and Dean of the Faculty of Arts, University of Strathclyde

Eleanor Gordon
Research Fellow in Economic History, University of Glasgow

Christopher Harvie
Professor in British Studies, University of Tübingen

W. Knox
Lecturer in Scottish History, University of St Andrews

N. Morgan
Lecturer in Scottish History, University of Glasgow

R.J. Morris
Senior Lecturer in Economic and Social History, University of Edinburgh

D.J. Morse
Research Fellow and Academic Computing Officer, Department of Economic and Social History, University of Edinburgh

R.H. Trainor
Senior Lecturer in Economic History, University of Glasgow

J.H. Treble
Lecturer in History, University of Strathclyde

Graham Walker
Lecturer in History, Birkbeck College, University of London

Illustrations

xi

Acknowledgements

We would like to thank Dorothy Kidd, National Museum of Antiquities, Country Life Section; Sara Stevenson, National Galleries of Scotland; and Sophie Leonard, Patrick Geddes Centre, University of Edinburgh, for help in finding illustrations.

W.H.F.
R.J.M.

Contents

INTRODUCTION
Scotland, 1830–1914
The Making of a Nation Within a Nation

R. J. Morris

In 1831, there were 2.4 million people in Scotland. By 1914 there were over 4.8 million, as well as many more in England and beyond who thought of themselves as Scottish. The search for coherence in the experience of those 80 years has always been difficult, especially if a specifically Scottish judgement is sought.

Start with the experience of two men. William Chambers came to Edinburgh on the back of one of those wrecks of domestic order which were characteristic of the economic changes taking place. His father was a cotton manufacturer and agent in Peebles. Economic change drove him into drapery and then bankruptcy. The family came to Edinburgh where father again failed to prosper in the dying hand-loom weaving trade. His son, William, with brother Robert, became a spectacular success in the bookselling, printing and publishing trade. They exploited not only Edinburgh's local resources, its active printing, publishing and literary culture and the local market demand for popular literature and for 'Scottish traditions', but also the skills of a submerged middle class to get credit and use 'domestic connections and conditions'. With the steam press on the supply side and the rational recreation movement on the demand side, the brothers established a publishing empire based upon *Chambers's Edinburgh Journal*. Reading the essays which brother Robert wrote for the early numbers provides a window into the marginal middle classes in which William began his life. William ended life with his statue in Chambers Street, as an improving paternalistic Lord Provost, and Robert in the house he built near St Andrews as he sought 'fresh air and tranquility'. Edinburgh and its Scottish culture was the base from which they gained a national and international market for their products.[1]

Tom Bell was a very different character. Born and bred in Parkhead, then a declining hand-loom weaving and mining village close to Glasgow, he became an ironmoulder in the massive Parkhead Forge which thrived

1

on the markets of war and imperialism. He was drawn into the ILP
in 1900, but eventually, by way of the Scottish Socialist Party, ended
as an activist in the Communist Party of Great Britain in the 1920s.
His part in the engineers' and foundry workers' strike of 1917 made
him a national figure.[2] He shared three crucial experiences with many
other Scottish people. He inherited a radical tradition which included
a respect for and love of reading:

> There were hand loom weavers in our village. . . These old men were
> notorious for their advanced views, and as a boy I frequented their
> shops. . . There was a local lending library in the village established for
> many years by these old radicals. . .

His family lived in squalid physical conditions which led to a collectivism
very different from the networks used by the Chambers brothers. But
above all he had a mixture of anger and pride in his own survival and
endurance when he considered his harsh work environment:

> The conditions under which the moulder worked were vile, filthy and
> insanitary. . . Smoke would make the eyes water. The nose and throat
> would clog with dust. Drinking water came from the same tap as was
> used by the hosepipe to water the sand.
>   Every night pandemonium reigned while the moulds were being cast. The
> yelling and cursing of foremen; the rattle of overhead cranes; the smoke
> and dust illuminated by sparks and flames from the moulten metal made
> the place a perfect inferno. . . All this did not deter me from study.[3]

There is little possibility of finding a balancing duo of women. Scotland
was a male dominated culture. Women like Flora Stevenson emerged from
anonymity because they were determined to exploit to the full the limited
niche which Scottish society allotted to them. More representative was
the experience of two very different women. Mary Barbour was amongst
those who turned the experience of being a 'housewife' in the respectable
skilled working-class and lower middle-class environment of Glasgow into
a powerful political movement. The mixture of poor housing, war, rising
rents, 'socialist' and feminist ideas on education and birth control were
drawn into the rent strike of 1915 and the labour movement which
became part of Scottish character in the twentieth century.[4] Less heroic
but equally representative was Elizabeth, Countess of Sutherland, who
died in 1839 with a reputation that has been one of the most fought over
in Scottish history, but one which tied together landlords and tenants,
economic development and older loyalties, English and Scottish capital,
industrial and landed capital, Scottish poverty with a London-based élite
using the Highlands as a playground. No-one ever spent so much gaining

so much dislike as she pushed the cash economy into the last corners of Scottish society.[5]

Each reader will have his or her own selection for the representative experience, but can we go on and give a general character to these experiences? In our final chapter, Christopher Harvie offers a double challenge. Is it true, as the old nationalists claimed, that Scotland 'vanished' in those years, and must we be left with no central interpretation?

As late twentieth-century Scotland once more reassesses its identity, the process is haunted by the stereotypes of history. The images of earlier centuries are very often episodic tableaux—Bruce, Bannockburn, Queen Mary, the good Prince Charles. Disconnected colour and violence, most were embedded in Scottish consciousness during the period covered by this volume, as they were helped along by Walter Scott, the encyclopaedic Robert Chambers, a dozen 'history' painters and an incipient nationalist movement. This was the period in which Stewart became royal, Prince Charles 'bonnie', and tartan just fun. The experience of industrialisation and urbanisation in the nineteenth century has given modern Scotland a 'character' which is a muted part of the current debate, sometimes imposed, sometimes self-imposed. The Scots are the people of the enlightenment, inheritors of an open democratic educational tradition; and indeed Scotland sends a higher proportion of the 18-plus age group to higher education than any other part of the United Kingdom.[6] The Scots are a sturdy and hardy people who migrated to become founders of new nations, and indeed everyone seems to have a cousin or an uncle in Canada, Australia or New Zealand.[7] The real Scots are hard men, football mad heavy drinkers at leisure and skilled male wage labour at work, the men of a McIlvanney novel.[8] Such men are central to this book, but as the chapters on women and on urbanisation indicate, they were only a part of the story.[9] By the late nineteenth century, Scottish culture had already gained an uneasy position between self-imposed anglicising destruction and assertive renaissance, a land of Burns Suppers, cultural colonialism and books on etiquette which carefully listed 'Scotticisms. Words and Phrases to be avoided'.[10] Scotland was a country with more respect for religion than the English, perhaps a little too much respect. The period confirmed and recreated Scotland as a land with a distinctive legal, religious and political culture. This was the cultural baggage which Scotland brought to the romantic European view of a nation as a cultural community with its own land area, language, customs and history, which originated in the nineteenth century.

The chapters of this book will leave these images battered and transformed, but as is proper with all good myths, never quite destroyed. Most were selections from the truth rather than fabrications. Drawing the conclusions together in a coherent way is much harder. Three general directions do emerge. The first two are contradictory. In this period, Scotland reasserted and recreated a national identity. It was the period in which North Britain disappeared from the map and Scotland returned for good. At the same time anglicisation was powerful and insistent. This contradiction can be resolved by the third and most important of the general observations. Scotland was part of a series of much larger economic and social processes which interacted with the national resources, cultural, social and economic which Scottish people brought into the nineteenth century.

Scotland lay not quite at the centre of a rapidly expanding world capitalist economy. That meant that the fortunes of Scottish people were driven by the search for profit and power in markets linked together by a cash economy. These processes interacted with local and national cultures the world over, hence the mixture of general and specific which fills this volume. Several major strands affected Scotland. Industrialisation was marked by a fall in the percentage of the labour force engaged in agriculture and a rise in that devoted to services and transport. The nature of industrial production itself changed. There were more large units of production which depended upon division of labour and new technologies for their increased productivity. Skills became more specific and less general. A distinctive feature of the Scottish economy was dependence on export markets and by the end of the century on export markets for capital goods. This made Scotland more vulnerable to the competitiveness and the boom and bust fluctuations which characterised the international economy. Scotland was, compared to England, a low-wage and low-wealth economy.[11] The differences were not large, but enough to suggest that Scotland lay at the margin of a larger economic structure. Urbanisation was later and more rapid than in England and the response followed patterns that very often had more in common with Europe than with England. The sense of economic marginality in Scottish history was not just a matter of poverty, with its consequent overcrowding, but also resulted in a lack of opportunity at all levels, leading to huge rates of out-migration. The response from urban and welfare authorities suggested a community that was less well endowed, more authoritarian and more collectivist than in England.[12] The regional structure of Scotland was transformed. Economic specialisation and migration produced a population and economic landscape which lasted into the mid-twentieth century. This regional imbalance had its influence on social structures as varied

as the Labour movement and the organisation of sport. It has also produced strikingly different images and life styles, notably in Highland and
Lowland Scotland. These often conceal the close social and economic
relationships of these two areas. Internal migration, product movements,
the authority and leisure activities of the property owning classes, the
cultural and leisure interests of the middle classes, as well as the growing
power of Edinburgh and London-based state structures like the Education
Department and the Board of Supervision, all tied the fortunes of the two
parts of Scotland closely together. The Report of the Napier Commission
on Crofting was full of evidence from witnesses who linked Highlands
and Lowlands. John Murdoch spoke for the Glasgow Islay Association.
John MacDonald, a shopman who had been 20 years in Glasgow, went
to Lochaline to speak for the people of Morven. 'They would be assisted
by their families in Glasgow; they are all in Glasgow', he said, speaking
of the people left in the parish.[13] Finally, Scotland became a class society.
One set of relationships after another from the factory and the cultivation
of the land to the schoolroom and the factor's knock on the tenement
door depended upon conflict over the control of the means of production
and the distribution of the resulting goods and services. These conflicts
and the identities and organisation which arose from them were closely
related to the division and recreation of gender roles just as they were
in England, but they were also closely involved with growing national
and religious identities in a manner which outsiders found hard to follow. Callum Brown's account of religion is typical of the reassessments
which have to take place. The coming of an urban and industrial class
society did not result in a decline of religion, despite the comments of
preachers like Thomas Chalmers. All the evidence for Scotland points
to the reverse. The great conflict of the 1843 disruption was linked with
quasi-nationalist sentiments in Edinburgh, class conflict in the Highlands
and status conflict in Aberdeen. Some of the reassessments in this book
relate to specifically Scottish issues; others contribute to accounts of much
wider social and economic changes. Some aspects of the story will be
familiar to historians of Wales and Quebec.

The outcome of these processes was the creation of a nation within a
nation, hence the enigmatic answers to questions about the nature of
Scottish social change in this period. Scotland was neither destroyed nor
gained independence. It was recreated as a state with a state; Edinburgh
as a capital without a government. The new administrative structures
of the Board of Supervision and the Scottish Office were added to the
older structures of the Court of Session and the General Assembly.
The Lothians even became a pale reflection of the wealthy economy

with bias towards services which was London and its hinterland.[14] This was Scotland's achievement. It puzzled Unionists and irritated Nationalists but the results are littered all over the modern social and culture landscape of Scotland. The legal and educational systems are still quite distinct. Religious traditions are very different. The Queen still performs the annual miracle of transformation from devout episcopalian to true presbyterian on crossing the border. An English game (soccer) is played within an intensely Scottish organisation.[15] Just as in the nineteenth century, when Scots asserted their political identity by voting for a Liberal Party which was led by an English anglican landowner, with ancestors in Scotland (Gladstone), who came to represent an ideology which was anti-landlord, non-conformist and free-trade, so, in the twentieth century, Scottish political culture asserts independence by voting for a British party (the Labour Party) which was largely founded by Scots who were elected for English constituencies. One of the most potent reminders of the incorporation of the newly remade Scottish identity into a British identity are those terrible memorials to the dead of British imperial wars. From that scarcely medieval castle at Edinburgh to a thousand country churchyards, these memorials were bedecked with thistles and images of kilts and clansmen. The cultural revival of the last twenty years exploits the technology and media of the North Atlantic market system with great gusto but uses perceptions and discoveries of Scotland's past as much as the experience of the present. Bill Bryden's play, *Willie Rough*, (Edinburgh 1972) was an excellent example of this. The folk singing revival depends as much upon historical reference as upon its own creativity.[16] Even in its 'pop' music form groups like Run Rig and the Proclaimers make frequent and often overtly political uses of history in their songs. Recent novels like Alasdair Gray's *Lanark* and Iain McGinness's, *Inner City* are firmly placed in the 1980s but deal with Scottish experience in terms of the subordinations of work and an often incomprehensible urbanisation—two of the strands of Scottish consciousness created in the period covered by this book.

So the outcome was a nation within a nation, a social system that was as much British as Scottish, just as both were part of a larger world system. It was a delicate and potentially explosive product that stabilised somewhere between self-destruction and assertive independence. It is in that almost unique stabilisation of a double and contradictory identity that Scotland's experience can be best understood.

NOTES

1. William Chambers, *Memoir of Robert Chambers, with Autobiographical Reminiscences of William Chambers* (Edinburgh, 1876).

2. Helen Corr, Tom Bell, in William Knox (ed.), *Scottish Labour Leaders, 1918–39* (Edinburgh, 1984).

3. Tom Bell, *Pioneering Days* (London, 1941), pp. 15, 19, 65.

4. Joe Melling, *Rent Strikes. People's Struggle for Housing in West Scotland, 1890–1916* (Edinburgh, 1983), p. 32.

5. Eric Richards, *The Leviathan of Wealth. The Sutherland Fortune in the Industrial Revolution* (London, 1973), pp. 3–18; R. H. Campbell and T. M. Devine, Chapter 2 carries some of these themes forward in time.

6. Helen Corr, Chapter 10 has a critical account of this myth.

7. Migration is an important theme in Chapter 1, M. Anderson and D. J. Morse.

8. William McIlvanney, *Docherty* (London, 1975).

9. See Chapter 10 by Eleanor Gordon and Chapter 3 by R. J. Morris.

10. *How to write English* (John Leng and Co., Dundee, c. 1910).

11. See Chapter 4 by N. Morgan and R. H. Trainor; Chapter 5 by W. Knox; Chapter 6 by J. H. Treble.

12. See M. A. Crowther, Chapter 9.

13. *Royal Commission on the Condition of the Crofters and Cottars of the Highlands of Scotland*, Parliamentary Papers, vol. 35, Q. 36,386.

14. John Langton and R. J. Morris, *Atlas of Industrialising Britain* (London, 1986).

15. See W. H. Fraser, Chapter 8.

16. Nigel Gatherer, *Songs and Ballads of Dundee* (Edinburgh, 1986).

CHAPTER 1
The People

M. Anderson and D. J. Morse

Population Growth and Distribution

In the 76 years between Webster's private census of 1755 and the fourth national census of 1831, the population of Scotland rose by 88 per cent (from about 1.265 million to 2.374 million). In the next eighty years, from 1831 to 1911, the population almost exactly doubled, to 4.761 million. As Figure 1 shows, the rise in numbers, though continuous until after the First World War, was unsteady. In particular, compared with the period as a whole, there was rather slower growth in the 1850s, the 1880s and in the years after 1900. In every decade of the period, Scottish population increase was at a lower rate than that of England and Wales.[1]

Locally within Scotland the growth was even more uneven, a first indication of the marked regional contrasts which are apparent in almost all aspects of Scottish demographic experience in this period. The pattern of broad regional growth, using the six divisions of the country first employed by Michael Flinn and his colleagues, is also shown in Figure 1. This reveals clearly the rapidly rising numbers in the Central Belt (the Eastern and Western Lowlands in the categories used here). Growth was particularly strong in Renfrew, Lanark and Ayr. In 1831, these three 'Western Lowlands' counties contained almost 27 per cent of the population (compared with 21 per cent in 1801) but by 1911 they were home to 46 per cent of the Scottish people. Meanwhile, as the national population rose, the share of the Eastern Lowlands remained almost constant and the share of the North-East fell only slightly. In marked contrast, the Highlands and the Far Northern counties, which had had 17 per cent of the national population in 1831, had a mere 7 per cent by 1911. The relative share of the Borders also fell, by nearly half, to 5.5 per cent.[2]

In absolute terms, the contrasts were even more dramatic. The swathe of Border counties from Berwick to Wigtown all saw their populations rise until some point between 1851 and 1891. Thereafter, decline set in, and, in spite of the expansion of some of their urban centres, all but Roxburgh contained smaller numbers of people in 1911 than in 1831

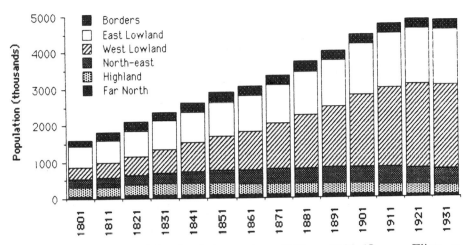

Figure 1. Population of Scotland, by region, 1801 to 1931 (*Source*: Flinn *et al.*: *Scottish Population History*, Table 5.1.3).

(the average decline across the five counties as a whole was about 4 per cent). In the North-East, from Nairn round to Kincardine, the pattern across the period was a mixture of slow growth and intermittent stagnation, producing an overall average growth of about 55 per cent over the 80 years. Elsewhere in the North (with the exception of Ross and Cromarty, where the pattern was affected by the continued growth of the Outer Isles) and right down through Perthshire and into Argyll, the pattern at county level was one of early peak (in the case of Argyll and Perthshire as early as 1831) and then of significant decline. Overall, the total population of these counties fell by about an eighth between 1831 and 1911. At the other extreme lay the counties in what now became the dominant manufacturing and mining centre of the country. The populations of Angus, Clackmannan and Fife, and of Midlothian, Renfrew and Stirling, all more than doubled. The populations of West Lothian and of Selkirk more than trebled, while Dunbarton's population grew more than four times and Lanarkshire increased its numbers by a massive 356 per cent. Throughout the country, and partly in association with these changes, the urban proportion in the population also rose.[3]

Although most discussion has in the past been conducted at the regional or county level, there are several important patterns in the changes that can only be identified if one goes below this level of analysis. Map 1 shows the changes between 1831 and 1911, using data either for individual civil parishes, or, where parish boundaries changed, small groups of parishes.[4]

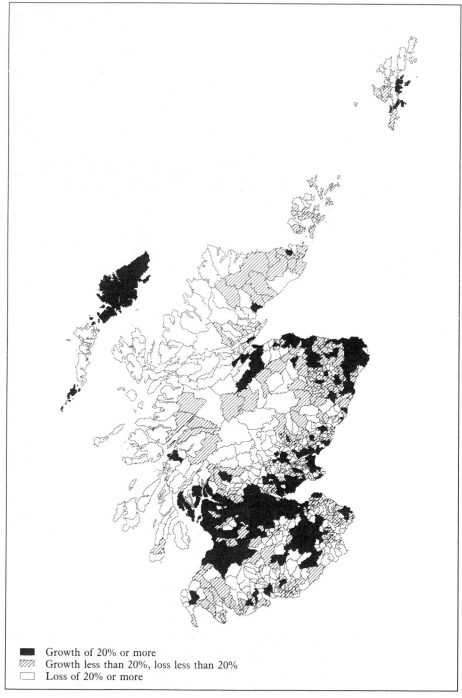

Growth of 20% or more
Growth less than 20%, loss less than 20%
Loss of 20% or more

Map 1. Percentage Population Change, 1831–1911

1. The nineteenth century was a world full of children. Several of Patrick Geddes's photographs show them in the threatening world of Edinburgh's crowded and unhealthy tenements. This group is in St Ann's playground by the Cowgate. *Patrick Geddes Centre, Edinburgh.*

It shows clearly that the changes in population distribution did not just result from a shift of population from the Highlands to the commercial, manufacturing and mining counties of the central belt. Rather, in almost every part of the country there were some places where populations rose between 1831 and 1911, and many where they fell, often dramatically (and in some cases as a continuation of a process that had already begun in the second half of the eighteenth century). Particularly important is the clear demonstration that depopulation was a chronic feature of significant parts of all rural areas of Scotland except the North-East. The experience of the Highlands and Islands, whatever their unique cultural and tenurial features, was demographically just part of a much more general Scottish (and indeed in many ways British) picture. The Highland area was only special to the extent that the populations of many areas in the West showed a more general and rapid rise rather than fall in the later eighteenth century, and because the nineteenth century fall in population in some areas, when and where it came, was rather earlier and more rapid than elsewhere.[5]

Natural Increase

Differences between areas in the directions and rates of population change
are the result of differences in the balance between their birth rates and
death rates, and in the balance between inmigration and outmigration
of their populations. Precise and reliable data on the factors involved
are only available from 1861 (when for the first time census data can be
combined with material from vital registration which began in 1855).
Thereafter, however, the Scottish micro-level data are among the best
in Europe because data on populations, on births, deaths and marriages,
and, from 1881, on age, sex and marital status distributions, are published
at parish level.[6]

In terms of overall population change, before 1855 there are only very
tentative clues available. Taking the national level first, there seems to
have been a severe check to growth in the 1830s and 1840s through a
temporary rise in the death rate; this is explored further in a later section.
The 1840s and 1850s also saw significant immigration from Ireland, but
this was more than offset by emigration of native Scots, a movement
which, as is discussed further below, seems to have been particularly
focused on younger men. Figure 2 shows how from the 1860s there was
almost continuous slow decline in the death rate (from 22 per thousand
population in the 1860s to 15 per thousand between 1910 and 1914).
Meanwhile, the birth rate fell gently from 35 per thousand in the 1870s
to about 30 per thousand around 1900, and then declined more steeply

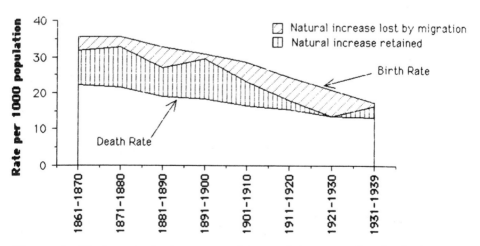

Figure 2. Birth and death rates and natural increase, Scotland, 1861 to
1939 (*Source*: Mitchell and Deane, *Abstract of British Historical Statistics*,
pp. 31–2, 3–7).

towards a low point of 18 per thousand in 1938. The difference between the birth and death rates gives a measure of the 'natural increase' in the population, and this remained high right up to World War I. Figure 2 also shows how at certain periods most of this natural increase was eroded by net emigration (to a point where in the 1920s the population actually fell by 0.8 per cent, in spite of a natural increase of 7.2 per cent in the period).[7]

Regionally, the pattern was one of very considerable diversity in all the components of population change. As Map 2 shows, substantial variation in natural increase was already present by the 1860s. In particular the low rate of natural increase in the whole north-western mainland is clear, and this pattern of somewhat constrained natural growth spread by the early twentieth century to the whole of the rural fringe of the country. Other points to be noted are the contrast between the Outer Hebrides (especially Lewis) and the remainder of the North-West, the continued buoyancy of population in the North-East, and the high natural increase recorded, not only in the mining areas, but also in much of the textile-dominated borders. The next sections explore each of the components of natural increase in turn and seek to explain some of these contrasting patterns of growth.

Migration, Immigration and Emigration

As Figure 2 makes clear, nationally the most important short run variable in Scottish population growth in this period was the fluctuating balance between immigration and emigration. Scotland's higher rate of emigration is also the main reason why her population grew more slowly than that of England and Wales throughout the period. Unfortunately, for most of our period, it is very difficult to discuss the details of immigration and emigration with any degree of precision. There are no reliable figures on total immigration, and, though attempts to collect information on numbers going overseas from Scottish ports began on a systematic basis in 1825, the returns are very incomplete and exclude in particular the not insubstantial numbers who left Britain from ports in other parts of the United Kingdom. Reform of the statistics in 1853 allows us to distinguish for the first time emigrants of Scottish origin, and the figures gradually became more comprehensive and complete as the century proceeded. In 1895 for the first time it becomes possible to identify returning emigrants, and it is only from that date that we can estimate with reasonable accuracy the real net effect of emigration on Scottish population change. The data plotted in Figure 3 are thus no

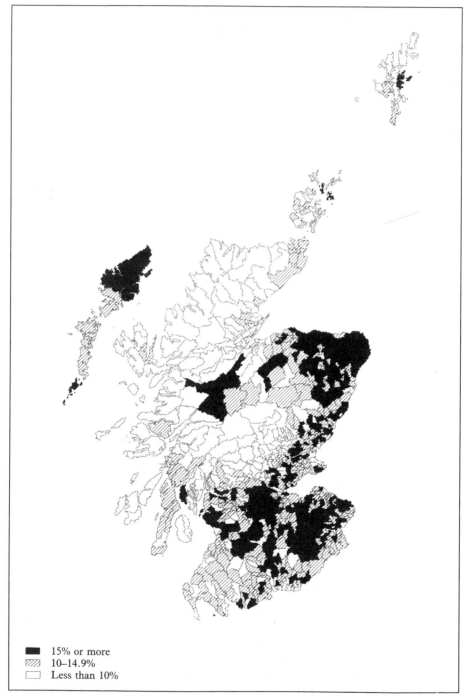

Map 2. Natural Increase (Per cent of Population), 1861–1871

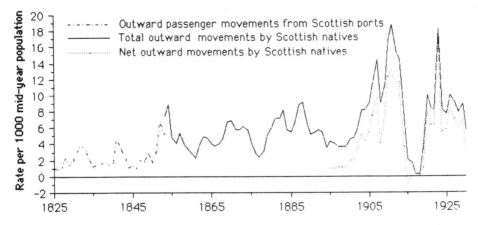

Figure 3. Overseas emigration from Scotland, 1825 to 1930 (*Source*: D. Baines, *Migration in a Mature Economy*, Appendixes 3, 5).

more than indications of the broad patterns of fluctuation and medium term trend in numbers of migrants.[8]

In aggregate, and allowing for omissions from the statistics, it seems that not far short of two million people left Scotland for overseas destinations between 1830 and 1914. This probably places Scotland in second place after Ireland in a European league table of proportion of population involved in emigration overseas, and it implies a gross emigration rate of around one and a half times that of England and Wales. As Figure 3 shows, Scottish emigration, like that of most of the rest of Europe, was characterised by fluctuations throughout the period, but it reached extremely high levels between 1906 and 1913. In 1906–7 and again between 1909 and 1913 more than one Scot in a hundred was sailing overseas *in each year*. In the years 1904–13 the total outflow exceeded 600,000 people, the equivalent of almost thirteen per cent of the 1911 Scottish population.

Up to the early 1840s, the outflow was strongly focused on Canada, a destination which again became fashionable in the years preceding the First World War (though by this date many were using it as a back door to the United States). Australia and New Zealand briefly flourished as attractions in the gold rush of the early 1850s and took a high proportion of emigrants in the low emigration years in the early 1860s and again in the late 1870s. There was a significant movement to South Africa around the turn of the century. Otherwise, the United States was the predominant destination, the immediate target of just under half of all emigrating Scots between 1853 and 1914.[9]

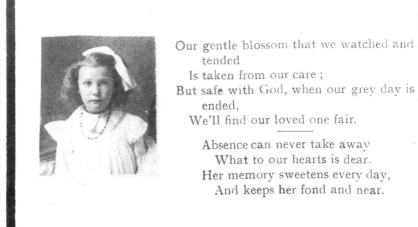

Our gentle blossom that we watched and
    tended
Is taken from our care ;
But safe with God, when our grey day is
    ended,
We'll find our loved one fair.
———
Absence can never take away
    What to our hearts is dear.
Her memory sweetens every day,
    And keeps her fond and near.

2. The high rates of child mortality were only just beginning to decline at the end of the century. This funeral card was one way in which one family faced the relentless distress and threat which the statistics represent. It came from Brechin in 1918. *Scottish Ethnographic Archive, National Museums of Scotland.*

Estimates of gross emigration overseas provide a rather misleading picture of the demographic impact of migration flows. They ignore the significant numbers of overseas migrants who returned to Scotland after spending a period of time abroad. They also ignore the substantial movements taking place between the countries of the United Kingdom (and also, for most of the period, the relatively small flows to and from continental Europe). Before 1895 it is not possible to estimate the quantitative impact of return migration from overseas, but it was clearly substantial, though highly variable. In the later 1890s, as is clear from Figure 3, net emigration was only about a quarter of the gross figures, but the reverse migration rates for the middle of the century seem to have been much lower than this (the high 1890s figures probably reflect the return, at a period when outward sailings were markedly depressed, of substantial numbers of those who had left in the peak years of the 1880s). Certainly, from 1901 to 1914 the gap between net and gross figures was much smaller than in the 1890s. Overall it seems likely that around one-third of those who left sooner or later returned. Even on a net basis, however, the demographic effect of emigration was substantial; the total loss to countries overseas in the years 1901–14 must have been

3. Many sought consolation in a 'decent' burial. These often spectacular funerals were evidence of the affection and respect of family and friends. William Baillie plied his trade at 24 Sciennes, Edinburgh, in the 1890s. *Scottish Ethnographic Archive, National Museums of Scotland.*

over 450,000—an average rate of around 7 per cent of the population per decade.

Estimating movement within the United Kingdom is a much more hazardous task. One plausible estimate suggests that, allowing for return migration, about 600,000 Scots-born persons moved to England, Wales and Ireland in the years 1841 and 1911. If this figure is as reliable as it seems to be, this would suggest that emigration to other parts of the United Kingdom must have been about half of the total net emigration from Scotland in the second half of the nineteenth century. Up to the middle of the century, this movement was heavily focused on London and the south-east of England, and on Lancashire. It particularly involved young single men and contained a markedly disproportionate number of the most educated and to some extent skilled section of the population. From the 1870s there is more evidence of movement into mining and heavy industry areas of England and Wales, and after 1900 the share of all migrants going to England and Wales fell markedly, to around a fifth.[10]

On the other side of the balance there was a steady and slowly growing influx into Scotland of people born in England and Wales, though this

4. Scottish nineteenth-century population was shaped by the massive emigration of young people, especially males. Here is one of them, 'Robbie the Sheep-shearer', Robert Harper of Caithness who turned up in Patagonia in 1908. *Scottish Ethnographic Archive, National Museums of Scotland.*

never matched the southward flow. Nevertheless, the English-born (who were particularly concentrated in the cities) made up 1.5 per cent of the Scottish population in 1841, and 3.5 per cent in 1911. This implies a total immigration over the period of perhaps a quarter of a million persons. There was also a significant influx of people from continental Europe from the 1880s to the early 1900s; this must have brought over 25,000 additional immigrants into the country, especially from Italy, Russia, Poland and the Baltic areas.[11]

The most important immigrant flow came from Ireland. Estimates, especially for the earlier part of the period, are made problematical by the high level of seasonal migration, but the Irish-born already made up nearly 5 per cent of the Scottish population at the 1841 census. Ten years later, the disaster of the Potato Famine had increased the Irish proportion to over 7 per cent and the Irish-born total to over 200,000: a 90 per cent increase over the 1841 figure. In 1851 almost 19 per cent of the Dundee population and 18.2 per cent of Glasgow's were natives of Ireland. Thereafter, the rate of Irish immigration slowed, and in both the 1880s and the 1900s there was probably net emigration of Irish-born persons from Scotland. Even so, the total net immigration from Ireland into Scotland between 1831 and 1914 must have exceeded a third of a million. However, even when this is taken into account, the total net Scottish loss of population through emigration over this period was around one million; this is a substantial figure if one bears in mind that the total population in 1911 was under five million.[12]

Migration also played a key role in the pattern of population changes within Scotland. There was a great deal of seasonal and other short-term movement, particularly by Highlanders (of both sexes) who worked in the fisheries or went south and east, to work in the potato, green vegetable, and grain fields of the Lowlands. In addition, there were substantial more enduring net outflows at the regional level, and these were extraordinarily widespread and persistent — certainly after the 1850s. Except for the Western Lowlands in the 1860s, 1870s and 1890s, all of Flinn's regions saw net out-migration at every intercensal period between 1861 and 1911. In no decade was the outflow in the Far North less than 10 per cent of the population, and it exceeded 10 per cent of the population in the Highlands in the 1860s, in the North-East in the 1880s and 1900s, and in the Borders in the 1860s, 1880s and 1890s. Even the cities were at times unable to provide enough opportunities to retain all their natural increase of population. There was net outflow from Glasgow in the 1870s, from Dundee in the 1880s, from Dundee and Glasgow in the 1890s, and from all four cities in the 1900s, when the average loss was almost eight per cent.[13]

But it is at the parish level that the full extent of population outflow can be observed. Map 3 shows the levels of net in- and out-migration by parish for the 1860s; this pattern seems to have continued throughout most of the century. The map shows clearly how, in the 1860s, the vast proportion of parishes in all parts of the country were experiencing net outmovement of population, with especially heavy losses in most of the south-west and on the east side of the country from Berwickshire to Moray. The few centres of attraction of population were almost entirely concentrated in the textile areas of the Borders and parts of the central belt.

Before the 1860s we cannot identify population outflow so precisely, but, even if we assume that population loss occurred from every parish with a population growth of less than 10 per cent per decade (and this, especially outside the Highlands, is almost certainly a significant under-estimate), it is the geographical spread of areas of out-migration which is striking. Map 4 shows this pattern for the 1830s. More detailed

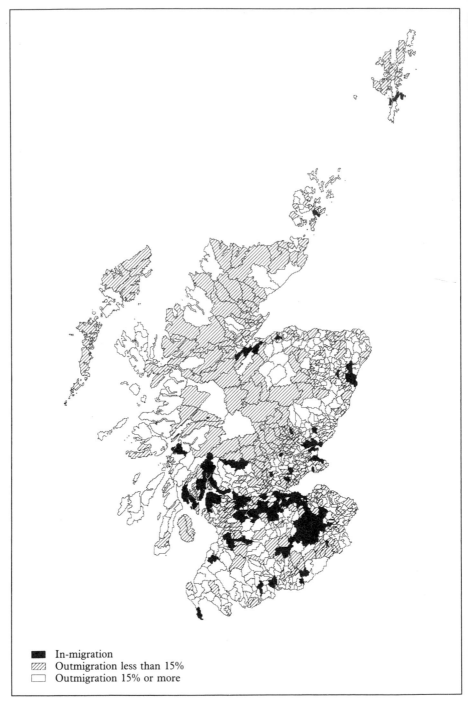

Map 3. Net Migration (Per cent of Population), 1861–1871

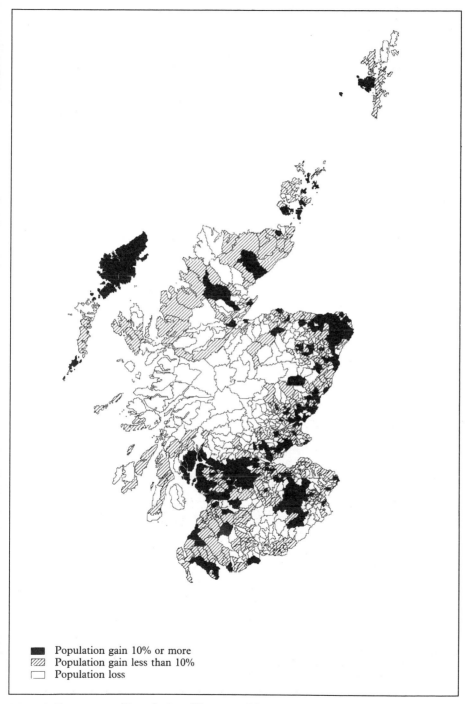

Map 4. Percentage Population Change, 1831–1841

examination of the data reveals that significant inflow was only occurring on a wide scale in Forfar, Selkirk and Peebles, parts of Fife, a few parishes in Aberdeenshire, and in Ayrshire and the west central belt. The conclusion must be that almost the whole of rural Scotland (and many of the more industrial and commercial areas also) were, throughout our period, unable to provide enough opportunities at home to absorb even quite modest rates of population growth. The implications of this for our understanding of the workings of Scottish economy and society are clearly profound.

Comparison of population age structure at successive censuses allows us to gain a reasonable picture of the age groups most involved in migrations of this kind. They show that by far the largest proportion of out-migration and emigration took place between the ages of 15 and 25; this was particularly the case for males, with young men leaving home to enter farm service or industrial apprenticeship or other juvenile employment, changing employers and frequently community of residence often on a six-monthly or yearly basis, searching out employment and residential niches in a varied and changing society. Even in relatively good years like the 1870s, more than a quarter of boys aged 15–19 at the start of the decade had left by its end from the Highlands and Islands, from the North-East, and from the South-West; more than a fifth had gone from the Borders; one in ten had left the country altogether. But in the 1850s the outflow was far more dramatic. In the early 1850s, rural depression in the aftermath of the potato failure of the 1840s coincided with a sluggish Scottish urban economy and the glittering attractions of gold discoveries and other opportunities overseas. In these years 24 per cent of the young men who had been in their late teens in 1851 left Scotland. The loss of young men between 1851 and 1861 was higher than between 1911 and 1921, years that had included the massive mortality of the First World War. In the 1850s, of all the counties of Scotland, only West Lothian saw net in-migration of men from this 15–19 age group, while 22 counties, including almost all those with any significant high ground, saw losses of one-third or more.

Mortality

No precise information on the trends and patterns of mortality in Scotland is available before the start of civil registration in 1855. It seems very likely, however, that the early years of the nineteenth century saw the national death rate at a lower level than it had been fifty years earlier or, indeed, than it was to be again until well after the middle of the century. The

5. The effect of migration on Scottish consciousness and culture is so universal it is scarcely reflected upon. Here is a medallion presented to W. Grant who left Carrbridge, Inverness-shire in 1910 for New Zealand. *Scottish Ethnographic Archive, National Museums of Scotland.*

crisis years of 1739–41 had been followed nationally by a sustained fall in both the severity and frequency of violent surges in mortality from hunger and disease, though local problems still continued, especially in the Western Highlands. Following the devastating crop failures of 1782, famine had only been avoided in the north-east by the prompt and concerted efforts of the landowners, and there was real hunger and some death from starvation in parts of the Highlands. Thereafter, until the 1840s, Scotland was freed from the threat of actual starvation, and the introduction first of inocculation and especially of vaccination, after 1803, produced a major reduction (at least in the short term) in the numbers dying from smallpox, a disease which had previously been the cause of about 15 per cent of all deaths.[14]

The good years did not last. A serious and lethal epidemic of measles in 1807–8 was followed in 1818–19 by another, accompanied this time by whooping cough and typhus. Worse still was to come. Cholera struck for the first time in 1831–2, killing perhaps 10,000 people, and it returned with almost equal severity in 1848–9. The third attack in 1853–4 was somewhat less lethal, and the final, in 1866–7, made little impact on the national death rates, though, like its predecessors, it caused widespread alarm. Meanwhile, the cities had been struck by two great epidemics of typhus. The first, in 1836–7, pushed Glasgow mortality some 60 per cent above its normal level, while the second, in 1846–7, temporarily doubled mortality in the city. Both epidemics hit many other urban areas as well, and in doing so severely accentuated a more general crisis in urban mortality, to which overcrowding, lack of effective sanitation, chronic poverty and the general dislocation caused by the panic migration in the aftermath of the potato failure in Ireland and in the Highlands of Scotland, all contributed in these years.

After 1849, devastating years of national crisis disappeared, though it was some time before mortality began to return to the levels of the beginning of the century, and it was not until the 1870s that the national death rate began a sustained decline. The crude death rate averaged 21.5 per 1000 living the for the years 1860–62 and 22.3 for 1870–72. Thereafter it fell to 19.7 for 1880–82, 17.9 for 1900–02 and 15.2 for 1910–12, a fall of 29 per cent in fifty years. By 1930–32 it was down to 13.4. More striking still were the regional and urban–rural contrasts in this decline, though absolute precision here is somewhat inhibited by boundary changes and by alterations in 1871 and in 1910 in the ways that data were presented. Figure 4 is derived from the extensive work of Michael Flinn and his colleagues, and circumvents the worst of these

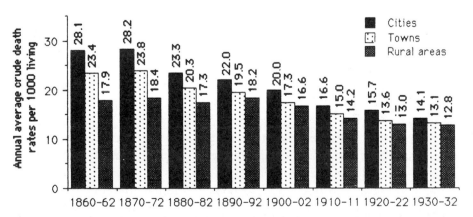

Figure 4. Crude death rates by settlement size, 1860–2 to 1930–2 (*Source*: Flinn *et al.*, Table 5.5.6).

problems. The graph clearly shows how in the early 1860s the crude death rate for the four cities was significantly (20 per cent) above the rate for 'towns' (settlements with populations of over 5,000 people) and very clearly (57 per cent) above the rate for rural areas. By 1910–12, city crude death rates were just 11 per cent above those of the 'towns'. More significantly, the city rates were only 17 per cent worse than those of the rural areas. Over the fifty-year period the fall in crude mortality had been 41 per cent for cities and 36 per cent for towns, but only 21 per cent for rural areas.

As we shall see below, some of these absolute and relative changes in crude rates were results of changing age structures in the different regions (in particular, the declining share of infants and small children in the overall population, and the increasing average age of rural communities, especially in the Highlands and the North). Alongside this went a corresponding concentration in the urban areas of younger adults (who had much lower mortality than the population as a whole). Other factors were also involved. A preliminary view can be obtained from Figure 5, which has been derived from annual averages of the three earliest and the three latest years in which the Registrar-General produced data on a comparable basis. It shows that, compared with rural areas on the mainland, the male death rate of the 'Principal Towns' (those with populations in excess of 25,000 people) showed a significantly greater

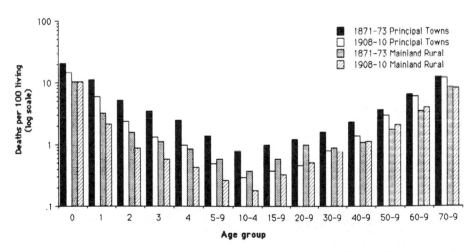

Figure 5. Male death rates in urban and rural districts, 1871 to 1873 and 1908 to 1910 (*Source: Detailed Annual Reports* of the Registrar-General for Scotland for 1871–73 and 1908–10).

tendency to fall at all ages under seventy, and a very marked tendency to fall much faster at all ages under fifty. Indeed, in the mainland rural areas any major fall in mortality was only apparent at ages between one and twenty-nine years. In absolute terms the urban changes were especially important among younger children, and especially among infants under the age of one. The 'Principal Towns' infant mortality rate fell from 161 per 1,000 live births in 1871–3 to 126 in 1908–10, while the rate for the rural areas actually rose slightly from 86 to 88 per 1,000 births.[16]

Of special importance in a country where most of the larger centres of population continued to expand at a rapid rate, was the fact that the fall in mortality was particularly noticeable in the cities and in some of the larger towns. Thus, the crude death rate in Glasgow, which had been 38 per cent above the national average in 1871–3 fell by 41 per cent to be only 14 per cent higher than the national figure in 1908–10. At the same time Glasgow's infant mortality rate fell from 172 per 1,000 live births to 130 (the national average figures for the two dates were 126 and 112). Even Dundee, where infant and child mortality remained at an appallingly high level (infant mortality was still 154 per thousand in 1908–10) saw a significant improvement in its death rate at most ages. Overall, there was a 29 per cent reduction in Dundee's crude death rate in these years.[17] Indeed, as Figures 6 and 7 show, by the end of the century it was not the largest cities which had the highest death rates. As early as the 1860s, Dundee, Aberdeen and Edinburgh, when compared with many of the smaller towns, had managed to get their death rates under a significant measure of control. When Glasgow began to catch up (as it did from the 1880s), it was places like Ayr, Coatbridge and Dumfries, and above all Montrose and Stirling, which had the worst mortality rates in the country.[18]

As elsewhere in Europe, the most significant element in this decline in mortality was changes in deaths from a quite limited number of infectious diseases. Reduction in deaths from the common diseases of childhood and from tuberculosis was particularly important. Between 1861–1870, and between 1911–1920, the crude death rate fell from 22.0 per 1,000 living to 15.2 per 1,000. The tuberculosis death rate fell from 3.6 per 1,000 to 1.6 per 1,000, and the share of tuberculosis in total mortality fell from 16.4 per cent of all deaths, to 10.3 per cent. The combined death rate for smallpox, measles, scarlet fever, whooping cough and diphtheria and croup fell from 2.8 per 1,000 to 0.9 per 1,000 and the share of these diseases in the total from 12.7 per cent to 5.9 per cent. Deaths from the typhus group of fevers almost disappeared, and mortality from diseases of the digestive system, and especially from the diarrhoeal

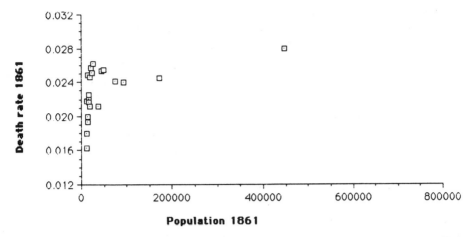

Figure 6. Death rates by population, urban centres, 1861 (*Source: Detailed Annual Reports* for 1861 and 1901).

group of diseases, also fell; in total, death rates from these groups of conditions fell from 3.2 per 1,000 to 1.1 per 1,000. After the 1870s, deaths from respiratory disorders (especially bronchitis) also fell, but the death rate from cancer and from heart and circulatory diseases rose significantly.[19]

Recent work on other parts of Europe has suggested that an understanding of the nineteenth century mortality decline requires a

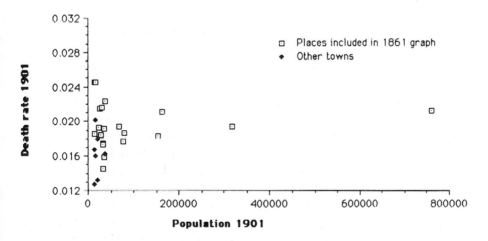

Figure 7. Death rates by population, urban centres, 1901 (*Source: Detailed Annual Reports* for 1861 and 1901).

clear perception of the relative importance of urban–rural variability in mortality patterns, of changes in the age structure of the population and in the incidence of death at different ages, and of variation in the impact of particular diseases. Figures 8 and 9 show the contribution to the overall death rate of some of the main causes of death at different ages. Contrasts are drawn between principal towns and mainland-rural areas. The figures are averaged across the first three and the last two years in which the Registrar-General used consistent area groupings. The data are confined to males to control for gender differences. Most importantly of all, all four graphs are standardised to a single population age structure — that of the principal towns for 1871–3. This last factor is of more importance than is usually credited to it. The crude death rates for the principal towns fell from 29.7 to 17.5 between the early 1870s and 1909–10. Crude rates for the mainland-rural areas fell from 17.4 to 14.4 over the same period. However, the standardised figures for principal towns moved much less (from 29.7 to 19.5) and for the rural areas the age-adjusted figures were 14.8 and 12.1. Overall, the standardised principal towns rate fell by 34 per cent over the period (compared with 19 per cent for the rural areas). The 1871–3 principal town rate was almost exactly double that of the rural areas, but their 1909–10 rate was only 61 per cent higher.[20]

Examination of Figures 8 and 9 shows clearly the age pattern of mortality, with high but falling infant and child deaths in the towns, and lower but more stable figures in rural areas. For the groups between the ages of five and 29 years there were significant reductions in both urban and rural areas, but among those in middle age the main changes again occurred in the towns. Little difference is observable among older age groups. The principal identified factor in the higher urban mortality at the older ages comes at both periods from a marked excess in deaths from respiratory conditions (and especially from bronchitis, a condition which is also a major factor in excess mortality among the middle aged). In the early 1870s, the high incidence of mortality from smallpox in what were European epidemic years is expected. The concentration of this mortality in young adulthood, however, must mean that much of the resurgence in the disease resulted either from a loss of immunity due to failure to re-vaccinate or, perhaps equally likely, given the geographical incidence of the cases revealed by more detailed research, the result of immigration of unvaccinated young men from Ireland in these age groups. The importance of high levels and significant declines in lung tuberculosis among young men in both urban, and especially rural areas, is to be noted. The significance of deaths from typhus and enteric fever

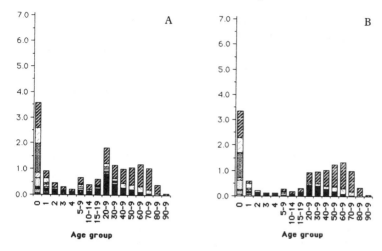

Figure 8. Contribution to overall death rate of some of the main causes of death at different ages in mainland rural areas, (A, From 1871 to 1873; B, From 1908 to 1910 (*Source: Detailed Annual Reports* for 1871 to 1873 and 1909 to 1910). For further details see text.

other
respiratory
infancy
other tubercular
diarrhoeal
typhus/enteric
diptheria
scarlatina
smallpox
whooping cough
measles
phthisis

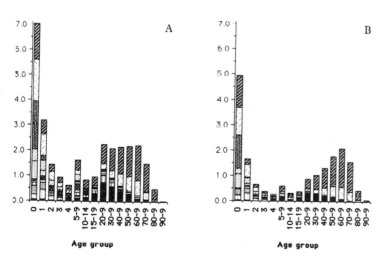

Figure 9. Contribution to overall death rate of some of the main causes of death at different ages in the principal towns, A, From 1871 to 1873; B, From 1909 to 1910 (*Source: Detailed Annual Reports* for 1871 to 1873 and 1909 to 1910). For further details see text.

in young urban adults shows how late typhus proper remained a major killer disease among sections of the urban poor.

At the younger age groups, the enormous mortality from respiratory disease (especially from bronchitis) and from congenital conditions and 'premature debility' in infancy is to be noted. Contrasts and changes in conditions directly affected by contamination of food or water are seen to be significant — note the role of non-lung tuberculosis and gut diseases — but less so than other factors, suggesting that administrative control may have been less important in this period than differences in exposure to infection, variations in physical condition at birth and nutritional state of babies and/or mothers, and contrasts and developments in child care and maternal support services. These all require further research that is only just getting under way. The significance for children (especially in the towns) of the probably spontaneous decline in the lethality of scarlatina may also be noted.

Expectation of Life

The impact of these changes on expectation of life at birth and on numbers surviving to particular ages is shown for Scotland as a whole in Table 1.[21] While survival to first birthday was not greatly affected nationally (in great part because of the increasing concentration of infants in the high death rate towns), the improvement among children and younger adults was marked.

Table 1. Expectation of Life at Birth and Survivors, 1871 and 1910–12

	Males		Females	
Percentage surviving to age	1871	1910–12	1871	1910–12
1	86.0	88.1	87.9	90.3
5	74.5	82.1	76.0	84.5
25	63.1	78.2	64.2	78.7
65	28.0	40.9	32.8	46.7
Expectation of life at birth	39.8	50.1	42.1	53.2
Percentage dying between ages				
0 and 1	14.0	11.9	12.1	9.7
1 and 5	13.4	6.9	13.5	6.5
5 and 25	15.2	4.7	15.5	6.8
25 and 65	55.6	47.6	48.9	40.6

The Age Structure of the Population

As Figure 10 shows, both in 1851, when for the first time we can obtain reasonably reliable data on the age structure of the Scottish population, and in 1911, the population remained young, and there was a significant excess of females.[22] The effects on the age structure of the declining birth rate were largely offset by the falling death rate, so that, in 1911, 32 per cent of the population were still under 15 years of age and 52 per cent under 25; the figures for 1851 had been 36 and 56 per cent; 5.4 per cent of Scots were aged 65 years and over in 1911, compared with 4.7 per cent in 1851.

The continuing excess drain of males through emigration, together with the higher male death rates at most ages, meant that there were always excess females at all adult ages. At one extreme, at the principal marriage ages of 25–29 years in 1861, there were only 77 men for every hundred women. As Figure 11 shows, thereafter the imbalance tended to lessen in every part of the country, at least up to 1901, though only in the Western Lowlands did the sex ratio even approach parity before 1911. In the Borders there were consistently fewer than 80 men per 100 women throughout the period.

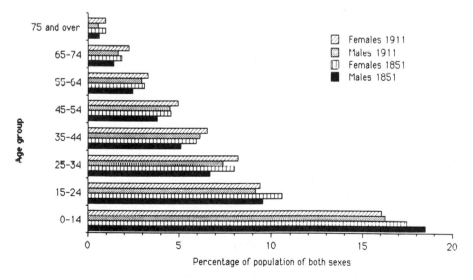

Figure 10. Age and sex structure of the population, 1851 and 1911 (*Source: Censuses of Population*, 1851 and 1911).

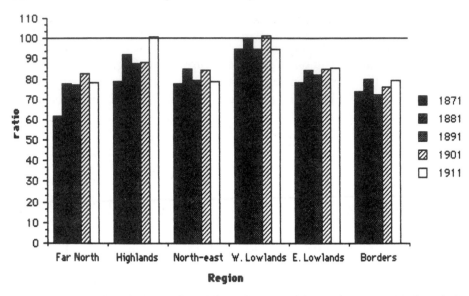

Figure 11. Regional sex ratios, 25 to 29-year-olds (males per 100 females) (*Source*: Flinn *et al.*, Table 5.2.2).

Nuptiality and Fertility

In the remainder of the chapter we return to two questions which have been briefly touched on above. Firstly, how do we explain the changes in the Scottish birth rate which, having (so far as we are aware) been fairly stable at around 35 per 1000 population from the 1830s to the late 1870s, then fell steadily to 25.4 per 1000 for the years 1911–15 (it was 17.7 per 1000 in 1936–39 and only 10.4 per 1000 in 1980–82). Secondly, what was the contribution made by differences in the birth rate to the marked regional differences in the patterns of natural increase noted above?

A pronounced and sustained decline in the birth rate in this period was by no means unique to Scotland. Europe as a whole went through what has become known as 'demographic transition', involving a historically unprecedented shift from a high fertility, high infant mortality régime, to one in which low fertility and low mortality were the norm. In Scotland, as elsewhere in Europe, this demographic transition was a fertility-led process; family size did not primarily fall in response to lower infant mortality, but fell before or in tandem with it.[23] Given this, there are three areas which require investigation as possible contributory factors in the birth rate decline: a fall in the level of fertility outside marriage (illegitimate fertility); a reduction in the proportions married and/or a change in the average age at marriage; and limitation of births within marriage (legitimate fertility).

Illegitimate Fertility

A stormy debate ensued when it was reported in The *Scotsman* in 1860 that the Scottish illegitimacy ratio was the second highest only to Austria in Europe: 'the average annual number of births . . . amounted, as nearly as possible, to 9 per cent [of all births]'.[24] In fact — as was rapidly realised — in many European countries the number of births occurring outside wedlock was undercounted, and Scotland's nine per cent put her in the lower half of Europe's illegitimacy league.[25] By the First World War, the national rate was down to 7.3 per cent.

However, behind the national average lay some striking and persistent regional differences, and this provoked further contemporary argument as to why illegitimacy should be higher in some areas than others. In 1855–60, the percentage of births illegitimate in the north-easterly county of Banffshire was 15.4. In the South-West, 13.8 per cent of births in Wigtownshire occurred outside marriage. Illegitimacy remained at around these levels in both these counties throughout our period. In some parishes in these areas the rates were even higher. Rhynie, in Aberdeenshire, had 20.2 per cent of its births illegitimate in the years 1859–63. At the same dates the figures for Rothiemay in Banffshire were 21.4 per cent, and Torthorwald and Lochmaben in Dumfriesshire were respectively 21.2 and 19.5 per cent. By contrast, in the far north, the figure for Ross and Cromarty for 1855–60 was only 3.8 per cent and for Shetland it was 3.9 per cent, though in both places, and against the national trend, the figures climbed by 1911–20 to be 5.8 and 4.6 per cent respectively. Even urban Lanarkshire had a rate of only 6.0 per cent in 1855–60 and 6.2 per cent in 1906–10.[26]

Why these major differences occurred between different parts of the country is still not entirely clear. Economic factors (particularly in the form of employment opportunities which allowed single women to raise children independently of paternal support) were probably important in some areas. It seems likely, though, that local social and cultural norms were also influential. Indeed, in both the north-east and the south-west, there appears to have been an 'illegitimacy subculture', in which the bearing of children outside wedlock was treated as normal, or, at any rate, did not attract opprobrium, and was prevalent in some families generation after generation.[27]

Whether or not illegitimacy was actively discouraged, nowhere in Scotland throughout our period did the fall in the number of births occurring outside marriage play more than a marginal role in the decline in overall fertility. The places in which illegitimacy was consistently above the national average were few, and being located for the most part in the North-East and South-West, involved a small percentage of the Scottish population.[28]

The Role of Marriage

Given that the contribution of illegitimacy to the late nineteenth-century fertility decline was minimal, it follows that the major factors must have involved changes in *marital* fertility. Historically, in European populations, little or no deliberate birth control was used within marriage, but women typically married in their mid-twenties — relatively late in their fertile years, which then (as now) normally fell between the mid-teens and late forties. Since few women had children before marriage, delayed marriage normally meant the loss of at least ten years of potential reproduction. In response to crises, such as a run of bad harvests, fertility could be further constrained by marrying later still, thus further restricting the numbers of years available for reproduction.

To what extent was the decline in Scotland's birth rate in this period due to the adoption, deliberately or otherwise, of this 'Malthusian' strategy of delayed marriage?[29] One factor that can markedly restrict marriage opportunities is a major imbalance between the numbers of men and women of marriageable age, but we have already seen that the sex ratio tended to become more balanced in the later years of the nineteenth century. In spite of this, as is shown in Figure 12, all the Scottish regions returned higher median ages at marriage in 1891 than in 1881, and the median age rose again by 1901, and in most areas further still by 1911. Significantly, though, the rise was least and the age at marriage remained lowest in those regions (the Western and Eastern Lowlands, and the north-east) which contained the majority of the Scottish population and where at a regional level actual population growth consistently occurred up to the First World War. Still, overall, no significant reduction in Scottish marital fertility can be attributed to changes in the age at marriage in this period.

Another way in which some older European populations had altered their fertility in response to economic change was by significant variations in the percentage of women who never married at all. Given the steady

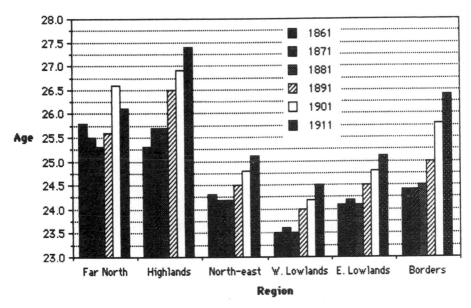

Figure 12. Regional median age at marriage, 1861 to 1911 (*Source*: Flinn *et al.*, Table 5.2.9).

improvement in the regional sex ratios of the 25–29 age group, and the patterns of the average age at marriage shown in Figure 12, it seems unlikely that the proportions of women marrying in Scotland would have fallen markedly over our period. Indeed, Figure 13 shows that at least from 1861 (and in contrast to England and Wales) there was a slight increase in the proportion of Scots women who were able to marry. Under these circumstances, it is clear that the onset of the demographic transition in Scotland must be almost entirely due to something historically quite new — limitation in the number of births *within* marriage.

Marital Fertility

The extent of the limitation of fertility within marriage in Scotland is apparent at the national level from the dramatic and persistent falls in the marital fertility and crude birth rates plotted in Figure 14. The two rates do not follow precisely the same course because of differences in the way in which they are calculated, and neither fully captures the extent of the fertility decline that was taking place. Fortunately, the wealth of information on marital status and legitimate births in Scotland in this period allows us to use a more robust and sophisticated measure of

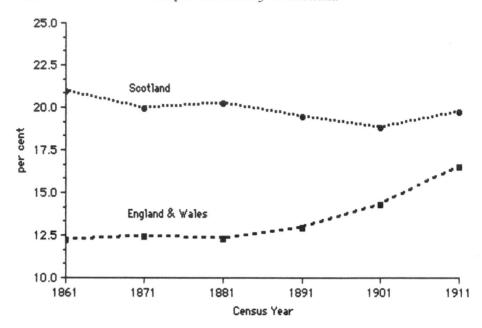

Figure 13. Percentage of females single at ages 45 to 49, Scotland and England & Wales, 1861 to 1911 (*Source: Censuses of Population*, 1861 to 1911).

fertility: I_g, Coale's index of marital fertility.[30] Put simply, I_g is an estimate of actual recorded fertility as a proportion of 'maximum' fertility. A figure of 1.0 is taken to represent the 'maximum' level of fertility. ('Maximum' is used here in an empirical sense, the standard set of rates used in constructing the I_g index being derived not from physiological data but from the fertility experience of the Hutterites, a North American religious sect noted for its practice of early and near-universal marriage, and for avoidance of all forms of deliberate birth control).

In recent European work on the demographic transition, two indicators of fertility decline have been widely used. Firstly, it has been found that when I_g fell by 10 per cent or more from an historically high 'plateau', it generally continued to fall thereafter. Determination of the decade during which a country's I_g fell by 10 per cent or more is therefore a good indicator of the onset of decline. Scotland had an I_g of 0.74 in the 1860s and achieved a 10 per cent decline in the 1890s, thus placing her among the leaders of the European trend.

Secondly, specific levels of I_g can be used as indicators of the degree to which a population is deliberately restricting its within-marriage fertility.

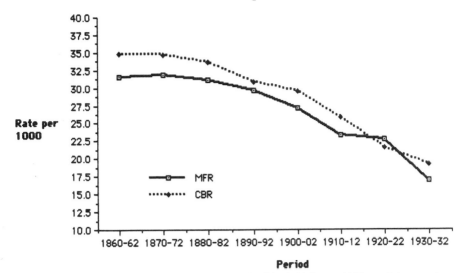

*The MFR's are 2-year averages of the number of legitimate births per 1000 married women in the age-group 15-44. The CBR's were computed from the number of births in each census year per 1000 population.

Figure 14. Marital fertility and crude birth rates, Scotland, 1861 to 1931 (*Source: Detailed Annual Reports*; Flinn *et al.*, Table 5.3.2).

As a rough guide, an I_g of above 0.7 is generally reckoned to indicate an 'uncontrolled' approach to child-bearing. A figure between 0.6 and 0.7 suggests that some control of fertility is being practised within marriage, while values below 0.6 indicate fairly widespread attempts to limit family size.

On this basis, in the years around 1881, I_g was below 0.6 in only twenty parishes in the whole of Scotland, and these accounted for just 0.6 per cent of the population. By 1891, 112 parishes (containing 4.8 per cent of the 1881 population) had an I_g of below 0.6, and by 1901, of the 856 parishes, 283 (accounting for 29.8 per cent of the Scottish people) were below this figure.

The high degree of variation of experience in Scotland is best demonstrated when the data are mapped by civil parishes, and this is done for I_g for 1881 and 1901 in Maps 5 and 6. The 1881 map clearly shows the unrestricted 'pre-modern' nature of marital fertility in Scotland at that time, with most of the parishes with I_g figures of above 0.7 and only a scattered handful below 0.6. By 1901, however, it is clear that most of Scotland was well on the way to its 'fertility transition'. By then it was only exceptional areas which had I_g levels above 0.7 and a substantial number showed values of less than 0.6.

Map 5. Marital Fertility Indicator (I_g), 1881

0.700 and over
0.600–0.699
Less than 0.600

Map 6. Marital Fertility Indicator (I_g), 1901

Further information on the nature of the early fertility decline comes from a study of its occupational pattern. The 1911 fertility census collected detailed information on family size, and detailed tabulations were prepared by age at marriage, year of marriage, and occupation. Unfortunately most of the Scottish material has subsequently been lost and the only surviving occupational analysis for Scotland is confined to marriages where the wife was aged 22–26 at marriage and the marriages had lasted at least 15 years.[31] Among this group, the average number of children born for the country as a whole was 5.8, though six per cent had twelve children or more and just over a fifth had ten or more.

Reverting to Map 6, the high fertility in 1901 in much of the North-West and in parts of Ayrshire, the Central Belt and western East Lothian is clearly to a great extent a reflection of one extreme pattern of child-bearing, in which crofters and miners averaged just over seven children. Fishermen, farmers and most agricultural labourers also had high average family sizes. A marked contrast can be seen in a number of professional groups (including doctors, lawyers, teachers and ministers) with an average family size of around four. Other groups with average family sizes below five included clerks, grocers, tobacconists, publishers and booksellers, printers and bookbinders, electricians and scientific instrument makers, watchmakers and inn and hotel keepers. At a local level, one effect of a clustering of low fertility groups was to pull down fertility in small market towns and in city suburbs like Broughty Ferry and areas to the west of Glasgow (see Map 6). Finally, among factory workers, a clear division emerges. On the one side were workers in heavy industry and shipbuilding (averaging over six children and holding up local fertility levels in parts of Lanarkshire). On the other were textile workers (especially those in woollens) who nationally averaged just over five children and pulled down fertility in parts of Fife and the Borders.

Figure 15 takes this analysis a little further and shows the distribution of family sizes for some selected occupations. It shows clearly that for two important upper middle-class groups (those who were the most ardent public opponents of artificial methods of birth control) the trend towards the normative two-child family of the twentieth century was already apparent by 1911. Woollen textile workers had an intermediate pattern, while many very large families remained among miners and crofters. The implications of these variations for living standards and especially for overcrowding of housing hardly need to be stressed. In addition, right from the start, the reduction in fertility was particularly important among older women, and this had the effect not merely of

Figure 15. Number of children born, by occupation of husband, Scotland, 1911 (*Source: Census of Scotland*, 1911, Table XLVII).

reducing family size but also of concentrating child-bearing into the earlier years of marriage. Already by the 1870s many wives of professional men were ceasing child-bearing entirely by their early thirties, and this pattern became almost normal for this group by the end of the century. By 1900 a similar tendency seems also to have been not uncommon among other pioneer groups.[32]

In seeking to explain this totally new pattern of fertility with marriage, research has concentrated on three sets of factors: the techniques or means that may have been employed to limit family size; the attitudes that made fertility restriction possible; and the social and economic circumstances that motivated couples to reduce their fertility.[33]

Among the pioneer middle-class groups there is a considerable measure of agreement that much of the motivation came from the costs of rapidly rising material living standards, and the increasing expenditures necessary to prepare children for careers. In Scotland, at least, these pressures were especially felt by those who were upwardly socially mobile into the professions or who were having to make their own way in highly competitive careers. Alongside this, new and more 'rational' or scientific attitudes to nature and to everyday life brought the possibility of active fertility limitation 'within the calculus of conscious choice'. When these motivations and attitudes were combined with more general ideologies of control and planning of one's life, and with high values placed by professional culture on restraint and purity, the scene was set for a ready adoption of ideas of planning one's family and probably for the widespread use of abstention rather than mechanical means of fertility limitation.

Among other groups, the precise balance of factors is still the subject of debate. Again, access to knowledge about birth control technology does not seem particularly important. Mechanical means were expensive, but coitus interruptus and abortion were probably quite widespread and, again, significant levels of abstention were possibly quite common. Economic and social pressures were especially strong among small shopkeeper and more privatised skilled artisan groups, with their strong desires to maintain status and social position in a fragile employment market. To this was probably added a wish to enjoy some of the increasing range of consumer goods which became available after the 1870s; this was the era when mangles and gas cookers, bicycles and pianos entered working-class and lower middle-class homes, and when those who had a little surplus cash and not too many familial encumbrances could begin to enjoy occasional trips by train or to the music-hall and even a week at the seaside.

NOTES

1. Material from Webster's census is presented in J. G. Kyd, *Scottish Population Statistics*, Scottish History Society, 3rd series, No 44, (1952). National census statistics are conveniently summarised in B. R. Mitchell and P. Deane, *Abstract of British Historical Statistics* (Cambridge, 1962), p. 6.

2. Calculated from M. W. Flinn *et al.*, *Scottish Population History from the 17th Century to the 1930s* (Cambridge, 1977), p. 306. Parts 5 and 6 of this book provide a comprehensive statistical survey of all the main national and regional trends in the period covered by this chapter, and can be referred to for more details of developments at these geographical units of analysis.

3. For urban data see Chapter 4. County figures from Mitchell and Deane, pp. 21–3.

4. The data for this large parish database were taken from Kyd's version of Webster's 1755 data (see note 1) and for the years 1801–1951 mainly from the valuable summaries in Table 3 in the *County Reports* of the 1951 *Census of Scotland*. Changes in boundaries are usefully summarised in the footnotes to these Tables.

5. Cf. also A. Collier, *The Crofting Problem*, (Cambridge 1953); M. Gray, 'Scottish Emigration: the Social Impact of Agrarian Change in the Rural Lowlands, 1775–1875', in D. Fleming and B. Bailyn (eds.), *Perspectives in American History*, (1973).

6. The population data are from the successive decennial censuses. The main sources for vital registration data are the *Detailed Annual Reports* of

the Registrar-General for Scotland, though convenient decennial summaries are reported in supplementary tables to some of the national censuses.

7. Mitchell and Deane, pp. 31–2, 36–7.

8. The data for Scotland are usefully summarised in D. Baines, *Migration in a Mature Economy* (Cambridge, 1985) pp. 300 and 304–6. More detailed data and commentary on the sources can be found in N. H. Carrier and J. R. Jeffery, 'External Migration: a Study of the Available Statistics'. *General Register Office Studies on Medical and Population Subjects*, No 6 (London, 1953). A useful commentary of the data are in Flinn *et al.*, pp. 91–6 and 441–55.

9. Destination data, mainly from Carrier and Jeffery, pp. 95–101, are usefully summarised in Flinn *et al.*, pp. 447–52.

10. Flinn *et al.*, p. 442. Migration destinations were derived from the birthplace tables of successive censuses of England and Wales. 1851 occupation data are from the national sample from the 1851 census of Great Britain.

11. Flinn *et al.*, pp. 458–9, and population census birthplace data for 1841 and 1911.

12. Flinn *et al.*, pp. 455–7.

13. See, for example. T. M. Devine, 'Temporary Migration and the Scottish Highlands in the Nineteenth Century', *Economic History Review*, 2nd series, XXXII (1979), pp. 344–59; Flinn *et al.*, pp. 304–5, 463–5, 472–9.

14. Mortality data in this and the next paragraph are mainly based on Flinn *et al.*'s summary (pp. 368–96) of the *Detailed Annual Reports* of the Registrar-General for Scotland. For the Highland 'famine' (which caused much more disruption of the population than actual mortality) see T. M. Devine, *The Great Highland Famine* (Edinburgh, 1988).

15. Flinn, *et al.*, p. 382.

16. *Detailed Annual Reports*, 1871–3 and 1908–10 (*Parliamentary Papers* 1875 XIX, 1876 XIX, 1877 XXV, 1911 XII, 1912–13 XIV, 1914 XIV).

17. *Ibid.*

18. *Detailed Annual Reports* for 1861 and 1901 (*Parliamentary Papers* 1865 XIV, 1904 XV).

19. Flinn *et al.*, pp. 398–9.

20. Recent work on England and Wales by Simon Szreter 'The Importance of Social Intervention in Britain's Mortality Decline, c 1850–1914: a Re-interpretation of the role of Public Health', *Social History of Medicine*, I (1988), pp. 1–38 and R. I. Woods *et al.* 'The Causes of Rapid Infant Mortality Decline in England and Wales, 1861–1921', Parts 1 and 2, *Population Studies*, XLII (1988), pp. 343–66 and XLIII (1989), pp. 113–32 have confirmed a subtle but significant shift in the interpretation of the nineteenth and early twentieth century mortality decline away from an orthodoxy established through the work of Thomas McKeown summarised in *The Modern Rise of Population* (London, 1976), and largely followed for Scotland by Flinn *et al.* The data used here come from the *Detailed Annual Reports* for 1871–3 and 1909–10.

21. J. C. Dunlop and R. M. Hunter, 'The Expectation of Life in Scotland in the Year 1911', *Transactions of the Faculty of Actuaries*, No. 70, VII (1915), pp. 357–83. Supplement to the 48th Detailed Annual Report (*Parliamentary Papers* 1906 XXI).

22. Mitchell and Deane, p. 13.

23. The course of the fertility decline in Europe is documented in A. J. Coale and S. C. Watkins (eds.), *The Decline of Fertility in Europe* (Princeton, 1986); the book contains a comprehensive bibliography, including reference to the many individual national studies conducted under the auspices of the Princeton University Fertility Project which began in 1963. For a more detailed study of the onset of the demographic transition in Scotland, see D. J. Morse, 'The Decline of Fertility in Scotland', (unpublished PhD thesis, University of Edinburgh, 1987).

24. G. Seton, *The Causes of Illegitimacy, particularly in Scotland* (Edinburgh, 1860), cited in Flinn *et al.*, p. 355. The Scottish figures had been significantly lower in the eighteenth century (L. Leneman and R. Mitchison, 'Scottish Illegitimacy Rates in the Early Modern Period', *Economic History Review*, 2nd series, XL (1987), pp. 41–63).

25. T. C. Smout, 'Aspects of Sexual Behaviour in Nineteenth Century Scotland', in A. A. MacLaren (ed.), *Social Class in Scotland, Past and Present* (Edinburgh, n.d.).

26. Flinn *et al.*, p. 364. Further debate on why some places had persistently higher illegitimacy than others can be found in Flinn *et al.*, Part 5, Chapter 4; Smout *op. cit.*, and T. C. Smout *A Century of the Scottish People, 1830–1950* (London, 1986), Chapter 7.

27. Flinn *et al.*, *Ibid.* See also P. Laslett and K. Oosterveen, 'Long-term Trends in Bastardy in England', *Population Studies*, XXVII (1973), pp. 255–86.

28. Flinn *et al.*, Table 5.4.2.

29. J. Dupâquier, A. Fauve-Chamoux and E. Grebenik, *Malthus Past and Present* (London, 1983) and R. A. Soloway, *Birth Control and the Population Question in England 1870–1930* (London, 1982) give excellent accounts of Malthusian and neo-Malthusian schools of thought.

30. Details of the calculations of these and other measures, and of their limitations, can be found under the appropriate entries in C. Wilson's edited edition of R. Pressat's *The Dictionary of Demography* (Oxford, 1985).

31. *Census of Scotland, 1911*, Table XLVII.

32. Flinn *et al.*, p. 346. Many of the ideas in this paragraph are based on the work of a group of Edinburgh University graduate students who have transformed our understanding of the nineteenth century fertility decline in Scotland. In the present connection note especially the work of: A. Gilloran 'Family Formation in Victorian Scotland', unpublished PhD thesis, University of Edinburgh, 1985; S. P. Walker, 'Occupational expansion, fertility decline and recruitment to the professions in Scotland 1850–1914' unpublished PhD

thesis, University of Edinburgh, 1986, and D. Kemmer 'The Marital Fertility of Edinburgh Professions in the Later Nineteenth Century', unpublished PhD thesis, University of Edinburgh, 1989.

33. There are excellent summaries of this work in the articles in Coale and Watkins cited in note 23 above.

CHAPTER 2
The Rural Experience
R. H. Campbell and T. M. Devine

The assumptions, attitudes and experiences of a rural society still permeated much of Scotland in 1830. The sights and sounds of the countryside were not far removed from the urban and industrial areas, many of whose inhabitants had known rural life at first-hand. Until the middle of the century only about half of Glasgow's Scottish-born population had been born in the city. By then the populations of some rural counties were passing their peaks: Argyll, Kinross and Perth in 1831; Inverness in 1841; Kirkcudbright, Ross and Cromarty, Sutherland and Wigtown in 1851; Berwick, Caithness, Orkney, Roxburgh, Shetland in 1861. Sharp falls were recorded in the Highlands, the south-west and in the Borders later in the century. Glasgow and Edinburgh were the destinations of most internal migrants, especially Glasgow, which took the greater proportion of the migrants from all regions except the Borders. The result was that by the beginning of the twentieth century the entire population was more thoroughly urbanised.[1] The diminishing importance of rural life was also evident in the fall in the proportion of the population engaged in agriculture, even taking into account the possible unreliability of some of the figures for the earlier years. It fell from around 25 per cent in the mid-nineteenth century to 11 per cent in the early twentieth century.

As more and more came to live and work in the industrial centres, many who wrote of Scotland's social history concentrated on the problems of an industrial society and, in geographic terms, gave attention to the experiences of the industrial and urban west. Such concentration provides a misleading interpretation for two reasons. Firstly, the effect of the increasing density of population in the central belt was that relatively thinly populated tracts remained elsewhere which showed little visible evidence of the transformation produced by industrialisation. The experience of rural society in the later nineteenth century concerned a diminishing proportion of the people of Scotland, but it was still the way of life found in a large part of the country. The conspicuousness of the land, especially its desolate lack of habitation, gave rise to its own problems. The second reason, less obvious but just as important, was the way in which the life of the countryside, particularly some of its social problems, were reflected back into the urban communities and engendered heated controversy far from their place of origin. Sometimes the bond was forged through the movement from the country to the towns, with migrants showing a more passionate zeal to remedy perceived injustices than those who remained at home. The interest was fostered further as the traditional bastions of political power, the landowners, found their privileges attacked.[2] The alleged evils of Highland proprietors attracted wide attention and radical burghs displayed a surprising interest in the total abolition of the game laws.[3] The rural experience had a political and social importance far beyond any quantitative evaluation of its significance.

The contrast between the urban and the rural areas had its counterpart in the variations between the rural areas themselves, which helped to give different economic opportunities and produced different social conditions. Most evident of all were sharp physical contrasts. Conditions and opportunities were so much bleaker and fewer further north and west of the Highland line that they have distracted attention from the variety within the Lowlands, between the intensely arable districts of Berwickshire and the Lothians, the arable and livestock region of the north-east and the dairying grasslands of the south-west.[4] In so far as the social structure was influenced by the form of agricultural production, generalisations based on the experience of one locality cannot easily be applied more widely. There were also major differences in agricultural practice in quite small areas, as between the grain-growing and the

6. A Land League Meeting in Skye (1884) being addressed by John Macpherson, a leading figure in the crofters' agitation of that decade. *Illustrated London News.*

livestock districts of the north-east and between the liquid milk producers of Ayrshire and the cheesemakers of Wigtownshire. The absence of local studies can lead to neglect of this diversity.

By 1830 all parts of rural Scotland, even the more remote, had experienced the effects of the commercialisation of agriculture. The process was deepened and intensified thereafter, especially by three forces which made for greater transformation of rural society. The first was the decline of older forms of industrial activity in the countryside, which contributed to rural depopulation and reduced the labour available for seasonal and part-time employment in agriculture. The decline in the traditional crafts or of their dispersal over the countryside followed improvements in distribution provided by the mass of branch lines added to the main railway network in the later nineteenth century.[5] The single most notable change came from the decline of hand-loom weaving as urban power-weaving spread in the second quarter of the nineteenth century. The weavers supplied many of the migrants of the nineteenth century to both the industrial areas of Scotland and to overseas, and their departure from the countryside deprived agriculture of a ready source of additional seasonal labour.[6]

The second transforming influence was the advent of new scientific and mechanical ways of agricultural production. Before 1914 scientific agriculture was still a small-scale pioneering activity. It began to spread its influence generally only with the emergence of the agricultural colleges at the end of the nineteenth and at the beginning of the twentieth centuries.[7] The improvements of the nineteenth century were more empirically based, conspicuously in the successful breeding of livestock, the Aberdeen Angus among beef cattle and the Ayrshire among dairy stock. An incentive to reduce labour requirements, especially of seasonal labour, when added to the empirical tradition of improvement, encouraged the spread of mechanical devices: the threshing machine, the reaper, and, though not always successful, milking machines. Mechanical improvements were less rapid where the need to economise in the use of labour was less pressing. The cultivation of potatoes was then mainly confined to meeting domestic needs, until later in the century, and led to the slow development of the rotary spinner lifter.

The third force which changed rural experience in the nineteenth century was the expansion of the market. The commercialisation of agriculture was intensified as more districts moved from supplying only the needs of their own locality to meeting those of a wider region. The nineteenth century produced new markets in the urban and industrial districts, which were more effectively exploited by improved transport.

7. Highland eviction, later nineteenth century. The Crofters Holding Act (1886) markedly reduced evictions among the rent-paying tenantry. *Royal Museum of Scotland.*

Railways gave quicker and more reliable access to wider markets at home, which helped the disposal of perishable products, such as the profitable sale of liquid milk for the dairy farmers of the south-west; steamships conveyed cattle and sheep to markets in London and other major conurbations in the south without the animals having to undertake the long and harmful trudge to them.[8] The opening of markets had another side. Producers elsewhere were given access to Scotland, an opportunity of particular importance from the 1880s, when the new methods of conveyance by refrigeration led to the penetration of the natural protection which perishability gave to home producers. The urban population gained from the increased supplies of cheap foodstuffs. The rural experience was more varied. Feeding stuffs and manures became more readily available. Those districts in the western Highlands which were net importers of grain benefited in the same ways as the urban areas. But rural areas suffered more generally from the difficulties of increased competition which followed the greater exploitation of world demand and supply through improved transport.

Though there were many regional variations in the consequences of changes in the supply of labour or through the adoption of more scientific methods, they were slight compared with those which came from the new methods of transport. Fortunately, Scottish agricultural production, which was directed less to the market for arable products and was much more concerned with livestock, suffered relatively less than elsewhere in Britain from the adverse effects of foreign competition until the later nineteenth century. In general, the Scottish countryside was comparatively prosperous throughout much of the century, provided it was able to break away from the restraints imposed by limited physical potential on the level of population that an area was able to support. The strains and stresses which affected the arable areas of England were not reproduced, except locally, in Scotland.[9]

The varied influence over time and place of the forces making for change in rural experience was most conspicuous in the contrasting experience of the Highlands from elsewhere. The western Highlands did not possess those advantages which led to a rising standard of living.[10] Their physical terrain and climate were unfavourable to many agricultural enterprises, while remoteness impeded both access to markets and the ease with which any surplus population could move permanently to take up employment elsewhere. Behind these obvious physical disadvantages were complex social attitudes which inhibited change in ways which no longer applied in the Lowlands, if they had ever done. They were rooted in attachment to the land, which led many to regard their tenancies as permanent, and to look to the landowner, not as someone with whom they had a merely legal and monetary relationship, but as someone to whom they owed a comprehensive range of social obligations as well, and from whom they expected a similarly widespread response. The tenants still looked for a paternalist relationship when it was neglected or denied by the proprietors, a contrast in attitudes which was bound to lead to an explosive situation in any subsistence crisis by the 1830s. Not all proprietors were unmindful of their tenants and of the difficulties which faced them in years of distress, especially in the potato famine of the 1840s. Some who achieved notoriety, among them the Sutherlands, took steps to alleviate hardship.[11] Yet, even the most generous could not accept that the social and economic structure should remain intact and unchanged when it was so patently unable to provide the bare necessities of life in many places for a rising population. Efforts to resettle the tenantry, harsh and unfeeling as they may seem to later generations, were not always attempts to clear the land to make way for sheep, or later for deer, without any concern for the welfare of the tenants. Some cases were thoughtless and insensitive, but others were designed to eliminate what seemed to be a perpetual subsistence crisis with only slight intermissions, attempts to provide a long-term solution which short-term relief could not do. Even altruistic efforts by some landowners — and there were many schemes which were not altruistic at all — encountered resistance because the objectives of landlord and tenant diverged widely and could not be reconciled.

The climax to the Highland problem came with the potato famine of the 1840s. Until then it had seemed possible to contain a potentially explosive situation as increasing population pressed against the limits of subsistence. Thereafter, as population pressure remained and subsistence and supplementary cash income collapsed, emigration had to increase.[12] Conditions deteriorated wherever proprietors withdrew support or gave none at all. Social tensions became acute as sheep prices fell later in the century, and more land was reserved for sport. Sporting proprietors or sporting tenants, while often willing to support their household and immediate dependents generously, were not interested in maintaining the traditional way of life of peripheral tenants and dependents.[13] Growing dissatisfaction with landowners in the Highlands coalesced with more general political criticism to provide the background to the crofters' agitation for more land in the 1880s. The outcome was a radical change in land tenure in the Crofter Holdings (Scotland) Act of 1886, by which the state curbed the power of the landowners in the interests of the tenants. Clearances became impossible as crofters were given security of tenure and a fair rent. The Act did not provide the additional land needed to support the population; that was the main objective of the Congested Districts (Scotland) Act of 1897. How effective these measures and their implementation were are matters of dispute. Their achievement was to introduce a land system more acceptable to the people in districts where social tension had been most acute in the previous century. But it is also possible to suggest that they were more concerned with resolving the problems of the past instead of looking to those of the future. No legislation could remove the fundamental economic difficulties which remained to plague the Highlands. The legislation which was passed may have made matters worse in the long-run by freezing the availability of land and so the structure of Highland society and economy.[14]

While the tenantry in the Highlands continued to cling to older conceptions of landownership, those in the Lowlands had accepted a strictly economic relationship with their landlords before the beginning of the period under consideration. In most cases too their labour force did not have land of their own to work, either as tenants or as proprietors. The commercialisation of agriculture in the Lowlands meant that the

8. Mechanical reaper at work near Dundee, c.1890. The harvest was only slowly mechanised. The numbers required show a significant fall from previous periods but female labour was still necessary to bind and stack the corn. *Scottish Ethnological Archive, Royal Museum of Scotland.*

social structure, and much of the social life, was determined by the nature of agricultural operations, particularly by the ways in which they affected the demand for labour. There were marked differences in what was needed, differences which are masked by generalisations derived from the experiences of one area. The chief operational distinction lay between east and west. The more arable areas were in the east, stretching from the Laigh of Moray to the Merse of Berwickshire, districts where agricultural needs gave priority to the work of the ploughman and his pair of horses. The more intensively arable an area, such as the Carse of Gowrie, the more dominating his role in the rural scene. To the north-east the concentration on livestock, encouraged when steam navigation facilitated the movement of cattle in good condition to the London market, did not change the dominance of the ploughman. The expansion of livestock increased the cropping of turnips, which required such frequent and intensive cultivation that even in these livestock areas the skilled activities of the ploughman and his team were needed. In the west the leading place of the ploughman and his horse team was rivalled by that of the dairyman or, on a higher social scale, by the bower, who often aspired to taking an orthodox tenancy.[15]

The nature of the labour required varied, but it is possible to distinguish four characteristics of the permanent labour force, which can be seen in all districts, though to varying extent.[16] The first was the method of engaging labour, the long-hire, which tied the Scottish farm servant to an employer for six months or more, and which perpetuated farm service long after it had disappeared elsewhere. The procedure which fixed the engagements varied. The hiring fairs, which were an important part of the life of the eastern lowlands, were to be found only in an attenuated form in the west. But everywhere the attractions of the long-hire were considerable to both sides. The mixed nature of Scottish farming did not involve significant seasonal fluctuations in the demand for labour. It required a steady and assured supply. Key workers could not be multiplied, so that, whether in the arable east, where the ploughman and his horse team dominated, or in the west, where he was supplanted in the hierarchy by the dairyman, essential labour had to be tied to the farm as firmly as possible to enable labour to be used economically. The perpetuation of the long-hire may then be interpreted as an attempt to maximise the control the farmer was able to exercise over his labour force. He had to be able to do so, because rural labour in Scotland could move more easily to the new industrial areas, which were so close that in some parts of the country, notably in the more scattered mining districts, it was possible for both rural and industrial work to be combined. The perpetuation of the long-hire was not merely the continuation of an older social arrangement, but a method of balancing the respective powers of the two parties to the engagement. Which side had the greater strength varied according to time and place. When the need for labour was high, as during periods of industrial expansion, the labourer was able to dictate terms, and the farmer had to pay for it in order to have his labour assured.[17]

The second characteristic which survived from an earlier age was also adaptable to modern needs. It was the responsibility which often fell on those who were employed on a long-term engagement to provide additional labour when it was required, or the expectation that they would do so whatever the arrangements. At one extreme the agreement was formal, as in the requirements of the East Lothian hind to provide — as part of his bond — a bondager, an extra pair of female hands, which may have been either from his own family or from outside, and which was available for any supplementary tasks which required extra labour. It was a permanent source of supply of labour for semi-casual tasks. In the dairying west the provision for the supply of additional labour was less formal but even more necessary as it was required for milking on an intensively regular part-time basis, except in winter when the output of milk declined. When either a bower or a dairyman was employed, the responsibility for the operation of the dairy was usually passed to him, and he had to ensure that the necessary labour was forthcoming, either from his own family, as was commonly the case, or from some other source. Since the additional labour supplied was in most cases generally female, the number of women employed in agriculture was relatively high.[18] The first two characteristics of Scottish agricultural labour ensured that labour was tied to its place of work. The third and fourth were corollaries, which again seem redolent of an earlier age. The third was the provision of some form of housing or accommodation on the farm for the regular workers, leading to the dispersal of the agricultural labour force and to the absence of any notable concentration in villages. Once again regional variations ensured that any attempt to generalise about the provision can be misleading. In the middle of the nineteenth century it was possible to distinguish three categories of housing,

9. The ploughman was the key figure in the production routine of the lowland arable farms. He was an aristocrat of labour with pride in his job and his horses. *Scottish Ethnological Archive, Royal Museum of Scotland.*

which are brought out clearly in the official reports of the time. These show how limited was the geographical incidence of the bothy system which is often taken to be the standard form of accommodation, perhaps because it made such an impressive mark on Scottish literature and has been highlighted by the modern cult of folk music. The classic bothy system, in which the unmarried males lived in varying degrees of communal squalor, was confined to arable areas in much of Kincardine and Angus, centred on the Howe of the Mearns, where the unmarried males formed a large part of the labour force. It spread in an attenuated form elsewhere but, while often referred to confusingly both by contemporaries and by later commentators as 'the bothy system', it was nearer to what was described as 'the kitchen system'. In this the labourers slept in accommodation external to the farmhouse — the chaumer of the north-east — often cleaned by some of the farm's domestic servants, and ate in the farm kitchen. The so-called kitchen systems covered many variations and merged into the bothy and became the practice followed generally for the accommodation of the unmarried workers in the nineteenth century.[20]

Both the bothy and the kitchen system met the needs of the regular unmarried workers. They did not meet those of the married workers, the ploughmen and the dairymen. They were concentrated on large farms, especially in the arable districts of the Borders and the east of Scotland. They were less common in the south-west, with its small farms worked chiefly by family labour, and in the north-east, where, as the area's traditional smallholdings fell, the proportion of unmarried workers grew.[21] The pattern of evolution was clear. In the past the cottar tenanted a cottage with a small piece of land but, out of considerable variety of practice, the cottar became the married farm servant living in the tied cottage, which has persisted to the present. The state of housing remained poor throughout the nineteenth century, though there were improvements from the 1840s. The resistance to alter the primitive provision of one room for the family was evident. In the first edition of the *Book of the Farm* (1844) Stephens was still thinking of one-roomed houses because 'nothing is more uncomfortable to work people than to be obliged to occupy a house much larger than the small quantity of furniture they usually possess can occupy'.[22] Improvements were slow. They came on the larger farms, notably in the later nineteenth century, as landowners paid more attention to housing. Some of the changes were distinguished by architectural embellishment to meet some preconceived external design than to meet the practical internal requirements of the occupants. Though poor, the housing for the married workers was no worse than in many industrial areas. The rural worker had the one great benefit of not suffering from the high density of population which was typical of urban housing.[23] The fourth characteristic of the permanent Scottish labour force was a more general case of the third. It was the practice of paying a substantial part of wages in kind, which was both an economical way of making payment for many farmers and a practical necessity for those living in relatively isolated farms and not in small villages, especially before the internal combustion engine enabled delivery vans to reach most locations easily. The allowances in kind varied depending on the agricultural specialisms of an area. Obviously, dairy produce loomed larger in the remuneration of those in the dairying districts than elsewhere, but an attempt was often made to provide a full range of the produce which could be grown in a district. Patches of potatoes were also cultivated to provide for the needs of the labour force.[24]

Two consequences followed from the greater extent of payment in kind. The first was the restriction it placed on the pattern of consumption of many agricultural workers, simply because they did not have the cash needed to exercise much freedom of choice. The restriction can be readily condemned on social grounds, too readily perhaps, because the high consumption of oatmeal it involved enabled the Scottish farm servant to enjoy a pattern of food consumption nutritionally superior to what was commonly followed with freedom of choice.[25] Second, and of wider implication, was the effect on the standard of living of payment in kind when prices fluctuated. Those paid in kind were protected from the fall in real wages which accompanied a period of inflation and did not gain when prices fell. The worker was isolated from many of the economic effects of the market place in the short-run, though changes in prices and profitability of farming forced gradual adjustment on subsequent agreements.[26] Though the characteristic feature of Scottish agricultural labour was the retention of servants and not labourers, some form of supplementary temporary labour was required for two groups of operations. The first, and more permanent, was the wide range of activities which were always taking place about any farm, irrespective of its specialisations: hedging, dyking, ditching, fencing, often essential supporting tasks, but distinct from others. They were the jobs which could have been, and were, undertaken by additional labour permanently employed on the farm. Only the larger farms had such workers and they had the greatest need for them. There was the same variety in the requirements from the other source of demand for casual labour: the seasonal needs of haymaking, harvesting, and the cultivation of turnips. The families of other workers were always a useful source of supply, and

10. Bondagers in the Lothians, c.1875. The extensive use of female labour was one of the distinctive features of Scottish agriculture. *Scottish Ethnological Archive, Royal Museum of Scotland.*

gave another boost to the employment of women workers, but it was often an inadequate one, and the main source of casual labour varied in different districts. The north-east was unusually well placed through the proliferation of smallholdings from which the inhabitants were unable to obtain full subsistence. They therefore welcomed the possibility of gaining additional income from occasional work on larger places. In areas near to the main districts from which temporary labour could be obtained, such as the Highlands and Ireland, these migrants joined the labour force and in many cases settled to become part of the permanent population. Such absorption was most evident in the south-west, where the Irish had long filtered through the local population. Provision for the temporary workers was inevitably poor and makeshift, for it met only a passing requirement. Bothies were sometimes provided, some of them for female workers; at other times the migrant labour force was left to fend for itself as best it could. The resulting poor conditions persisted into the twentieth century, notoriously those of the Irish potato lifters which became a matter of public discussion in the early years of the century.

A superficial examination of the life of Scottish agricultural labourers in the nineteenth century can leave the impression that they suffered from the perpetuation of practices redolent of an earlier age of servility.

In another way also the labourer seemed to be at a disadvantage, especially when compared with his opposite number in England, in the lack of any formal provision for the relief of the able-bodied in the Scottish poor law. Its absence was not entirely without gain as it prevented the emergence of a demoralised labour force, paid inadequate wages on the assumption that supplementation in the form of poor relief was always available. Some modicum of subsistence had to be paid to their workforce by Scottish farmers if they were to retain them, especially to those who could move easily to the industrial opportunities. They could not rely on the basic support being provided from another source.[27]

It can be suggested, however, that the trappings of servility often masked a high degree of independence in the workforce. Behind the apparent survival of the old features of service which had died out in England, two characteristics of the environment in which the labourer lived gave him a more independent, and so a more secure position. The first was the greater flexibility of agricultural production in Scotland, which enabled farming enterprises to be changed to meet new market conditions. There was no area in Scotland which suffered so acutely in the later nineteenth century as parts of the grain-growing areas of England. There were still economic difficulties in the Lothians, though less so in the important sectors of Scottish agriculture in the north-east and south-west which relied on the fattening of livestock and on dairying.[28] The flexibility of agriculture depended on the possibility of moving from less to more profitable lines of production. Efficient practices were encouraged by some of the old characteristics, notably the long-term engagement. The productivity of Scottish agriculture owed much to the way in which an assured labour supply both enabled the farmer to plan his use of labour efficiently and compelled him to do so.

The consequences of the second feature were more widespread: they followed from the ability to move to openings elsewhere. In most districts away from the western Highlands, and so in most areas which suffered from the more depressed economic conditions of the later nineteenth century, the agricultural labourer could move more easily to alternative employment, as he was not remote from the main centres of industrialisation. The consequence was that migration from the land, which had been characteristic of some areas in the earlier part of the nineteenth century, spread to all by its later years, changing the distribution of the population throughout the Scottish countryside radically in the long-run.[29] In the short-run the possibility of moving from the land enabled the Scottish agricultural labourer to retain his standard of living more easily.

11. 'Kitchie deem', c.1890. Women workers of this type were required to labour both in the house and in the fields. They were commonly found in small and medium-sized farms and often worked the longest hours for the lowest pay. *Scottish Ethnological Archive, Royal Museum of Scotland.*

Those who concluded the various bargains with farm servants and made the day-to-day decisions on farming operations were usually tenant farmers. The pattern of working the land was fixed by the early nineteenth century and experienced little change until after the First World War. Even then the old pattern persisted. Dramatic change came to the social structure of the countryside only after the Second World War, with the emergence of owner-occupation on a large scale.[30] The system of tenant farming ensured a measure of social mobility which was lost as owner-occupiership grew. The mobility worked both up and down. The upward movement is the more obvious. The capital requirements for entry to owner-occupation have become increasingly onerous, but, when a range of tenancies was open, it was possible in some localities for those with limited capital to enter farming and to progress from small to large holdings. However, there were always complaints that those with more modest means were prevented from assuming tenancies because those with outside capital bid up the rents offered. Complaints about hobby farming are not new. The criticisms also sometimes came from sitting tenants against the tendency of the would-be small tenants to offer high rents recklessly as they had nothing to lose by doing so.[31] The downward movement was a form of social mobility which was to become even less evident with the growth of owner-occupation. The limited number of tenancies which were available, and the frequency with which they were passed on, but to one member of the family only, meant that the modern assumption that all, or at least most of the farmer's sons — though not his daughters — should continue somehow in father's occupation, did not exist. Some had to leave the land or work as farm labourers. They did both.

Mobility depended on the availability of tenancies of an appropriate size.[32] A survey published in 1906 and based on valuation rolls gives a convenient summary of the position. Physical conditions and tenurial systems ensured a high proportion of low rented holdings in Scotland. Of the total of 89,065 in Scotland in 1906, 62,303, or 69.9 per cent, had rentals of under £50. Their geographical distribution was uneven. The counties which had high percentages were in the Highlands and Islands, ranging from 73.6 per cent in Argyll to 99.0 per cent in Shetland. The counties with low proportions were not necessarily those with many large farms but were often dairying or other specialist districts near to the large urban centres. Five were in that category: Ayrshire, Renfrewshire, Lanarkshire, West Lothian and Wigtownshire, where the bulk of the holdings were in the middle range. Ayrshire had the highest proportion of the five in the top range of those with rentals of over £300 annually. Even then only 6.8 per cent of holdings were in that category. Three other counties had similarly small proportions of holdings of under £50 annual rentals, but they had high proportions in the high rental category of over £300 annually: Midlothian, always a special case, as it included Edinburgh, with 47.1 per cent of its holdings rented at over £300 annually; Berwickshire, with its large arable farms, had 32.6 per cent; Peeblesshire, with its large sheep farms, had 18.2 per cent. East Lothian (24.8 per cent), Roxburghshire (16.2 per cent), and Selkirkshire (16.3 per cent) were the only other counties with percentages of farms rented at over £300 annually in double figures which confirmed the unique nature of the tenurial arrangements of south-east Scotland. To portray that region's agricultural practices and the social structure which accompanied it as representative of Scottish agriculture as a whole is therefore misleading. So too is any belief that the substantial farms of either the arable areas or the large sheep walks were typical of the Scottish tenantry. Even if the mass of smallholders to be found in the Highlands and Islands, or to a lesser extent in parts of the north-east, are excluded, the Scottish farming tenantry were often to be found in modest holdings, most of all in the dairying districts of the west. Ayrshire had 53.1 per cent of its holdings in the range of £50 to £200, and Renfrewshire had 50.7 per cent.

The number of smaller and medium-sized holdings reduced the social gulf which existed between large tenants and their workers. Many of the smaller masters did the same work as their employees, and some of their family became labourers. Social mobility was also increased by the way in which the availability of smaller tenancies gave the opportunities for those with limited resources to move into the ranks of tenant farmers — notably in the west through the system of bowing. It was a more egalitarian social structure. The lot of many of the tenants and their families was no better than that of their workers. They often endured a life of slavish toil.[33]

The long leases which were common in Scottish agriculture gave a measure of stability to the tenant farmers. More important than this, however, was general agricultural prosperity. The decline in the long lease at the close of the nineteenth century was symptomatic of the uncertain conditions which led more dramatically to the removal of many tenant families of long standing who could not adapt to the new conditions. The change can be illustrated in the differing responses in the arable east and in the dairying west. In the former, and especially in East Lothian, some of the established were unable to adapt to the new conditions; in the west a new race of tenants moved from Ayrshire and spread dairying and a more arduous way of life throughout the south-west and further afield, notably to Essex and other eastern counties of England, where, even as arable farmers, they were able to succeed because of their low costs of production. The composition of the tenantry changed more than is often recognised, though the only way of examining how it did so is by detailed investigation of localities, and that has not been carried out.

Not all tenants enjoyed a sufficient margin of profit to allow them to be generous to their workforce; many also felt exploited by the landowners from whom they held the land they worked. A whole range of contentious issues led the landowners to be blamed for all manner of difficulties by the later nineteenth century. Some matters of dispute of an earlier age were removed or had diminished in importance by the later nineteenth century. Hypothec, by which the landlord had a prior security of the crop and livestock for a year's rent, that old problem 'which no Englishman can pronounce and few Scotsmen defend',[34] had been virtually brought to an end by 1880, though the objections raised to it were advanced less by tenants and more often by articulate seed and manure merchants who objected to the landlord's position as a preferred creditor. Even the restrictive conditions in leases — to follow a certain rotation or to consume all the produce on the land, which had become theoretically more onerous with the increased availability of cheap fertilisers and feeding stuffs — were generally mitigated. Many landlords allowed greater freedom of cropping than was permitted in the lease, though often still insisting that the farm should be in a regular rotation at the end of a lease. Controversy centred more on the allegation that the tenants were given inadequate compensation for improvements, leading, as in other matters, to legislation in the early years of the twentieth century to control the landowners in the interests of the tenantry.

One bone of contention which was of more general importance was the question of the preservation of game. The topic must be treated with care. It is one where the dissatisfaction could prove to have had greater repercussions than was justified on any rational basis because of the ways in which it was given maximum publicity by those increasingly anxious to portray the landowners in as unfavourable a light as possible. Disputes varied geographically. There were relatively few parts of Scotland where hunting, which increased markedly in the late nineteenth century, was the dominating field sport. It gave rise to less widespread opposition, especially if some compensation was paid for the loss of poultry or to make good cut wires. In Scotland the enforcement of fishing rights was more important. Preservation was mainly designed to protect the game from poachers. This was a policy which tenants usually supported, though it was the source of more general conflicts and contributed to the popular conception of the topic. For the smooth and co-operative operation of agriculture in the countryside it was less harmful than the potential damage done to crops through the prohibitions of tenants controlling the depredations of ground game. Winged game was not so harmful, its main damage being confined to the consumption of grain crops. Some of the worst effects were mitigated by the tenants being allowed to control ground game. Allegations of any kind, whether of extensive destruction or of minimum damage are, by their nature, difficult to substantiate. But mournful tales from tenants were useful evidence to back appeals

12. A group of prominent farmers, Kintyre, c.1900. *Scottish Ethnological Archive, Royal Museum of Scotland.*

for reductions of rents in agricultural depression, and were powerful assertions to be used more generally in the contemporary campaign against the landowners. The clearance of parts of the Highlands to make way for deer forests gave rise to some of the best known and most bitterly contested actions by proprietors. In other areas of Scotland the preservation of game was not a matter of such controversy as in parts of England. Yet there were complaints that when more impecunious landowners leased properties to shooting tenants less attention was paid to the requirements of those who were directly concerned with agricultural operations.[35]

In the eighteenth century the possession of land had been the way to economic and political power. In the nineteenth century it gave no such passport. Economic success was more likely in the new commercial and industrial activities, and political power was being spread to a wider electorate. Even the possession of a peerage, traditionally a more effective path to political power than the mere possession of land, no longer had the influence of former years. In the urban districts of Scotland landowners counted for little. The political challenge of Liberalism, always strong in the cities and in the small burghs, ensured solid opposition to the landowners, most of whom became Conservative in politics, after the disputes over the Liberal support for Home Rule for Ireland in the 1880s. Though denuded of much of its political power, the possession of land was still the source of social prestige, especially as the break-up of many large estates had not yet begun. It encouraged many to apply their newly acquired riches to its possession. However, partly because the scale of this new demand was relatively limited, and also because few suitable properties came on the market except in the impoverished north and west, the new landowners never held a dominating share of the land.[36]

This was also a period when some fortunate landowners found their economic position transformed by industrialisation. In most cases they had given up earlier attempts to exploit directly the industrial potential of their estates, and gained through the exploitation of their properties by others. Revenue came to them often as mineral royalties, though minerals were wasting assets in a way the land was not. A report on the ownership of land in 1874[37] showed how some of the great landowners became greater still when they had the good fortune to possess mineral rights. In Lanarkshire the Duke of Hamilton's 45,731 acres had an annual land rental of £38,441, while his minerals yielded £56,920; his 3,694 acres in West Lothian gave £7,445 and £8,076 respectively; 810 acres in Stirlingshire yielded £911 and the minerals £2,011. Some lesser proprietors were relatively even more fortunate. David Carrick-Buchanan of Drumpellier at Coatbridge had 8,549 acres in Lanarkshire, with an annual rental of £8,693 and minerals producing £15,180. In some cases the transformation through the ownership of particularly valuable minerals was even more notable. William Gillespie's 709 acres of Torbanehill on the shale measures gave a rental of £776 while its minerals gave £13,125 annually. The transformation in the position of a landowner brought about by the possession of mineral-bearing property or the opportunity to tap some profitable industrial concern is a warning against any tendency to classify landowners by the quantity of land they held. The visible evidence of proprietors with large acreages made them more conspicuous and so more likely to be subjected to public criticism. But the answer to the question, 'Who owned Scotland?' is much less instructive than knowledge of which parts of Scotland were owned. The extensive landowners were in the Highlands and Islands, but their widespread possessions did not make them wealthy landowners. Caithness had only two with gross annual values in excess of £10,000 each; Inverness-shire had four and Ross-shire had five, but their acreages were among the largest of any proprietors in Scotland. In 1874 the Duke of Sutherland was the leading example of this type of proprietorship. His ownership of 1,176,343 acres or 90.5 per cent of the total in Sutherland was likely to attract more public attention than its gross annual value of £56,395, more attention even than the Duke of Buccleuch's 254,179 acres or 37.4 per cent of the total in Dumfriesshire, which gave him annually £95,239 as well as £3,012 from minerals, or the Earl of Dalhousie's 136,602 acres in Angus, 24.7 per cent of the county's total, which yielded £55,601.

When mineral and industrial rents are included, the Duke of Hamilton's £67,006, when added to the annual values of his Scottish estates, gave him an annual rental of £132,505, which reduced the gap with Buccleuch, who had only £15,692 annually from minerals and from Granton harbour, providing for him an annual total from his Scottish properties of £187,521. Other Scottish proprietors, notably the Marquess of Bute, with Scottish estates of 93,170 acres, giving £45,266 annually, and minerals in Ayrshire of £2,506 and Sutherland's much more extensive but only slightly more valuable property, were swamped by their Welsh and English possessions, which enabled them to play more influential roles in Scottish rural society than would have been possible if they had depended only on the income from their Scottish estates.

In view of the criticism which has been levelled at the large Scottish proprietors it is worth noting that only a few had truly large holdings. Their reputation arose partly from their geographical concentration. Of the 117 landholdings of an annual value of £10,000 and above in one county,[38] excluding non-agricultural rentals, the largest county concentration was in Perthshire, which had eleven. Aberdeenshire and Ayrshire had nine each and Berwickshire had eight. Taken together in each county these large holdings did not account for most of the counties: 433,613 acres or 34.5 per cent of Aberdeenshire; 264,677 or 36.7 per cent of Ayrshire; 688,171 acres or 42.7 per cent of Perthshire. Even a grandee of the territorial significance of the Duke of Buccleuch owned only 37.4 per cent of Dumfriesshire, 27.4 per cent of Roxburghshire, 37.4 per cent of Selkirkshire. For much of the rural society of Scotland, the smaller proprietors were more significant.

In retrospect, the most striking feature of such possessions is how they and the rural society which rested on them seemed securely based before 1914. The signs of opulent living, which so incensed contemporary social critics, and have been noted ever since, continued unabated. Newly acquired wealth found its way to rural pursuits, especially in rivalry to provide bigger and better sporting estates, often as though they were the main objectives of rural life, which is what they became in some districts. Yet, there were two notable flaws in the apparently stable edifice. The first, the one more often stressed by contemporaries, though of less fundamental importance, was the increased social criticism of the landowners and its translation into political criticism. The emergence of Estate Duty in 1894 was only the most dramatic result of this development. There was a whole series of other measures directed towards controlling the unfettered power of the landowners, concerned, among other issues, with compensation for improvements or tenants' rights to destroy game. In addition, landowners thought that the general burden of taxation seemed to fall inordinately heavily on them. They were increasingly resentful of how their traditional social and political powers were under attack, and banded together in 1906 to form the Scottish Land and Property Federation, particularly in response to the proposal in the Small Landholders (Scotland) Bill of 1906 to extend provisions of the Crofters Act of 1886 to the whole of Scotland. The proposal fell foul of the House of Lords, and led in Scotland to as much condemnation of the peers in the elections of 1910 as did their rejection of the Budget in that year. In 1911 the Small Landholders (Scotland) Act introduced powers of compulsory purchase, if necessary, to make provision for smallholdings. This demonstrated clearly that it was not only in the Highlands that the power and position of the landowners were greatly diminished from a century earlier.

The second crack in the edifice of the power of the landowners in the countryside was less fully recognised, though it was the more fundamental. It was the declining capacity of the estates to support the traditional way of life. To many landowners the political and fiscal attacks on their power lay behind the economic difficulties of their estates, but that was not so. The burden of taxation was insufficient to explain the difficulties of many. These problems had emerged much earlier in the nineteenth century before the political measures had been adopted or had effect.

The ability of many landowners to continue to live as they had in the past and so to leave their estates to be run in traditional fashion, with all the stable continuity that meant for tenants and others, was dependent on the buoyancy of rents. That, in turn, relied on the possession of good land or of revenue from non-agricultural sources such as mineral royalties, or, better still, of both. Large parts of Scotland did not have fertile land, and general agricultural conditions even detracted from the prosperity of those parts where the land was good. The industrial potential was declining in some cases, especially through the exhaustion of mineral fields, the revenue from which had supported some of the grandest styles of living. Such conditions made the old problem of expenditure exceeding revenue even more acute. But it was not a problem which influenced the conduct of the estates and the way of life of their owners, because these aspects were rarely linked in the minds of proprietors or of their agents. Two features of estate management encouraged this approach. The first was that many landowners were heirs of entail. Though legislation to free land from some of the more inhibiting fetters of entail was passed in the nineteenth century and no new entails were possible after 1914, heirs of entail were still largely life tenants with little incentive to adapt their estates to changing external circumstances.[39] The second, very simply, was that the method of accountancy on an estate frequently did not draw the proprietor's attention easily to any deterioration in its economic conditions, even if, as is doubtful, the proprietor was interested in being informed. In these circumstances an able agent could not easily ensure action to deal with an impending financial crisis, and many agents did not perceive that any were emerging.

As with the tenants, so with the landowners, their financial liquidity determined their action before 1914. Only a cessation of cash flow interrupted the grandeur of the lifestyle of many. An immediate short-term solution was sought by letting property, often to sporting tenants, whose insatiable demand provided a rational, economic justification for the concern of many proprietors to meet sporting requirements. Unlike tenants, landowners could borrow more readily. They did so on a large scale. Estates became crippled with a burden of indebtedness, and the key to their survival was often the ability to obtain enough cash from rents or outside lenders to service existing debt.[40] To a greater or lesser extent it was a rake's progress, which had to come to an end one day, and which was brought to an end more suddenly than it might have been by the social changes of the First World War and the economic collapse of agriculture thereafter. The unprofitable nature of agriculture, which was to increase after 1918, ensured that many more could not continue along traditional ways. The break-up and sales of estates which followed ensured that farms were often sold to sitting tenants, and the owner-occupier began to emerge with major effects on the social structure and social mobility of the rural areas. The seeds of that dramatic change had been sown before 1914, though the harvest was reaped only after 1918, and more so after 1945.

NOTES

1. See Chapters 1 and 3.

2. Examples were common in the crofters' agitation in the 1880s, notably in the activities of the Highland Land League whose 'success was to force the highland question to the forefront of British politics'. J. Hunter, 'The Politics of Highland Land Reform, 1873–1895', *Scottish Historical Review* [*SHR*], liii (1974), p. 67. Earlier studies are D. W. Crowley, 'The Crofters' Party, 1885–1892', *SHR*, xxxv (1956), and H. J. Hanham, 'The Problem of Highland Discontent, 1880–1885', *Transactions of the Royal Historical Society*, xix (1969), pp. 21–65. See also J. Hunter, *The People's Cause* (Edinburgh, 1986).

3. The President of the Scottish Chamber of Agriculture, William Smith, told the Select Committee on the Game Laws of 1872 '. . . some of the Radical boroughs [sic] wanted to co-operate with us immediately when, as they said, we had at last put ourselves right with the country by advocating the total abolition of the Game Laws'. *British Parliamentary Papers* [*BPP*]. 1872. X. Q.6118 The support of the burghs was a factor which encouraged the Chamber to move between 1866 and 1871 from the limited objective of seeking to have rabbits and hares dropped from the list of preserved game to the advocacy of the total abolition of the game laws.

4. *Report on the Present State of Agriculture in Scotland, arranged under the auspices of the Highland and Agricultural Society to be presented at the International Agricultural Congress at Paris in June 1878* (Edinburgh, 1878) gives a useful summary of the differences between districts in Scotland. The perpetuation of variations to modern times is shown in J. T. Coppock, *An Agricultural Atlas of Scotland* (Edinburgh, 1976). I. Carter suggested that much Scottish agricultural history has failed to recognise the 'distinctively different agrarian structures of the Lowlands and has taken the experience of the Lothians to be representative of all'. *Farm Life in Northeast Scotland 1840–1914* (Edinburgh, 1979), pp. 178–9.

5. Gavin Sprott, 'The Country Tradesman' in T. M. Devine (ed.), *Farm Servants and Labour in Lowland Scotland 1770–1914* (Edinburgh, 1984), pp. 143–154. The persistence of older methods is evident in John Shaw, *Water Power in Scotland 1550–1870* (Edinburgh, 1984).

6. N. Murray, *The Scottish Hand Loom Weavers 1790–1850* (Edinburgh, 1978) pp. 144–7. A representative comment from a farmer in Lanarkshire in 1881 was '. . . there used to be no difficulty [in the supply of labour at harvest time] so long as hand-loom weaving was kept up, but that is done away with now. Our cottages were largely filled with hand-loom weavers when I began farming, but that trade has gone down. These men were always available for a push'. *Royal Commission on Agriculture, 1881–2. BPP*, 1881. XVII. Q.40,280.

7. The three colleges — West, East and North of Scotland — were established between 1889 and 1904. County councils provided much of the initiative for them under programmes for technical education.

8. The effects are evident in many parochial accounts in the *New Statistical Account*, especially in the North-East. R. C. Michie, 'Trade and Transport in the Economic Development of North-east Scotland in the Nineteenth Century', *Scottish Economic and Social History*, 3 (1983) pp. 69–70. Later competition from the railways is considered in Geoffrey Channon, 'The Aberdeenshire Beef Trade with London: a Study in Steamship and Railway Competition 1850–69', *Transport History*, 2 (1969) pp. 1–24.

9. The differences are clear in the evidence of witnesses to the two Royal Commissions on Agriculture in the 1880s and 1890s. Pioneering studies of the contrasts were E. H. Whetham, 'Prices and Production in Scottish Farming, 1850–1870', *Scottish Journal of Political Economy*, ix (1962) pp. 233–243 and, though concerned with England, T. H. Fletcher, 'The Great Depression of English Agriculture, 1873–1896', *Economic History Review*, xiii (1961) p. 417.

10. A brief but comprehensive survey of the difficulties of adjustment in the Highlands is D. Turnock, 'The Highlands: Changing Approaches to Regional Development' in G. Whittington and I. D. Whyte (eds.), *An Historical Geography of Scotland* (London, 1983), Chapter 9. More concerned with recent changes is J. M. Bryden and G. Houston, *Agrarian Change in the Scottish Highlands* (London, 1976). For the economic and social crisis in the nineteenth century Highlands and its aftermath, see T. M. Devine, *The Great Highland Famine: Hunger, Emigration and the Scottish Highlands in the Nineteenth Century* (Edinburgh, 1988).

11. The more considerate response grew. By the mid-nineteenth century the factor to the Duke of Sutherland was kept so firmly in his place by the Duke that 'he could neither clear the tenants, nor punish the rioters'. Eric Richards, *A History of the Highland Clearances* (London, 1985) ii, p. 364.

12. Devine, *Great Highland Famine*, Chapters 6–11.

13. The development of a Highland estate for sport is studied in Philip Gaskell, *Morvern Transformed*, second edition (Cambridge, 1980). See more generally Willie Orr, *Deer Forests, Landlords and Crofters* (Edinburgh, 1982) and T. M. Devine, 'The Emergence of the New Elite in the Western Highlands, 1800–60', in T. M. Devine (ed.) *Improvement and Enlightenment* (Edinburgh, 1989) pp. 108–142.

14. A Collier, *The Crofting Problem* (Cambridge, 1953); James Hunter, *The Making of the Crofting Community* (Edinburgh, 1976).

15. Though the detail varied, under the system of bowing the farmer supplied working as well as fixed capital, such as the dairy herd and fodder.

16. A. Orr, 'Farm Servants and Farm Labour in the Forth Valley and South-East Lowlands' in Devine (ed.), *Farm Servants and Labour*, pp. 31–3.

17. Some indication of the procedure followed in different areas and views on the methods are in a 'report by a Committee of the Highland and Agricultural Society on Hiring Markets', *Transactions of the Highland and Agricultural Society* [*THAS*], fourth series, v (1873) p. 311. R. Hunter Pringle, 'The Agricultural

labour of Scotland — Then and Now', *THAS*, fifth series, vi (1894), p. 238 deals with this and other distinctive features. See also T. M. Devine, 'Social Stability and Agrarian Change in the eastern Lowlands of Scotland, 1810–1840', *Social History*, 3 (1978), 331–346.

18. T. M. Devine, 'Women Workers, 1850–1914' in Devine (ed.), *Farm Servants and Labour*, pp. 98–124. For an example of how bondagers and other form of apparently casual labour were required all the year round on a large farm see *Royal Commission on Agriculture, 1881–2. BPP* 1881. XVII. Q.36,530–1.

19. The distinction is drawn clearly in the *Fourth Report of the Commission on the Employment of Children, Young Persons, and Women in Agriculture. BPP*. 1870. XIII. para.52. The main report is based on those of assistant commissioners, which show greater variety in the provision than is often recognised. See also, Pringle, *The Agricultural Labourer of Scotland*, pp. 251–9.

20. Its origin, especially in the Carse of Gowrie and in the lower part of Strathearn, is described in the report by an assistant commissioner to the *Commission on the Employment of Women and Children in Agriculture. Report on Perthshire*, etc. para. 17. *BPP*, 1870. XIII. See also, Carter, *Farm Life in Northeast Scotland*.

21. The change in the North-East, which had a special characteristic of smallholding is described in Malcolm Gray, 'North East Agriculture and the Labour Force 1790–1875' in A. Allan MacLaren (ed.), *Social Class in Scotland* (Edinburgh, n.d.) pp. 86–104.

22. H. Stephens, *Book of the Farm* (1844), iii, p. 1370. See also David Low, *Landed Property and the Economy of Estates* (London, 1856), pp. 175–6.

23. A major source of information is again the *Fourth Report of the Commission on the Employment of Children, Young Persons, and Women in Agriculture. BPP*. 1870. XIII. The persistence of complaints about the number and standard of housing continued and was a major source of grievance between tenant and landlord. To one tenant of the Duke of Fife in Banffshire in 1895 lack of cottages was 'the greatest grievance that farmers have to contend with'. *Royal Commission on Agricultural Depression, 1894–6. BPP*. 1896. XVII. Q.51,872. See, more generally, Alexander Fenton, 'The Housing of Agricultural Workers in the Nineteenth Century', in Devine (ed.,), *Farm Servants and Labour*, pp. 188–212.

24. 'Not as a necessary, but as a very natural accompaniment of the farm cottage and yearly hiring comes the payment in kind, a custom which prevails throughout my district [central and south-east Scotland], with however some exceptions which I am afraid indicate its extinction or at least curtailment at no very distant date.' *Commission on the Employment of Children, Young Persons, and Women in Agriculture. BPP*. 1870. XIII. Report on Assistant Commissioner (Culley) on central and south-east Scotland, para. 6.

25. R. Hutchison, 'Report on the dietaries of Scotch Agricultural Labourers', *THAS*, fourth series, ii (1868–9) p. 1 and 'On the economic condition of the

English agricultural labourer, in relation to his food and its mode of cooking, considered in contrast to the dietary of the Scottish agricultural labourer', *THAS*, fourth series, iii (1870–1) p. 349.

26. T. M. Devine, 'Scottish Farm Labour in the Era of the Agricultural Depression 1875–1900' in Devine (ed.), *Farm Servants and Labour*, p. 245.

27. R. Mitchison, 'The Creation of the Disablement Rule in the Scottish Poor Law' in T. C. Smout (ed.), *The Search for Wealth and Stability* (London, 1979) pp. 199–217.

28. A useful summary of the variety of experience in Scottish counties based on an analysis of the agricultural statistics for 1891 is in Section ii.D of the *Miscellaneous Memoranda, Abstracts and Statistical Tables*, prepared for the Royal Commission on Labour, *BPP* 1893–4. XXXVII. Part II.

29. See Chapter 1. Also, Malcolm Gray, 'Scottish Emigration: the social impact of agrarian change in the rural Lowlands, 1775–1875', *Perspectives in American History*, vii (1973); Marjory Harper, 'Emigration from North East Scotland', *Northern Scotland*, 6 (1985), pp. 171–3.

30. By 1966 only 49 per cent of holdings in Scotland were tenanted.

31. In 1881 one witness commented that 'reckless rents' were being offered by 'ignorant and uneducated men'. *BPP*. 1881. XVII. Q.40,934. There were also complaints that capital was being directed from trade to agriculture, and so forcing up rents.

32. *Return showing the Number of Occupiers of Farms (whether owners or tenants) in each County and Parish in Scotland with the Gross Rental according to the Valuation Roll, for the Year ending Whitsunday 1906. BPP*, 1907. LXXIII. 411.

33. This comment remained unchanged for many years. In 1865 James Drennan told the *Royal Commission on Hypothec* that the small tenants 'work as hard, and live almost as frugally, as ploughmen, and they have much anxiety on their minds'. *BPP* 1865. XVII. 413; in the 1890s John Spier gave evidence to the *Royal Commission on Agricultural Depression* that '. . . they are by far too hard working; they work, and work, very hard'. *BPP*, 1896. XVII. Qs.47,001 and 47,003. Conditions remained similar until the First World War; J. Drysdale, 'The Management of a Dairy Farm', *THAS*, fifth series, xxv (1913), p. 58.

34. Sir J. C. Dalrymple-Hay to Disraeli, 11 March 1876, quoted in I. G. C. Hutchison, *A Political History of Scotland* (Edinburgh, 1986) p. 104. The reality was less dramatic than some of the objectors implied. One witness in 1865 compared hypothec to the privileges which had brought disaster to the French aristocracy: 'The law has created now more than ever an uncomfortable and injurious feeling, that the landlords, as a class, are disposed to be selfish, and jealous of those with whom their tenants require to have pecuniary transactions, and all for an object which is not worth its odium'. *BPP*. 1865. XVII. 413. p. 273.

35. Hutchison, *Political History of Scotland*, pp. 242–5. Page v of the *Report of the Select Committee on the Game Laws, 1873*, remarked that in Scotland

'a much stronger feeling has been evoked by the preservation of game than in England', partly because of the excessive preservation of ground game on some large estates. *BPP*, 1873. XIII. In 1880 occupiers resident on rented land were allowed to kill hares and rabbits and complaints were less in the evidence given to the *Royal Commission on Agriculture in 1881*.

36. A detailed study of the movement of many successful industrialists into the nearby countryside is in J. T. Ward, 'Ayrshire landed Estates in the Nineteenth Century', *Ayrshire Archaeological and Natural History Collections*, 8 (1967–9), pp. 93–145.

37. *Return of Owners of Land*. Part III (Scotland). *BPP*. 1874. LXXII. Reprinted with revisions and additions in John Bateman, *The Great Landowners of Great Britain and Ireland*, (fourth edition, 1883; reprinted, Leicester 1971).

38. Twenty-one of the 117 had land of this amount in more than one county, so the number of individuals in the group was 96.

39. The criticism of entail was clear in the evidence given to the Select Committees of 1828. *BPP* 1828. VII. James Loch, a member of the committee as well as a witness, was less critical than most, but he felt the system was least favourable when rents were falling. (page 87).

40. The need to borrow often led Edinburgh lawyers, who had ready access to the potential sources of borrowing in trust funds and insurance companies, to become the factors on estates, providing a frequent occasion for complaint in the late nineteenth century.

CHAPTER 3
Urbanisation and Scotland

R. J. Morris

To understand Scottish urbanisation we need to think at two levels. These towns were part of a British, perhaps even a European cum North American industrial urban system. They also formed a coherent and distinctive Scottish network. Hence much of the language of this chapter could apply equally well to Manchester and Chicago, to Lille or Montreal: the language of suburbs, central business districts, municipal authority, public health and building regulations. We also need a distinctively Scottish language of Dean of Guild, of feu charters and Royal Burghs. We need a language in which burgh is spelt differently and police and tenement have meanings which differ from their connotations south of the border. To understand these complex and rapidly changing forms of social and economic organisation we need to acknowledge that the idea of urban itself has a double reference. Urban refers to a distinctive physical environment noted for its relative size, density and complexity. It also refers to a specific form of local authority, located in space and associated with distinctive powers; in Scotland that meant the burgh in its various forms. It is often easier to follow some of the tensions and confusions of Scottish urban history by remembering that both these meanings were and are equally valid for those who live in or think about towns.

Between 1831 and 1911 Scottish urbanisation increased steadily (Table 1). The rate of urban growth did slow down in the last decade to 8.1 per cent, but this did nothing to dislodge Scotland from the place it had gained in the league table of European urbanisation in the late eighteenth century (Table 2).

Indicators of Scottish urbanisation followed those of England and Wales, but a larger proportion of the population remained in rural and in smaller settlements. Scottish urbanisation was increasingly dominated by the big four cities: Glasgow, Edinburgh, Dundee and Aberdeen. Although Scottish urbanisation was more than the big four, it must be remembered that in 1851 one in five (22 per cent) of the Scottish people lived in these four cities and that by 1911 the proportion had risen to one in three (30 per cent). If Govan, Partick and Leith were

*Table 1. Percentage of the Scottish
Population in Settlements of More
than 5,000, 1831–1911*[1]

Year	Total (per cent)
1831	31.2
1861	39.4
1891	53.5
1901	57.6
1911	58.6

*Table 2. Scotland and the Rank Order of European Urbanisation, 1910–11.
Percentage of Population in Towns and Cities of More than 20,000*[2]

Country	Per cent	Country	Per cent
England and Wales	60.6	Belgium†	26.6
Scotland	49.5	Ireland	21.5
Netherlands	40.4	Switzerland	21.1
Germany	34.7	Norway	18.1
France*	32.5	Austria	16.9
Italy	28.2	Sweden	16.1
Denmark	27.0	Finland	9.3

*in 10,000 plus cities; †in 25,000 plus cities.

included, as geography, though not politics and local loyalty, would require, then the 1911 share was 35 per cent. Scotland had no primate metropolitan city like London and Paris, Glasgow was only 2.5 times the size of Edinburgh in 1911 compared to London's 5.9 advantage over its nearest rival. Nor did Scotland fit the rank size rule of an economy like the United States.[3] The Scottish pattern, in which a small number of very large cities dominated was reflected by several other countries in which politics and the national economy were dominated by London, countries otherwise as different as Ireland, India and Canada. It is not surprising that Scotland has been presented as a series of 'city regions' dominated by urban centres so distinctive that they defy generalisation.[4] There were many smaller urban centres. Haddington and Dumfries were typical of the agricultural market and service centres. Some, like Ayr and Perth, attracted or retained an industrial sector, usually textiles.

Then there were the rapidly growing industrial towns of the west, like Coatbridge and Hamilton. In addition, there were a series of specialised networks like the Fife burghs and the Border textile towns. Specialist groups included a series of fishing burghs, the new spa towns, some small seaside resorts and the independent suburban burghs. Volume 1 has shown the economic basis of this urbanisation and the importance of these towns for middle-class culture.[5] The nineteenth century saw a massive increase in the size, scale and dominance of urban places in Scotland. Glasgow's growth must be seen in terms of space as well as population and wealth. Between 1831 and 1911, the population of the City of Glasgow increased 3.9 times, whilst acreage went up 5.9 times to 12,669. Between 1856, when comparable figures become available, and 1911, the rateable value of the burgh increased 4.4 times, whilst population and area both increased 2.4 times. This increase in scale required a new urban technology of sewers, piped water, gaslight and tramways together with a need for organisational forms to regulate the growing complexity of urban economy, society and environment.

The substantial changes experienced by the big four have dominated the historical record and urban consciousness of Scotland. By 1830, Glasgow already contained a massive accumulation of urban capital and labour. Important on the capital side was the growing number of textile factories at the east end of the city, the quays by the Broomielaw and beyond as well as the investment in improving the Clyde Navigation. Prominent in the labour force was a massive army of hand-loom weavers, their wages depressed by a ready supply of labour from immigrants.[6] The first of the major employers were beginning to emerge. Tennants at St Rollox produced bleaching powder for textiles. The works and the tall chimney, Tennant's stalk, became a landmark. The product enabled manufacturers to economise on land and capital when finishing cloth, thus assisting urban concentration. Dixon's gathered a massive concentration of iron and coal production on the south bank of the Clyde.[7] Coal, iron, the river, the experience of steam that cotton spinning brought, plus the availability of labour and capital, provided a potent mixture from which iron shipbuilding and the associated engineering industry grew in the later part of the nineteenth century. Part of the power of a developed urban economy was and is an ability to generate economic development from a variety of economic resources and relationships. Glasgow possessed this variety in full, and was thus able to serve those 'distant markets' which brought it wealth. By 1900, the landscape was dominated by a series of major employers, Sir William Beardmore at Parkhead Forge, the Albion Works, the locomotive building shops at Springburn and Cowlairs to

13. The 'unimproved' city. Probably a Thomas Annan photograph of the Calton district of Glasgow in the 1860s. Urban by-laws had not yet got rid of the chickens which supplemented someone's family income. *Strathclyde Regional Archives.*

the north of the city, Elder's Fairfield Yard at Govan and Templeton's carpet factory, like a Venetian palace, by Glasgow Green. Although some textiles survived, Glasgow became the skilled man's city. In 1911, less than 30 per cent of the occupied male labour force was identified as unskilled. The rest were the basis of an aggressive male wage-earning culture formed in the face of harsh work environments and the vicious bargaining of a boom bust market economy.[8] Around these clustered a host of smaller concerns supplying the goods and services required by the big exporters and serving the needs of the growing population.

If Scotland had a 'shock' city then it was Glasgow. In the 1840s, Edwin Chadwick, the Benthamite civil servant, who led the utilitarian campaign for British public health, had his correspondents there. He was led through the narrow courts south of Argyle Street, which had produced 754 out of 5,000 cases in the fever hospital; dirty, narrow courts each with a dunghill of 'the most disgusting kind', 'worse off than wild animals . . . the dwellers of these courts had converted their shame into a kind of money by which their lodging was to be paid'. Even the hardened utilitarian was shocked by this effective working of the market economy.[9] Contemporaries were fearful and fascinated. 'Shadow', the letterpress printer, Alexander Brown, recorded his 'social photographs' in 1858. He saw beneath the merchant wealth, returning from the coast on Tuesday, and the mechanics throwing off the effects of Monday lethargy, the world of the Bridgegate and Trongate:

An immense concourse of men, women and children . . . preferring the open air of the street to the vitiated atmosphere of their pestilential dwellings. Rows of women with folded arms . . . oaths, recriminations, and abuse . . . the thundering noise of vehicles . . . the incongruous cries of apple women, fish and other dealers . . . the idiotical jeer and senseless laugh of drunkards . . . the horrid oaths and imprecations of low prostitutes . . . the roar of this social volcano . . . the disease of the body social in its acute form . . . .[10]

There was a sense of impending clash. By the 1850s, the crowding and poverty effects of the boom slump economy on which the human ecology of Glasgow was being established were being entombed in table after table of statistics, as if those endless threads of figures would provide a means to control and direct, as in some cases they did.[11]

During the nineteenth century Edinburgh became the extra-ordinary city which it is to-day. Its imposing physical presence was the work of those who re-made the city as a capital without a government. St Giles was encased in new ashlar in 1829 and its interior cleared of divisions and prepared as a vast presbyterian cathedral. The Castle and its esplanade were remoulded as a great monument and stage upon which Scotland displayed its new identity as a nation within a nation.[12] The Tolbooth Church (Pugin 1839–44) and New College (William Playfair 1845–50) dominated the new skyline, together with the transformed Bank of Scotland (1864). Holyrood Park was landscaped and lost the wild extra-urban character which was portrayed in Scott's *Heart of Midlothian* and James Hogg's *Confessions of a Justified Sinner*. Buildings like the North British Hotel (1895) and Jenner's department

14. The Gorbals, c.1870. These tenements were being built on land cleared of slum property by the Glasgow City Improvement Trust set up in 1866. *Strathclyde Regional Archives.*

store, a great Renaissance scrapbook in stone, (1893–94) confirmed Princes Street as a great shopping and hotel street.[13] These buildings reflected the economic, social and political function of Edinburgh. Although second in size, Edinburgh dominated the authority structure of Scotland. The Court of Session and the General Assembly of the Kirk still met there. Sir Walter Scott had talked of 'the bankers of Edinburgh who are in general zealously loyal, and who held the commerce of Glasgow and all the west of Scotland in the hollow of their hand'.[14] Glasgow had banks all right, but they, like the City of Glasgow Bank in 1878, were the ones which went bankrupt. By the 1890s, as the Scottish banking system was consolidated, Edinburgh's authority can be measured in terms of the number of branches which were directed from headquarters in each of the major cities (Table 3)[15].

New forms of government authority were added to the economy and society of Edinburgh. The Board of Supervision (Poor Law) was established in 1845 and attracted an increasing range of functions. Government agencies like this not only brought employment and government spending to Edinburgh, but meant that an increasing

Table 3. Bank Branches in the Major Scottish Cities, 1891

	Edinburgh	Glasgow	Dundee	Aberdeen	Inverness
City in which headquarters were located					
Edinburgh	52	83	11	6	5
Glasgow	14	30	2	3	1
Dundee	0	0	0	0	0
Aberdeen	0	0	0	9	1
Inverness	0	0	0	0	1

number of Scottish people looked to the city for the policy, authority and resources which only the capital of a national state could provide.[16] This 'post industrial' service function concealed a powerful industrial sector. In 1861, Youngers, Dryborough, Campbell, Usher and the others were employing 250. This rose to nearly 1,000 in 1891, producing beer for both the home and export markets. An engineering industry grew upon the back of the paper industry of Fife and the Lothians which in turn grew on the back of the printing and publishing trade of Edinburgh, itself stimulated by the demand from Law Courts, University and General Assembly, but now through firms like Chamber's and Nelson's, serving a wide leisure and educational market. The vulcanised rubber industry was brought to the west of the city by United States' capital in 1855. The North British Rubber Company and the Scottish Vulcanite Company (Limited) produced a wide range of footwear, clothing and other goods based upon the hardened rubber.[17] This provided Edinburgh with its distinctive occupational structure. By 1911, 15 per cent of occupied males were 'professional'. The figure for Glasgow and Aberdeen was 10 per cent.[18] The wealth of the middle and upper classes of Edinburgh, and indeed of many of the better paid artisans was reflected in the 40 per cent of the female labour force engaged in domestic service. The figure in Glasgow was 20 per cent and Aberdeen 23 per cent.[19] These functions were also the basis for the status-conscious hierarchies for which Edinburgh became famous:

> There are now ten or twelve well defined castes in our city . . . The merchants — not great with us — stand between the professionals and the shopkeepers; these are getting up: the Big Panes despise the Little Panes. The latter expel the Tradesmen, who erect a *nez retroussé* against the labourers. And these lord it over the Irish Fishdealers who will cut

an Applewoman of a Sunday . . . the pressure upwards has become a war of pride and envy . . . everyone castigates castes and is building one of his own.[20]

Dundee began the period as a port and hand-loom weavers' town. Five thousand were there in 1838; some 700 in the village of Lochee dominated by merchant weavers, Messrs Cox. In 1832 there were 36 flax spinning mills in the town, and by 1841 'the sulphurous atmosphere' gave the local sandstone 'a bloated and unseemly appearance'.[21] Power-loom weaving came later, led by the Baxter family in the Dens works. By the 1860s the Cox family employed several thousand in the massive Camperdown Works at Lochee and had moved into jute which, in many markets, displaced the coarse linens which were Dundee's speciality. The result was a grubby, hard working ill-balanced economy dominated by its female labour force. There were only 74 males aged over ten to every 100 women above the same age in 1911. Glasgow had 95 and Edinburgh and Aberdeen around 80. According to the census, 52 per cent of this teenage and adult female group were 'occupied', 38 per cent of them in textiles. In the other big three the total was around 37 per cent, 6 per cent of which were in textiles in Glasgow and Aberdeen. The result was a raucous shawl-clad mill-girl culture which shocked male observers with its coarseness and loud laughter. The high proportion of female-headed households and married women in waged work worried the enquiry writers of the Dundee Social Union as they studied the consequences for family life and infant mortality.[22] Aberdeen nearly became a Dundee but lost the bulk of its textile firms in the slumps of 1832 and 1848, and gathered a balanced economy based upon regional services and trade, shipbuilding, the export of granite and the fishing which came and went.[23]

Although Scotland has been seen understandably as four regional urban networks, closer examination shows a national network bound together by the influence and authority of Edinburgh, notably in banking, legal and church affairs and in government. By 1850, the new rail network and improved sea transport brought this network closer. Improved transport, together with the increased efficiency of the cash economy, increased the specialisation between towns which was a major feature of the period. Dundee, as we have seen, produced the coarse end of the linen trade and jute products. Dunfermline was fine table linen; Kirkcaldy floor covering; Galashiels soft tartans (doubtless wrapped in Dundee sacking); Dumfries and Hawick were stocking knitters' towns; Selkirk for tweed; Kilmarnock for carpets and Alloa for woollen yarn. The same sort of specialisms existed in the metal and engineering trades.

The growth, specialisation and integration of the Scottish urban network produced much more than the big four cities. In 1901 there were 75 burghs with over 5,000 inhabitants. If we consider the economic activity of the population aged over ten years in each place and compare the percentages obtained with the mean value for all 75 burghs (Table 7), then several distinctive groups of towns begin to emerge. The metal-bashing towns of the West were male and proletarian. There were few jobs for women and a relatively small number of commercial and professional men (Table 4).

Table 4. The Metal Towns in 1901

Burgh	Per cent metals (male)	Sex ratio m/f	Per cent professional (male)	Per cent commercial (male)	Per cent domestic servants (female)	Per cent unoccupied (female)
Clydebank	56.9	123	0.6	1.8	3.3	76.4
Port Glasgow	56.8	105	1.1	2.0	3.3	69.0
Renfrew	55.7	107	1.3	2.5	4.4	72.9
Dumbarton	51.5	107	1.7	2.4	7.6	73.9
Coatbridge	44.1	127	1.4	2.7	7.7	79.7

The textile towns were by no means as simple. Woollen towns, like Galashiels and Selkirk, had a male bias in their demand for labour, whilst the linen towns, like Brechin, Forfar and Dundee had a strong female bias. The stocking-knitters' town of Hawick was more balanced. All were a little more hospitable to the professional and commercial classes and displayed higher rates of 'occupation' for women (Table 5).

The metal and mining towns of the West were one urban frontier. The other was more sedate. In 1901, the douce burgh of St Andrews led a distinctive group noted for their high proportion of professional men, armies of domestic servants and consequent female bias in the sex ratio (Table 6).

If commercial men had been taken as the basis of ranking, then Broughty Ferry would have been top, and places like Helensburgh and Partick would have joined this list of resorts and suburban burghs. By 1901, social status and environmental specialisation in Scotland had taken place not just within burghs but between burghs. The three largest

Table 5. The Textile Towns in 1901

Burgh	Per cent textile (female)	(male)	Sex ratio m/f	Per cent professional (male)	Per cent commercial (male)	Per cent domestic servants (female)	Per cent unoccupied (female)
Dundee	38.0	22.6	74	2.2	4.9	4.1	48.3
Hawick	34.3	35.0	72	2.9	4.0	8.3	49.6
Forfar	32.6	22.8	70	3.3	3.7	5.6	51.7
Brechin	31.4	22.7	68	3.4	2.9	6.6	51.1
Selkirk	29.5	34.5	74	3.0	2.9	6.1	55.2
Dunfermline	27.1	13.4	79	2.7	3.4	4.7	59.3
Galashiels	27.0	34.9	78	2.3	3.7	6.4	57.7

Table 6. Resorts, Suburbs and Douce Burghs, 1901

Burgh	Per cent professional (male)	Sex ratio m/f	Per cent domestic servants (female)	Per cent unoccupied (female)
St Andrews	7.7	61	24.1	60.4
Elgin	6.0	71	16.2	65.4
Edinburgh	5.9	80	16.0	62.3
Crieff	5.6	72	19.1	64.3
Dunoon	5.0	67	14.4	70.8
Dumfries	4.8	79	12.5	58.6
Broughty Ferry	4.7	69	20.0	64.3

Table 7. Mean Value for the 75 Burghs over 5,000 Population, Scotland, 1901

sex ratio	92.0 (90.0)	% textiles (male)	5.8 (4.8)
% professionals (male)	2.8 (2.8)	% textiles (female)	8.8 (10.1)
% commercial (male)	3.9 (5.5)	% metals (male)	14.0 (17.3)
% domestic servants (female)	9.1 (8.9)	unoccupied females	67.9 (64.4)

The figure in brackets is the value for the total population of the 5,000 burghs

towns can all be paired with commuter burghs: Glasgow/Helensburgh, Dundee/Broughty Ferry and Edinburgh/Portobello. This specialisation reached its most complex around Glasgow. Helensburgh had a greater share of professional men. Partick and Gourock were for the commercial classes. Kinning Park, with its active co-operative society, was for skilled artisans; Clydebank and Greenock for heavy industry.

The distinctive forms of Scottish urban government were part of the forces which shaped the development and experiences of these urban places. The Royal Burgh had an ancient origin but still formed the basis of Scottish urban authority in the nineteenth century. The seventeenth-century Dean of Guilds Court was crucial for regulating the built environment. The slow decline of these courts was halted in the mid-nineteenth century when they were revived as a powerful agency enforcing stringent building regulations in the industrial cities.[24]

The supply of housing to all but the highest income groups in Scottish cities was dominated by the tenement. This was a high-rise building of some three to four storeys. Each storey would contain several flats or 'houses' which were reached by a common stair, sometimes with galleries.[25] Scottish law provided for the supply of building land through feuing. This was a once-and-for-all perpetual rent charge agreed on the initial transfer of occupancy and building rights. Thus the initial holder of ground rights had a motive for withholding land to gain the maximum return from the feu. This and the high legal cost of property transfer pushed up the initial cost of land and increased the motive for the intensive use of that space — hence the density of building.[26] The cost of housing was further increased by a tradition of building in stone and the stringent building regulations issued by the Dean of Guild Courts. Observers commented upon 'the excessive solidity of the Scottish tenement'. The result was a supply of urban housing with a very high structural quality of building but very poor facilities and a very limited supply of space to each family. In Edinburgh, in 1913, there were 7,106 one-roomed houses or single ends. 94 per cent shared a common water-closet and 43 per cent shared a common sink. In Glasgow there were 44, 354 such houses. Of these, 93 per cent shared a water-closet, but most had their own sink. Even in the 111,451 two-roomed houses or room-and-kitchen, 62 per cent still shared the water-closet. Thus, by 1914, the Scottish housing problem was very clearly identified as overcrowding.[27] The difference between Scottish and English experience was widened by levels of urban working-class income which were in general five per cent lower in Scotland. The result was levels of rents and of overcrowding that were not exceeded in any English town, with the exception of parts of London and the naval town of Plymouth. In general, the Scots paid a little less for their housing than the English, and as a result got a lot less. Housing was only one aspect of urban poverty which had roots in the countryside. The distinctive discipline of the hiring fair, the long hire, living in service and the tied cottage, together with the limitations of the Scottish Poor Law, both old and new, meant that surplus labour in Scotland tended to emigrate or move to the towns rather than stay in the countryside, as it often did, especially in southern England. This added to the endemic poverty and relatively low wages of the urban centres (Table 8).[28]

Table 8. Rents and Crowding in 1908[29]

| | Weekly rent | | | | Percentage of |
| | two rooms | | one room | | population in houses |
	s.	d.	s.	d.	of one or two rooms*
Aberdeen	4	3	5	7	39.3 (50.4)
Dundee	3	10	6	1	63.0 (71.8)
Edinburgh and Leith	4	4	6	5	41.3 (50.4)
Falkirk	4	3	5	1	no data (63.2)
Galashiels	3	0	3	10	no data (61.7)
Glasgow	4	2	6	8	55.1 (69.7)
Perth	3	6	5	2	31.5 (41.5)
London	6	0	7	6	22.2
Bradford	3	6	4	6	14.8
Leeds	3	3	4	0	9.9
Middlesbrough	3	6	4	0	5.7
Plymouth	4	6	6	0	30.3
Rochdale	2	9	4	1	11.4
Sheffield	3	1	4	1	4.4

*The figure in brackets shows the percentage of families in one- or two-roomed houses from the 1901 census.

Although the four-storey tenement dominated the history of nineteenth-century housing, there were places, moderate-sized towns like Galashiels, Arbroath and Musselburgh, where the two-storey flatted house predominated. The same house style can be found in late nineteenth-century areas of Kirkcaldy and the parts of Edinburgh built by the Edinburgh Co-operative Building Society, suggesting that it was the house type preferred by the prosperous working class.[30] It will require a much closer study of the smaller towns of Scotland to fully understand the mixture of law, tradition, income and rents which created the urban housing of nineteenth century Scotland.

The regulations which helped to push up the prices of Scottish urban housing derived from a tradition of urban authority which Scotland inherited and developed from the Royal Burghs. The resulting problem of shortage, crowding and a standard of accommodation in single and double ends outraged the growing standards of privacy between sexes and age groups which spread from middle-class to working-class people during the nineteenth century. The spokesmen for the Edinburgh Trades and Labour Council even objected to the galleried housing provided by Edinburgh City in Tron Square because 'the stairs and landing have to be cleaned by the people, and it is objectionable for the wife to come out and clean those stairs outside'. The Rev. Dr Watson of Glasgow reported: 'The children are forced out of doors to give the housewife room to work. . . . they play in the dark evil smelling courts, . . . They see sights which demoralize and hear language which corrupts'.

The attempts to combat the overcrowding reflected the authoritarian tradition of Scottish urbanism. Under the Glasgow City Improvement Act of 1866, the Corporation took power to ticket houses not exceeding 2,000 cubic feet. A metal ticket inscribed with the maximum number of occupants allowed by law was fixed to a door or lintel. That done, the police and sanitary inspectors were allowed to raid the house at any time of day or more usually night.[31] The practice was extended to Edinburgh and Greenock through local acts, and made available to all burghs through the Burgh Police Act of 1903. These raids or 'repressive efforts', in the words of Dr Russell, long-time medical officer of health for Glasgow, were seen to be 'degrading . . . to have any family living under conditions where they are apt to be stirred up at any time during the night by men coming in with lanterns and books and taking notes'.

Housing regulation found itself at the sharp end of class conflict. The raids were continually frustrated by warnings passed from close to close. 'Sometimes the people have got into presses, into barrels, and into enclosed places above the bed — sometimes on the roof, hiding behind the chimney head'.[32]

When the full impact of urban industrial growth hit Scotland between 1820 and 1850, Scotland already had a structure of locally specific power structures — the royal burghs. By the chance of geography, all major and most medium-sized urban centres grew within the existing network. No major city grew within a web of parish, manorial and ad hoc institutions like Manchester or Birmingham. As urban problems, the dis-economies of

15. Such plates were attached to the doors of 'ticketed houses' in Glasgow from 1862 onwards, in an attempt to curb overcrowding. They gave cubic capacity and the number of permitted dwellers. Sanitary inspectors made night-time swoops. *People's Palace, Glasgow Museums.*

concentration, the problems of fire, disease and traffic congestion, became clear, solutions based upon a dual structure of urban authority became dominant. The Municipal Reform Act of 1833 made the royal burghs rate-payer elected. Twelve parliamentary burghs were added, notably Leith, until then subordinate to Edinburgh, Paisley and Falkirk. The reformed royal burghs still retained fragments of the older structures. In Edinburgh, Glasgow and Perth, the guilds or trades still appointed two councillors. The guilds were, for practical purposes, private associations of citizens. In Edinburgh, they elected two councillors and the Dean of Guild. So great was the distrust of the corporations that a parallel system of police commissioners was created with the power to raise and spend rates for a variety of purposes. By the 1840s, most corporations and police commissioners were, in practice, the same membership, but they kept separate minute books and accounts. The term 'police' had a much wider meaning in Scotland. Their powers included not just paving, lighting and watching but extended to issues covered by public health legislation in England.[33] In terms of national legislation, Scotland lagged well behind England. The Public Health (Scotland) Act did not appear until 1867. Its weak powers of central direction belonged to the Board of Supervision (the poor law authority) in Edinburgh. Other attempts to legislate verged on the absurd. The 1866 Sanitary Act proved unworkable in Scotland, because, amongst other reasons, the ultimate court of enforcement was the English Court of Queen's Bench. Several Scottish burghs took an interest in the Artisans Dwellings Acts passed between 1868 and 1882, but the Royal Commission on Housing in 1885 was told that they were a 'dead letter'.[34] The gap was not as great as might appear for several reasons. The early English acts were not as effective as their supporters claimed. The Scottish towns carried out a great deal of cleansing and draining under the 'police' acts. For a large part of Scotland's urban population urban 'improvement' was directed by a series of local acts obtained by the major cities. The 1866 City of Glasgow Improvements Act cleared or remodelled 88 acres of the central area of Glasgow. Between 1871–74, some 15,425 houses were demolished. The initial intention had been to rely upon profit-seeking builders to provide new housing. This was only partially successful. The Trust which acted for the Corporation in this matter was drawn into building in the late 1880s, and by 1902 the Corporation owned 2,488 houses. The Edinburgh Act of 1867 paid as much attention to improving communications as to public health, but by supervising large-scale demolitions and rebuilding around the city centre reduced death rates, population densities and housing supply.[35] Other places did little and were lucky. In Galashiels water flowing across a steep-sided site and a powerful river cleansed the town. This left a few substantial centres, places like Coatbridge and Greenock, at risk. By the 1890s the gaps in Scotland were in the smaller towns where aspects of health regulation were partial and primitive.

The pattern of national legislation for urban Scotland had several distinctive features. Most important was the Lindsay or Burgh Police (Scotland) Act of 1862. This was adoptive only, and so enabled towns like Coatbridge simply to ignore it. The police authorities could form Dean of Guild Courts to enforce extensive building regulations. The number of such courts increased from 20 in 1880 to 189 by 1912. Sanitation, water supply, street regulation and, for places with a population over 7,000, police, in the English sense, were to be undertaken. In the following decades there was a substantial growth in the permanent officials employed by the burghs. The town clerk was joined by medical officers of health and sanitary inspectors. These urban powers were increased by the Police Act of 1892 and the Public Health (Scotland) Act of 1897. Central supervision under the Local Government Board (Scotland), created in 1894 under the recently formed Scottish Office, was also strengthened.[36]

16. Urbanism could take many forms. Turning on the water at Ladybank in Fife (1908) attracted great curiosity, although the men entering the public house seem unwilling to join the enthusiasm. *Scottish Ethnographic Archive, National Museums of Scotland.*

Lindsay's Act, in its anxiety to improve urban government, provided extensive powers for the self creation of police burghs. Seven or more householders in 'any town, village, place or locality' containing over 700 people could apply to the Sheriff of the County. After appropriate investigation, usually involving a poll of householders whose property was valued at over £4 a year, the Sheriff would 'mark out, define and specify' the boundaries of the new police burgh. The results of a poll were often close, as property holders balanced the benefits of urban regulation against the pressure of increased rates and the obligations of building regulations. In 1886, the rapidly growing settlement of over 5,000 around Thomson's shipyard in the parish of Kilpatrick, down river from Glasgow, only became the Burgh of Clydebank by 497 votes to 496. By the 1900s, Robert McAlpine and Sons, builders, were putting up working-class tenements on Kilbowie Hill, thus, said burgh officials, escaping the higher urban rates and the more stringent building regulations of the Dean of Guild Court. McAlpine smartly pointed out that his rents were some 20 per cent less than the average in Clydebank.[37]

As a means of easing the creation of local government structures, the Scottish Acts worked well, but they had unintended and less desirable

17. Civic pride and social order: the laying of the foundation stone of the Glasgow City Chambers in October 1883. *Strathclyde Regional Archives.*

results, adding to the scatter of detailed and specific power structures which already littered the Scottish landscape. Tax shelters for the wealthy, like Portobello and Hillhead, appeared. Industrial interests sheltered from the influence of county and big-city government in places like Govan and eventually in Coatbridge. The resulting inefficient and often unjust distribution of power and responsibility appeared in its most extreme form around Glasgow. By 1887 Glasgow was hemmed in by a ring of police burghs to the south and west. They were of two kinds. The residential or villa burghs, Hillhead, Kinning Park, Pollokshields, Pollokshields East, Govanhill and Crosshill all had lower rates than Glasgow, but a very limited range of local government services. Hillhead had a fire brigade of eleven men, but only one was full-time. Police were provided by the county and water by Glasgow. Pollokshields was composed only of self-contained villas and thus, its commissioners told the 1887 enquiry, it needed to make no arrangements for the treatment of infectious diseases. The three industrial burghs of Govan, Partick and Maryhill all had higher rates than Glasgow, but equally ineffective urban services. Provost Craig, of Maryhill, when asked if the manual fire engine (eleven part-timers and

18. Patrick Geddes's contribution to town planning owed much to his upbringing and work in Scotland. He used many photographs in his 'Cities and Town Planning Exhibitions' in 1911 and 1912. Here is East Crosscauseway in Edinburgh with its mixture of commercial, industrial (the brewery) and residential property which well illustrated a theme he called 'chaos'. *Patrick Geddes Centre, Edinburgh.*

a full-timer who doubled up as the sole detective officer on the police strength), was adequate, replied: 'Well, for a small fire, I daresay it would be . . .' The Glasgow authorities were insistent that efficiency and justice required wholesale boundary extension. The population of the residential burghs worked mostly in Glasgow. The others were firmly tied to the Glasgow economy. Glasgow provided the capital costs of the water, gas, tramway, police and fire services which the smaller places borrowed, albeit at a charge, but only when they needed them. In 1891, Glasgow got the residential places, and Maryhill, Partick and Govan stayed out until 1912.

The motivation of the small places which agreed to amalgamate with Glasgow indicates many of the pressures for the growth of urban power in Scotland. It was more than a matter of public health and building regulations, as the Ratepayers' Committee for the Burgh of Hillhead and the District of Kelvinside explained: 'Annexation is the only means of affording adequate protection to person and property in the police, sanitary and fire arrangements'. They only had 25 county police stationed locally, so, 'in the event of any sudden riot or disturbance arising in the surrounding labouring or mining districts of Maryhill, Anniesland, Knightswood or Partick, or in the City, and coming into Kelvinside or Hillhead, police reinforcements would . . . [be] . . . widely scattered over a large county.'

They had memories of recent riots in Blantyre. In addition, there was 'a recent Socialistic meeting, between 500 and 600 men were collected on the Green', and 'During the summer of 1887, several cases of housebreaking and robbery occurred in Kelvinside and Hillhead, in none of which were the parties discovered.' Things were not happy in Hillhead. Change was clearly worth risking an increase in the rates.[38]

Emerging from all this is the sense of a Scottish perception of urbanisation which increasingly identified the urban place with higher levels of authority and order than was expected by the English. The Scots accepted and expected strong, positive forms of locally specific authority in their towns. The town was a place of order. The countryside and the unbounded mining settlements like Blantyre were the sources of violence and chaos. In Scotland, urban traditions of authority were strong whilst central direction was weak. Scotland's image of its towns was as places of order and discipline. Here is Willa Muir, writing about Montrose in 1912:

> All this late summer peace and fragrance belonged to the municipality. The burgh of Calderwick [Montrose] owned its golf and its bathing, its sand and its gorse. The larks nested in municipal grass, the cows waddled on municipal turf . . . the burgh of Calderwick was busy about its jute mills, its grain mills, its shipping, schools, shops, offices and dwelling houses.

When the minister's sister [Free Kirk] goes out, she did not:

> expect to be surprised by anything in the streets . . . the baker's van was precisely at the head of the street and the buckets of house refuse were still

waiting by twos and threes at the kerb . . . everything had its time and place; that streets were paved and gardens contained within iron railings, that children were in school . . . hundreds of shopkeepers waiting behind clean counters for the thousands of housewives who like herself were shopping . . . She could hear the prolonged whistle of the express from King's Cross as it pulled out of the station. Punctual to the minute.[39]

The 1851 religious census provided another indicator. If we take a very crude attendance index, namely total attendances in morning, afternoon and evening, divided by population adjusted for missing returns, then, with the exception of a few rural areas, mainly along the Scottish border, English urban areas had a lower level of attendance than the surrounding countryside. In Scotland, the result was different (Table 9).

Table 9. Church Attendance per 100: Urban/Rural Contrasts, Scotland, 1851[40]

Aberdeen/rest of Aberdeenshire	59/59
Edinburgh-Leith/rest of Midlothian	63/45
Haddington/rest of East Lothian	112/34
Peebles/rest of Peebleshire	64/53
Glasgow/all Lanark and Renfrewshire	43/43
Dundee/rest of Forfarshire	64/53

These figures are the distorted shadows of reality, but they are enough to suggest that Scottish cities were better able to sustain the social discipline of religious attendance. In urban government the sense of the importance and the legitimacy of strong municipal collective action was inherited from the royal burghs. The better ordered of the royal burghs brought with them into the nineteenth century an account called the common good fund. It had been amassed from rents on land and tolls on trade and markets held in the burgh. It became the basis for active and innovative interventions into urban affairs. In 1904 Glasgow endowed a lectureship in social philosophy from its fund, and Edinburgh kept a town observatory. Sometimes this strength could hinder development. In Selkirk, corporation and trades were strong. The privileges of the weavers and of the commons were actively defended. The Common Riding was a survival rather than a revival, and the huge common with its grazing was well worth defending. As a result the first wave of industrialisation passed Selkirk by. The lead was taken by Galashiels with its weak municipal tradition and the freely constituted Manufacturers' Corporation.[41] In Stirling, the common good fund, with its revenue from

19. Houses and shops in Anderston, c.1850. The horse-driven omnibuses facilitated greater ease of movement to the suburbs. *Graham Collection, Mitchell Library, Glasgow.*

rents and customs dues, was used to finance paving, drainage and water supply, thus delaying the day the town had to form a police commission and raise a rate until 1857. So great was the antipathy to rates, that the proprietors of the principal streets helped finance improvements by subscription between 1834 and 1841.[42]

Overall the impact of this tradition of urban authority emerged by the end of the century in the great sense of collective action which was so important for Scottish towns. Edinburgh had begun the period with a glorious bankruptcy related to its development of the New Town and Leith docks, and so was understandably cautious.[43] Glasgow finished the nineteenth century as the municipal trading capital of the world.[44] The Loch Katrine water scheme, opened in 1859, was followed by the work of the 1866 Improvement Act and the gas takeover in 1869. In the 1890s, on the back of economic growth, the city authorities expanded their activities into trams, electricity, libraries, museums, art galleries, golf, tennis and housing. Local taxes per head of the population rose from 12p in 1846/7 to 134p in 1913/14, or from 4p to 19p in the pound in terms of the retail value of the city.[45] The revenue and spending pattern of Scottish burghs as a whole was very striking (Tables 10a, b).

Table 10A. Expenditure and Receipts in All Scottish Burghs of more than 5,000 Population

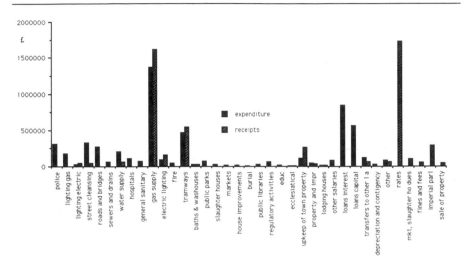

Table 10B. Net Expenditure, 1901

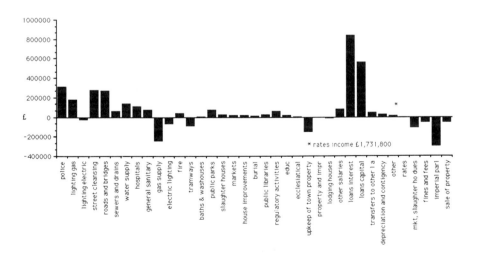

The pattern was dominated by the collective consumption of many things, from water to trams, where the authority and ability to raise capital inherent in local government provided extensive and effective services. Public health policies eventually contributed to substantial falls in Glasgow's death rate, but the proportion of the population living in

Golf Club House and Grand Hotel, St. Andrews

The Lodge is a little way further along from where I marked + hope you are well ... ... Peggy

20. A very different sort of town! Postcard from Peggy. 'The Lodge is a little way further along from where I marked x. hope you are well'. What else can you say about St Andrews in 1903? *Scottish Ethnographic Archive, National Museums of Scotland.*

one- or two-roomed houses had only fallen from 73 per cent to 66 per cent of the population between 1861 and 1911.

In urban politics Scotland was liberal and anti-landlord. The 1832 and 1833 parliamentary and municipal reforms brought a property-owning ratepayer electorate to the towns. Before 1832, Scotland's politics were managed by a Tory alliance of lawyers and landlords. The post-1832 reaction swept the Tories from the towns more thoroughly than anything that happened in England. Urban electoral contests were either non-party or between liberals. Radical/moderate or Free Church/moderate clashes lay behind most mid-century contests. Towards the end of the century, the Irish Home Rule issue and early labour success brought a mild weakening of liberal dominance. Patronage did have some effect. The Tories made occasional gains in the Ayr Burghs, influenced by the Lords Eglinton, Bute, Argyll and Buccleuch, and in the Falkirk Burghs, which included Coatbridge, where the evangelical Tory Bairds of Gartsherrie were major ironmasters. Influence worked more easily when it ran with the prevailing liberal sentiment, as it did for the Fergusons of Raith in the Kirkcaldy Burghs.[46] Despite the late-century importance of home rule and the large number of Irish Catholics, Glasgow never became a base for effective sectarian politics. These remained a matter for the football terraces. The Orange order was strong in the iron and steel towns around the city, places like Coatbridge and Hamilton, and in some of the shipyards down river. Organisations like the Scottish Protestant Alliance gained support in the 1930s but were never able to counter the influence of the urban liberal tradition. This linked the anti-state Presbyterian tradition with the anti-landlord tradition of the Highland and Irish migrants. That tradition was remade in late century. Housing was a major issue for the Independent Labour Party and the landlords and their factors were the target for the rent strikes of 1915. Thus Glasgow was set to become the labour city of the 1930s and not to follow the sectarian politics of Liverpool and Belfast. Such a result against the blandishments of many eager sectarian organisations must stand as one of the major achievements of the people of Glasgow.[47]

Anti-landlord urban politics was not limited to Glasgow. The hosiery town of Hawick was a liberal stronghold which lay in the County of Roxburgh, territory of the Duke of Buccleuch, de facto leader of the Scottish Tories. The Duke dominated rural voters with ease and was happy to create 'faggot' votes to bolster his score. Unfortunately these people had to get into the centre of Hawick (and out again) in order to vote. During the 1830s and 1840s, the stocking weavers and their allies surrounded the Tower Inn where the polling station was and mobbed any farmer who came to town to vote Tory. Several were caught, stripped and dropped in the Slittrig Burn. In 1841, police and dragoons were brought from Edinburgh. The police were plied with missiles and drink. The dragoons charged and cleared the main street. As they turned at the top of the hill, the local population emerged from the courts and wynds to which they had retreated and barricaded the street with carts and the guns normally used for poaching. The soldiers wisely considered that their job was done and left the scene. Buccleuch must have seen the formation of the Hawick Burghs in 1868 with some relief.[48] The confrontation of urban dwellers and landlords may well have been much clearer and more intense in Scotland than in England.

The nineteenth century added several significant physical elements to the Scottish City. The names of suburbs like Morningside in Edinburgh and Kelvinside in Glasgow gathered a rich association of social overtones. Smaller areas of high-status housing appeared in the other towns, like the King's Park district south of the castle in Stirling, where the arrival of the railway added a commuter population to the existing rentier inhabitants.[49] In the larger cities the growth of the suburbs was made possible by the tram. Horse-drawn, and then in the 1890s, electric, they followed the builders down Great Western Road in Glasgow and along Morningside Road and Minto Street in south Edinburgh.[50] Behind the new suburban dwellers came the working classes and the middling sort filtering up in areas like Nicholson Street in Edinburgh.[51] The quality of these new areas was often protected by feu charters drawn up and enforced. In 1877 Arnothill in Falkirk was restricted to single and double villas. In the 1870s, Sir George Warrender laid out his estate south of the Meadows in Edinburgh. His feu charters ensured a uniform and homogeneous development for the white-collar population which came to inhabit the great castles of respectability which form some of the finest tenements in Scotland. Although many areas of Scottish cities began to get increasingly specific social identities during the second half of the century, the separation of middle-class and working-class people, of skilled and unskilled wage earners, must not be exaggerated. Morningside had its working class in noisy, smoky Balcarres Street by the railway; Gorbals in Glasgow retained a middle-class population to the end of the century.[52]

The growing towns attracted a series of massive and specialised institutionalised buildings. In 1867–9, Edinburgh's new poor house was placed at the edge of the built-up area to take advantage of low rents. Glasgow University was pushed from its city-centre site by a need for space and the high prices which the railway companies were willing to pay for that land. The baronial poor house and the Gothic university were no mere utilitarian buildings. They celebrated the purpose and importance of the communities which built them. Shops, offices and warehouses gathered in the expanding central business districts. In Glasgow large parts of Argyle and Sauchiehall Streets were renewed in late century to create prestigious retail areas.[53] In Edinburgh, the 1867 City Improvement Act created Chambers Street, a broad street dominated by educational institutions, the completed University, the Church of Scotland Normal School (1878–9), the Watt Institute (1872) and the Royal Scottish Museum (1861–75). Echoes of the Renaissance announced civic purpose. In all parts of Scotland, warehouses and offices were built which no longer looked like overgrown houses or utilitarian blocks, but asserted themselves with street frontages that selected from the whole scrapbook of European architectural history. The railways added to the specialised architecture and played a major part in reshaping inner-city areas. By 1900, railways and their related buildings covered 7.6 per cent of the land area of central Glasgow.[54] As Scotland began to feel its way towards a new sense of national identity, the cities became the focus for a complex system of symbols. Statues of Burns and Sir Walter Scott appeared everywhere. The border towns responded to the traumas of industrial change and immigration from the South with the cult of the border reiver. As the city centres became complex and functional symbol systems, the greatest symbol of all arrived in George Square, Glasgow. The foundation stone of the Glasgow Municipal Buildings was laid in October 1883. The ceremony celebrated every aspect of the power, history and social structure of the city. In its detail it laid bare the proud soul of urban Scotland. The day began with a massive procession from the Cathedral to George Square, 'our local Pantheon'. The Lord Provost was accompanied by the magistrates and councillors, by members of the Clyde Trustees, the Glasgow Guilds and the Dean of Guild. Dozens of masonic lodges marched with banners and emblems and the band of the 93rd Highlanders. The Trades marched from Glasgow Green. Carters, bricklayers, ropemakers, lathsplitters, hand-loom weavers and many others marched with banners and the emblems of their trade. Under the stone were deposited coins, newspapers, copies of the Acts of Parliament upon which the municipal authority of Glasgow depended, from the Public Parks Act of 1859 to the Loans Act of 1883, together with the municipal and parochial accounts. Hymns, prayers, speeches and banquets followed as Glasgow asserted its identity and its legal, moral and financial ability to impose order upon its own size, density and complexity.[55]

By the end of the century the Scottish city had become a powerful agency for organising production and reproduction. The concentrations of population were formidable. The concentration of state power was equally important. To represent this power by its spending patterns and legislative framework presents only the bare bones of its impact and ambitions. There were already many tensions. Amalgamation with neighbouring police burghs and central government grants provided some relief. Labour politics and the urban technology of pipes and sewers and trams provided other means of change. Scotland had an ambitious and powerful urban structure with which to face the economic blizzards of the inter-war period. It was a structure which gave considerable power and freedom to Scottish towns and cities to use or neglect as local political élites thought fit.

NOTES

1. M. W. Flinn *et. al.*, *Scottish Population History, from the Seventeenth Century to the 1930s* (Cambridge, 1977), p. 313.

2. Peter Flora, Franz Kraus and Winifred Pfennig, *State, Economy and Society in Western Europe, 1815–1975. A Data Handbook*, *vol.* 2 (Frankfurt, 1987), pp. 247–81; Flinn *et. al.*, p. 302.

3. This rule suggests that balanced urban industrial growth produces a pattern whereby the second largest city is half the size of the largest, the third a third of the largest, and so on. Brian T. Robson, *Urban Growth. An Approach* (London 1973), pp. 23–4.

4. Sydney and Olive Checkland, *Industry and Ethos. Scotland, 1832–1914* (London, 1984), pp. 34–47.

5. T. M. Devine, 'Urbanisation', and Stana Nenadic, 'The Rise of the Urban Middle Classes', in T. M. Devine and Rosaline Mitchison (eds.), *People and Society in Scotland, vol. I, 1760–1830* (Edinburgh, 1988).

6. In 1831, there were 15,217 weavers and winders in Glasgow, 15 per cent of the total occupied population of 103,001. There were also 9,856 (9.5 per cent) cotton spinners and steam-loom weavers, James Cleland, *Enumeration of the Inhabitants of the City of Glasgow . . . 1831* (Glasgow, 1832).

7. A. Slaven, 'Earnings and Productivity in the Scottish Coal Mining Industry During the 19th Century: the Dixon Enterprises', in Peter L. Payne (ed.), *Studies in Scottish Business History* (London, 1967), pp. 217 49.

8. Jim Treble, 'The Market for Unskilled Male Labour in Glasgow, 1891–1914', in Ian MacDougall (ed.), *Essays in Scottish Labour History* (Edinburgh, 1978); Sylvia Price, 'Rivetters Earnings in Clyde Ship-building, 1889–1914', *Scottish Economic and Social History*, vol. I, (1981), pp. 42–65.

9. M. W. Flinn (ed.), *The Sanitary Condition of the Labouring Population of Great Britain by Edwin Chadwick, 1842* (Edinburgh, 1965), p. 98; Dundee has an equally strong claim for the title of shock city, see G. Lewis, *The Filth and Fever Bills of Dundee, and what might be made of them* (1841).

10. Shadow [Alexander Brown], *Midnight Scenes and Social Photographs, being Sketches of Life in the Streets, Wynds and Dens of the City*, (Glasgow, 1858; reprinted Glasgow, 1976), ed. John McCaffrey, pp. 17 and 43.

11. A. K. Chalmers, *The Health of Glasgow, 1818–1925* (Glasgow, 1930).

12. That Portcullis Gate which forms the backdrop to so many tourist photographs is a sixteenth-century fabric, but its appearance and the nearby gatehouse are the work of the 1880s.

13. John Gifford, Colin McWilliam and David Walker, *The Buildings of Scotland, Edinburgh* (London, 1984).

14. S. G. Checkland, *Scottish Banking. A History, 1695–1973* (London, 1975), p. 284.

15. *Edinburgh and Leith Post Office Directory, 1894–95* (Edinburgh, 1894), pp. 717–28

16. John S. Gibson, *The Thistle and the Crown. A History of the Scottish Office*, (Edinburgh, 1985); Ian Levitt, *Government and Social Conditions in Scotland, 1854–1919* (Edinburgh, 1988). Note that the Scottish Office itself was not physically transferred to Edinburgh until 1939. The nineteenth-century developments refer to the fragmented structure of the Boards which mediated between Scotland and Whitehall.

17. David Bremner, *The Industries of Scotland. Their Rise, Progress and Present Condition* (Edinburgh 1869), pp. 363–73, 437–43; *Stretch a Mile, Gorgie–Dalry Living Memory Project* (Edinburgh, 1985).

18. The 1901 census recorded 1,102 lawyers in Edinburgh.

19. Note that 'servants' were often employed in retail, hotel and lodging establishments, and thus the figure reflects the service function of Edinburgh as much as the high standards of domestic comfort gained by its citizens. Edward Higgs, 'Domestic Servants and Households in Victorian England', in *Social History*, vol. 8 (1983), pp. 201–10.

20. John Heiton, *The Castes of Edinburgh* (Edinburgh, 1861), p. 7.

21. A. Fullarton and Co., *The Topographical, Statistical and Historical Gazetteer of Scotland*, vol. 2 (Glasgow, 1841), p. 372.

22. William M. Walker, *Juteopolis, Dundee and its textile workers, 1885–1923* (Edinburgh, 1979); Dundee Social Union, *Report on the Housing and Industrial Conditions and Medical Inspection of School Children* (Dundee, 1905).

23. Alastair Durie, 'Balanced and Unbalanced Urban Economies in Aberdeen and Dundee, 1800–1914', *Scotia*, vol. 7 (1984), pp. 16–25.

24. R. G. Rodger, 'The Evolution of Scottish Town Planning', in George Gordon and Brian Dicks, *Scottish Urban History* (Aberdeen, 1983).

25. Frank Worsdall, *The Tenement. A Way of Life. A Social, Historical and Architectural Study of Housing in Glasgow* (Edinburgh, 1979).

26. R. G. Rodger, 'The Law and Urban Change', *Urban History Yearbook* (1979), pp. 77–91; *Second Report of the Royal Commission for Enquiring into the Housing of the Working Classes*, BPP, 1884–85, vol. 31, Q.18,514.

27. *Royal Commission on the Housing of the Industrial Population of Scotland, Rural and Urban, BPP*, 1917–18, vol. 14, pp. 42–4, 77.

28. R. G. Rodger, 'The Invisible Hand, Market Forces, Housing and the Urban Form in Victorian Cities', in Derek Fraser and Anthony Sutcliffe, *The Pursuit of Urban History* (London, 1983).

29. *Report of an Enquiry by the Board of Trade into Working Class Rents, Housing and Retail Prices . . . in the Principal Industrial Towns of the United Kingdom, BPP*, 1908, vol. 108.

30. R C 1884–84, Q.18,680; R C 1917–18, pp. 47–59; Rosemary Pipes, *The Colonies of Stockbridge* (Edinburgh, 1984).

31. John Butt, 'Working Class Housing in Glasgow, 1851–1914', in S. D. Chapman, (ed.), *The History of Working Class Housing* (Newton Abbott, 1971), pp. 55–92; Sean Damar, 'State, Class and Housing: Glasgow 1885–1919', in J. Melling (ed.), *Housing, Social Policy and the State* (London, 1980).

32. R C 1917–18, p. 113–15.

33. Mabel Atkinson, *Local Government in Scotland* (Edinburgh, 1904), pp. 29–67; Robert Miller, *Guide to the Procedure of the Dean of Guild Court of Edinburgh* (Edinburgh, 1891).

34. G. F. A. Best, 'Another Part of the Island', in H. J. Dyos and M. Wolff, *The Victorian City*, vol. I (London 1973), pp. 389–411; *Second Report of the*

Royal Commission into the Housing of the Working Classes, *BPP*, 1884–85, vol. 31, qq.18,466–18,478.

35. C. M. Allan, 'The Genesis of British Urban Redevelopment with Special Reference to Glasgow', *Economic History Review*, second series, 18 (1965), 598–613; John Butt, 'Working Class Housing in the Scottish Cities', in George Gordon and Brian Dicks, *Scottish Urban History* (Aberdeen 1983), pp. 233–67; David Cousin and John Lessels, *Plan of Sanitary Improvements of the City of Edinburgh* (Edinburgh, 1866).

36. Ian Levitt, *Government and Social Conditions in Scotland, 1845–1919* (Edinburgh, 1988).

37. John Hood, (ed.), *The History of Clydebank* (Clydebank, 1988), pp. 24, 36.

38. *Report of the Glasgow Boundaries Commission*, vol. I, *BPP*, 1888, vol. 46.

39. Willa Muir, *Imagined Corners* (London, 1935; reprinted Edinburgh, 1987).

40. *Census of Religious Worship (Scotland)*, *PP*, 1854, vol. 59.

41. John Gilbert (ed.), *Flower of the Forest, Selkirk: A New History* (Selkirk, 1985).

42. Finlay McKichan, 'A Burgh's Response to the Problems of Urban Growth: Stirling, 1780–1880', *Scottish Historical Review*, 57 (1978), pp. 68–86.

43. Thomas Hunter and Robert Porter, *Report on the Common Good Fund of the City of Edinburgh* (Edinburgh, 1905); A. J. Youngson, *The Making of Classical Edinburgh* (Edinburgh, 1966).

44. Bernard Aspinwall, *Portable Utopia, Glasgow and the United States, 1820–1920* (Aberdeen, 1984), pp. 151–88.

45. Tom Hart, 'Urban Growth and Municipal Government: Glasgow in a Comparative Context, 1846–1914, in Anthony Slaven and Derek H. Aldcroft (eds), *Business, Banking and Urban History* (Edinburgh, 1982), pp. 193–219.

46. J. G. C. Hutchison, *A Political History of Scotland, 1832–1924* (Edinburgh, 1986), pp. 53, 87, 114–15; William Miller, 'Politics in the Scottish City, 1832–1982', in George Gordon (ed.), *Perspectives of the Scottish City* (Aberdeen, 1985), pp. 180–92; Alan B. Campbell, *The Lanarkshire Miners* (Edinburgh, 1979), pp. 205–14.

47. Joan Smith, 'Class, Skill and Sectarianism in Glasgow and Liverpool, 1880–1914', in R. J. Morris (ed.), *Class, Power and Social Structure in British Nineteenth Century Towns* (Leicester, 1986), pp. 157–204.

48. *History of Hawick from 1832* (Hawick, 1902); J. I. Brash, *Papers on Scottish Electoral Politics, 1832–1854* (Edinburgh, 1974).

49. R. C. Fox, 'The Morphological, Social and Functional Districts of Stirling, 1798–1881', *Transactions of the Institute of British Geographers* (1979), pp. 153–67; Charles McKean, *Stirling and the Trossachs* (Edinburgh, 1985), pp. 51–7.

50. A. D. Ochojna, 'Lines of Class Distinction: An Economic and Social History of the British Tramcar with special reference to Edinburgh and Glasgow', unpublished PhD Thesis, University of Edinburgh, 1974.

51. Rev. Thomas Brown, *Alexander Wood, Sketch of his Life and Work* (Edinburgh, 1886), p. 178.

52. Michael Barke and Tony Johnson, 'Emerging Residential Segregation in 19th century Falkirk', *Scottish Geographical Magazine*, 98 (1981), pp. 87–100; Malcolm Cant, *Marchmont in Edinburgh* (Edinburgh, 1984); J. G. Robb, 'Suburb and Slum in Gorbals. Social and Residential Change, 1800–1900, in George Gordon and Brian Dicks (eds.), *Scottish Urban History* (Aberdeen, 1983), pp. 130–67.

53. J. W. R. Whitehand, *The Changing Face of Cities* (Oxford, 1987), pp. 118–27; John Tweed, *Guide to Glasgow and the Clyde* (Glasgow, 1872), pp. 16 and 45; John Gifford, Colin McWilliam and David Walker, *The Buildings of Scotland, Edinburgh* (London, 1984), p. 536.

54. John R. Kellett, *The Impact of Railways on Victorian Cities* (London, 1969), p. 290.

55. *Description of Ceremonial on the Occasion of Laying the Foundation Stone of the Municipal Buildings in George Square, Glasgow, October 1883* (Glasgow, 1885).

CHAPTER 4

The Dominant Classes[1]

Nicholas Morgan and Richard Trainor

The Classes and the Issues Defined

This chapter is an analysis of the number, occupations, wealth, education, lifestyle, institutions, interconnections and influence of the upper and middle classes of Victorian and Edwardian Scotland. The analysis includes the relationship between the landed upper class and the middle class. However, as the towns were arguably the quintessential habitats of the nineteenth-century middle class,[2] and as rural society is covered in Chapter 2, this chapter concentrates on the urban middle class and its leaders. In doing so the chapter focuses on the middle class of Scotland's four major towns—Aberdeen, Dundee, Edinburgh and Glasgow—which contained almost a quarter of the country's population in 1861, rising to almost a third by 1911. Indeed, if the suburbs and separate adjoining urban districts of these towns are included, this proportion would be signficantly greater. Nevertheless, as many Victorian and Edwardian Scots inhabited towns quite apart from the four major centres, it would be foolish to ignore the category of small and medium-sized towns whose distinctive individuality reflected the extreme variability of Scottish urban life. To this end, some analysis is devoted to Lochgelly, Paisley, Peebles and Perth. In large towns as well as small the middle class is explored with particular reference to the benchmark years of 1861, 1881 and 1911.

The people we are concerned with in this chapter cover a broad range of Victorian and Edwardian society. At one extreme there was the upper class properly defined, the nobility and gentry, men such as Sir John Stirling Maxwell of Pollok who possessed immense rural wealth but also sometimes significant urban territorial and political influence. The middle class, of course, was far more heterogeneous, encompassing all Scots who fell between the lairds and the manual labouring class. The Scottish middle class ranged from, say, Sir William McEwan, the Edinburgh brewer and wielder of political influence (who left £1.5 million in 1913) to the growing army of clerks and such representatives of small business as the cautious and conservative parents of Sir Thomas Lipton, who preserved a precarious existence through a grocer's shop in the back streets of Glasgow.[3] Between these extremes of upper- and lower-middle class lay the numerous ranks of the inelegantly named but numerous middle-middle class. Here were to be found the leading retailers, middling manufacturers and ordinary professional men of nineteenth-century Scotland, such as John Buchan's fictional Glasgow grocer, Dickson McCunn, lovingly portrayed in Buchan's post-war adventure, *Huntingtower,* as the backbone of Scottish society.[4]

What is known about Scotland's Dominant Classes

The study of the middle class, and of the urban élites largely drawn from it, is currently a lively field of investigation in nineteenth and early twentieth century British history.[5] Historians have begun to recognise that social history cannot afford to neglect a group which was even more influential than it was numerous. Yet the middle class and its leaders have started to attract serious attention only during the last few years. Moreover, despite the fact that Scottish professional men such as Andrew Sinclair, estate manager to the Bellamy estate on the BBC series 'The Archers', are ubiquitous in popular drama and literature, the systematic study of the Victorian and Edwardian middle class in Scotland has hardly begun.[6] Nevertheless, the sources for the subject are far-ranging, encompassing not only British materials such as the census, but also distinctively Scottish records resulting from the country's tightly-knit administrative structure.[7] While the existing literature is used extensively, the chapter also deploys such sources to suggest ways in which the understanding of the Victorian and Edwardian Scottish middle class can be broadened and deepened in the future.

In addition to considering how patterns of resources and leadership varied among types of community, and shifted during a long and complex period, the chapter addresses some central issues of Scottish (and British) social history, raising questions for others to pursue. We shall be concerned with topics such as: How far were wealth, property and power concentrated? To what extent did friction among the various occupational, political and sectarian groups put the middle class at a disadvantage in its relations with the local working class, the Scottish landed class and élites based in London? How far did patterns of wealth and power differ among Scottish towns, and did the élites of Edinburgh (perhaps in conjunction with those of Glasgow) dominate Scottish society? The chapter is also concerned with how far and why the dominant classes in Scotland differed from their counterparts south of the Border. This issue will be pursued with particular reference to: the role of the professions in social structure and public life;

21. A Group of Visitors to Mar Lodge. This well dressed selection of the landed classes with hints of highland dress, was photographed by Victor Prout in 1864.

the possible existence of a distinctive, even gentrified 'Scottishness'; the degree to which the Scottish landed classes held aloof from the urban property-holding and leadership which increasingly engaged their English cousins; and the extent to which the élites of the Scottish middle class (which had already achieved considerable coherence and impact by the 1830s[8]) resembled their counterparts south of the Border in retaining an increasingly embattled but still potent influence.[9] Attention will also be paid to the suggestion made recently for Britain generally by W. D. Rubinstein that the professional, financial and mercantile groups within the middle class kept disproportionate resources and influence even well after the onset of rapid industrialisation.[10]

SOCIAL STRUCTURE

Middle-class Numbers and their Distribution

The Scottish middle class formed a substantial and increasing proportion of the population. Even the census of 1831, with its conservative category of 'capitalists, bankers, professionals and other educated men', reveals 5.3 per cent of Scotland's males of 20 years of age and over falling comfortably within the middle class.[11] A more inclusive measure of middle-class status from the same period—the proportion of adult males enjoying the parliamentary vote—locates Scotland's cities and its towns such as Paisley and Perth in a middle range of British towns generally, with a sixth to a fifth of men aged more than 19 having the vote.[12] More definitively, information in Table 1 regarding the numbers of Scots enumerated with middle-class occupations in 1861, 1881 and 1911 reveals a substantial and increasing proportion.[13] The levels and trend are similar to those found for supposedly more prosperous England and Wales.[14]

Yet, as Table 1 also suggests, the relative size of the middle class varied significantly among our sample towns. This variation was wildly exaggerated by the category in the 1831 census of 'capitalists and educated',[15] which enumerated 20.4 per cent of adult males in Edinburgh but only 8.0 per cent in Dundee, 7.5 per cent in Aberdeen, 5.9 per cent in Glasgow, 4.4 per cent in Peebles and a mere 2.7 per cent in Paisley. A measure less biased against industrial and commercial centres, the percentage of adult males having the parliamentary franchise, gives a more reliable if perhaps a slightly compressed range, from 19.6 per cent in Edinburgh (excluding Leith) to 16.9 per cent in Aberdeen, 15.4 per cent in Dundee and 15.1 per cent in Glasgow.[16] Analysis of the census in Table 1 reveals similar but growing levels, with Edinburgh comfortably ahead and Dundee well behind its rivals in 1861. This rank order remained

Table 1. Individuals with Middle-class Occupations as a Percentage of Occupied Population

| | Year | | |
	1861 (per cent)	1881 (per cent)	1911 (per cent)
Aberdeen	22.5	27.2	30.4
Dundee	11.6	17.1	17.8
Edinburgh	29.3	36.0	37.0
Glasgow	17.6	16.4	27.6
Perth	22.2	23.5	33.4
All Scottish Towns	16.6	23.5	n/a
Scotland	21.6	23.2	25.1

Source: Census of Scotland 1861, 1881, 1911.

in 1911, but with some contraction of the range. On the eve of World War I even Dundee had almost a fifth of its occupied population in middle-class jobs. More importantly, each of the towns had a significantly larger middle class, even allowing for substantial population increase, in 1911 than fifty years earlier: the middle class of Scotland's larger towns was growing especially rapidly. Such disporportionate middle-class growth in the four largest towns evidently reflected both suburban boundary extensions and urban Scotland's participation in the rapid expansion of the service sector in the late Victorian and Edwardian decades.[17] By the end of the period, even more than at its start, Scotland differed from England and Wales in the extent to which its middle class was concentrated in a few large towns: as early as 1881, 22.6 per cent of the Scottish middle class lived in the four cities, which had 79.1 per cent of all the middle-class inhabitants of towns of 10,000 or more.[18] Nonetheless, the rapid expansion of the middle class in all Scottish towns above that threshold suggests that these trends also prevailed in substantial market towns.

In all five towns both the industrial and service sectors made a major contribution to the middle class. Although those engaged in manufacturing never formed a majority of the middle class,[19] industrial entrepreneurs, managers and clerks constituted a significant proportion, especially in Glasgow and Dundee. Not all of these were to be found in the large enterprises which dominate the historiography of the Scottish economy;[20] for example, many members of the industrial middle class made their living from the building trade, whose structure illustrates the social complexity of urban Scottish society. The construction industry supplied a large base of employers and aspiring self-employed tradesmen who made up a distinct element in each of the towns' middle classes, men who were closely associated with both manual labour and high finance, and who could provide at one extreme a civic leader such as Sir James Steel, property developer extraordinaire and Lord Provost of Edinburgh between 1900 and 1903.[21] By 1911 the capital claimed nearly 900 employers and self-employed in this sector; in Aberdeen the figure was 366 and in Dundee 275. Glasgow had nearly a thousand employers of labour in the building trades, and another 289 self-employed—here as elsewhere an important group in social, political and religious affairs. As the Glasgow builder, Thomas Binnie, frequently exhorted his more 'steady' employees, employment in building as a clerk of works or cashier, aided by regular savings, could also provide a route to independence in business, property and enhanced social status.[22] The career pattern of many a successful (and for that matter unsuccessful) Scottish builder shows how this transition could easily be made, making the industry one of the most important in providing the middle classes in Scottish towns with a regular and expanding supply of new recruits.

Within the service sector, there were significant variations in the relative importance of the professional[23] and commercial groups (Table 2). Clearly, Edinburgh deserved its reputation as a stronghold of professionals, just as Glasgow was a hub of commerce. Yet, when we retreat from percentages to raw numbers, the significant presence even of relatively small groups becomes clear. In 1881 Dundee had more than a thousand professionals, and Aberdeen almost double that number in commercial occupations. Contrariwise, similar percentages can hide significant contrasts in raw numbers. Despite comparable proportions of the occupied population in commercial occupations, Glasgow enumerated 11,119 in this category, while Edinburgh mustered only 5,005. Similar points apply at the level of individual occupations. In 1861 Edinburgh, as the centre of Scotland's legal system, had 710 lawyers to Glasgow's mere 222, but the Clydeside metropolis had nearly as many clergymen and medical practitioners as did the capital, and Glasgow domiciled more civil engineers. Similarly, despite Edinburgh's reputation as Scotland's financial centre, Glasgow, with its thriving stock exchange, dominated the capital as a provider of financial services: in 1911 there were 1,979 bankers, bill discounters, accountants and insurance agents in Glasgow, 1,231 in Edinburgh. Likewise, Aberdeen had twice as many bankers

Table 2. Males Occupied in Particular Middle-class Groups as Percentages of Occupied Males, 1881

	Professional (per cent)	Commercial (per cent)
Aberdeen	6.5	5.6
Dundee	2.8	4.8
Edinburgh	10.9	7.5
Glasgow	3.5	7.1
Perth	4.9	5.1
All Scottish towns	4.5	5.7
Scotland	4.4	4.3

Source: 1881 Census.
Note: Professional = Order 3, including new as well as old professions;
Commercial = Order 5, including commercial clerks and salesmen.

and lawyers as did Dundee, despite the reputation of the latter as the centre of the Scottish investment trust movement.[24] Commercial clerks and bookkeepers were ubiquitous. In 1911, while Perth and Aberdeen had an apparently unimpressive 0.8 per cent in this category, this translated into 294 and 1,361 respectively, while Dundee counted 1,709, Edinburgh 3,839 and Glasgow a staggering, 12,684 clerks (compared to 3,982 employed in shipbuilding) in the same census.[25]

These humble members of the commercial sector had numerous counterparts in each of the towns' retailing and drink-trade occupations. On the one hand there were clothiers and outfitters, offering an increasingly specialised retailing function not provided by tailors and dressmakers. Only a small number of such institutions flourished in 1861, giving employment to 334 men in Glasgow, 118 in Edinburgh and only 9 in Aberdeen. By 1911 the respective numbers had increased to 459, 275 and 105, with Dundee and Perth claiming 66 and 33 each. In Edinburgh nearly 30 per cent of these were employers, in Glasgow only 17 per cent, and in Dundee 13 per cent. Far more appealing to those seeking a firm rung on the ladder to middle-class security was the grocery trade. Serviced by a small number of provision dealers, grocers were the most numerous and vulnerable group in retailing. Many were like Thomas Lipton's parents:

> They had only a few pounds saved up and failure would have meant disaster. But they had faith and energy and determination; all they desired was a bare living and the thought of 'success'—in the ordinary sense of the word—and of money making never entered into their calculations.[26]

Individuals such as these must have made up a large number of the men and women returned as grocers in the 1911 census, marking a startling increase in a business which accounted for the employment of only 1,767 Glaswegians in 1861; in Glasgow there were 4,898, of whom nearly 500 were employers, and another 254 self-employed. In Edinburgh the figures were 2,344, 401 and 618, the self-employed being dominated by 525 women. Even in Dundee, Aberdeen and Perth, where the global figures were much smaller, there were 398 employers and 230 self-employed out of a total of 2,388 grocers. But all of those involved would have shared at least the modest ambitions of the Liptons, if not the more audacious schemes of their enterprising son.

No less important an occupation at all levels of the Scottish middle class was the drink-trade, which furnished a few (like Thomas Lipton's good friend, Thomas Dewar, or his brother John) with massive fortunes and influence, and many with but a tenuous foothold on the path to

22. The Cox Family at Invertrossachs in 1880. Less elegant and well dressed than the Mar Lodge group, but very powerful Dundee millowners. The photograph was taken by James Cox, a man of second generation wealth whose hobby was photography.

security and a sort of respectability. For, regardless of the practices of the frequently parodied Scottish abstainers, and the notions of temperance reformers, drink was firmly intertwined into the economic and social base of all Scottish towns. In Glasgow alone in 1861 there were 1,296 wine and spirit merchants, and an additional 118 publicans, compared to Edinburgh's 474 and 51. The capital may have been the city that provided much of the nation's drink from its breweries and bonds, but it was in Glasgow where most of it was drunk in the city's bars, beer-houses and brothels. By 1881 Glasgow had 2,259 publicans and wine and spirit merchants; by 1911 there were 1,954, reflecting a fall that was shared by Dundee, where the numbers rose from 56 in 1861, to 270 in 1881, declining to 190 in 1911. In all these towns a large proportion of drink traders were either employers or self-employed: 70 per cent in Dundee, 76 per cent in Aberdeen and 52 per cent in Edinburgh, contrasted with 28 per cent in Glasgow, where the large number of outlets were owned by a significantly smaller group of businessmen. These entrepreneurs were men such as Gray Edmiston, who 'came a youth from the country almost penniless'; subsequently finding himself 'the capitalist of thirty shillings' he 'invested in a pastry business of little pretensions', moving on 'by close application to business' to own the Lyceum Vaults in Glasgow, 'one of the most luxurious bars in Scotland'. Here was a man for whom even 'the Town Council has no allurements', preferring to spend 'whatever time he has to spare in the bosom of his family, except for now and again when he takes a run to a race-course'.[27]

Whether at the level of major sectors or of significant subgroups or of individual trades, therefore, there was considerable social as well as occupational complexity within the middle classes of Scottish towns. The urban Scottish middle class was richly textured within as well as between cities.

Incomes

The abundant figures on Scottish income tax assessments indicate that the middle class north of the Border was only marginally poorer than its English counterpart. In 1880, for example, Scottish property and profits assessed per capita were 81.6 per cent of the English and Welsh level on Schedule D (income derived from the professions and from partnerships, but not from land ownership or occupation, government securities and funds, or public offices or corporations) and 85.8 per cent on all the schedules.[28] The comparable per capita figures for Wales alone, and for Ireland, were far lower. Moreover, Scotland's share of British assessments did not decline thereafter.[29]

The income of the dominant classes was not, of course, equally distributed around Scotland. In the counties, as Table 3 shows, there were marked inequalities, roughly corresponding to the most prosperous and least prosperous agricultural systems. As expected, southern and central areas emerge as well-to-do, while the Highlands fare less well. What is more surprising is the poor performance of the industrial counties adjoining Edinburgh and Glasgow.

That phenomenon may be explained, in part, by the extraordinary advantage that Scotland's two leading cities enjoyed over other burghs in terms of income tax assessments. Their leads reflected real concentrations of middle-class income, but also the tendency for urban centres with company headquarters to have artificially inflated totals (Table 4). As some industrial towns are in the 'highest' list, some in the 'lowest,' it seems difficult to argue that, in Scotland, industrial areas yielded

Table 3. Income Assessed per capita on All Schedules in Pounds, Selected Scottish Counties, 1880

Highest nine counties		Lowest nine counties	
Roxburgh	£24.84	Orkney & Shetland	£3.93
Berwick	£23.50	Ross & Cromarty	£7.65
Peebles & Selkirk	£21.00	Sutherland	£7.71
Dumfries	£20.71	Caithness	£8.18
Haddington	£20.70	Inverness	£8.47
Kirkcudbright	£18.62	Banff	£8.79
Perth	£17.74	Renfrew	£9.29
Forfar	£16.32	Lanark	£9.33
Wigtown	£16.09	Linlithgow	£10.24

Source: PP 1882 lii (149), 28–9.

especially low concentrations of middle-class incomes, though those towns which combined industrial, financial and commercial functions fared especially well. The major Scottish cities and towns do not stack up badly against their English counterparts on this measure, always excepting the wholly exceptional figures for the City of London. Thus, the Glasgow figure, though well behind Westminster's £65.99, was comparable to the London average of £34.72, Manchester's £33.64 and Liverpool's £27.49, and exceeded major English centres such as Cardiff (£21.03), London without the City (£20.93), Newcastle (£18.84), Birmingham (£15.47), Leeds (£12.76) and Leicester (£12.37). Even the poor figures

Table 4. Income Tax Assessments per capita, All Schedules, 1880. Pounds per capita, Selected Scottish Burghs

Highest nine burghs		Lowest nine burghs	
Edinburgh	£30.74	Forfar	£5.31
Glasgow	£24.00	Dysart	£5.99
Inverness	£19.86	Port Glasgow	£6.27
Leith	£15.45	Peterhead	£6.84
Galashiels	£15.28	Rutherglen	£6.86
Paisley	£15.25	Dunfermline	£7.24
Greenock	£14.52	Arbroath	£7.25
Aberdeen	£14.02	Kirkcaldy	£7.40
Dundee	£13.06	Hamilton	£8.39

Source: PP 1882 lii (149), 28–9.

for places such as Port Glasgow and Rutherglen are no worse than those for comparable English industrial localities.[30]

Wealth

Another view of the middle classes is provided by the analysis of wealthholding at death, using valuations of personal estate submitted by executors for confirmation at Sheriff courts.[31] These data are fraught with problems of interpretation, and should be used only with extreme caution. While not sufficiently reliable to support detailed investigation of the social and economic origins of the very wealthy,[32] they can provide general signposts for the distribution of wealth within the whole community, as the following analysis of all personal estates confirmed in Scotland in 1881 shows.[33]

In 1881, 5,300 estates were confirmed in Scotland, representing only 12 per cent of the adults dying that year:[34] 88 per cent of the Scottish dying population either left no estate, or contrived to have their estates escape the due process of the law. Nonetheless, the 12 per cent which left confirmed estates could nearly be doubled in order to include those widows of the wealthy whose possessions were held only in life-rent, and who thus left nothing at their death. In other words, confirmations allow us to examine the scale and the source of wealth left by the best-off fifth of the population—a group roughly equivalent in size to the middle class as defined by occupations. Clearly not all wealthleavers would be defined as middle class by their occupational descriptions; at the lowest level (those few below the sum of £10 at which estates were obliged to be submitted for confirmation) there was a miner and a labourer. Some labourers were recorded as leaving in excess of £70, as were a pithead man, and a lady's-maid who left £99. However, no matter how much money these people left, it is probably safe to assume that once they reached the sum of about £50 they stood head and shoulders above the majority of the population in terms of accumulated wealth.

The distribution of confirmees across ranges of wealthholding was fairly consistent in the four major centres of population, as Figure 1 shows. In each case the majority of confirmees left between £100 and £1,000, ranging from no fewer than 50 per cent in Edinburgh to no greater than 57 per cent in Glasgow; in Scotland as a whole, too, 57 per cent were to be found in this central range. At the top there was slightly more variation; less than 1 per cent of Dundee's confirmees left more than £10,000, compared to 5 per cent in Glasgow, 6 per cent in Edinburgh and nearly 4 per cent in Scotland as a whole. Edinburgh's

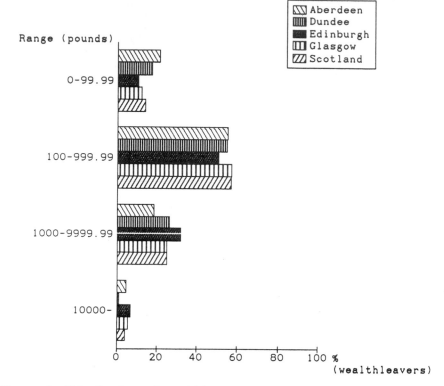

Figure 1. Distribution of wealthleavers in Scotland, 1881, by range of wealthholding. (*Source*: Morgan and Moss, Calendar of Confirmations database).

lead, with the greatest number of top wealthleavers, might seem to confirm its dominance as the core of middle-class Scotland. Overall, nearly 39 per cent of the capital's population left in excess of £1,000 as compared to 30 per cent in Glasgow, and 28 per cent in Scotland as a whole. Globally however, Glasgow dominated wealthholding in 1881 (Figure 2), as one suspects it would have done in any year in the late nineteenth century. Whilst Aberdeen and Dundee accounted between them for less than 3 per cent of the total wealth left in the 1881 confirmations, Edinburgh claimed 16 per cent and Glasgow a massive 23 per cent. In reality, Glasgow's dominance over Edinburgh was even greater, for included in the Edinburgh confirmations are a large number of estates of expatriates who chose to nominate Scotland as their domicile at death. Moreover, the distribution of wealth in Glasgow was far more extreme than in the other towns, and in Scotland as a whole.

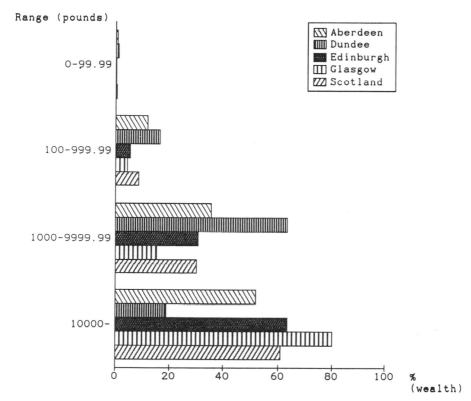

Figure 2. Distribution of personal wealthholding at death in Scotland, 1881, by range of wealthholding. (*Source*: Morgan and Moss, Calendar of Confirmations database).

The nationwide 4 per cent of confirmees who left in excess of £10,000 accounted for 60 per cent of wealth left in Scotland. In Edinburgh the 6 per cent of confirmees in this group accounted for 63 per cent of all wealth left in the city, but in Glasgow the 5 per cent of such confirmees accounted for over 80 per cent of the city's wealth.

An analysis of the occupational distribution of wealth, although not entirely satisfactory due to a significant number of missing values, provides further insights into the structure of the middle classes. In all the towns except Glasgow, and in Scotland as a whole, occupations classified as professional left a disproportionately large amount of wealth. In Aberdeen, 8 per cent of confirmees classified as professional left 25 per cent of the city's wealth, in Dundee 11 per cent left 15 per cent and in Edinburgh 12 per cent left 31 per cent. In Scotland as a whole professionals accounted for nearly 10 per cent of all confirmees (double their share of occupations), leaving 18 per cent of all wealth. Yet industrial and manufacturing occupations were, overall, more important, accounting for 23 per cent of all wealthleavers and 18 per cent of all wealth in Scotland. Surprisingly, in Glasgow, although 30 per cent of confirmees were from this group they could muster only 13 per cent of the city's wealth; however, this can clearly be accounted for by the fact that a significant number of those with no recorded occupations in the Calendar were involved in manufacturing. In addition, industry provided some of the largest wealth-holders in both the city and the country. Men such as the chemical manufacturer, John White (the largest wealth-holder in 1881 with £886,496) and the distiller Archibald Walker (£148,602) appear in this group. As an analysis of confirmations for Glasgow in 1901 tends to confirm, Glasgow was the wealthiest city in Scotland, with its prosperity based firmly on industry and manufacture.[35]

This is not to claim that either Glasgow industrialists or Edinburgh professionals dominated wealth-holding in nineteenth-century Scotland. Perthshire, with the whisky industry firmly established in the county town and surrounding district, produced Robert Moubray, the distiller, who left £215,350 in 1881. Traditional wealth was also well represented; Earl Home left £108,231, in addition to estates (whose value was always excluded from the confirmation process) totalling in excess of 140,000 acres. The Earl of Dalhousie, former MP for Liverpool, left £138,820 and land covering nearly 200,000 acres.

Landed wealth was ever present in Scotland, as in England,[36] throughout the period; of the 380 largest personal estates left in Scotland between 1876 and 1913, 27 per cent were left by landowners, dominated by the Duke of Portland, who left £1.6 million in 1880, and the Marquis of Bute (£1.1 million in 1901). However, only 5 per cent of these top wealthleavers came from the professions; and whilst 24 per cent came from commerce, many of these, with the ambiguous description of 'merchant', more properly belong with the industrialists who accounted for 34 per cent of these large estates. Here were some of Scotland's wealthiest, and in the terms of urban centres at least, most powerful men, notably: Archibald Orr Ewing, turkey red dyer, landowner, and sometime MP for Stirlingshire, who left just over one million pounds in 1894; and Thomas (d. 1884), James (d. 1912), Archibald (d. 1912), and James Coats (d. 1913), four members of what was possibly Scotland's wealthiest non-landed family, and threadmakers to the world.

The pattern of Scottish wealth-holding revealed by confirmations, then, both reinforces and modifies the suggestion that the professional and mercantile groups within the middle class retained disproportionate wealth even after the onset of rapid industrialisation. In urban Scotland professionals and, to a lesser extent, merchants accumulated wealth well beyond their share of the middle-class population, but in no city was the industrial share of wealth negligible, and the largest concentration of wealth was to be found in a mainly industrial city, Glasgow. Meanwhile, the high proportion of small wealth-holders underscores the significant numbers and considerable cumulative resources of the Scottish lower middle class.

Landowning

Sources abound in Scotland for the study of urban and rural landowner-ship. The Register of Sasines and the annual Valuation Rolls provide information as to the identity and occupations of owners, and data relating to the price or value of property. But far more convenient for the study of the owners of land in Scotland are the returns made to Parliament in 1872 and 1873 which made up what became known as the 'new domesday book', containing details of all owners of one or more acres of land in England, Wales and Scotland.[37] In this source, the 'Scotch returns' were 'undoubtedly the best'. Doubts remained about the accuracy of some returns,[38] but such problems were less acute for the nine burghs (Aberdeen, Dundee, Edinburgh, Glasgow, Greenock, Kilmarnock, Leith, Paisley and Perth) with populations of over 20,000, which were separately enumerated. Similarly, the returns for those highly profitable rural estates that impinged upon the fringes of urban settlements would undoubtedly have been more precise than those for holdings in Ross or Invernesshire.

In each of the nine burghs 90 per cent or more of landowners owned less than an acre of land (Figure 3): typically these were landlords whose feus and property occupied a relatively small plot, such as the 10,681 owners in Glasgow (97 per cent of the total), whose combined holding nonetheless amounted to only 1,811 acres, or 37 per cent of the burgh's total area (Figure 4). Only in Aberdeen, where they accounted for 57 per cent of all land, did these small owners dominate landholding. Yet the cumulative value of these diffuse property holdings was not trivial; the 37 per cent of property held by small owners in Glasgow made up 73 per cent of the total annual value of the burgh—some £1,713,789. Thus the typical Glasgow property holding had an average annual value of £160.45, making it worth some £2,166. In Aberdeen, the small owners who held 57 per cent of all property, accounted for 74 per cent of the

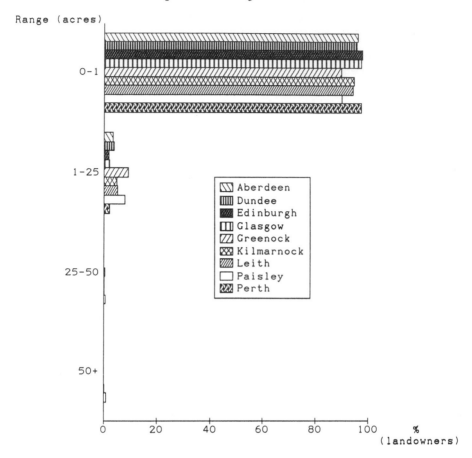

Figure 3. Distribution of landowners in the major Scottish burghs, 1872, by range of landholding. (*Source*: Return of landowners for Scotland, 1872–73).

value; in Edinburgh, where nearly 98 per cent of the owners held only 31 per cent of the acreage, the value stood at 80 per cent of the city's total. Land ownership in Scottish towns was for the most part widely spread amongst large numbers of the middle classes, and of considerable value to them.

At the other extreme, in all these towns, with the exception of Aberdeen, a handful of prominent men owned large concentrations of property, with consequent advantages for income and, even more so, potential influence. In Glasgow, 13 owners held 30 per cent of the burgh's acreage, in Edinburgh, ten owners held 36 per cent of all land, in Dundee eight owners owned 46 per cent of all land, and in Kilmarnock one owner

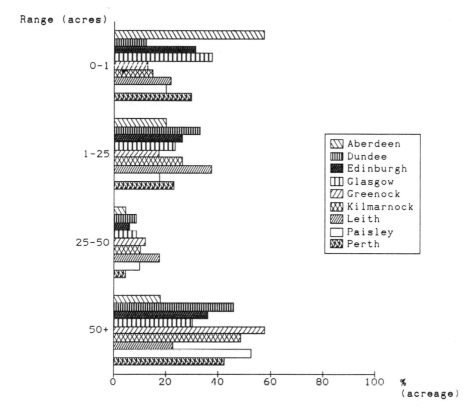

Figure 4. Distribution of land in the major Scottish burghs, 1872, by range of landholding. (*Source*: Return of landowners for Scotland, 1872–73).

held 49 per cent, whilst in Greenock two owners held over 57 per cent of land. The value of such holdings was generally small. In Greenock, for example, the two largest owners held less than 1 per cent of the total value of land in the burgh; it was only in Leith that a significant proportion of the burgh (22 per cent) with a high value (16 per cent) was owned by less than 1 per cent of owners. The largest landowner in Leith was the Trinity Hospital, reflecting the general importance of institutional owners that was found in the capital. In Edinburgh, the three largest owners were the Crown, the city fathers, and the Governors of Heriot's Hospital. With other significant owners, including the Governors of George Watson's College, and of Donaldson's Hospital, the city's legal professionals, who serviced these bodies and frequently managed their property holdings, were given an unprecedented influence in determining the city's spatial and physical growth. In Glasgow, upper-middle-class individuals were well represented among those seven owners who owned 100 acres or more in the city, including the chemical manufacturer, Charles Tennant, who later represented the city in Parliament, the trustees of the coalmaster William Dixon, and the dyer and bleacher Alexander Dennistoun. In Paisley, the largest landowner (by acres and value) was the millionaire, Thomas Coats, of Ferguslie, partner in the thread manufacturers, J. & P. Coats, who owned 326 acres worth annually £1,080, and whose family exerted considerable political influence in the burgh.[39] However, the other large owners in the burgh were of a more traditional stripe, including the Duke of Abercorn, the Earl of Glasgow, and Sir Michael Shaw Stewart of Ardgowan. Shaw Stewart was the largest owner in Greenock, where he held 1,130 acres worth £2,378 annually, and amongst the largest in the rest of Renfrewshire, providing an urban and a rural power-base which members of the family did not fail to exploit in local and national politics in the late Victorian and Edwardian era.[40] Other aristocrats with significant urban interests included the millionaire Duke of Portland, who owned 518 acres in Kilmarnock.

As in England,[41] traditional landed influence on towns could also be exerted from the periphery by those owners who controlled the destiny of urban settlements, sometimes struggling to expand beyond outdated boundaries. Here were opportunities for both tensions and reconciliations. The Shaw Stewarts provide one example, but another can be found in the Stirling Maxwell family who, with extensive interests amounting to over 5,500 acres in 1872, were fêted by Glasgow's middle class at numerous civic occasions, providing dignified presidents for endless philanthropic ventures and voluntary societies.[42] Even more enthusiastically received by his urban neighbours was the third Marquis of Bute; he had already served as Lord Mayor of Cardiff between 1890 and 1891, but in 1896 he was projected into Scottish local government when he was elected to serve as Lord Provost of Rothesay. Although the Marquis was the largest landowner on Bute, in the town itself landownership was dominated by the Burgh in conjunction with a large number of small proprietors. Here were great opportunities for tensions between the scholarly and eccentric nobleman, an antiquarian who made his mark on Scotland partly through the careful restoration of ancient monuments, and the commercially-minded middle classes of Rothesay, seeking to exploit the town's (and island's) potential as a tourist resort serving both middle-class visitors at its hotels and two impressive Hydros, and also day-trippers deposited by the bustling Glasgow steamer services.[43] Nonetheless, the third Marquis was the sixth member of his family to be Rothesay's Lord Provost, 'applying himself to the duties of the position with his habitual assiduity and care, not infrequently travelling long distances to attend the meetings of the corporation'. Such was his success in the office (during his incumbency the harbour had been extended and electricity introduced into the burgh) that the Corporation re-elected him for a further period of office in 1899.[44]

Thus, despite the wide diffusion of Scottish urban landownership, there were significant concentrations which, like the clusters of urban income and wealth, laid the basis for influence from above.

CLASS FORMATION

Education

Mythical as the educational opportunities supposedly open to the 'lad o' pairts' may have been for the Scottish working class, the country's Victorian and Edwardian middle class was on the whole well served by schools, colleges and universities. When rapid industrialisation and urbanisation overwhelmed the towns' parochial schools, the middle class responded with waves of agitation, philanthropy and collective self-help. By the end of the period they had reformed the existing burgh schools and devised new private schools in forms which suited bourgeois needs. Until the last quarter of the century the burgh schools bore few traces of the English public school ideal; commercial influences on the curriculum were strong. Moreover, day- rather than boarding-schools remained the norm for middle-class Scottish education down to 1914 and beyond, suggesting a persisting Scottishness in the mores of the middle class north of the Border. However, in the 'endowed and higher class' schools the growing middle-class demand for higher standards evidently encouraged the English model of classical education, which also affected the cheaper, less socially exclusive 'higher grade' schools. Thus, as R. D. Anderson argues, the Scottish secondary school system which emerged during the second half of the period both unified the middle class and accentuated its social distinctions.[45]

For most Scottish middle-class children secondary education had to suffice, supplemented by on-the-job training and, in exalted circles, sometimes by tours of industrial establishments abroad. University education, increasingly taking students at an older age than secondary schools, usually seemed an irrelevance for boys destined for commercial or industrial jobs.[46] Yet there was a significant role for Scottish higher education, entry to which became an obsession in late Victorian secondary schools. Later nineteenth-century Scottish universities surged ahead of their English counterparts in the production of science graduates,[47] and Scotland was comparatively well endowed with colleges such as the Glasgow and West of Scotland Technical College which provided high-quality technical training. Moreover, Victorian Scotland was relatively well provided, for its day, with positions for schoolteachers; entry to the kirk and the legal system required specifically Scottish training; and Scots were well used to filling professional jobs abroad. There was, therefore, significant Scottish demand for the degrees earned in institutions which, compared to England, were well supplied with places. Thus, the Scottish middle-class male (and, from the 1890s, female) adolescent had both a greater incentive and a greater opportunity to attend university than his or her English counterpart. In Scotland, unlike south of the Border, even unfashionable schools had considerable success in sending students to university, as suggested by the ample shares which comparatively humble middle-class parental occupations held in student numbers.[48]

Thus, education was not so divisive a force in Scottish middle-class society as it was in England. Not only was there less distinction in terms of intra-middle-class social inequality, the sectarian question was also dormant.[49] To a significant degree, belief in the utility of education and the experience of a comparative meritocratic system helped to bind together the diverse elements of the Scottish middle class.

Lifestyles

For many members of the Scottish middle class, lifestyles were shaped by two other pervasive forces—work and religion; 'Glasgow, like most towns given over to industry and commerce, has no leisured class', suggested a guide to the city in 1901.[50] For the majority engaged in work, leisure time was hard to find. The would-be grocer, Thomas Lipton, recalled, without any sense of exaggeration, that

> I stuck to my work all day long and fast into the night. Often I was on duty from six in the morning until midnight. Frequently indeed, I slept in the little back shop so that I could be up bright and early to take advantage of some bargain in butter, or eggs, or bacon which I knew would be on offer.[51]

J. J. Bell, in his reminiscences of Glasgow in the 1880s and 1890s, describes the fathers of Hillhead rushing to work at 8.30 in the morning, returning home from the office at around 8.00 in the evening, confirming the degree to which weekdays remained, both for the middle and working classes, the preserve of Mammon up until 1914. Saturday, or the better half of it, was also subsumed by work, both in the office, shop (where work often continued for employer and employee until late on a Saturday evening) and factory. It was followed by Saturday afternoon, 'where men shed convention and reveal their nature', an occasion where 'time is very precious. A few hours and it will be Sunday, which was not made for pleasure.'[52]

For the middle class church going was, almost without exception, an indispensable token of the respectability which they so cherished.[53] Nor were acts of devotion necessarily confined to one or two (or even perhaps three) services on the Sabbath. In some households the Bible dominated all 'in daily family prayer and long Sabbath sessions'.[54] Moreover, the shadow of Sabbatarianism was broad and dark over the country's day of rest; in Glasgow's West End (now Kelvingrove) Park, the Loch Katrine Memorial Fountain was switched off on Sunday mornings. In towns throughout the country museums and art galleries remained firmly closed, as did bars, theatres and music halls. With the exception of divine worship, and the opportunities it afforded for sometimes lengthy walks to and from church, middle-class families by and large found themselves confined to home on Sundays. Even within this private space leisure pursuits were mediated by spiritual concerns, although, as Bell's memoirs show, the growth of popular and respectable periodical literature, such as *Sunday at Home* and *Leisure Hour*, gradually saw a relaxation in some homes of the prohibition of secular Sabbath reading. There was, he recalled, a 'slow but sure decline from standards'. Even where prohibition remained, all was not lost for the imaginative, who like John Buchan were able to discover 'a fruity line in missionary adventure'.[55]

Sundays were tolerable for the middle class because, unlike many of Scotland's working-class population, they had homes to live in, rather than houses that simply afforded venues for shelter and sleep. There were, of course, many shared features of middle- and working-class housing; even as late as 1911, for example, the common form of house tenure in Scotland's major urban centres was rental. The middle classes might increasingly clutter their homes by the accumulation of furniture, pictures, books and even holiday souvenirs,[56] but they were reluctant to burden themselves with house ownership.[57] Moreover, many middle-class as well as working-class homes were located in multi-occupied dwellings, tenement houses, where the privacy of exclusive doorways and private entrances was sacrificed for closes, common stairs and back greens.[58] By the late nineteenth century all Scottish towns and cities had some distinctly middle-class developments, but these housed only a few. The strictly defined patterns of social segregation that urban geographers have attempted to impose on towns are not helpful for our understanding of the Scottish middle classes; for many, segregation entailed simply being on the right side of the road, or at the better end of a street.[59] Indeed, much of the strength of Glasgow's famous wartime rent-strikes rested on the promiscuous mixing of working- and middle-class tenants in areas such as Thornwood in Partick, where grocers and their assistants, engineers, commercial travellers and insurance agents, lived in close proximity to skilled artisans from the shipyards. The articulate, respectable and well-organised protest that emerged was far more alarming to the authorities than it would have been without this distinctive flavour.[60]

Given the burdens of work, and the restrictions that over-furnished and sometimes quite small houses could place on the home life of the middle class,[61] it is not surprising that by the 1880s and 1890s the annual holiday loomed so large on the calendar. For the very wealthy manufacturer, such as the thread maker John Clark, or the grocer Thomas Lipton, this could mean taking the steam yacht out to sea accompanied by family or friends. Clark was also lucky enough to have an extensive villa at Largs (Curling Hall) where he could entertain.[62] Others with great fortunes had country retreats that offered beauty, sport and solitude. For the less well-off such pursuits could be parodied by the possession of small seaside villas, or more often by taking a house in an appropriate location for the summer, to be reached for west-coast residents by an almost obligatory cruise down the Clyde. These were not boorish Glasgow Fair trippers, but rather assiduous searchers after the moral and physical benefits of the countryside and seaside. Detailed guidebooks were prepared to enable the visitor to appreciate the historical and antiquarian associations and natural wonders of their chosen venues.[63]

As publishers' catalogues show, history and antiquarianism ranked high among the titles avidly consumed by the middle class at home. Nationalistic sentiment, expressed in history and literature, was a rallying point for these 'middling' Scots. For many, such attitudes probably mixed with a rarely articulated romanticism that made the fictional (and presbyterian) grocer, Dickson McCunn, 'a Jacobite not because he had any views on Divine Right, but because he had always before his eyes a picture of a knot of adventurers in cloaks, new landed from France, among the western heather'.[64] The annual calendar was dotted with ceremonial occasions where males from all sections of the class would meet over elaborate (and rarely temperate) dinners to celebrate shared cultural or sometimes regional backgrounds; they also provided a meeting point for the urban middle class and the rural gentry and aristocracy. Foremost were those devoted to the memory of Robert Burns, whose centenary had been universally celebrated in January 1859, and for whom annual suppers were held in towns and cities throughout the nation.[65] Nor were opportunities for the middle and upper classes to come together confined to such ceremonials. Voluntary associations (at least at their annual general meetings) provided such occasions, as could the most unlikely sporting pursuits. Bowling clubs reflected a shared status among their members, and competition provided an unparalleled arena for fraternisation, as the Earl of Eglinton discovered when he found his Ayrshire side playing in Glasgow against the Kingston Bowling Club's team of 'decent shopkeepers from Tradeston':

> The bearing of the handsome nobleman was, no doubt, in marked contrast to that of several of his competitors; but what of that? They were all, I take it, respectable in their sphere, and nothing could exceed the unaffected courtesy of his manner to the humblest, as if in recognition of the fact that on the bowling-green the highest and the lowest were for the moment on perfectly level ground.[66]

Of course, social mixing between peers and shopkeepers was unusual, and in many respects lifestyle divided rather than united the propertied classes. There were significant differences between the usual social rounds of the upper- and lower- middle classes, notably with regard to clubs, foreign travel and rural pastimes.[67] Conviction also differentiated the leisure of the propertied classes, notably with regard to drink, an abiding controversy of the period, and religion, where the divisive effects of the Disruption of 1843 complicated middle-class social routines and public activities for many decades. Yet attitudes to the bottle and to the Kirk cut across the status divisions within the propertied classes and, indeed, provided points of contact with those of similar beliefs in the working class.[68] In fact, given the widespread acceptance of notions such as respectability and improvement which permeated all but the seamiest aspects of the leisure of these groups, the variety of Victorian and Edwardian Scottish lifestyles was more a safety valve than a source of aggravation for the propertied classes.

ÉLITES AND THEIR INFLUENCE

The Changing Institutional Structure

Who were the élites, or active social leaders, who emerged from the Scottish middle class during the Victorian and Edwardian periods?

This question requires examination of the major public institutions available to Scots during these decades, especially for politics, local government and voluntary service. Of course, it is possible for people with massive economic power and prestige to exercise power behind the scenes without holding prominent positions in major institutions. Yet such 'godfather' figures, rare in Britain as a whole during the Victorian era, at least outside London,[69] were also uncommon in Scotland: even late in the period most of the wealthiest Scots held honorific or active offices in the institutions of their counties and towns.

The top upper middle class could not have monopolised such leadership even if they had wished to do so, for the number of responsible positions in Scotland (despite the lesser importance there of the justices of the peace) had grown in line with the rapidly increasing quantity of institutions, especially in the towns. Although Scotland's cities did not get their fair share of MPs until 1918,[70] they increased their representation in 1832, 1867 and, especially, in 1885. Thus Glasgow, which had shared members with Rutherglen before the First Reform Act, had two MPs of its own from 1832, three from 1867 and seven from 1885, thereby significantly increasing its potential vote in a House whose membership expanded much less quickly. Similarly, the reform of urban local government from the 1830s added new 'parliamentary burghs' (and eventually a large number of small police burghs, extending even to such humble localities as the Fife mining village of Lochgelly) while augmenting the prestige of the older burghs by opening them to semi-popular election. The councils also soon enjoyed enhanced revenue raising and spending powers, and the number of responsible local government posts was further increased by special purpose authorities for poor relief and education. From 1889 the counties, too, had elected local government. Meanwhile, all forms of local administration gradually developed a 'civil service' which provided positions of considerable informal influence to a significant and growing number of middle-class Scots.[71]

At the same time, the proliferation of institutions and of posts for the making and execution of policy was at least as rapid in voluntary societies, even if the many primarily devoted to middle-class instruction, agitation and amusement are excluded. The voluntary sector was as active and, adjusting for wealth, apparently as generously funded in Scotland as in England, especially in 'Generous Glasgow'.[72] Thus, by the early twentieth century, even Dundee, which had been only moderately well-endowed with voluntary institutions in the mid-nineteenth century, boasted thirty-two 'charitable and benevolent institutions', including the Royal Infirmary, the Dundee Orphan Institution, the Dundee and Lochee

Mission to the Outdoor Blind, and The Home ('for the Reformation of Females') as well as branches of the Charity Organisation Society and the Society for the Prevention of Cruelty to Children.[73] Moreover, Scottish towns were amply supplied with prestigious institutions which straddled the boundary between the private and public sectors. These were legion in Edinburgh with its concentration of national institutions, but even Glasgow had its Trustees of the Clyde Navigation, Chamber of Commerce, Trades House, Merchants House, Institute of Accountants and Actuaries, Faculty of Procurators, and Faculty of Physicians and Surgeons, to say nothing of a host of employers' associations.

Identity and Background of Scottish Leaders

The upper class played an important role in Scotland's representation in Parliament. By definition it formed the whole of the country's delegation in the House of Lords. Lairds and the relatives of noblemen also sat in the Commons for many Scottish constituencies, notably in the counties and in the smaller towns. For example, the Hon. A. F. Kinnaird, a younger son turned diplomat and banker, was the member for Perth for 28 years before being ennobled. Even these controversially privileged Scots had significant local ties, usually to the county's deputy lieutenancy and magistrate's bench, as well as to an estate in their constituency.

Moreover, in urban Scotland the connections between the local middle class and MPs were very close, at least during the Victorian decades. Despite the informal barriers to Commons membership suffered by the urban middle class,[74] the MPs for Scottish cities consisted largely of middle-class men, usually with active connections to local business or professions, enhanced by ties based on local government involvements as well as birth and education. This description fits four of the six members for the four cities in 1861, and at least seven of their nine members twenty years later. For example, Duncan McLaren, Liberal MP for Edinburgh between 1865 and 1881, a merchant in the city, was also Lord Provost, a JP and deputy lieutenant, and past president of the chamber of commerce. The same link with the Edinburgh council held true three decades later, but by then only about half the Scottish cities' members had strong local ties, and even fewer were local businessmen. Many had previously sat, or attempted to sit, for other constituencies, frequently in England. In short, the Scottish urban MP was becoming a semi-detached, professional politician, of whom Dundee's member, Winston Churchill, was the starkest example.[75] On the other hand, because the MPs were less often home-grown, and because they were no longer virtually all Liberals, the members of 1911 included more current or future office-holders than their predecessors, thereby enhancing the prestige and the potential influence of their constituencies.[76] Also, even at the end of the period local ties appealed to Scottish electors, doing much, for example, to rescue the Glasgow member A. Cameron Corbett from the effects of four changes of party between 1885 and 1910.[77]

Throughout the period, the truly Scottish MP, like the extremely successful Scot on the British or Imperial stage generally, was usually the product of a well-off middle-class family and a privileged local education.[78] Urban employers as well as rural lairds enjoyed considerable electoral influence, at least down to the 1880s, as did the well-off middle-class leaders of urban Liberal associations.[79] Politics, then, both enhanced and reflected the position of the better-off members of the Scottish propertied classes.

Strengthened until late in the period by links with their local MPs, Scotland's urban local government institutions attracted a large proportion of well-off middle-class members to their elected offices. Between the 1830s and the 1870s, in Scottish cities[80] as in many of their English counterparts, the prestige of reformed local government and growing civic pride enticed a significant number of leading businessmen (often merchants or merchant manufacturers) and professional people to become members of the councils, especially as baillies and provosts. Thus, between the first two Reform Acts, Aberdeen's Lord Provosts consisted of two shipping owners, two manufacturers, a copper merchant, an insurance promoter and two advocates.[81] Such positions were particularly attractive to Liberals, preferred by the reformed municipal electorate which, like its parliamentary equivalent, roughly coincided with the middle class between 1832 and 1867.

Yet even before the 1870s the councils were not monopolised, either by top businessmen or by Liberals. Such diversity sometimes brought disputes about rates and party privileges onto the Council floor. Nevertheless, as partisanship and other divisive factors evidently usually remained within narrow bounds,[82] it was ultimately an advantage, both to the effectiveness of the councils and to the cohesion of the urban middle class, that council members varied in their partisan and sectarian affiliations and included members from the middle as well as the upper middle class.[83] Such diversity became even more marked in the last quarter of the century, as some wealthy businessmen became increasingly absorbed in country houses and far-flung investments. Workingmen's leaders gained seats for the first time, and professional men and retailers increased their share both of seats and of leadership positions at the expense of merchants and industrialists.[84] However, in Scotland as elsewhere in Britain, well-off businessmen usually remained close enough to their urban bases to continue some civic as well as business involvement.[85] Merchants and industrialists retained a significant presence on Scottish councils down to 1914, paralleling trends south of the Border. Thus, as late as 1900 in Glasgow and 1905 in Edinburgh, more than a quarter of councillors were businessmen from outside the retailing sector; this proportion had fallen only to a sixth by 1914.[86]

Key voluntary societies such as hospitals and mechanics' institutes also enjoyed a continuing leadership input from the better-off members of the urban middle class.[87] The case of Aberdeen suggests that Scottish worthies devoted energy and money to such bodies for a variety of reasons: religion, humanitarianism, social anxiety and, not least, zeal for personal distinction in an era when the voluntary sphere still included many important social services.[88] In Paisley, for example, 'the leading men in the thread trade . . . [were] to be found on the governing boards of every institution and society, educational, philanthropic and religious', hoping thereby, in part, to 'knit together in bonds of mutual sympathy and help, the various classes of the people'.[89] Especially in Edinburgh and Aberdeen, the nobility and gentry also played a role, but more as benefactors and ceremonial officers than as active managers.[90] The latter function may have begun to appeal less to top businessmen in Scottish cities, as it did in English towns such as Reading.[91] Also, by 1914 working-class leaders held seats on the boards of Scottish charities.[92] Nevertheless, an increasingly diverse voluntary society leadership did not mean withdrawal by the upper levels of the middle class, whose ranks were increasingly reinforced by women who assumed leading roles in organisations such as the Dundee and District Female Nursing Home and the Scottish Women's Liberal Federation.

The Achievements of Power

What did these élites accomplish with their prominent positions? Well-off urban leaders had to deal, of course, with the landed élite itself: in this respect the pervasive Liberalism of the middle class in Scottish towns until the late nineteenth century was a source of strength as well as of conflict. An even more important aspect of leadership by individuals largely drawn from the upper- and middle-middle classes was the reinforcement of their influence over the middle class as a whole. In philanthropy, prominent and generous leaders secured ascendancy over the ordinary middle-class members who, however, gained satisfaction through 'subscribers democracy'.[93] The glorification of the almost uniformly wealthy Lord Provosts suggests that this trend also operated in local government, where frequent elections and the existence of minor local government bodies served as safety valves for the discontents of the lower middle class.[94] More generally, large industrial employers may have been especially influential members of the élites because they provided jobs and, it was hoped, social discipline where they were most required.[95] Other parts of the middle class were not ciphers: professionals in particular exerted considerable influence, especially in matters where their expertise was directly relevant, as when doctors advised councils as medical officers of health or hospital boards as consulting surgeons.[96] Yet such professionals were members at worst of the middle-middle class.

Concerning the relationship of the élites with the working-class majority of the population, they enjoyed very substantial power, especially in the first half of the period. In large measure, of course, this was private power, exercised individually by civic leaders who were primarily employers and landlords. Yet in Scotland, as south of the Border,[97] private power reinforced public authority, not only because of implicit coercion, but also because of the civic credibility that accrued to those who generated employment and proved their capacity to manage large private concerns.

Such credibility also depended on strenuous and imaginative public policies, in philanthropic as well as municipal affairs: at least as much as their English counterparts, the Scottish dominant classes used their privileged positions to undertake initiatives striking by the standards of their day. In the voluntary sphere, the Scottish urban middle class, in particular, created an intricate web of active institutions, the apex of which were the voluntary hospitals of the four cities. For example, it was said of James Lumsden, sometime Lord Provost of Glasgow, that

> For nearly twenty years he was honorary treasurer to Glasgow Royal Infirmary, and . . . he rarely allowed any gentleman to escape him in the street from whom he thought he could extract a subscription in its behalf.[98]

Admittedly the credit arising from philanthropic donations often exceeded their proportion of the donors' disposable income, and aid was delivered on terms that suited the philanthropists. Also, working-class support of voluntary hospitals became increasingly important later in the period. Yet individual middle-class subscriptions provided a crucial core of support for efforts which delivered substantial assistance.[99]

In local government, Victorian and Edwardian Scottish urban leaders expanded the traditional Scottish tolerance for broad 'police' powers into a network of accomplishments epitomised by Glasgow's pioneering and internationally famous water supply and tram systems.[100] These efforts had particular impact because of a neat dovetailing of private and public effort, notably in Glasgow Corporation's assuming responsibility in 1891 for funding the Mitchell Library which had been privately founded 14 years previously.[101]

Appalling gaps remained in public social provision, in part because of the vested interests of property owners on local government bodies, but the shortfall would have been much greater without the positive leadership of the better-heeled members of the 'dominant classes'. Until the end of the period it was the radicals, not the established members of the élites, who were the economisers. Only in the years immediately preceding the First World War, when working-class and Labour influence started to assert itself significantly, did municipal intervention and philanthropic innovation begin to seem inimical to the upper and middle classes of Scottish towns.[102] In the meantime Scotland's urban élites gained credit, especially with the less prominent members of the middle class, but to a significant extent also with the working classes as well, for its vigorous public profile. Even in 1914, the Scottish dominant classes had lost little of the confidence which characterised the city fathers of Glasgow at the laying of the foundation stone of the City Chambers in 1885, when tens of thousands of Glaswegians watched a procession which included working men's organisations, but gave pride of place to an urban élite which in the day's speeches praised the productive alliance between its own imaginative leadership and the progressive outlook of the urban masses.[103] Both the substance and the spectacle were reinforced by the strong connections among the élites of Scotland's major towns and by the links to power centres in London enjoyed by these leaders, especially but not solely those in Edinburgh.

Thus, because of their numbers, resources, institutions and leadership strategies the Scottish "dominant classes", and in particular the urban middle class, were still surprisingly influential as late as 1914. Indeed, any resident of late twentieth-century Scotland can testify that an obituary of these social groups would still be very premature. Yet, as John Buchan realised in retrospect, the First World War was a watershed for the aristocracy and middle class in Scotland, as in so many other countries: 'I realised that we were at the point of contact of a world vanishing and a world arriving, and that such a situation was apt to crush those who had to meet it'.[104]

NOTES

1. A grant from the Carnegie Trust for the Universities of Scotland has assisted us with the research on which this chapter is partly based.

2. R. J. Morris, 'The Middle Class and British Towns and Cities of the Industrial Revolution', in D. Fraser and A. Sutcliffe (eds.), *The Pursuit of Urban History* (London, 1983), pp. 286–306.

3. As occupational, rating, house size and income tax information all indicate, the lower middle class was by no means unusually small in Scotland (Compare H. J. Hanham, *Scottish Nationalism* (London, 1969), pp. 21–2).

4. John Buchan, *Huntingtower* (London, 1922), p. 123.

5. For references to the literature see: R. H. Trainor, 'Urban Elites in Victorian Britain', *Urban History Yearbook* (1985), pp. 1–17; S. Gunn, 'The Failure of the Victorian Middle Class: a Critique', in J. Wolff (ed.), *The Culture of Capital: Art, power and the 19th century middle class* (Manchester, 1988), pp. 17–43.

6. For notable exceptions see: E. Knox, 'Between Capital and Labour: the *petite bourgeoisie* in Victorian Edinburgh', unpublished PhD thesis, University of Edinburgh, 1986; C. Lee, 'The Glasgow Business Community c. 1840–1870', unpublished Ph.D. thesis, University of Strathclyde, 1985; A. A. Maclaren, *Religion and Social Class: the Disruption Years in Aberdeen* (London, 1976), and (ed.) *Social Class in Scotland Past and Present* (Edinburgh, 1976); S. S. Nenadic, 'The Structure, Values and Influence of the Scottish Urban Middle Class: Glasgow 1800 to 1870', unpublished PhD thesis, University of Glasgow, 1986, and 'Record Linkage and the Exploration of Nineteenth-century Social Groups; A Methodological Perspective on the Glasgow Middle Class in 1861', *Urban History Yearbook* (1987), pp. 32–43 and 'The Rise of the Urban Middle Class' in T. M. Devine and R. Mitchison (eds.), *People and Society in Scotland,* vol. 1, 1760–1830, pp. 109–26; S. P. Walker, 'Occupational Expansion, Fertility Decline and Recruitment to the Professions in Scotland 1850–1914, with special reference to Edinburgh Chartered Accountants', unpublished Ph.D. thesis, University of Edinburgh, 1986.

7. Notable examples are confirmations of estates at death, inventories of personal estates, the register of sasines (property transfers) and valuation rolls (property ownership and occupation).

8. Nenadic, 'Rise'.

9. Trainor, 'Urban Elites'.

10. W. D. Rubinstein, *Men of Property: The very wealthy in Britain since the Industrial Revolution* (London, 1981); with significant qualifications, Nenadic, 'Structure', finds similar patterns in Glasgow for the period to 1870.

11. *Census of Scotland 1831*, vol. 2, Enumeration Abstracts.

12. Cf. Morris, 'Middle Class', pp. 287–8.

13. Despite many difficulties enumerated by Alan Armstrong ('The Use of Information About Occupation', in E. A. Wrigley, (ed.), *Nineteenth Century*

Society (Cambridge, 1972), pp. 191–310) figures derived from the published census provide rough approximations of the relative size of major social categories. We are grateful to Ms Fiona Watson, Department of Scottish History, University of Glasgow, for her expertise on the occupational tables of the census.

14. C. Erickson, *British Industrialists: Steel and Hosiery 1850–1950* (Cambridge, 1959), pp. 20–4, 233–4.

15. By excluding middle-class people in manufacturing or trade (*Census of Scotland 1831*, vol. 1, p. vi), it was particularly unfair to industrial cities such as Glasgow which that year had 19,313 men enumerated in manufacturing or the making of machinery, compared to a mere 792 in Edinburgh.

16. Compare the much lower subjective estimates for Dundee and Glasgow in H. Pelling, *Social Geography of British Elections 1885–1910* (London, 1967), pp. 388–90, but also note indications of middle-class suburban residence (*Ibid.*, 400, 406–8).

17. C. H. Lee, 'Modern Economic Growth and Structural Change in Scotland: the Service Sector Reconsidered', *Scottish Economic and Social History*, iii (1983), pp. 5–35 emphasises the relatively small size of the service sector outside the Lothians. Cf. R. Tyson, 'The Economy of Aberdeen', in J. S. Smith and D. Stevenson (eds.), *Aberdeen in the Nineteenth Century: the making of the modern city* (Aberdeen, 1988), pp. 30–1.

18. Cf. R. D. Anderson, 'Secondary Schools and Scottish Society in the 19th Century', *Past & Present*, 109 (1985), p. 188.

19. Cf. Nenadic, 'Structure', p. 64.

20. R. Rodger, 'Concentration and Fragmentation: Capital, Labor and the Structure of Mid-Victorian Scottish Industry', *Journal of Urban History*, xiv (1988), pp. 178–213.

21. N. J. Morgan, 'The Construction Industry', and R. G. Rodger, 'Sir James Steel', in A. Slaven (ed.), *Dictionary of Scottish Business Biography*, vol. 2, (Aberdeen, 1990).

22. T. Binnie, *Memoir of Thomas Binnie, Builder in Glasgow, 1792–1867* (Glasgow, 1882) pp. 90–2.

23. Surprisingly enough, Scotland was below the British average in professional occupations, though it was drawing closer (Lee, 'Modern Economic Growth', pp. 15–18, 31–2).

24. H. W. Macrosty, *The Trust Movement in British Industry: a Study of Business Organisation* (London, 1907).

25. Cf. G. Anderson, *Victorian Clerks* (Manchester, 1976).

26. Thomas Lipton, *Leaves from the Lipton Logs* (London, n.d.), pp. 39–40.

27. *Scottish Wine, Spirit and Beer Trades Review*, 20 September 1887, p. 259.

28. Calculations based on PP 1882 lii (149), 28–9. The use of all the schedules rather than Schedule D alone is more appropriate for consideration of a country

with significant rural as well as urban areas, though this method does of course include upper-class income where relevant.

29. Rubinstein, *Elites and the Wealthy in Modern British History*, (Brighton, 1987), pp. 92–5, 98–9.

30. Cf. T. C. Smout, *A Century of the Scottish People 1830–1950* (London, 1986), pp. 110–12 for similar comparisons based on Schedule D.

31. J. G. Currie, *The Confirmation of Executors in Scotland according to the Practice in the Commissariot of Edinburgh*, revised by J. Burns (Edinburgh, 1923), fourth edition.

32. Rubinstein, 'British Millionaires, 1809–1949', *Bulletin of the Institute of Historical Research*, xlvii (1974), pp. 202–23; R. Britton, 'Wealthy Scots, 1867–1913', *Ibid.*, lviii (1985), pp. 78–94; M. S. Moss & N. J. Morgan, 'Listing the Wealthy in Scotland', *Historical Research*, lix (1986), 189–95.

33. Morgan and Moss, Calendar of Confirmations Database.

34. Of the 5307 estates confirmed in 1881, 61 per cent were for deaths in that year, 25 per cent for deaths in 1880, and the remainder for earlier years.

35. Moss and Morgan, 'Urban Wealthholding and the Computer', in P. Denley *et. al.* (eds.), *History and Computing II* (Manchester, 1989), pp. 181–92.

36. Rubinstein, *Men of Property*, chapter 2.

37. PP 1874, lxxii, Part III, *Return of Owners of Land: Scotland 1872–3*.

38. J. Bateman, In D. Spring (ed.), *The Great Landowners of Great Britain and Ireland* (Leicester, 1971), reprint, x, xvii–xviii.

39. C. R. Dod, in Hanham (ed.), *Electoral Facts from 1832 to 1853 Impartially Stated*, (Brighton, 1972), reprint, p. 243.

40. I. G. C. Hutchison, *A Political History of Scotland 1832–1924: Parties, elections and issues* (Edinburgh, 1986), pp. 219–20.

41. D. N. Cannadine, *Lords and Landlords: The aristocracy and the towns 1774–1967* (Leicester, 1980), and (ed.), *Patricians, Power and Politics in Nineteenth Century Towns* (Leicester, 1982).

42. J. R. Kellett, *The Impact of Railways on Victorian Cities* (London, 1969), chapter 8.

43. *The Beauties of Scotland: the North British Railway Official Tourist Guide* (Edinburgh, 1915).

44. David Hunter Blair, *John Patrick, Third Marquis of Bute* (London, 1921), pp. 209–14.

45. R. D. Anderson, 'Secondary Schools', pp. 176–203, and *Education and Opportunity in Victorian Scotland: Schools and Universities* (Oxford, 1983), chapters 4–6.

46. A. Slaven and S. G. Checkland (eds.), *Dictonary of Scottish Business Biography*, vol. 1 (Aberdeen, 1986), *passim*.

47. P. Robertson, 'Scottish Universities and Scottish Industry 1860–1914', *Scottish Economic and Social History*, iv (1984), pp. 39–54.

48. Anderson, 'Secondary education', p. 201, and *Education*, pp. 308–18.

49. Anderson, 'Secondary education', p. 186.

50. J. H. Muir, *Glasgow in 1901* (Glasgow, 1901), p. 153.

51. Lipton, *Leaves*, p. 91.

52. J. J. Bell, *I Remember* (Edinburgh, 1932), pp. 27–37; Muir, *Glasgow in 1901*, pp. 178–81.

53. Cf. Chapter 10 and C. G. Brown, *The Social History of Religion in Scotland since 1730* (London, 1987).

54. John Buchan, *Memory Hold the Door* (London, 1940), p. 14. Cf. F. M. L. Thompson, *The Rise of Respectable Society 1830–1900: a social history of Victorian Britain* (London, 1988), pp. 251–2; G. Best, *Mid-Victorian Britain* (Frogmore, 1971), pp. 213–18.

55. Bell, *I Remember*, pp. 39–50; Buchan, *Memory*, pp. 15–16. Cf. Smout, *Century*, pp. 182–3.

56. In the spring of 1895 the Marquis of Bute visited Dumfriesshire, where he 'bought some mugs. . .—"Presents from Sanquhar"—for the children, and found on investigation that they were made in Germany': Blair, *Bute*, p. 203.

57. In Glasgow, for example, an analysis of all residential property for 1911 using the valuation rolls shows that less than 2 per cent of houses in the city were owner-occupied.

58. For a fictional account of lower middle-class tenement life at around the turn of the century see J. Cockburn, *Tenement* (Glasgow, 1925).

59. For a discussion of these points, see M. A. Simpson, 'The West End of Glasgow, 1830–1914', in Simpson and T. H. Lloyd (eds.), *Middle Class Housing in Britain* (Newton Abbot, 1977); J. G. Robb, 'Suburb and Slum in the Gorbals: social and residential change 1800–1900', and G. Gordon, 'The Status Areas of Edinburgh in 1914', in Gordon and B. Dicks, (eds.), *Scottish Urban History* (Aberdeen, 1983), pp. 130–67, 168–96.

60. Cf. J. Melling, *Rent Strikes: Peoples' struggle for housing in West Scotland 1890–1916* (Edinburgh, 1983).

61. Modest entertaining at home was, however, characteristic, at least in the more comfortable reaches of the middle class (Simpson, 'West End', pp. 83–4; Bell, *I Remember*, Chapter 7).

62. Morgan, 'John Clark', *Dictionary of Scottish Business Biography*, i. 326–8.

63. Bell, *I Remember*, pp. 54–71; Muir, *Glasgow in 1901*, pp. 197–8, 214–29; North British Railway *Guide*.

64. Buchan, *Huntingtower*, p. 19.

65. J. Hedderwick, *Backward Glances* (Edinburgh, 1891), pp. 153–5; Scott was also a favoured son, bringing the Marquis of Bute to Glasgow to share table with the city fathers for his centenary banquet (*Ibid.*, pp. 218–19).

66. *Ibid.*, p. 204.

67. Anderson, 'Secondary Education', p. 190; S. and O. Checkland, *Industry and Ethos: Scotland 1832–1914* (London, 1984), p. 40.

68. For an example regarding temperance see Smout, *Century*, p. 245.

69. Trainor, 'Urban Elites'.

70. M. Dyer, " 'Mere Detail and Machinery': the Great Reform Act and the effects of redistribution on Scottish representation, 1832–1868', *Scottish Historical Review*, lxii (1983), pp. 17, 25, 27.

71. M. Atkinson, *Local Government in Scotland*, (Edinburgh, 1904), p. 51.

72. O. Checkland, *Philanthropy in Victorian Scotland: Social welfare and the voluntary principle* (Edinburgh, 1980), pp. 312–13; Morris. 'Voluntary Societies and British Urban Élites, 1780–1850: an analysis', *Historical Journal*, xxvi (1983), pp. 95–118. Compare MacLaren, 'Bourgeois Ideology and Victorian Philanthropy: the contradictions of cholera' in MacLaren, *Social Class*, pp. 36–54.

73. *Slater's Directory of Scotland*, 1860, 1907. Cf. also: *Handbook to the Charitable Institutions of Dundee* (Dundee, 1907); *Glasgow Charitable and Philanthropic Institutions*, (Glasgow, 1892).

74. J. Garrard, 'The Middle Classes and Nineteenth Century National and Local Politics', in Garrard *et. al.* (eds.), *The Middle Class in Politics* (Farnborough, 1978), pp. 35–66.

75. Cf. Hanham, *Elections and Party Management: Politics in the time of Disraeli and Gladstone* (London, 1959), p. 158.

76. Scottish MPs had been notoriously ineffective (K. G. Robbins, *Nineteenth-Century Britain: Integration and Diversity* (Oxford, 1988), pp. 101–2).

77. Pelling, *Social Geography*, pp. 402–3.

78. Cf. Anderson, 'Secondary Education', pp. 202–3.

79. Pelling, *Social Geography*, Chapter 16, especially pp. 373, 377, 395, 407, 409; Hanham, *Elections*, pp. 163–4. From the 1880s party affiliation less often divided urban leaders from their rural counterparts.

80. Throughout the period, the councillors in smaller towns such as Peebles and Perth evidently were less eminent though still highly respectable in their own setting.

81. Nenadic, 'Structure', pp. 306–14; *Biographical Sketches of the Hon. the Lord Provosts of Glasgow* (Glasgow, 1883); *Memorials of the Aldermen, Provosts and Lord Provosts of Aberdeen* (Aberdeen, 1897). We are indebted to Ms Irene Sweeney, Department of History, University of Strathclyde, for information on Glasgow's local government leaders, on whom she is completing a thesis.

82. On party, see: Atkinson, *Local Government*, p. 43; B. Elliott *et. al.*, 'Property and Political Power: Edinburgh 1875–1975', in Garrard, *Middle Classes*, p. 101.

83. Cf. Trainor, 'Authority and Social Structure in an Industrialized Area: a Study of Three Black Country Towns', unpublished D.Phil. thesis, University of Oxford, 1981, chapter 6, and P. Hills, 'Divisions and Cohesions in the Nineteenth-century Middle Class: the case of Ipswich, 1830–1870', *Urban History Yearbook* (1987), pp. 42–52. For significant if lesser diversity in Scottish

counties in the era of the commissioners of supply, see A. Whetstone, *Scottish County Government in the 18th and 19th Centuries* (Edinburgh, 1981).

84. Elliott, 'Property'; Nenadic, 'Structure', pp. 306–14; T. Hart, 'Urban Growth and Municipal Government: Glasgow in a Comparative Context, 1864–1914', in Slaven and D. Aldcroft (eds.). *Business, Banking and Urban History* (Edinburgh, 1982), p. 278, n. 59. The ancillary local government bodies evidently had never been so attractive to the upper middle class.

85. Trainor, 'The Gentrification of Victorian and Edwardian Industrialists', in A. L. Beier *et. al.* (eds.), *The First Modern Society* (Cambridge, 1989), pp. 167–97.

86. Elliott, 'Property', p. 107; R. Baird, 'The Machinery of Local Government and Justice', in J. Cunnison and J. B. S. Gilfillan (eds.), *The Third Statistical Account of Scotland: Glasgow* (Glasgow, 1958), pp. 426, 859.

87. Checkland, *Philanthropy*, pp. 5, 7, 156, 160–1, 311–14.

88. J. L. Duthie, 'Philanthropy and Evangelism among Aberdeen Seamen 1814–1924', *Scottish Historical Review*, lxiii (1984), 153–73.

89. M. Blair, *The Paisley Thread Industry and the Men who created and developed it* (Glasgow, 1907), pp. 108, 89.

90. Checkland, *Philanthropy*, p. 8; *Slater's Directory of Scotland 1907*.

91. S. Yeo, *Religion and Voluntary Organisations in Crisis* (London, 1976).

92. Cf. D. A. Dow, ' "Lost to his Country as well as to his Friends": voluntary hospitals and working men', *Scottish Industrial History*, viii (1985).

93. Morris, 'Voluntary Societies', *passim*; Nenadic, 'Record Linkage', p. 39.

94. See, for example, the tribute to John Ure, a well-off flour miller who was Lord Provost of Glasgow 1880–83 (*Biographical Sketches*, pp. 374–81).

95. Nenadic, 'Businessmen and the Middle Classes: the "Dominance" of Manufacturers in Glasgow 1800–1870' (unpublished paper, Scottish Economic and Social History Society Conference, Edinburgh, November 1987).

96. Checkland, *Philanthropy*, p. 163.

97. E. P. Hennock, *Fit and Proper Persons: Ideal and reality in nineteenth century urban government*, (London, 1973); Garrard, 'Middle Class'.

98. Hedderwick, *Glances*, p. 164.

99. Dow, 'Lost', p. 35; Duthie, 'Philanthropy', p. 172.

100. Hart, 'Glasgow', p. 210; Best, 'The Scottish Victorian City', *Victorian Studies*, xi (1967–8), pp. 329–58.

101. Checkland, *Philanthropy*, pp. 139–40.

102. Hutchinson, *Political History*, p. 132; Smout, *Century*, pp. 46, 50; I. Levitt, *Poverty and Welfare in Scotland 1890–1948* (Edinburgh, 1988), Chapter 5.

103. 'Description of Ceremonial on the Occasion of Laying the Foundation Stone of the Municipal Buildings. . .' (Glasgow, 1885).

104. Buchan, *Memory*, p. 174.

The Political and Workplace Culture of The Scottish Working Class, 1832–1914

W. Knox

Outside of the necessity of having to work for a wage in order to survive and reproduce the next generation of workers, working-class experience under industrial capitalism is by no means homogeneous. The division of labour, the differences in pay and access to social necessaries, as well as ethnic, geographical, national, religious and sexual factors ensure discontinuities of experience which make fragmentation inevitable and solidarity difficult to realise. How does one begin to relate the experience of a working class of a small town based on craft production and sharing a fairly uniform culture with a large industrial town with a diverse and cosmopolitan population? Not only is the occupational structure markedly different, but the social and religious structures produce different levels of experience which create greater or lesser impediments to the development of class consciousness. Furthermore, within these local economic and social structures there is also a divergence of experience among groups of workers which makes generalisation on class methodologically hazardous. Is it scientifically possible to universalise the experience and attitudes of such diverse occupational groups as agricultural labourers, bakers, coalminers, dockers, engineers, printers, shopworkers, and talk of a homogeneous working class? Perhaps we can, since each shared a common relationship to the means of production, but their level of class awareness and organisation was so different that generalisation in terms of class identity becomes a minefield of contradiction. Therefore, it becomes apparent that the constraints of time and space and the sheer scale of methodological problems surrounding the nature of social class means that some sort of selection process is necessary to bring order and shape to experiences so disparate. Because of this the chapter will concentrate on the industrial working class in general, particularly those members of it working in the industries of the west of Scotland, as it was this section of the working class which not only was to become numerically dominant, but also was vital in mapping out the landscape of working-class political culture in Scotland. However, whenever appropriate, evidence will be drawn from other parts of Scotland to distinguish between the specific and the general trends in working-class history.

This chapter will also attempt to establish that culture is not a static concept but that it is located within a complex and shifting set of relationships, as much influenced by the traditions and customs of working-class life as it is by the changing imperatives of capital accumulation. Specifically, it questions whether changes in the workplace are necessary harbingers of changes in political behaviour, arguing that it is important to see political change as the product of a number of different and sometimes contradictory factors, of which the workplace is only one, albeit an important one. Thus the chapter draws attention to the role of such social agencies as religion, temperance and gender, in shaping the content of working-class political culture. It also examines the role of the more exclusively class institutions such as trade unions, co-operatives and political organisations in this process. However, although giving recognition to changes in working-class political culture, particularly the rise of Socialist politics in the late nineteenth century, emphasis will be placed on the continuance and strength of a political tradition traceable back to the Enlightenment and firmly established in working-class consciousness in the Radical struggles of the 1790s through to Chartism in the 1830s and 1840s. What is of major concern is the inability of Socialists effectively to overturn the political consensus established in the mid-Victorian period, and the failure of the more class-conscious members of the working class to produce anything better than a Labourist synthesis between collectivist ideas of state intervention and the social ethos of popular Liberalism.

1. The Culture of the Workplace

The nature of workplace culture was largely determined by the pace of economic and technological change. During the course of the nineteenth and early twentieth centuries the Scottish economy underwent a structural transformation. From a narrowly-based industrial structure heavily reliant on textiles, with limited growth in coal and iron production, the economy took on a more recognisably modern form, with coal, shipbuilding and steel the leading sectors in terms of output and employment.[1] The more the economy became based on heavy industry, the more it was dependent on overseas markets. By 1870 Glasgow's economy was more dependent on overseas trade than any other region in Britain. The reliance on the export trade made manufacturing industry

23. Photographs are as much an art form as are engravings and paintings. This studio photograph represents the culture of skilled male work which dominated Scotland from Aberdeen to Glasgow. This newly-apprenticed blacksmith from Aberlady in East Lothian was posed with his work clothes and the tools of his trade more carefully than a modern student for a graduation portrait. *Scottish Ethnographic Archive, National Museums of Scotland.*

sensitive to shifts in world demand and, therefore, particularly vulnerable to the workings of the trade cycle. From the 1880s the emergence of the USA and Germany as industrial giants added to the pressures on the Scottish economy. Continued expansion involved improvements in technology and workforce management if Scottish industry was to retain its share of world trade. Industry also encouraged the trend towards urbanisation set in motion by the growth of foreign trade. From an early date Scotland was one of the most urbanised countries in the world. In 1841, 70 per cent of the population of the west of Scotland was urban, with three-quarters of them living in six towns: Glasgow, Paisley, Greenock, Kilmarnock, Airdrie and Ayr. Much of the rise of the urban population was due to immigration from the Scottish Highlands and Ireland. Rural poverty and agricultural change pushed immigrants towards the labour hungry industries of the west of Scotland, Dundee and, to a lesser extent, Edinburgh. By 1841 the percentage of Irish born in Glasgow amounted to 16 per cent of total population, or 44,000 out of 270,000, and this influx maintained its momentum until the 1860s when it began to slow.[2]

Industrial and urban grown was dependent to some extent on the pace of technological change. The first phase was associated with the industrial revolution, and the changes occurring in this period saw the breakdown of the all-round skills of the pre-industrial craftsman and a dramatic deterioration in the condition of handworkers such as weavers.[3] The division of skilled tasks among less skilled workers and the subsequent decline in wages and status led to frequent outbursts of complaint within the artisan community. The intensive innovation which characterised the early phase of industrialisation slackened in the third quarter of the nineteenth century. Emphasis was placed on reorganising the workplace to raise output, and firms began to specialise in the production of a particular product. The growth of manufacturing industries, particularly heavy engineering, dramatically increased the demand for skilled labour, while, at the same time, there was the creation of new categories of skilled workers, such as boilermakers and railway enginemakers. The demand was such that tradesmen still continued to exercise control over the planning and execution of work. The final phase of technological development coincided with the onset of the 'Great Depression' and the growth of foreign competition. Scottish employers were under strong pressure to rationalise production and increase the exploitation of labour. The chief characteristics of their response to changing economic conditions were: firstly, the introduction of semi-automatic machinery in engineering, shipbuilding, coalmining and construction; secondly, the increasing use of semi- and unskilled labour in areas of work hitherto the exclusive preserve of skilled men; thirdly, the extension of the scale and size of plant; and, finally, the introduction of aspects of Taylorism, particularly the premium bonus system, and new specialist categories of workmen concerned with the design and planning of work, that is, draughtsmen, production engineers, and so on. These innovations, although experienced on a less than even basis over industry, led to a general downgrading of skill[4] and increased discontent among skilled workers.

The rationale behind much of the technological change was to reduce production costs, but it also created opportunities to break down skilled labour's independence in the workplace and reduce labour costs by opening the trades to greater intrusion from semi- and unskilled labour. Thus accompanying changes in technology were changes in the ways workers were subject to supervision and industrial discipline. This was apparent from the earliest phases of the industrial revolution. As Landes points out, the factory was preferred to the domestic system because it offered the best possible method of imposing discipline and supervision on the workers.[5] From the early 1820s there were numerous strikes in cotton mills over the question of the prerogatives of management. Similar tight supervision was not possible, however, in non-factory

24. Large-scale work dominated cities like Glasgow and Dundee. The Lower Dens Works, Dundee, in 1866. They were built in the 1850s by Baxter brothers and their engineer partner Peter Carmichael for flax production. *Scottish Ethnographic Archive, National Museums of Scotland.*

workplaces where employers found it difficult to subordinate labour to the imperatives of accumulation. The dispersed nature of the work in coalmining, or the high levels of skill in printing, were all obstacles to strict regulation. Employers therefore experimented with different methods of control, from direct supervision, through the use of foremen and/or managers, to indirect control, using sub-contracting, gang work and piece-rate payment. In many areas of work the latter meant ceding control of the labour process to the workers. Key workers would be contracted by employers to carry out work at an agreed price, and they would be responsible for the recruitment and payment of their assistants.[6] This method of labour organisation was used extensively in mining, iron works and shipbuilding. Such a system of control had obvious disadvantages for employers, as it allowed key workers to set the intensity of the work rhythm, to delimit areas of skill and, hence, reward. The loss of managerial control implicit in this arrangement led employers to opt where possible for more direct forms of control. Foremen were used in this capacity. They took responsibility for most of the tasks of management, from hiring and firing to quality control.[7]

Such strategies may have enhanced employer control and increased the commitment of the worker to the goals of management, but, as Newby has recognised, 'no matter how much emphasis is placed upon strategies for obtaining employee commitment within the factory gate, the worker will be open to alternative definitions of his situation outside in the locality . . . A common solution [to the problem] has been [for employers] to extend the boundaries . . . of the factory gate to encompass a complete locality'. Patrick Joyce, in his study of the Lancashire cotton industry, has convincingly demonstrated how a paternalistic strategy was used by employers to obtain the social adhesion of the workforce.[8] There has been little systematic attempt to extend this type of analysis to Scotland. However, Lothian coalowners provided libraries and reading rooms, housing (in some cases free), pensions for widows of colliers killed in mining accidents and other benefits. Scottish shipyard owners were involved in providing cheap housing, not only to attract workers, but also, as Pollard notes, to extend the social power of the yard. Similarly, railway companies offered welfare benefits and job security to their workers in return for militaristic obedience.[9]

As reflected in managerial strategies workers until the 1880s enjoyed a fair degree of autonomy in the planning and execution of work. However, coinciding with developments in new technology, management imposed stricter disciplinary controls on labour and introduced new methods of cost accounting to regulate the work effort. The introduction of electric light made shift work more common and excessive overtime working a major problem for trade unions. In engineering the extension of the incentive payments system was extremely effective in intensifying the work effort. By 1914, 46 per cent of fitters and 37 per cent of turners were on piece-rate payment, compared to only 5 per cent of all engineering and boilermaking workers in 1886.[10] Added to this was the premium bonus system, which involved the measuring and recording of job times by stopwatch. But this only affected 10 per cent of engineering workers in 1909, and an even smaller number of other metal workers.[11] The complexity of calculation involved in the new payments systems saw the creation of wages departments and workers began to receive 'payment through the office'. As a consequence, internal sub-contracting, and with it the gang or piece master, declined.[12] The new method of calculation also had implications for the role of the foreman. Time measurement of jobs eroded his all-round authority in the workplace as it involved the separation of planning from the execution of work; the former became the concern of works management.[13] Personal recruitment was also gradually disappearing as large firms set up employment departments. The decreasing role of the foreman and the decline of internal sub-contracting gradually made clear to workers the relationship of authority and power in the workplace. Increasingly workers were confronted by capital or, at least, its managerial representatives, rather than by a host of authority figures.

These changes had implications for employers utilising paternalistic schemes to achieve worker commitment. Although there is evidence to suggest that companies continued to provide welfare benefits and housing in a variety of occupations, it was being stripped of any notion of reciprocity. As Melling points out, welfare provision was the result of 'deliberate calculation of economic costs and benefits . . . with an overtly strategic purpose in mind'.[14] Employer-sponsored friendly societies were introduced to discourage workers from joining trade unions. The introduction by the Engineering Employers' Federation of a Foreman's Mutual Benefit Society has to be interpreted in this light, in as much as it was designed to attract foremen away from membership of the Amalgamated Society of Engineers.[15] Housing was also used as a form of social control, as striking workers and their families were liable to be evicted during industrial disputes. Employers, however, could use housing more subtly to reproduce the status hierarchies of the workplace in the wider society. The Edinburgh and Glasgow Railway Company's housing in Springburn Hill, Glasgow, was arranged in such a way that 'the houses on the top of the hill were of a better standard and were

25. Ironmoulders with their skills and relatively high wages were among the aristocracy of labour. *Falkirk Museums.*

for the top drivers, engineers and supervisors, while the lower blocks were for other drivers and lower grades'.[16]

The impact of economic and technological change, as well as the sharpening of relationships between capital and labour, brought about changes in what the journeyman engineer, Thomas Wright, called the 'inner life of the workshop', that is, they led to changes in the customs, values and organisation of workers. Prior to 1850 artisan culture in Scotland was predominantly male and Protestant. Female work was synonymous with low paid unskilled labour, usually in domestic service, textiles or sweated trades. Similarly, the Irish Catholics were confined to low-grade work in spinning factories, coal mines, iron works and casual labouring jobs.[17] The main elements of the skilled workers' culture were literacy, drink and an elaborate system of ceremonials and rituals. Mechanics' Institutes and literary and scientific societies provided access to knowledge in a wide variety of forms. But balancing the world of self-improvement was the culture of drink. Alcohol was interwoven into the fabric of Scottish society, and most occasions in the workplace routine were used as an excuse for excess. In the stonemason's trade, for example, drinks were served on the men when an apprentice joined the squad, when his 'apron was washed', and again when his time was out.[18] John Dunlop, in his study of drinking usages, has itemised the customs relating to drink in each occupation and showed how endemic they were in Scottish industry.[19]

The role played by drink in industrial relations was important at this time. Employers plied their workers with drink at strategic times of the year or at the completion of a certain workload. Drinking in this context had the effect of legitimising the social relations of production. However, it could also symbolise the independence of labour from capital. Thomas Stewart, the Larkhall collier poet of the 1840s, recalled how, on the slightest pretext, the colliers would decide to retire to the pithead for a 'social glass'.[20] Drink also had a part to play in the creation of group loyalties within the workplace. It was an integral ingredient of workplace ceremonials and rituals, such as apprentice initiations, which, in turn, were of symbolic importance in the creation of craft pride, independence and solidarity among the artisanate. The ceremonials and rituals were important indicators of the significance attached to work and to one's position in the culture of the workplace. They were also reference points in the determination of status hierarchies within the occupational structure and the wider society. According to artisanal logic, apprenticeship and work experience had meant that they had acquired a property in their skill which was the equivalent of bourgeois private property, with the exception that it was collective rather than individual property. A skilled worker thus inherited a 'use right to be expressed within the regulations and constraints of the trade'.[21] This 'use right' to the trade was seen as the inheritance, indeed, the birthright of the artisan's son. Upon this logic was built a whole system of patrimony which extended to most skilled work, including coalmining.[22]

A strong sense of independence was derived from traditionally inherited ideas of skill as a definition of one's property and status, and this was further emphasised by craft customs and the ownership of tools. The latter not only advertised the 'relative independence of the artisan from management, but, even more clearly, his monopoly of skilled work'.[23] In the building trade, bricklayers' labourers were not allowed to use the trowel; Edinburgh stonemasons let their hammers fall without striking if time was called, as an assertion of their right to control their own pace of work.[24] Colliers would refuse to work if observed by management. Even in the new trades of the industrial revolution, such as engineering and boilermaking, there developed a complex system of rituals and ceremonies to impress upon members the essentials of craft pride and solidarity.[25]

This culture suffered a series of damaging blows brought about by the economic and technological change in the closing decades of the nineteenth century. The ceremonials and rituals disappeared in the larger works as journeymen, tied to piece work and responsible for more expensive and sophisticated machinery, had less time to indulge in them or the drinking usages associated with them. Such had been the specialisation of skill there was less of an achievement to celebrate. Even in the smaller workshops the old process of socialisation was stripped of intrinsic value and symbolism. The washing of the mason's apron, an important event in the *rites de passage* of the apprentice, was abandoned, and the more 'modern masons were satisfied by taking the youth to a public house and making him drink a pint of beer'.[26] True, the ritual smearing of the genitals with ink, grease or oil continued, but these actions were more the product of a closed male environment than surviving traditions of a once powerful culture of ceremony and ritual. As such they have their parallels in public schools, sea-going vessels and other exclusively male institutions.[27] Patrimony became less relevant as a carrier of traditions and customs. The expansion of employment and population ensured that trades were no longer the preserve of tight-knit networks. Increasingly the agent of socialisation and the defence of trade practices lay with the trade union.

Although associations of workers existed in pre-industrial times, trade unions were a response to the pressures of industrialisation. The early unions were small, local, based on skilled workers, and concerned to limit the supply of labour and control the labour process. They operated around the notion of the trade or craft as a community of interests, and it was mainly those employers who trangressed against the customs of the trade who were singled out for action. The 'good' or 'honourable' employer was from the early nineteenth century allowed membership of the craft society. More bitter relations tended to be commonly associated with the highly capitalised industries, such as cotton and mining. The unionism which developed in these industries was a mixture of pre-industrial and modern forms of protest and organisation. Ear-cropping was occasionally used to deal with blacklegs in mining areas, and intimidation and violence, including murder, occurred in the cotton industry. Signs, oaths and rituals were also part of the same process and were used to impress upon union

26. The metal trades in towns across central Scotland included a range of intricate and developing skills. These stove fitters were in a Falkirk Iron Co. workshop c.1910. *Glasgow University Archives.*

members the seriousness of their undertaking, and to build an identity of interests. Secrecy was a consequence of weakness and as unions became established tended to disappear, though remnants remained in a body like the mystical Free Collier Movement of the 1850s and 1860s which emerged in response to the collapse of union organisation in the Lanarkshire and Lothian coalfields.[28] But alongside the violence and the secret rituals there existed the more recognisable forms of modern trade unionism, that is, a visible leadership, an administrative structure based on membership cards and dues, established meeting places, conferences, and so on. In spite of this, unions in this period had a reputation for violence enhanced by the events surrounding the cotton spinners' strike of 1837. The strike and the 1838–42 depression, inflicted a crushing blow on Scottish trade unionism. National unions of miners and spinners broke up and were replaced by weak local associations.[29]

Since alcohol was thought to have been the cause of much of the violence in Scottish unions, the search for respectability led them away from pubs into coffee houses for their meetings at an earlier stage than happened in England.[30] This conscious action was part of a desire for respectability and acceptance by the trade unions which some labour historians, taking their lead from the Webbs, have seen as opening up a new era of class collaboration. On the surface there does seem to be strong evidence to suggest that craft unions were actively collaborationist. New members of the Boilermakers' Society were informed by branch presidents that 'We are united not to set class against class but to teach one another that men are all brothers. Our greatest desire being to cultivate a close and lasting relationship between all those with whom we have to do with in undertaking our daily work'.[31] The miners' rule book in the west of Scotland 'emphasised that strikes tended to fail and that collaboration was to be preferred'.[32] However, the degree of industrial pacifism was greatly exaggerated by the leadership, and when economic conditions were favourable strikes could flare. Demands for a nine-hour day in the 1860s led to frequent strikes among building workers, engineers and boilermakers. Twenty thousand Clyde workers were out in 1866. The boom of the early 1870s, when the demand for labour was almost insatiable, allowed major gains to be made, generally without strikes. However, in the worsening trade conditions of the late 1870s some major stoppages occurred, with prolonged strikes in 1876 and 1878 on Clydeside.[33] Strikes in mining were said to be more frequent and bitter 'by the standards of mid-Victorian Britain'.[34] Added to these direct forms of protest were the more discrete actions such as 'ca'canny', refusal to teach apprentices or to set up work for handymen, memorials, shop meetings and deputations.

Where labour collaborated with capital it was not as equal partners, since the former was weakly organised. During the 1860s trade unionism was all but wiped out in the shipbuilding and mining industries.[35] As late as 1892 there were only 147,000 trade unionists in Scotland, which amounted to only 3.7 per cent of total population. The figure for England and Wales was significantly higher at 4.9 per cent of the population. More recent studies have shown that Scotland's level of trade union membership as a percentage of the employed population was half that of South Wales and Humberside, and only a quarter of the north-east coast of England. This, of course, masked the higher density of membership in the capital goods sector, but even here it rarely accounted for more than 25 per cent of the workforce.[36] Weakness was not only the result of labour market insecurity or employer resistance, but also the outcome of community and workplace relationships. Miners' and iron workers' communities, exhibiting a high degree of shared ethnic origins and religious convictions, as well as low in/out migration patterns, were better placed to sustain stable organisations and independence from employer authority systems than those which were unstable and culturally diverse. As Alan Campbell has shown, there was a marked contrast between the patterns of unionisation in a village like Larkhall, with its largely native, stable population and the more mixed community of Coatbridge. At Larkhall the culture of the independent collier was more easily sustained against pressures from capital, whereas Coatbridge was amenable to the social control of the employers.[37] However, although stable local unions by their very nature were weak, localist traditions meant that Scottish unions generally opposed amalgamation with English unions. Local autonomy was preferred to centralised control. In 1892 two-thirds of trade unionists in Scotland were members of exclusively Scottish unions.[38] As a result, a multitude of small and insular unions existed, with the Clyde alone able to boast a hundred unions active in the early years of the twentieth century. Of these only 21 could claim 500 or more members, while 37 had less than 100.[39] Inevitably demarcation disputes arose, particularly in construction, metals and shipbuilding, and this kind of sectionalism was intensified by the existence of sectarian division in these industries.[40]

Organisational weakness led to informal modes of resistance among workers. For most of the nineteenth century the workplace remained the unit of organisation. Basic pay and conditions were fought for on a plant-by-plant basis through ad hoc activity. Price estimates that around 50 per cent of restrictions imposed in the workplace in engineering in the 1860s emerged out of 'informal workgroup decisions rather than [shop] steward or union policies'.[41] Among female workers ad hoc organisation was commonplace, as their position as low-paid workers and wives and mothers made trade unionism irrelevant.[42] Absence of formal organisational structures did not inhibit industrial action. Strikes were common in the female dominated jute industry of Dundee, and were said to occur regularly with 'the appearance of the spring sun'.[43] During the 1894 miners' strike Arnot estimated that of the 70,000 workers on strike only 30,000 were union members.[44] Although institutional studies of workers' organisations have failed to give due prominence to this form of unofficial collective defence, the existence of strong work-group responses should not lead to the conclusion that the level of class-awareness was high among Scottish workers. It was the immediate work-group and the locality which were important rather than the working class, or even the industry as a whole.

In contrast to the weakness of the unions, the employers in Scotland were remarkably strong. Subscription to the ethos of individualism and self-help did not prevent association or federation, especially when faced with challenges from organised labour. The East of Scotland Association of Engineers, the North West Engineering Trades Employers' Association, the Shipbuilding Employers' Federation, the National Association of Master Builders, were some of the more active employers' associations. Federated or not they took a hardline in industrial disputes and refused to accept trade-union constraints on their power to manage. It was not until the late 1880s that Clydeside shipbuilding employers recognised the Boilermakers' Society. Supplementing the abrasiveness were the paternalism and welfare schemes already mentioned. Thus, major impediments to the formation of a strong trade-union movement existed, and this ensured that the majority of workers remained unorganised. However, the latter should not blind us to the fact that while trade unionism was not strong in Scotland, it was growing and encompassing groups of workers hitherto unorganised, such as carters, dockers and farm workers. A greater need to combat the growth of employers' associations was demonstrated in the move among some unions towards amalgamation with English unions. The founding of the Scottish Trades Union Congress (STUC) in 1897 was a recognition of this and of the wider political problems faced by Scottish labour. The established unions witnessed an increase in their numbers in this period as well.[45] This phenomenon is equally deserving of explanation as are the already discussed weaknesses.

The intensification of exploitation through the implementation of new technology and stricter codes of industrial discipline fractured the reciprocity between capital and labour, which historians, such as Patrick Joyce,[46] had seen as a distinguishing feature of mid-Victorian industrial relations, and elicited a more class-orientated response from labour. An important example of heightening class antagonisms in industry was the reaction of apprentices to changes in the labour process. From the 1890s apprentices were confronting grievances at work by withdrawing their labour. Allied to this was the high turnover rate which indicated a lack of job satisfaction and a growing awareness of exploitation.[47] In this climate workers' values and concerns underwent a transformation, and this resulted in an improvement in the mechanisms of collective self-defence. Previously the work-group had been the unit of organisation, but as capital became more organised this was seen as increasingly inadequate. Trade unionism was the only viable form resistance could take, and this realisation saw numbers sharply increase. However, although objectively this situation of rising trade-union membership and intensifying class antagonisms might have been thought to have radicalised the workers politically by opening them to alternative definitions of their experience, as we will see, the relationship between economic and political change was by no means unproblematic.

The Political Culture

Working-class political culture in Scotland rested on the pillars of democracy, nationalism, republicanism and social justice. These political principles were underscored by a value system which derived its strength from independence, temperance and religion. The first was the product of workplace notions of skill and status; the last two enhanced this by emphasising the respectability and social worth of the worker. Like trade unionism, working-class politics in Scotland were predominantly male and Protestant, and were shaped by the concerns and ideology of skilled workers. The social ethos and the political principles, however, were not exclusively confined to the working class, but were shared by other groups, particularly the petty bourgeoisie, and this made political alliances possible and a noted feature of working-class political development. Although the political practice which emerged from this cross-class ethos was threatened on occasion by the more volatile culture of the unskilled and immigrant communities, particularly in the first half of the nineteenth century, it proved remarkably durable and should caution the historian against periodising working-class history. It has been the practice until recently to divide working-class history in the nineteenth century into three distinct phases of development; firstly, the struggle for the six points of the Charter, which was evidence of a militant working-class consciousness; secondly, the mid-Victorian consensus in which the radicalism of the Chartist years dissipated itself and degenerated into class collaboration; and thirdly, the rise of Socialism in which, under pressure from economic and technological changes from the late 1880s onwards, the working class rediscovered political radicalism. This section of the chapter will argue that such an approach distorts our understanding of nineteenth-century Scottish labour history. Therefore, emphasis will be placed on the continuity of the political tradition, while, at the same time, recognising that the tradition was open to a continuous process of renegotiation and redefinition.

Part of the reason for the continuing strength of the political tradition lies with the social ethos which underscored it, of which religion, temperance and the culture of respectability, were elemental parts. From the Chartist period onwards working-class political leaders were linked to temperance societies. Most of the Glasgow Chartist leaders, including Brewster, Fraser, McFarlane and Cranston, were officials in temperance societies. In Aberdeen, the Total Abstinence Society had 3,000 members and was made up 'almost entirely' of Chartists and other political radicals. These societies not only preached temperance but also campaigned for the Charter. This connection carried over into the decades of the third quarter of the nineteenth century and beyond. The mid-Victorian labour leaders held their meetings in coffee houses, and teetotalism, although with a subscribing middle-class membership, was still largely based on skilled workers.[48] What attracted the politically motivated to temperance was that it provided an ideological critique of industrial capitalism, which linked poverty and alcohol abuse to exploitation, and gave experience to working men in the mechanics of pressure-group politics and in administration.[49] The idea of raising workers, both morally and socially, as well as criticism of the social effects of industrial capitalism, made temperance equally appealing to the emerging Labour Party. Keir Hardie was a strong temperance advocate, as was the Scottish Independent Labour Party (ILP) whose main mouthpiece — *Forward* — refused to take adverts from the drinks trade and constantly preached teetotalism. The Scottish Co-operative movement also took a hostile attitude to drinking among its members and as a result 'Co-operation and Temperance became synonomous'.[50]

Anti-drink was part of a strategy of moral improvement, in order that workers could be made into the kind of people Socialism was thought to require. Various organisations were formed to offer wholesome entertainment and healthy pursuits for young workers. Rambling clubs, ILP cycle scouts, vocational courses, musical societies and choirs were all part of the culture of Labour in the late nineteenth century. These initiatives were part of the artisan tradition of self-improvement and respectability, and as such had their forerunners in mechanics' institutes, literary societies, debating clubs, and so on, during the first phase of industrialisation. In the relatively more affluent period of the 1860s and 1870s skilled workers joined voluntary societies, such as golf and bowling clubs and volunteer societies, in increasing numbers, and by doing so were actively rejecting 'certain aspects of the older popular culture, especially drinking customs'.[51] Even among Marxist organisations, such as the Socialist League, the Socialist Labour Party (SLP), and so on, classes were held in history, politics, philosophy and literature, including English grammer. For children, Socialist Sunday Schools were introduced by the ILP in the 1890s, and were attended by the better off.[52] The slum dweller, the unskilled and the poor were ignored, as they were incapable of attaining the status of respectability. *Forward* praised itself for not being read in the slums of Glasgow.[53]

Respectability was not restricted to one social class; it cut across all social classes, and direct involvement in movements such as the Scottish Temperance Association forged social contacts between skilled workers

27. Many workplaces were still small in scale at the end of the century. These men in Aberdour were keen to show that Scotland was very much part of the British Empire. Notice the careful display of the cabinetmakers' tools by the front row. *Scottish Ethnographic Archive, National Museums of Scotland.*

and the petty bourgeoisie. Religion did likewise. Although throughout the nineteenth century the majority of workers did not attend church, the majority of congregations were dominated by the working class, particularly the skilled workers.[54] Many Chartists were members of dissenting churches, and, later in the century, leaders of the ILP were linked to the Free Church and the United Presbyterian. These churches, as a consequence of being locked out of the corridors of power, if not wealth, took a more critical attitude to the status quo and to the dominant institutions of Scottish society. Moreover, the laity and the ministry were drawn from the ranks of the skilled and the petty bourgeoisie.[55] The influence of religion on politicised workers meant that the political emphasis was placed by the labour movement on brotherly love and social justice rather than on class hatred. Labour leaders like Keir Hardie espoused a brand of ethical Socialism which preached class reconciliation, and it tended to be only among those workers who had abandoned religion that a class-based brand of revolutionary politics was articulated.[56] The secularism of the latter alienated them from the workers and from the leadership of the labour movement. Owenite Socialism was disowned by the Chartists and by the Glasgow trade societies because of its secularism; likewise, the smaller Marxist parties of the late nineteenth century, such as the Social Democratic Federation (SDF) and SLP, found atheism a difficult concept to sell to the working class.

Tensions between the labour movement and the churches did exist, particularly regarding the middle-class bias of some ministers' utterances on social questions. This did not lead to an abandonment of the faith — rather it led to the establishment of independent working-class churches. Both Chartism and late nineteenth-century Socialism produced their own Chartist and Labour churches, a common theme of which was anti-clericalism. Ministers were generally seen as being in alliance with employers, and the chief task was to reclaim the faith from the clutches of Mammon. According to James Connolly, Scottish and, later, Irish revolutionary, 'It is not Socialism but Capitalism that is opposed to religion'.[57] As the churches began to champion ideas of state intervention and trade unionism from the mid-1880s the tensions began to ease considerably and a general rapprochement between Labour and the churches took place.[58]

Knowing that God was on their side gave moral conviction to the political demands of the working class, but the influence of religion was not always positive. The social framework implicit in Christian scriptures stressed the importance of the family and subordination of women. No changes were envisaged in the traditional role of women in society by working-class radicals. Women were seen as helpmates rather than equals in the political struggle. Chartists campaigned for adult male suffrage, and it was not until 1912 that the labour movement agreed to oppose any extension of the franchise which did not include women.[59] Socialists condemned capitalism because it could not provide the family wage. Women, if they played a part at all in political struggles, did so in a supporting role. Indirectly, religion was part of the process of fragmentation of the working class along the lines of gender. Sectarianism, however, was a more explicit form of fragmentation, and this was evident from the political struggles of the early nineteenth century. Orange societies were active from this period onwards, and in 1836 a Glasgow Operative Conservative Society was formed, committed to Presbyterianism and Toryism.[60] However, since the main flood of Irish immigration did not occur until after the Famine and was fortunate to coincide with a favourable upturn in economic activity anti-Catholicism did not enjoy a mass following. What intensified the problem was the influx of Ulster Protestants in the years 1876–81. By 1913–14 Glasgow had 107 Orange lodges out of a total of 400 for the whole of Britain, and certain occupations, such as boilermaking, became recruited on a sectarian basis.[61] Religious bigotry saw the Irish Catholics retreat from the embrace of the Scottish labour movement. The Irish refused to co-operate with the Chartists until the death of Daniel O'Connell in 1847, and later in the century the demands of the STUC for secular education in state schools and the attacks on Irish publicans by the Scottish ILP led the Irish to withdraw into their own community, which naturally centred on the Church.[62] This had important consequences for the development of working-class politics in Scotland.

The operation of a shared value system allowed for the construction of political alliances with other social classes, particularly the petty bourgeoisie. This was evident during the struggles for reform of the franchise in the early 1830s, when the Scottish Political Union was set up to promote close ties between the middle and working classes. The triumph of the middle classes in 1832, and the continued exclusion of the workers from the franchise, increased political tension between the classes, as did the failure of the Glasgow MPs elected under the reformed franchise to give support to the short-time factory movement; however, the links were never severed. During the campaign for the six points of the Charter workers continued to co-operate with the middle class, especially over the repeal of the Corn Laws. Relations were strained when the Anti-Corn Law League stressed repeal before the Charter, but, on the whole, the workers accepted the political premise that economic distress and social injustice were the consequence of the corrupt monopoly of power by the aristocracy, and the only solution was a radical restructuring of the British state. Operating within a political economy determined by the interests of capital meant that alternatives to mainstream Radicalism were rendered peripheral. Owenite Socialism, with its critique of competitive capitalism and its emphasis on co-operation, failed to make a significant impact on

28. Carters, like these at Dundee docks, were among the many unskilled workers whose earnings were low and irregular. *Dundee District Libraries.*

Scottish workers. Owenism lacked a theory of politics in general and the state in particular. Moral regeneration rather than political change was seen by Owenites as the central goal of labour. For this reason they found the Chartist programme irrelevant.[63] Similarly, those advocating violent revolution failed to overcome artisanal commitment to constitutionalism. Violence did not figure as a political strategy during the reform struggles of the 1830s, and even in the Chartist years commanded insignificant support.

Chartism's failure to achieve its aims or develop a critique of class or property relationships is unsurprising. Its leaders were mainly petty bourgeois, and split over such questions as moral v. physical force, attitudes to the Anti-Corn Law league. It was also adversely affected by the structural and ethnic divisions among the workers, and by the realities of artisanal culture, which was independent, but reformist and rational, sharing a part of a common value system subscribed to by the industrial bourgeoisie. However, the democratic/radical tradition of which Chartism was a part was important in laying the foundations of

the future political development of Scottish workers. The acceptance of
the Liberal/capitalist framework was the outcome of the struggles of the
1830s and 1840s as the alternatives of Owenism and revolution failed to
attract mass support. Because of this there are no grounds for seeing
the decades which followed as marking a discontinuity in working-class
history in Scotland. Working-class energies in this period continued
to be directed towards the fight for parliamentary representation, the
democratisation of municipal politics and the development of a stable
trade union movement. The political language remained broadly similar,
although the tone was more conciliatory. Labour attacked the denial of
the vote to the respectable working-class householder as unjust, since it
failed to recognise the 'growing virtue and intelligence of the worker'.[64]
One should not read this as simply a case of accepting the assumptions
and values of the middle class. In spite of the fact that the language
and ideology were borrowed from Liberalism, the interpretation was
ambiguous. Sometimes the demands of the workers were articulated
within the dominant value system, as with the vote, and on other
occasions, as with trade-union reform, within a more class-based
language. It also did not mean that workers accepted an exclusively
middle-class interpretation of Liberalism or middle-class patronage.
In local politics there were frequent cases of separate working-men's
electoral committees being established precisely because of distrust
of middle-class Liberal politics.[65] Keir Hardie's decision to stand as
independent candidate in Mid-Lanark in 1888 was largely made on the
issue of the need for class representation.

Notwithstanding these qualifications, attachment to radical philosophy
meant that workers did not clearly comprehend how the political system
was organised to protect and nurture the class ownership of property.
To Scottish workers politics still revolved around the Radical slogans
of 'masses versus classes' and the object was to establish standards
of 'fairness', 'justice' and 'morality' in politics and civil society.
These objectives were shared by Radical middle-class Liberals. Once
anti-trade union legislation was abolished in the 1870s, politically all that
separated the latter from the working class was the issue of working-class
representation. The question was, would the rise of Socialism in the 1880s
and the worsening of industrial relations following rapid technological
development and economic change allow greater space for an alternative
version of class experience?

The Socialist revival of the 1880s and its subsequent progress did not
mark large discontinuities in the social profile of the leadership, which
remained within the skilled/petty bourgeoisie alliance. Socially, Labour

leaders were teetotal, pacifist, rational, untheoretical and evangelical in religion; politically, they were radical, republican, anti-landlord and nationalist. Their heroes were Jesus, Shelley, Mazzini, Whitman, Carlyle and Burns. Marxism was introduced from without by Hyndman and Morris. Thus, Socialists in Scotland drew on an eclectic range of sources to provide an analysis of capitalism and a challenge to the hegemony of the Liberal Party. The starting point was land reform, with Henry George's *Progress and Poverty* (1880) the key text. Anti-landlordism was tied up with demands for Scottish Home Rule, and Labour leaders were prominent in Liberal-dominated organisations such as the Young Scots, the Scottish Home Rule Association and the Highland Land League. Land reform and nationalism cut across class and ethnic barriers and tied together different strands of Scottish society. The ILP's anti-landlord ideology led to a 'strategy of housing agitation rather than an industrial agitation'.[66] Most of Glasgow's housing was owned by small property owners who owed allegiance to the Liberal Party, and they became prime targets in the ILP's political strategy. The ILP equated the agricultural landlords of the Highlands and Ireland with urban landlords and drew on the immigrant communities' hatred of landlordism. The stress on non-workplace relationships meant that the ILP was incapable of theorising the link between industrial and political action. The only capitalists that *Forward* attacked were monopolistic mineowners.[67]

Politically there does not seem to have been a great difference between the ILP and the Liberals. Glasgow was turned into the leading practitioner of municipal socialism in Britain by the Liberals and to the ILP 'any municipalisation was socialism'.[68] In spite of the formation of the Labour Party in 1906, Labour's two Scottish MPs, George Barnes and Alexander Wilkie, had pronounced Liberal sympathies. It was only the legal setbacks that the trade unions suffered in the 1890s and in the early twentieth century, of which the Taff Vale judgment of 1901/2 was the most important which convinced organised labour of the need for independent political representation. Thus the shift of the unions towards Labour was based on expediency rather than ideology. However, since the overwhelming number of Scottish workers were outside the labour movement, the Liberal position prior to the First World War remained impressively strong. It was only the Liberals that could deliver on the issues of Home Rule for Ireland, which retained the Irish vote, and land reform, which assured them of the Scottish Highland vote. With three MPs and two hundred councillors of various kinds Labour was able to dent the Liberal edifice but not topple it.

However, what progress Labour had achieved was at the expense of the

29. Before 1914, men still controlled the clerical jobs. The office of Lowrie's, Washington Street, Glasgow. *Glasgow University Archives.*

revolutionary left, and this begs the question of why Labourism advanced where revolution had failed to attract the dissident worker. Part of the answer lies with the commitment of the trade unions to Lib/Labism, but attention also has to be paid to the importance of the radical political tradition, of which Scottish Labour was a part, and the way this was linked to perceptions of respectability. The Social Democratic Federation of Hyndman and the Socialist League of Morris and their various splinter groups, such as the SLP and the British Socialist Party were seen as imported products and not organisations organically rooted in the political tradition. With the exception of the SLP, organisations of the revolutionary left were London-based at a time when the Scottish labour movement had a separate national identity and Home Rule was part of its political baggage. Anti-parliamentarianism was also anathema to the Liberal/democratic tradition of Scottish workers. Finally, a large part of the membership of the Socialist movement was atheistic, and intemperance, particularly among London members, alienated potential Scottish members like Keir Hardie. Greater success was achieved by the revolutionary left in the industrial arena. The SLP and the shop stewards who had graduated from John Maclean's classes in Marxist economics were active in promoting militancy among skilled workers on Clydeside which culminated in the series of events known as 'Red Clydeside'. However, until the crisis of the war years and the shackling of the official trade-union movement by war agreements, there was little space for them to operate in. It was significant that during the 1908 depression, which threw thousands of skilled workers on relief when a Liberal government was in office, it was the ILP and not the revolutionary left which took the lead in uniting the various strands of the labour movement against unemployment.[69] Whatever the future political development of the Scottish working class it would be the eclectic, élitist and Calvinist ILP and not the Marxists which would have the decisive say.

3. Conclusion

The electoral failure of Labour and the minimal impact of the Marxist left pose important questions regarding the relationship between the labour process and politics. Restructuring the labour process produces positive and negative tendencies in advancing class consciousness among workers. On the one hand, technological change and the intensification of industrial discipline and the work/effort ratio constantly threatened the autonomy of the skilled worker in the planning and execution of his work. The trend towards skill specialisation also led to greater labour mobility and minimised the division between the honourable and dishonourable sections of trades. Control of the labour process became an increasingly important aspect of industrial bargaining as a result. This allowed Socialists the space to articulate an alternative version of class experience, but as Penn points out, the effect was profoundly contradictory. Socialism 'stands for the unity and equality of all labour, something which poses a dilemma for the exclusiveness of the craft worker' in their desire to retain status and pay differentials *vis-à-vis* other workers.[70] Restructuring also results in divisions being created within skilled trades. Changes in shipbuilding, particularly from wood to iron and steel, accelerated the frequency of demarcation disputes among shipyard workers and fragmented the response of labour to increased exploitation. The marginalisation of women's issues and the policy of restricting women to low-grade work further intensified the fragmentation of the working class. Sectarianism acted as another agent in this process. Moreover, in spite of the fact that issues connected with control of work became of increasing importance to workers as the nineteenth century wore on, it remains true that most strikes were still concerned with wages and hours. A unified working-class response to changes in the labour process would therefore seem questionable.

It would also seem that while the introduction of new technologies and work routines engendered discontent within the site of production there is no evidence that it was of such a magnitude as to politicise the majority of workers in the direction of Socialism. Workers may have opposed managerial strategies in the workplace but this was not translated into a political offensive against the rule of capital, as they continued to vote Liberal in large numbers. What motivated the working class more than anything else in political terms in the later period was Lloyd George's 'People's Budget' and the election campaigns of 1910. This was a crucial reminder of the strength of the radical tradition, as the campaign against the House of Lords was reminiscent of the struggles of the Scottish Radicals a century ago to reform parliament, and touched on the residual hatred of landlordism endemic among Scottish and Irish workers. This seems to underline the fact that political consciousness is shaped by a wide range of social experiences, and that the world of work does not exercise an overdeterministic ideological influence. As a result of differences in the standard of living, gender, religion, geography, language, recreational and residential patterns, as well as past political experiences and memories, the Scottish working class remained culturally diverse. As such it was only a party which was philosophically eclectic and politically elastic that could weld the variety of experience into a coherent political force. In spite of the gradually increasing criticism and tensions, the Liberals performed that role until the aftermath of war saw their hegemony breakdown. The spaces created by economic and social change were not large enough for Labour to redraw the political boundaries in Scotland.

Labour's eventual triumph was in many ways the result of external factors beyond its control. The crisis of the war years and the political changes in the immediate aftermath would seem to represent a climacteric in Scotland's development. Until then the strength of the radical political tradition and the social supports it rested upon were enough to maintain the Liberal hold over the majority of Scottish workers.

NOTES

I would like to thank Hamish Fraser, Eleanor Gordon, Mark Gray, Andy MacDonald, Bob Morris and Christopher Smout for reading and commenting on this chapter. Needless to say, they bear no responsibility for any errors or misinterpretations on my part. I should also like to thank the Carnegie Trust for the Universities of Scotland for generously financing archival research in Amsterdam and London.

1. S. & O. Checkland, *Industry and Ethos: Scotland, 1832–1914* (1984), pp. 19, 22, 24–5; A. B. Campbell, *The Lanarkshire Miners: a Social History of Their Trade Unions, 1775–1874* (Edinburgh, 1979), pp. 101–2; J. Butt, 'The Scottish Cotton Industry During the Industrial Revolution, 1780–1840', in L. M. Cullen and T. C. Smout (eds.), *Comparative Aspects of Scottish and Irish Economic and Social History* (Edinburgh, 1977), p. 123; T. Dickson and T. Clarke, 'The Making of a Class Society: Commercialisation and Working Class Resistance, 1780–1830', in *Scottish Capitalism: Class, State and Nation from Before the Union to the Present* (1980), pp. 142–3; A. Slaven, *The Development of the West of Scotland: 1750–1960* (1975), pp. 120–1, 178.

2. Slaven, *op. cit.*, pp. 141–5; A. Campbell, *loc. cit.*

3. N. Murray, *The Scottish Handloom Weavers* (Edinburgh, 1978); J. B. Jeffreys, *The Story of the Engineers, 1800–1945* (1945); R. W. Postgate, *The Builders' History* (1923).

4. N. Dearle, *The Problem of Unemployment in the London Building Trades* (1908), pp. 46–8; A. L. Levine, 'Industrial Change and its Effect on Labour', unpublished PhD thesis, University of London, 1954, pp. 462–3; K. McClelland and A. Reid, 'Wood, Iron and Steel: Technology, Labour and Trade Union Organisation in the Shipbuilding Industry, 1840–1914', in R. Harrison and J.Zeitlin (eds.), *Divisions of Labour: Skilled Workers and Technological Change in Nineteenth Century Britain* (1985), pp. 170–4; Slaven, *op. cit.*, p. 168; Working Man, *Reminiscences of a Stonemason* (1908), p. 255; J. Zeitlin, 'The Labour Strategies of British Engineering Employers, 1890–1922', in H. F. Gospel and C. R. Littler (eds.), *Managerial Strategies and Industrial Relations: an Historical and Comparative Study* (1983), pp. 27–8.

5. D. Landes, 'What do Bosses really do?', *Journal of Economic History*, XLVI, No.3, (1986), p. 602.

6. C. R. Littler, *The Development of the Labour Process in Capitalist Societies: a Comparative Study of the Transformation of Work Organisation in Britain, Japan and the USA* (1982), p. 67.

7. K. Burgess, 'Authority Relations and the Division of Labour in British Industry, with Special Reference to Clydeside, c.1860–1930', *Social History*, 11, No. 2, (1986), pp. 211–33; *Builder*, 10 October 1870.

8. H. Newby, 'Paternalism and Capitalism', in R. Scase (ed.), *Industrial Society: Class, Cleavage and Control* (1977), pp. 16, 67–8; P. Joyce, *Work, Society and Politics: the Culture of the Factory in Later Victorian England* (1980).

9. J. A. Hassan, 'The Landed Estate, Paternalism and the Coal Industry in Midlothian', *Scottish Historical Review*, LIX, No. 167, (1980), pp. 86–7; S. Pollard, 'The Economic History of British Shipbuilding, 1870–1914', unpublished PhD thesis, University of London, 1951, p. 216; R. Price, 'Structures of Subordination in Nineteenth century British Industry', in P.

Thane *et al.* (eds.), *The Power of the Past: Essays for Eric Hobsbawm* (1984), pp. 133–4.

10. E. J. Hobsbawm, *Labouring Men* (1964), p. 320.

11. Littler, *op. cit.*, p. 85

12. *Ibid.*, pp. 73–6; A. Reid, 'The Division of Labour in the British Shipbuilding Industry, 1880–1920: with Special Reference to Clydeside', unpublished Ph.D. thesis, University of Cambridge, 1980, pp. 207–8.

13. Burgess, *op. cit.*, pp. 226–7.

14. J. Melling, 'Scottish Industrialists and the Changing Character of Class Relations in the Clyde Region, c.1880–1918', in T. Dickson (ed.), *Capital and Class in Scotland* (Edinburgh, 1982), p.101.

15. Burgess, *op. cit.*, pp. 224–5.

16. F. McKenna, *The Railway Workers, 1840–1970* (1980), pp. 52–3; J. Melling, 'Employers, Industrial Housing and the Evolution of Company Welfare Policies in Britain's Heavy Industries: West of Scotland, 1870–1920', *International Review of Social History*, XXXVI, (1981), pp. 280–1.

17. R. Duncan, *Conflict and Crisis: Monklands' Miners and the General Strike of 1842* (1982), pp. 4–5.

18. H. Miller, *My Schools and Schoolmasters* (Edinburgh, 1854), p. 151.

19. J. Dunlop, *The Philosophy of Artificial and Compulsory Drinking Usage in Great Britain and Ireland* (1839).

20. T. Stewart, *Among the Miners* (Larkhall, 1893), pp. 4–5.

21. J. Rule, 'The Property of Skill in the Period of Manufacture', in P. Joyce (ed.), *The Historical Meanings of Work* (1987), p. 111.

22. Duncan, *op. cit.*, pp. 5–6 and A. Campbell, *op. cit.*, pp. 44–5 for coalmining; W. W. Knox, 'British Apprenticeship, 1800–1914', unpublished Ph.D. thesis, University of Edinburgh, 1980, pp. 382–3 for building.

23. E. J. Hobsbawm, 'Artisan or Labour Aristocrat?', *Economic History Review*, XXXVII, (1984), pp. 365–6.

24. R. J. Morris, 'Skilled Workers and the Politics of the Red Clyde', *Journal of the Scottish Labour History Society*, No. 18, (1983), p. 8.

25. J. E. Mortimer, *History of the Boilermakers' Society, vol. 1, 1834–1906* (1973), p. 199.

26. A. Gilchrist, *Naethin' at A'* (Glasgow, 1940), p. 21.

27. Knox, *op. cit.*, pp. 190–1.

28. Hassan, *op. cit.*, p. 82; A. Campbell, *op. cit.*, pp. 278–9; R. P. Arnot, *A History of the Scottish Miners from the Earliest Times* (1955), p. 49.

29. A. Campbell, *op. cit.*, p. 83; Fraser, *op. cit.*, p. 80.

30. *Ibid.*, p. 97.

31. Mortimer, *op. cit.*, p. 200.

32. G. M. Wilson, 'The Strike Policy of the Miners of the West of Scotland', in I. MacDougall, (ed.), *Essays in Scottish Labour History* (Edinburgh, 1979), pp. 44–5.

33. Mortimer, *op. cit.*, pp. 57–8.

34. Wilson, *loc. cit.*

35. Mortimer, *op. cit.*, p. 68 for shipbuilding; A. Campell, *op.cit.*, pp. 278–9, Hassan, *op. cit.*, p. 82, and Arnot, *op. cit.*, p. 49 for coalmining,

36. R. H. Campbell, *Scotland Since 1707* (Oxford, 1965), p. 315; H. Southall, 'Unionisation', in J. Langton and R. J. Morris (eds.), *Atlas of Industrializing Britain, 1780–1914* (1986), pp. 189–93.

37. A. Campbell, *op. cit.*, pp. 34–5.

38. G. Brown, 'The Labour Party and Political Change in Scotland: the Politics of Five elections', unpublished PhD thesis, University of Edinburgh, 1982, p. 46.

39. D. C. Unger, 'The Roots of Red Clydeside: Economic and Social Relations and Working Class Politics in the West of Scotland', unpublished Ph.D. thesis, University of Texas, 1979, pp. 257–8.

40. P. L. Robertson, 'Demarcation Disputes in British Shipbuilding before 1914', *International Review of Social History*, XX, (1975), pp. 220–35, Webb Collection XXIII, ff. 209–14, X, ff. 82–3 for demarcation disputes; W. Stewart, *Keir Hardie* (1921), pp. 11–2, T. Gallagher, 'A Tale of Two Cities: Communal Strife in Glasgow and Liverpool Before 1914', in R. Swift and S. Gilley (eds.), *The Irish in the Victorian City* (1985), p. 111; H. McShane and J. Smith, *No Mean Fighter* (1978), pp. 19, 56, for sectarianism.

41. R. Price, *Masters, Unions and Men* (Cambridge, 1980), p. 62.

42. E. Gordon, 'Women, Trade Unions and Industrial Militancy, 1850–1890', in *Uncharted Lives: Extracts from Scottish Women's Experiences, 1850–1892*, Glasgow Women's Studies Group (Glasgow, 1983), pp. 56–8.

43. W. M. Walker, *Juteopolis: Dundee and its Textile Workers, 1885–1923* (Edinburgh, 1979), p. 15.

44. Arnot, *op. cit.*, p. 78.

45. A. Tuckett, *The Scottish Carter: the History of the Scottish Horse and Motormen's Association, 1898–1964* (1967), p. 43; Unger, *op. cit.*, p. 186; J. H. Smith, *Joe Duncan: the Scottish Farm Servants and British Agriculture* (Edinburgh, 1973), p. 34; STUC, *Reports* (1900, 1910); Knox, *op. cit.*, p. 373.

46. P. Joyce, 'Languages of Reciprocity and Conflict: a Further Response to Richard Price, *Social History*, 9, No. 2, (1984), pp. 225–31.

47. W. Knox, '"Down with Lloyd George": the apprentices' strike of 1912', *Journal of the Scottish Labour History Society*, 19, pp. 20–35.

48. A. Wilson, *The Chartist Movement in Scotland* (Manchester, 1970), pp. 256–8; R. Duncan, 'Artisans and Proletarians: Chartism and Working Class Allegiance in Aberdeen', *Northern Scotland*, 4, (1981), p. 61; D. C. Paton. 'Drink and the Temperance Movement in Nineteenth Century Scotland', unpublished Ph.D. thesis, University of Edinburgh, 1977, p. 394.

49. I. S. Wood, 'Drink, Temperance and the Labour Movement', *Journal of the Scottish Labour History Society*, 5, (1972), p. 30.

50. E. King, *Scotland Sober and Free: the Temperance Movement, 1829–1979*

(Glasgow, 1979), p. 23; W. Knox, *Scottish Labour Leaders, 1918–1939: A Biographical Dictionary* (Edinburgh, 1984) p. 25.

51. R. Q. Gray, 'Thrift and Working Class Mobility in Victorian Edinburgh', in A. A. MacLaren (ed.), *Social Class in Scotland: Past and Present* (Edinburgh, 1976), p. 100.

52. F. Reid, 'Socialist Sunday Schools in Britain, 1892–1939', *International Review of Social History*, 11, (1966), pp. 32–3.

53. C. Harvie, 'Tom Johnston: A Patriot's Progress', *Scotsman*, 16 May

54. C. G. Brown, *The Social History of Religion in Scotland since 1730* (1987), p. 165.

55. A. L. Drummond and J. Bulloch, *The Church in Late Victorian Scotland, 1874–1900* (Edinburgh, 1978), p. 145.

56. T. Bell, *Pioneering Days* (1944), p. 33.

57. O. D. Edwards, *The Mind of an Activist — James Connolly* (Dublin, 1971). p. 33.

58. Knox, *Labour Leaders*, pp. 28–9.

59. J. Smyth, 'Women, Socialism and the Suffrage', *Radical Scotland*, June/July 1984.

60. J. T. Ward, 'Some Aspects of Working-Class Conservatism in the Nineteenth Century', in Butt and Ward, *op. cit.*, pp. 147–51; A. Campbell, *op. cit.*, p. 25.

61. I. C. G. Hutchinson, 'Glasgow Working-Class Politics', in R. A. Cage (ed.), *The Working Class in Glasgow, 1750–1914*, (1987), p. 128.

62. J. H. Treble, 'O'Connor, O'Connell and the Attitudes of Irish Immigrants towards Chartism in the North of England, 1838–1848', in J. Butt and I. F. Clarke, *The Victorians and Social Protest*, (Newton Abbot, 1973), pp. 63–9; Knox, *Labour Leaders*, p. 25.

63. J. Hodge, 'Owenism in Scotland', *Socialist Review*, (July-August 1918), p. 277; G. S. Jones, *Languages of Class: Studies of English Working Class History, 1832–1982* (1983), p. 110.

64. R. Q. Gray, *The Labour Aristocracy in Victorian Edinburgh* (Oxford, 1976), pp. 156–7.

65. Hutchinson, *op. cit.*, p. 112.

66. J. M. Smith, 'Labour Tradition in Glasgow and Liverpool', *History Workshop*, 17, (1984), p. 35.

67. *Ibid.*

68. J. M. Smith, 'Commonsense Thought and Working Class Consciousness: Some Aspects of the Glasgow and Liverpool Labour Movements in the Early Years of the Twentieth Century', unpublished PhD thesis, University of Edinburgh, 1980, p. 307.

69. Smith, 'Commonsense Thought', p. 330.

70. R. Penn, 'The Contested Terrain: a Critique of R. C. Edwards' Theory of Working Class Fractions and Politics', in G. Day (ed.), *Diversity and Decomposition in the Labour Market* (Aldershot, 1982), pp. 100–1.

CHAPTER 6

The Occupied Male Labour Force

J. H. Treble

This chapter[1] is concerned with a number of questions. To what extent did the national pattern of employment change over time, and how far did regional trends diverge from that pattern? Which industries generated new employment outlets and which had contracting work forces? Finally, what did these trends imply for the buoyancy or stagnation of regional job markets and for spatial and occupational mobility within Scotland as a whole?[2]

Male Employment in Scotland as a Whole

Part of the answer to the first of these questions is outlined in Appendix 1, which examines what occurred between 1851 and 1911 in the sectoral distribution of Scotland's male workforce. Collectively considered these data draw attention to three significant trends. At one level, they point to a marked fall in the percentage of the total occupied population that was employed in agriculture, forestry and fishing — from 19.86 per cent of the labour force in 1851 to 13.24 per cent in 1911. Most of this reduction can be explained as the product of a secular decline in the number of agricultural labourers in the second half of the nineteenth century. Between 1851 and 1891 the number of such workers fell by 40.8 per cent, with slightly more than half of that decline occurring in the 1851–71 decades when Scottish farming was experiencing a period of relative prosperity.[3] Scarcely surprisingly, those who have examined the agrarian labour market during the 1850s and 1860s have attributed this outward movement from the land more to the farmworker responding over time to the pull of increased opportunities for employment in urban areas than to the decision of the farming community to economise in its use of labour. But these 'pull' influences were not confined to the third quarter of the century. During the Agricultural Depression which coincided with the years 1873–96 and which was characterised both

167

by falling prices for most farm products and by intensified foreign competition in the domestic market, more use was made of machinery by Scotland's farmers. In part this was an attempt to improve efficiency by substituting, where appropriate, capital for labour intensive methods of production. However, in the context of the post-1873 rural labour market, it is also clear that mechanisation was often a consequence, not a cause, of the reduction in the supply of farm labourers who continued to be attracted by the burgeoning range of jobs in Scotland's towns, but who were rarely turned off the soil by employers seeking to contain their labour costs. Reinforcing this point, the buoyancy in the real wages of male farm servants during these years is further proof that farmers were forced to compete with urban employers in a bid to retain their most effective workers for their own needs.[4]

Second, an increasing proportion of the occupied male population was located in the mining (6.21 per cent in 1851; 11.16 per cent in 1911), transport (5.65 per cent in 1851; 10.75 per cent in 1911) and service (11.84 per cent in 1851; 17.7 per cent in 1911) sectors of the economy. The initial surge in employment in mining was primarily determined by favourable trends that operated within the domestic coal market, in particular the increasing use which was made of coal by the metallurgical and other industries, and the enhanced role that was allocated to the fuel in the budgets of working-class consumers. However, in the closing twenty years of our period the growth in work outlets in mining was also powerfully sustained by the rapid development of the Fife coalfield (Central/Fife region), a development which was in some measure assisted by the emergence of a vigorous export trade. As in mining, the rising number of economically active males engaged in a heterogeneous range of transport industries was profoundly influenced by an economy increasingly receptive to the stimuli of market forces. Thus, in the main industrial counties the evolution of a railway network catering for the long haul, and of a system of horse-drawn transport for the short haul, of goods, acted as mutually reinforcing agencies in maintaining a buoyant market for jobs. Nevertheless, they did not act alone, for the secular growth in transport employment was also underpinned by the proliferation of outlets in the merchant marine, in Scotland's ports and, in the post-1880 years, in an evolving tramway system. Clearly these changes proceeded furthest in towns and cities. Yet they were never an exclusively urban phenomenon. For, as Michie has shown in his study of the connections that subsisted between improved communications and the primary industries of fishing and agriculture in the north-east, they also had an impact, albeit in a

30. Skilled masons building the Technical Institute in Dundee in 1887. They would have shaped their own stones in the adjoining sheds. *St Andrews University Photographic Collection.*

more muted form, in impeccably rural parts of the country.[5] Last, but not least, the enhanced role of the service sector as a provider of work can, for the most part, be attributed to the maturing of the economy and a steady but by no means uninterrupted rise in real incomes in society at large. The sequel to both of these interrelated developments was the generation of a demand for a stronger and more complex tertiary sector, although at the margin this process was also abetted by the more intrusive role played by national and local government from the 1870s onwards in key areas of social life (education, public health etc.). For one of the consequences of such intervention was the creation over time of an enlarged pool of employees who had benefited from a professional training.

Third, Appendix 1 reveals what at first glance appears to be a striking similarity in the employment patterns of manufacturing industry and the construction trades for the three selected dates. Both claimed a rising share of the occupied population between 1851 and 1881, and both recorded, in percentage terms, a marginal drop in their significance as sources of male employment between 1881 and 1911. In reality, however, the degree of synchronisation between their economic fortunes was much less close than these data imply. For one thing, employment in the building industry was, from the late 1860s onwards, powerfully affected by the long swings associated with the house building cycle. And one of the most distinctive features of that cycle — the phenomenon of over-building — building, that is, ahead of demand for new homes — led to massive fluctuations in levels of employment. Between 1881 and 1891, a dull decade for house building, the number of construction workers fell by 5.1 per cent, only to expand by a phenomenal 43.4 per cent during the ensuing ten years which coincided with a vigorous upsurge in the level of residential provision. Between 1901 and 1911, however, when the building cycle entered its downswing phase, the numerical strength of the labour force again contracted sharply, on this occasion by 21.4 per cent.[6] On the other hand, the multi-faceted nature of manufacturing employment made it much less vulnerable to this kind of violent oscillation. What, therefore, was taking place in this segment of the economy in each decade between 1881 and 1911 was a deceleration in the rate of growth of its occupied population rather than an absolute decline in numbers. Indeed, it can be claimed that the overall statistic for manufacturing employment in 1911 presents a bleaker picture than was actually the case, since it was powerfully affected by the composition of the 'not classified' order. In 1881 that order accounted for 11.24 per cent of the total occupied population, in 1911 for 7.19 per cent. But at the latter date there had been a systematic attempt at reducing the size of the 'general' occupations that formed the core of this order by transferring part of their membership to more precise occupational headings. Given that an element of these general hands was probably reallocated from the place which they had occupied in the 1881 classification system to the transport and construction sectors, we can conclude that the percentage figure for manufacturing employment in 1911 was to some extent depressed by inconsistencies in the way that individual occupational categories were defined.

None the less, assessed overall, the most striking feature of the manufacturing sector was the relative stability of its share of Scotland's total occupied male population for over three selected dates, fluctuating between a minimum figure of 38.66 per cent in 1851 and a maximum of 40.68 per cent in 1881. Yet such stability at the sectoral level was quite compatible with considerable changes in the structure of its constituent parts, a point forcibly underlined by the relevant data in Appendices 2A, B and 4. Of these sources Appendix 4 is probably the most useful for this type of analysis since it tabulates the net gains and losses in the size of the occupied population by region and for the nation between 1851 and 1911. During those six decades there was a net increase in the number of males returned as occupied of approximately 618,000 in Scotland as a whole. And as has already been implicit in our previous discussion, an important part of these net gains was achieved in the non-manufacturing areas of the economy. Transport and communications were themselves responsible for 17.8 per cent of this net growth in employment, mining and quarrying for 18 per cent and the service sector for a further 25.8 per cent.[7] But in each of these sectors these positive trends owed something to parallel changes which were occurring in manufacturing industry. Of fundamental significance in this context was the sustained growth of employment in the metallic trades, which accounted for 11 per cent of the net increase in the total occupied population between those two dates; mechanical engineering, which was responsible for a further 10.7 per cent; and shipbuilding, whose contribution amounted to 7.5 per cent.[8]

But on the debit side, the size of the male labour force engaged in textiles underwent a reduction of such dimensions that it ranked second only to agriculture, forestry and fishing as a source of shrinking employment opportunities, while the numbers in clothing and footwear also dropped markedly during these sixty years. In analysing this less favourable outcome it must at the outset be conceded that the fall in the numerical strength of the male workforce in textiles was not an unbroken process. In 1881–91 and again in 1901–11 the pattern of decline was reversed, although the scale of increase was, in each decade, of the most modest proportions.[9] Nevertheless, the existence of this mitigating factor does not obscure the general picture. Between 1851 and 1881 both of these industries had recorded a substantial shake-out of their male labour force; after 1881 that pattern continued, for the minor recoveries that took place in the case of textiles were never sufficiently powerful to reverse the underlying trend. This process of contraction was partly a reflection of the increasing use that was made in cotton and the garment trades of female workers by employers anxious to contain their costs. Yet this aspect of the gender division of labour was also to some extent a defensive measure, prompted by the difficulties that the Scottish ready-made clothing industry was encountering from English centres of production and the challenge that was posed to cotton millowners by more dynamic rivals in Lancashire and later in India.[10]

The implications of these internal shifts within the manufacturing sector were profound. In 1851 textiles and clothing employed 20.29

per cent of the total occupied male population, and shipbuilding, the metallic trades and mechanical engineering 6.71 per cent. In 1911 the comparable statistics were 7.22 per cent and 16.02 per cent respectively, an important indicator of how far the frontiers of employment had moved during the second phase of Scotland's industrial revolution. It is against this backcloth that we now turn to examine the more diverse patterns of employment which were to be found in Lee's eight regions. (In this context the regional boundaries referred to coincide with those of present-day local government authorities).

Patterns of Male Employment in the Regions

In general terms the regions can be divided into three main groupings. The first consists of those regions — Dumfries and Galloway, Grampian and Highland — where, throughout the period under review, agriculture, forestry and fishing remained the largest source of male employment; where manufacturing industry was considerably less significant as a pro-vider of work than in the country as a whole; and where, notwithstanding the presence of granite quarries in and around the city of Aberdeen, mining exercised little more than a token presence in each labour market. Even between these regions, however, Highland possessed a unique characteristic. It remained the only region in Scotland which, in 1851, 1881 and 1911 had more than half of its occupied population engaged in the agrarian sectors. In 1851 agriculture, forestry and fishing claimed a massive 64.59 per cent of total employment within the region, in 1911, 50.07 per cent, an outcome which was in part shaped by the ability of crofting communities to survive recurring cycles of economic adversity.

Outwardly our second grouping which comprises of only one region — Border — had much in common with these rural parts of Scotland. Thus, mining and quarrying never afforded work to more than 1 per cent of its occupied population, while agriculture and its associated industries accounted for 45.28 per cent of economically active males in 1851 and 30.08 per cent sixty years later. On the other hand its experience appears strikingly different from those other bastions of primary production when we analyse the position that was assumed by manufacturing industry within its boundaries. In 1881 and 1911 manufacturing absorbed a larger share of the region's workforce than any of the other five categories of industrial employment that are listed in Appendix 1, an outcome that was primarily determined by the presence of high-quality tweed production

31. Dockers unloading jute at Dundee docks in 1907. These men would have been employed on a casual basis and subject to the vagaries of season and demand. *St Andrews University Photographic Collection.*

centred upon the town of Galashiels in Selkirkshire and of hosiery and knitwear based upon Hawick in Roxburghshire. In other words, and to revert to the relevant data in Appendix 4, the overall decline in textile employment in Scotland between 1851 and 1911 did not exclude the existence of specialist producers whose fortunes moved in a radically different direction.

The labour markets of our final group of regions — Strathclyde, Lothian, Central and Fife and Tayside — were distinguished by a manufacturing sector which was consistently the most important focus for male employment; by a secular fall in the number of jobs generated by agriculture, forestry and fishing; and by a dynamic transport sector. However, alongside these continuities have to be placed points at which the employment histories of these regions diverged from one another. Thus, the metropolitan role of Edinburgh meant that Lothian had a consistently higher level of service provision than the other regions.[11] On the other hand, if Tayside, containing the 'high farming' area of the Carse of Gowrie, was much more heavily committed to agrarian employment, it lacked coal deposits to enable it to develop jobs in mining on the scale that had taken place in Lothian, Strathclyde and, above all, Central and Fife. Last but not least, within the manufacturing sector there were inter-regional differences that were highly significant. The essence of these differences is adequately defined in Appendix Tables 2A, B and 4. Among other things they show that Strathclyde, between 1851 and 1911, more than recouped the job losses that took place in the West of Scotland cotton industry through a vigorous rate of expansion in work outlets in mechanical engineering, shipbuilding and the metallic trades, and through steady but less spectacular progress in other areas of manufacturing industry; that while the Lothian never possessed a significant textile industry, it remained an important focus for employment in the timber and furnishing and paper, printing and publishing trades; and that Tayside failed to depart, in any meaningful fashion, from its dependence upon jute and linen for manufacturing employment.

However, to probe more effectively the topic of regional diversity in the context of the labour market the historian must supplement these data with the table of location quotients in Appendix 3. In interpreting these tables we must remember that a ratio in excess of 1.00 demonstrates that a category of industrial employment was proportionately more concentrated in a region's labour market than in that of Scotland as a whole, and that a ratio of less than 1.00 means that it was proportionately of less importance in the job market of a region compared with the contribution it made to employment at the national level. To take one example from the returns of 1911, a ratio of 3.78, recorded for agriculture, forestry and fishing in Highland, indicates that there were proportionately almost four times as many males in that sector of the regional economy as in the country as a whole. Conversely, with a ratio of 0.34 the same occupational grouping was markedly under-represented in Strathclyde's structure of employment. Used in this way these data are of crucial significance in advancing our understanding of how far regional patterns conformed to, or departed from, the distribution of the labour force between the various industrial groupings nationally. Nevertheless their utility is not confined to this single area of analysis. For if these tables of location quotients are examined in conjunction with Appendix 4 which, as we have seen, records net gains and losses in employment by sector and by region, we can secure further insights into the dynamism or otherwise of each regional labour market as a generator of jobs over time. In general terms, Strathclyde and Lothian tended to possess high location quotients — that is, location quotients in excess of 1.00

— in several of the industrial groups whose workforce expanded most rapidly between 1851 and 1911 and, by 1911, low location quotients in the two key areas of shrinking job outlets, textiles and agriculture. In stark contrast, Dumfries and Galloway, Border, Tayside, Grampian and Highland had, with few exceptions, high location quotients in industrial categories where the occupied population was either declining or growing at a relatively slow rate, and low location quotients in those parts of the labour market which, nationally, were the principal sources of increasing employment opportunities. Finally, while Central and Fife recorded low location quotients (ratios below 1.00) in the growth areas of transport and service employment — in this last case an experience it shared with Strathclyde — it could claim by 1911 to have the most intense concentration of miners within its boundaries, of any region in Scotland.

This complex series of relationships is explored from a slightly different perspective in Tables 1 and 2. Table 1 exposes the huge disparities that surfaced during the period 1851–1911 in the percentage rate of growth of the occupied population of each region. Strathclyde, with a growth rate considerably in excess of 100 per cent, Lothian, whose numbers had doubled in the intervening sixty years, and Central and Fife, all achieved rates of expansion that were considerably higher than those for Scotland as a whole. But four of the five remaining regions yielded results which fell short of the national average, while uniquely in Dumfries and Galloway the occupied population actually fell by 6 per cent between these two dates. Table 2, which examines the regional distribution of the occupied male population in 1851 and 1911, underlines the degree to which the Scottish economy conformed over time to a core-periphery model. The inner core of dynamic regions (Strathclyde, Lothian, Central and Fife) accounted for 57.57 per cent of the occupied population in 1851 and 71.48 per cent in 1911. But the almost inevitable corollary of this outcome was that each of the five peripheral regions lacking coal and/or iron deposits and, on a sufficient scale, the accumulating volume of skilled labour to be found in the central belt, was responsible for a declining percentage of the country's labour force over the same timespan.

As Hunt has demonstrated, such wide disparities at the regional level were underpinned by parallel shifts in the distribution of Scotland's total population, a trend which raises further queries about the links that existed between economic development and labour mobility.[12] Did the more advanced regions obtain their expanding supplies of labour from a high rate of natural increase (the difference between the crude birth and death rates within their borders) or did they depend upon substantial

Table 1. Percentage Rates of Growth (+) or Decline (−) of the Occupied Male Population in Scotland and the Regions, 1851–1911

Area	Employment growth rate (per cent)
Scotland	+ 72.14
Strathclyde	+124.74
Dumfries, Galloway	− 6.00
Border	+ 13.48
Lothian	+100.26
Central and Fife	+ 85.45
Tayside	+ 18.80
Grampian	+ 35.02
Highland	+ 2.22

net inflows of migrants from Ireland and other parts of Scotland? In this instance it is easier to formulate this question than to answer it, partly because Hunt's data in this field contain a slight drawback. Instead of our eight regions, he divides the country into three more extended areas

Table 2. Regional Distribution of the Occupied Male Population, Expressed in Percentage Terms, 1851–1911

Area	1851 (per cent)	1911 (per cent)
Strathclyde	37.22	48.60
Dumfries, Galloway	5.34	2.91
Border	3.79	2.50
Lothian	11.19	13.02
Central and Fife	9.16	9.86
Tayside	11.85	8.18
Grampian	11.47	9.00
Highland	9.98	5.92
Scotland	100.00	99.99

Source: My calculations are based on the relevant data in Series A, C. Lee *British Regional Employment Statistics 1841–1971 (Cambridge, 1979).*

— South Scotland whose boundaries are conterminous with those of Dumfries and Galloway and Border; Central Scotland which covers the territory of Lothian, Central and Fife and Strathclyde minus Bute and Argyll; and Northern Scotland which consists of Grampian, Tayside and Highland plus Bute and Argyll. But this sharp reduction in the number of regions involves more than the rearrangement of geographical boundaries. It also yields a less refined picture of the relationship between economic growth and demographic change. We cannot, for example, on the basis of Hunt's statistics, explore any contrasts or similarities between patterns that surfaced in this field in Strathclyde, Lothian and Central Fife. None the less, this obstacle has to be kept in perspective. For the fact that, with the exceptions which have been noted, our eight regions can be incorporated into his spatial framework means that his work can still be effectively utilised to examine, albeit on a broader canvas (Central, Northern and Southern Scotland), major aspects of the topic under review.

The relevant information for such an analysis is presented in Table 3, which succinctly summarises the key factors which influenced the demographic history of each of Hunt's three regions between 1861 and 1911. From that source three conclusions emerge. First, each region experienced a loss of part of its natural rate of increase during 1881–91 and 1901–11 through out-migration, two decades of heavy emigration from Britain as a whole. However, not all of those losses were in response to the pull of America or the white areas of the British Empire; part at least represented movement from Scotland into the labour markets of England and Wales. Second, there were wide differences between the demographic régimes of these regions. Central achieved consistently high rates of decennial growth over the entire period; Northern was characterised by low rates of increase until 1901–11 when a 'nil' result was recorded; and South experienced a decline in its numbers at every decade after 1871–81. Third, these inter-regional differentials were much more decisively shaped by differences in migration rates than differences in their natural rate of increase. This last conclusion does not, of course, fully reveal all of the complexities of the process of internal movement during these years. For instance, gross migration between these regions was clearly on a much larger scale than the figures for net movement which are returned in Table 3, imply. Again, there was considerable interchange of people between the counties that make up each of these regions, and short-distance intra-county movement — from rural to urban Lanarkshire (Central region) — which these data effectively conceal.

Yet even when these caveats have been entered, these results still

Table 3. Population Change, Natural Rates of Increase and Net Migration Rates 1861–1911, Expressed in Percentage Terms

	1861–71			1871–81			1881–91			1891–1901			1901–11		
	a	b	c	a	b	c	a	b	c	a	b	c	a	b	c
South of Scotland (per cent)	nil	13	-13	5	12	-8	-2	11	-13	-6	8	-13	-1	7	-8
Central Scotland (per cent)	15	14	1	16	15	1	13	15	-3	17	14	3	10	14	-4
Northern Scotland (per cent)	4	12	-8	5	12	-7	1	12	-10	2	10	-8	nil	8	-9

Note: Column (a) = population change; Column (b) = natural rate of increase; Column (c) = net migration rate.
Source: E. H. Hunt, Regional Wage Variations 1850–1914 (Oxford 1973), p. 226.

demonstrate that changes in the total population of a region were for the most part determined by the state of the labour market. Thus, as Hunt has argued, the consistently high out-migration rates of the south of Scotland were a rational response to the lack of job opportunities within the region, although the sequel to this self-regulating mechanism was that the South had emerged as a high wage area by the late nineteenth and early twentieth centuries, for that considerable segment of its occupied population which was employed in the textile and agricultural industries. On the other hand, the secular rise in the total population of the Central region was causally linked with the buoyancy of its labour market and, from the late 1880s onwards, its lofty ranking in the wages league of the United Kingdom. But economic man did not reign unchallenged in northern Scotland. For the evidence at our disposal strongly suggests that, notwithstanding the loss of part of its natural rate of increase through out-migration, its demographic régime did not adapt sufficiently quickly to the lack of dynamism in its job market. Retaining a much more tenacious hold upon its people than the south of Scotland, it was for the most part a bastion of low pay, relieved only by isolated pockets of urban development, largely in Tayside and Grampian.

Levels of Skill in the Male Labour Market

None of these data, however, tells the reader anything about the levels of skill of labour. Here again there are difficulties in defining the broad categories of skilled, semi-skilled and unskilled. How do we distinguish between the perceptions of the worker and those of society when they were in conflict over the location of a particular occupation in that broad spectrum which embraced the skilled at the apex of the labour hierarchy and the unskilled at the bottom? Renfrewshire farmworkers, for example, complained bitterly in the 1890s that 'we are not estimated as other trades. We object to being called unskilled labourers. A man cannot be a ploughman in a day'.[13] At one level they were correct, for the ploughman enjoyed a considerable degree of autonomy in his work and was regarded as the élite element of the agricultural labour force. But the validity of their claim for higher status was not easy to reconcile with their rates of remuneration. Living in a high-wage county for agricultural labour, they still earned less than certain grades of unskilled hands employed in the construction industry in the adjacent towns of the West Central belt. On the other hand, problems could also arise in relation to groups who considered themselves to be skilled. Thus, where, in a stratified occupational structure, should the historian place

32. Although working with metal was a highly-skilled task, the work environment was still very harsh. These ironmoulders are in the Falkirk Iron Works c.1910. *Falkirk Museums.*

those bespoke tailors in Glasgow who had received an all-round training in their craft, but who, by the late 1880s and perhaps earlier, risked their union membership by descending into the sweated sector of the trade during periods of slackness?

Yet notwithstanding these difficulties, an attempt must be made to dissolve the world of manual labour into its constituent parts. One such exercise was undertaken by N. B. Dearle in his classic study of industrial training, published in 1914. According to Dearle, skilled employments 'require a long period of training, whether this is obtained under a definite contract or agreement and in a single firm, or whether without any agreement the worker is teaching himself his business in one or more firms'. Semi-skilled occupations on the other hand 'do not need a long period of education' although they were always clearly distinguished from the unskilled 'by the moderate level of knowledge, skill and power that they require'. Finally, unskilled work, possessing 'the minimum of skill and knowledge', was rarely associated with 'any definite period of training'. Mastery of those rudimentary techniques necessary to discharge a given unskilled task was speedily acquired 'by practice alone'.[14]

This conceptual framework, when applied to the world of work in post-1850 Scotland, has several merits. It emphasises the significance of training as an analytical tool for differentiating the skilled hand from other groups in the manual labour market; it recognises the existence of a growing semi-skilled workforce which formed the subject of intense debate, in the post-1880 era, in the engineering industry in connection with 'the machine question', but which was of much wider dimensions than the factory system itself; and it underlines the point that skill was acquired through more than one avenue. But alongside its strengths has to be placed a weakness that is inherent in all definitions of this nature, namely, it cannot fully encapsulate the process of change which characterises labour markets over time. To argue thus is not to overlook the fact that Dearle's detailed analysis of individual trades sought to grapple with the shifting frontiers of skill in late nineteenth- and early twentieth-century Britain. It is simply to claim that over a longer timespan, but in a more concentrated spatial context, we need to examine how far such concepts as skill were interpreted in the workplace, and whether de-skilling and/or upgrading were major features of the Scottish economy in the period that we are reviewing.

Given that definitions per se cannot illumine several of these more dynamic aspects of change, it is not surprising that in recent years historians have sought to enlarge our understanding of the impact of new technology and new forms of organisation upon the work process itself. Much of this research has in turn focused upon the socio-economic environment within which skill was defined and redefined. It is therefore appropriate to launch this part of the discussion with a consideration of what skill actually meant in Victorian and Edwardian Scotland, and how far the skilled worker's status was eroded by the assertion, in new forms, of the prerogatives of management.

At the outset it must be emphasised that the skilled worker was not the exclusive creation of the post-1830 maturing of the manufacturing base of the Scottish economy. Rather some of the post-1830 attributes of the skilled can be traced back to those urban incorporations of trades whose origins antedate the industrial revolution. These earlier craftsmen, tailors and shoemakers among them, and artisans working in such precision trades as jewellery production and watchmaking had usually acquired an extensive knowledge of the mysteries of their particular occupation during a five or seven years' apprenticeship. The skill which they possessed was real; that is, skill which gave them mastery of all aspects of their craft, enabling them to exercise a considerable amount of personal initiative at their place of work. And since, over considerable parts of Scottish industry, output remained after 1850 tied to labour intensive methods of production, catering for highly specific customer orders, real skill in this sense was bound to remain an important hallmark of whole segments of those workers who have been labelled 'labour aristocrats'.

Yet, while these continuities with an earlier tradition can be emphasised, they have to be kept in perspective.[15] For discontinuities in experience must also be highlighted. In the first place, by the 1880s indentured apprenticeship was no longer the principal route to entering a skilled trade. This does not, of course, mean that apprenticeship itself disappeared, for its presence can be discerned in many of the new trades that surfaced with the rapid growth of heavy engineering and iron and steel shipbuilding in the post-1850 era. But in most cases apprenticeship was no longer formalised by the signing of indentures. This adoption of more flexible modes of entry to a trade — the granting, for instance of apprenticeships by informal or verbal agreement — pointed towards another trend which had implications for the skilled. There was a general weakening of the apprenticeship system across swathes of Scottish industry, a point that was made with monotonous frequency by many of the representatives of Scottish labour who appeared before the 1891–4 Royal Commission on Labour. One indicator of this development was the disappearance of fixed ratios between craftsmen and apprentices in certain trades. Another was the introduction of a greater degree of flexibility in the length of any apprentice's period of training, while yet another was the acceptance by some trade unions of the 'halflin' — the apprentice who had failed to complete his apprenticeship — to follow his trade provided that he agreed not to undercut the standard rate. Last, but not least, apprenticeship in some sectors of the economy became more narrow in its focus. In engineering, for instance, the all-round skills that had been exercised by the millwright were replaced by the division of skills into more narrowly defined fields. By the 1870s and 1880s fitters and turners were two distinct groups of craftsmen, although they drew upon a common inheritance. Again, the advent of the iron and steel shipbuilding industry generated a range of new skilled jobs which were restricted in scope.

By themselves these changes did not automatically subvert real skill, even in the post-1880 era when machinery, allied to the principle of the sub-division of labour, spread across a heterogeneous range of industries. For one thing they should not be interpreted as signs that skilled manual labour had unilaterally conceded control of its craft to managerial initiatives that could bring in their wake the reality of de-skilling. Stratagems could be devised within the context of the workplace to prevent the flooding of the labour market through a more open-ended system of apprenticeship; craft unions in the post-1880 era pledged themselves to resist assaults upon traditional ways of working; and limitations were placed upon the spread of machinery, both by the non-standardised nature of many consumer and capital goods and, in the post-1880 decades, by the sturdy survival of small units of production, which were more resistant to mechanisation. The scope, therefore, for employers to launch a frontal assault upon all those who possessed real skill should not be overstated. Overall gradualism, rather than profound and concentrated change in the modes of production, characterised many areas of the post-1880 Scottish economy.

This national picture could, however, still conceal areas where real skills were challenged by adverse pressures from a range of sources which were making their presence felt in factory and workshop. Among them were secular shifts in the demand for specific skills; new modes of control and remuneration, including under this heading schemes that either modified or abolished the system of the standard rate; the beginnings of scientific management; and the spread of machinery, usually but not exclusively power-driven. Recent research has emphasised the problems posed for the craftsman by some of these socio-economic forces in Clydeside's engineering and steel shipbuilding industries in the post-1880 years. Thus, by the early 1900s, increasing preoccupation among employers with labour costs had led in a handful of shipbuilding trades to apprentices being employed on a limited scale at the expense of time-served adults. Another indicator of this type of change was the general stress placed upon the 'speeding up' of work in engineering, which innovative forms of payment such as the premium bonus system were designed to foster.

How far did the introduction of such practices result in de-skilling? To answer this question adequately it is necessary to revert to Dearle's definition of skill. As we have seen, skill could be acquired through more than one channel. Real skill was usually but not invariably associated with a programme of 'on job' training, imparted through an apprenticeship system that was itself exposed to the winds of change. Not all apprenticeships, however, led to the acquisition of real skill. For example, while shipyard rivetters insisted upon a five years' apprenticeship, mastery of the essential techniques of rivetting could be achieved within six months. But that very fact made the rivetter more vulnerable to pressures from below. It helps to explain why apprentices operating hydraulic machinery were used to replace a segment of time-served rivetters in Clydeside yards, and why there was, after 1890, a significant rise in the apprentice–journeyman ratio in that particular trade. In this case we can conclude that the proletarianisation of apprenticeship and the loss of control over the rate of recruitment of apprentices had resulted in a measure of dilution of the rivetter's crafts. The extent of this process should not, however, be exaggerated. Before 1914 pneumatic rivetting machinery was only introduced at a slow pace and the skilled status of the rivetter continued to be acknowledged by the maintenance of wage differentials between himself and other members of the black squad. Nevertheless, the pattern of limited dilution that I have been describing underlines the point that the rivetter's skill was not real, but socially constructed, and that the preservation of that skill was largely dependent upon the strength of custom and the ability of the specific work-group to exercise a degree of authority over its segment of the labour market.

Socially constructed skill — skill which 'was not intrinsic to the technical requirements of production but "'artificially" created' by restricting entry into the trade — was not, however, the sole preserve of narrow areas of specialism that accompanied the multi-faceted growth of the engineering and shipbuilding industries. It can in fact be located in any industry where homogeneous groups occupied a strategic position which they could exploit to distance themselves from their fellow workers. Thus, earlier in the nineteenth century, the skills of the male cotton spinner and later, with the coming of the railway, those of the engine driver, were clearly socially constructed. In each instance skill was ultimately the product of learning by 'following up' — securing knowledge, that is, by progressing through an internal occupational hierarchy, rather than through the route of apprenticeship. But the socially constructed skills which were associated with such occupations could only be sustained over time if their practitioners, with or without the sanction of management, had control over key facets of the work process.[16]

This discussion of socially constructed skill leads us back to consider the position of engineering craftsmen who, in the post-1880 world, were among those most threatened by sub-division and the introduction of new machine tools. Indeed the adverse nature of these trends appeared to be confirmed by the 'Terms of Settlement' which followed in the wake of the defeat of the Amalgamated Society of Engineers in the 1897–8 lockout, and which conceded to the employer formal prerogatives over the pace at which innovation should proceed within the industry. And in the decade and a half before 1914 moves towards greater specialisation and

33. Housing improvements created new employment opportunities, but working conditions remained unhealthy and primitive. Cast-iron baths being enamelled in Falkirk in 1910. *Falkirk Museums.*

increased employment of semi-skilled hands undoubtedly intensified. For both fitters and turners there was, therefore, some loss of the less skilled parts of their trade to the 'handy man' machinist. Yet down to 1914 these losses were never massive. Partly that was because of the extent to which the non-standardised character of much of the industry's output continued to depend upon the real skills that such artisans possessed. Partly that was because the position of the engineering craftsman was upheld in workshops and small factories, where the drive towards technological innovation was much slower than in the large factory. But what was perhaps more crucial in determining this outcome, these skilled groups accepted that their status was no longer automatically guaranteed, because they possessed real skill, since such skills could be superseded both by mechanisation and more intrusive methods of job control, and acted upon that perception. In short, their defence of their position in the labour hierarchy came to depend upon their recognising that their skills were also socially constructed, and using tactics which reflected that fact. Hence struggles at the local level over recruitment of hands to man the more simple machine tools, over the rate to be paid to such workers, and over the rate of innovation itself. And if not all of these struggles were won, they were conducted with sufficient vigour to leave largely unrealised most of the wilder fears that had been expressed about de-skilling which had followed the events of 1897–8.[17]

Summing up and examining the 1850–1914 period as a whole, it can be argued that the composition of the skilled workforce underwent considerable changes as new skills were created and some of the pre-1850 skills declined; that the avenues to acquiring skilled status were more complex than in that earlier era which had been dominated by the incorporation of trades; that socially constructed skill could co-exist with, but also remain separate from, real skill; and that de-skilling was not always the logical sequel to mechanisation. Thus, the progress of the power loom in Scotland's cotton industry in the 1840s and 1850s destroyed the livelihoods of coarse-grade hand-loom weavers who at best could be classified as semi-skilled workers, while leaving intact the skills of websters who were engaged in the production of fine fabrics such as Paisley shawls. Indeed, the disappearance of the remnants of this last group from the labour market in the late 1870s owed everything to the whim of fashion and nothing to competition from power-driven machinery.[18] Viewed from another perspective, mechanisation in several areas of the Scottish economy, far from exercising a baleful effect, actually added to the range of skilled employment, although those skills were often socially constructed. In other words, technical change only destroyed or downgraded skill when artisans were unable to exert any form of control over its application.

Yet while the numbers of skilled workers expanded during these decades, it has been claimed that the actual rate of growth of this grouping decelerated during the concluding quarter of a century of our period. To some extent this outcome was shaped by the severity of the post-1903 slump in the building industry which resulted in an actual decline in the number of building craftsmen who were returned as occupied between the 1901 and 1911 censuses. But it also owed much to the proliferation of semi-skilled machinemen in key segments of the economy, including under this heading not merely heavy industry, but also parts of the ready-made clothing trades and bookbinding. In each of these industries such hands came to occupy an intermediate niche between artisan and the unskilled, primarily because they had mastered one of the 'the numerous specialized processes, which involved considerable skill within a very narrow range'.[19]

Scarcely surprisingly, the high profile which was given to the machine operator as late nineteenth-century observers tried to draw the contours of the semi-skilled labour market, led some contemporaries to conclude that the boundaries of that market were conterminous with that type of worker. The better informed commentator, however, was aware that the nature of semi-skilled work could never be fully understood within such a constricted framework. For instance, while in 1907 Sir Benjamin Browne began by identifying 'the semi-skilled man' as a 'man who works a machine or does something of that sort', he ended by incorporating into that category 'coalminers and navvies and all these men'. At a more sophisticated level Dearle listed four discrete areas of semi-skilled labour, only one of which was associated with 'a great deal of machinery'. The other three comprised of men 'who are employed as mates or assistants to other workmen'; occupations 'which may be called semi-skilled *par excellence*, in that they have always been so, and have not required the development of machinery or of specialization to make them so' (navvies, carmen, for example); and 'jobs which may be placed in this grade on account of the responsibility and the often high degree of care and trustworthiness required of the workmen' (crane drivers, scaffolders).[20] Of course, not all aspects of Dearle's model are themselves free from criticism. It is, for instance, difficult to endorse his location of some occupations in one or other of these categories, since they possessed many of the attributes of unskilled work. Thus, it is impossible to sustain the classification of carman as a semi-skilled hand in the light of the complaints uttered by the Horsemen's Union in Glasgow in the early 1890s: 'When other unskilled labour is dull, a large number of men flock to drive horses: the trade is thus injured.'[21] Yet notwithstanding such qualifications the thrust of Dearle's thesis is undoubtedly correct. Above all, he was right to emphasise the heterogeneous nature of semi-skilled employment and to underline the unreality of any analysis which interpreted the labour market in terms of a dichotomy between the artisan and the unskilled.

What in fact the surge towards a more mature economy had yielded by 1911 was both a more complex manufacturing structure and a considerably extended supply of semi-skilled labour. Furthermore, this development had consequences, not only for the skilled, but also for the unskilled labour markets. In the first place it enhanced the opportunities for upward occupational mobility among the ranks of the unskilled, although the rate at which such openings occurred varied enormously from industry to industry, and on occasion even with the same industry.[22] As a result of this kind of mobility some of the adverse pressures were eased upon the unskilled labour market

34. Heavy engineering was at the heart of industrialised Glasgow. Among the largest companies was William Beardmore and Co. whose No. 2 engine shop is shown above. *Glasgow University Archives.*

which, in the 1830s and 1840s, had been chronically overstocked with hands. Secondly, between 1850 and 1914 there took place a reduction in the size of the unskilled workforce, expressed as a percentage of the total occupied male population. Thirdly, the growth of the semi-skilled was one factor responsible for the contraction over time in the reserve army of labour.

Mobility

Earlier in the nineteenth century the number of casual workers — those who were hired on an irregular basis to meet erratic surges in demand — had expanded vigorously as a result of the close and continuing interaction between the work rhythms of urban Scotland's seasonal and casual trades and, what was the corollary of that interaction, the practice among many employers of cultivating their own pools of surplus labour which would never be fully employed even on the busiest day. By the

1890s, however, as a result of deceleration in the rate of population growth; of organisational changes that were set in motion in several, but by no means all, of the main strongholds of casual and seasonal labour; and of those more favourable trends in occupational mobility that I have been outlining, the percentage of the occupied male population which was exposed to irregular patterns of employment, shrank during years of good or normal trade. Whereas, for example, Cleland, in 1831, estimated that virtually one in four of Glasgow's workforce were casual hands, that figure had fallen to between 4 and 5 per cent by the early years of this century.[23]

None the less, even if of declining significance, the very existence of sizeable groups of workers whose patterns of employment were disfigured by broken time illumines aspects of labour mobility which the static profiles presented to us by the censuses cannot elucidate. Clearly, the inner rationale of both the casual and seasonal labour markets demanded that many workers should follow more than one occupation in any period of twelve months if they were to have an opportunity of eluding the grip of poverty. However, this kind of movement within the market was rarely accompanied by widespread physical mobility. Because of the general surplus of unskilled labour, such individuals tended to seek outlets within the circumscribed area of their own neighbourhood where they could forge links with, and become known to, local foremen and hirers of unskilled labour. For, as casual hands in industries such as the docks realised, the cultivation of these ties played a crucial role in enhancing their prospects of being hired.

Differing fundamentally from this static pattern which was reproduced in the urban unskilled labour market as a whole, we can point to other groups of unskilled and semi-skilled hands, largely based in the countryside, who traversed huge distances in their search for employment. This conclusion applies with especial force to those men and women who left the crofting fastnesses of the north-west Highlands and to those who crossed the Irish Sea to participate in seasonal fishing and/or farm work in other parts of Scotland, and those semi-skilled navvies whose peripatetic lifestyle was dictated by the changing locations of public works' projects and a burgeoning railway network. In these instances, of course, we are not comparing like with like when we contrast mobility on the heroic scale with the immobility of the casual, since the economic stimuli which buttressed each labour market produced two distinctive patterns of demand for labour. In this context, therefore, it is more apposite to examine how far within towns and cities the skilled hand conformed to, or departed from, the neighbourhood-oriented mobility

35. From the 1850s a tradition of skilled iron shipbuilding developed on Clydeside. These rivetters are working on the inner bottom of the *City of New York* at the Fairfield Yard c.1900. *Glasgow University Archives.*

of the unskilled, rather than to compare this last element with groups of rural-based hands exposed to quite different social and economic pressures.

At one level qualitative evidence at our disposal strongly suggests that the majority of artisans lived within a short walking distance from their place of employment, although proximity to their place of work owed nothing to the job insecurity of the casual, and everything to the fact that factories tended to be built in or near localities which could meet their needs for skilled labour. However, in the closing twenty-five years of our period, when cheap railway transport and the tram helped to widen the horizons of the artisan, relatively well-paid segments of the skilled occupied population were prepared, on a daily basis, to travel considerable distances to practise their craft, among them shipbuilding workers employed in the yards of the Upper and Lower Clyde.[24] For some, this type of movement was a product of unfettered consumer choice — the preference, for instance, of working for a particular employer. But for others it was dictated by the culture and traditions of their craft. If work was scarce locally, they were prepared to incur transport costs in order to pursue their trade elsewhere, rather than transfer to alternative forms of employment nearer to their place of residence. Nor was such loyalty to the values of the artisan's craft discarded during the downswing phase of the trade cycle when this option was largely removed. Thus, while the prolonged slumps of 1884–7 and 1907–10, which scarred the strongholds of the shipbuilding and engineering industries, led to an expansion of the size of the reserve army of labour, as hands discharged from hitherto regular unskilled and semi-skilled jobs competed for a shrinking volume of work, they did not stimulate many unemployed craftsmen to make a similar descent into the ranks of the unskilled. For the artisan was only too well aware that downward occupational mobility, from whatever cause, was accompanied by a profound loss of status which encompassed not merely himself but also his family.

NOTES

1. I am very grateful to my colleague, Dr Arthur McIvor, both for supplying additional material and for his critical comments on the section of this chapter devoted to the issue of skill.

2. There are major difficulties in using the census data. Those who wish a full discussion of the problems of interpreting and reclassifying the census data should consult C. Lee *British Regional Employment Statistics 1841–1971* (Cambridge, 1979); J. M. Bellamy, 'Occupational Statistics in Nineteenth Century Censuses' in R. Lawton (ed.), *The Censuses and Social Structure* (London, 1978); W. A. Armstrong, 'The Use of Information about Occupation', in E. A. Wrigley (ed.), *Nineteenth Century Society* (Cambridge, 1969); and J..H. Treble, 'Parliamentary Papers and Analysis of Aspects of the Urban Labour Market in Britain 1820–1914' in *The Journal of Regional and Local Studies*, 8(2) (1988), 43–56.

3. My calculations are based upon the data in T.M. Devine (ed.), *Farm Servants and Labour in Lowland Scotland 1770–1914* (Edinburgh, 1984) p. 251.

4. For discussion of the agrarian labour market in this period, see T. M. Devine, 'Scottish Farm Labour in the Era of Agricultural Depression 1876–1900', in T. M. Devine (ed.), *op. cit.*, and Lord Eversley, 'The Decline in Number of Agricultural Labourers in Britain', *Journal of the Royal Statistical Society*, 70 (1907).

5. R. C. Michie, 'Trade and Transport in the Economic Development of North-East Scotland in the Nineteenth Century', *Scottish Economic and Social History*, 3 (1983).

6. My calculations are based upon the relevant data contained in Lee's Series A, C. Lee, *op. cit.* While not all construction workers were engaged in house building, that segment of the construction industry clearly played the dominant role in determining prevailing levels of employment over time in the industry as a whole.

7. My calculations are based upon the relevant data in Lee's Series A, *ibid.*

8. My calculations are based upon the relevant data in Lee's Series A, *ibid.*

9. See the relevant data contained in Lee's Series A for these years, *ibid.*

10. For the west of Scotland cotton industry see A. Slaven *The Development of the West of Scotland 1750–1960* (London, 1975) pp. 163–6 and R. H. Campbell, *The Rise and Fall of Scottish Industry 1707–1960* (Edinburgh, 1980), pp. 56–60. As these sources make clear, a general contraction in employment in the cotton industry conceals the emergence of a prosperous specialist thread industry in and around Paisley. For the drift of several clothing firms in the 1880s from Glasgow to Leeds see *Fourth Report of the House of Lords on the Sweating System, PP.* (381), 1888, qq.26043–5, 26156.

11. For an excellent survey of the role of service employment in the Scottish regions, see C. Lee, 'Modern Economic Growth and Structural Change in Scotland: the Service Sector Reconsidered', *Scottish Economic and Social History*, 3 (1983) pp. 5–35.

12. This part of the discussion is based upon E. Hunt *Regional Wage Variations in Britain 1850–1914* (Oxford, 1973), Chapters, 1, 4, 6, 7.

13. Royal Commission on Labour. *The Agricultural Labourer*, vol. III, *Scotland Part I, PP* [C–6894–IX] 1893 p. 57.

14. N. B. Dearle *Industrial Training* (London, 1914) p. 142.

15. Those parts of this discussion devoted to the artisan and semi-skilled elements of the labour force are based in part upon the following sources: C. More, *Skill and the English Working Class 1870–1914* (London, n.d.); S. Price, 'Rivetters' Earnings in Clyde Shipbuilding, 1889–1913'. *Scottish Economic and Social History*, I (1981); W. Knox 'Apprenticeship and De-skilling in Britain 1850–1914', *International Review of Social History*, XXXI, Part 2, (1986); K. Burgess, 'Authority Relations of Labour in British Industry with Special Reference to Clydeside, *c.* 1860–1930'; *Social History*, 11 (1986); C. K. Harley, 'Skilled Labour and the Choice of Technique in Edwardian Industry'. *Explorations in*

Economic History, 11 (1973–4) and J. Melling, 'Non-Commissioned Officers': British Employers and their supervisory workers 1880–1920', *Social History*, 5 (1980).

16. Because of weaker unions in Scotland than in England, socially constructed skill was more difficult to sustain in Scotland, as the history of the cotton spinners showed. I am grateful to Dr Arthur McIvor for this point. On the strength of Scottish *vis-à-vis* English trade unionism in this period, see W. H. Fraser, 'Trade Councils in the Labour Movement in Nineteenth Century Scotland', in I. MacDougall (ed.) *Essays in Scottish Labour History*, (Edinburgh 1979), pp. 1–28. The quotation in this paragraph is taken from K. Burgess, *art. cit.*, p. 215.

17. For the success of the artisans in resisting 'The Terms of Settlement' in the engineering industry, see J. Zeitlin, 'The Labour Strategies of British Engineering Employers 1890–1922' in H. F. Gospel and C. R. Littler (eds.), *Managerial Strategies and Industrial Relations* (1983).

18. N. Murray, *The Scottish Hand Loom Weavers 1790–1850* (Edinburgh, 1978), pp. 71–2, 75.

19. N. B. Dearle *op. cit.*, p. 143.

20. The quotations in this paragraph are taken from N. B. Dearle, *op. cit.*, pp. 142–4.

21. *Royal Commission on Labour. Answers to the Schedules of Questions, Group B. PP* [C.6795–VIII] 1892, No. 328 Horseman's Union, Glasgow.

22. For how this process was viewed by the unskilled, see A. McIvor, *Scientific Management: The British Response 1890–1914*, (Research Paper, Polytechnic of Central London (1984), p. 55.

23. For discussion of the seasonal and casual labour markets in Scotland, see J. H. Treble, 'The Seasonal Demand for Adult Labour in Glasgow 1890–1914', *Social History*, 3 (1978); J. H. Treble, 'The Market for Unskilled Male Labour in Glasgow 1891–1914', in I. MacDougall (ed.), *op. cit.*; J. H. Treble, *Urban Poverty in Britain 1830–1914* (London 1979), paperback edition, 1983, Chapter 2; and J. H. Treble, 'Unemployment and Unemployment Policies in Glasgow 1890–1905', in P. Thane (ed.), *The Origins of British Social Policy* (London 1978). The figure for Glasgow, provided by Cleland in 1831, is quoted in T. M. Devine and R.Mitchison (eds.), *People and Society in Scotland Vol. I 1760–1830* (Edinburgh, 1988), p. 49. It is at best an informed guess. The figure for Glasgow's casual male labour force in the early twentieth century is based upon my ongoing research into that market.

24. *Glasgow Municipal Commission on Working Class Housing* (1902–3), q. 13441.

General Notes on Appendices

These Appendices are all based upon Lee's Series A, in C. Lee, *British Regional Employment Statistics 1841–1971* (Cambridge, 1979) to which the reader is referred for further details.

The six sectors of Appendix 1 consist of the following orders which are listed in Appendices 2A, B:

Sector 1: Agriculture, forestry, and fishing consist of order 1

Sector 2: Mining and quarrying consist of order 2

Sector 3: Manufacturing consists of orders 5–19, 21 and 28

Sector 4: Construction consists of order 20

Sector 5: Services consists of orders 3 and 23–27

Sector 6: Transport consists of 22.

The placing of order 3 in the services sector creates certain methodological problems, since its membership consists not simply of innkeepers, publicans, tobacconists etc. but also of workers in the food and drink processing industries. However, I have followed Lee's incorporation of this order in the service sector. See C. Lee, *art. cit.*, on this point. Again, order 28, 'not classified', contains workers who belonged to more than one sector. However, examining the range of general occupations which it represents, it is clear that the bulk of its membership worked in the manufacturing sector; hence my decision to locate it there.

The calculation of the location quotients of each industrial category for each region (Appendix 3) is a time-consuming but relatively simple process. The first step is to calculate the percentage of Scotland's total occupied population living in a given region. Next we calculate the percentage of the total occupied population of each individual industrial category which was located in that region. The location quotient is finally arrived at by dividing this last figure by the percentage of Scotland's total occupied population which lived in that region. To take a concrete example, in 1851 Strathclyde contained 37.22 per cent of Scotland's male occupied population. On the other hand, it possessed only 20.29 per cent of Scotland's workers in agriculture, fishing and forestry (order 1). Hence its location quotient for order is 20.29 divided by 37.22 — or 0.55. This last figure means that there was a less concentrated representation of such workers in the region than in Scotland as a whole. Conversely, a ratio of 2.16 means that this same grouping was more heavily represented in Highland region than in Scotland as a whole.

APPENDIX 1. *Sectoral Breakdown of the Occupied Male Population for Scotland as a Whole and in the Labour Market of Each Region in 1851, 1881 and 1911 (Expressed in Percentage Terms)*

Sectoral Breakdown for the Year 1851

Sector	Scotland	Strathclyde	Dumfries & Galloway	Border	Lothian	Central and Fife	Tayside	Grampian	Highland
1. Agriculture, Forestry and Fishing	29.86	16.27	48.63	45.28	16.63	21.70	27.21	52.04	64.59
2. Mining, Quarrying	6.21	10.73	2.75	0.91	6.31	10.65	1.32	1.07	0.72
3. Manufacturing	38.66	47.58	25.58	29.55	36.76	44.73	47.06	25.39	17.66
4. Construction	7.78	7.41	8.36	10.06	10.25	7.88	8.35	6.71	5.71
5. Services	11.84	11.26	10.48	11.29	22.23	9.75	10.94	10.47	7.90
6. Transport	5.65	6.75	4.18	2.90	7.85	5.29	5.13	4.32	3.42
Totals	100.00	100.00	99.98	99.99	100.03	100.00	100.01	100.00	100.00

Sectoral Breakdown for the Year 1881

Sector	Scotland	Strathclyde	Dumfries & Galloway	Border	Lothian	Central and Fife	Tayside	Grampian	Highland
1. Agriculture, Forestry and Fishing	19.12	7.43	38.07	32.39	8.81	15.75	20.05	42.02	57.59
2. Mining, Quarrying	7.57	11.33	3.20	0.62	7.35	14.25	1.25	2.17	0.78
3. Manufacturing	40.68	49.03	25.05	36.56	38.96	40.16	45.91	27.88	17.10
4. Construction	9.84	9.40	12.00	11.79	12.67	9.04	10.11	8.75	7.71
5. Services	14.98	13.65	16.16	15.12	22.42	13.83	15.57	13.53	12.27
6. Transport	7.81	9.19	5.50	3.54	9.81	6.98	7.11	5.65	4.54
Totals	100.00	100.03	99.98	100.02	100.02	100.01	100.00	100.00	100.01

Appendix 1 continued

Sectoral Breakdown for the Year 1911

Sector	Scotland	Strathclyde	Dumfries & Galloway	Border	Lothian	Central and Fife	Tayside	Grampian	Highland
1. Agriculture, Forestry and Fishing	13.24	4.46	36.73	30.08	6.25	8.59	17.75	35.28	50.04
2. Mining, Quarrying	11.16	12.13	4.99	0.66	14.23	28.70	1.50	2.91	0.60
3. Manufacturing	39.36	48.82	20.91	34.40	33.44	31.74	41.90	26.59	14.43
4. Construction	7.78	7.36	9.65	9.00	8.60	8.34	8.64	7.15	6.91
5. Services	17.70	15.56	20.00	20.14	24.58	14.25	19.96	17.51	20.85
6. Transport	10.75	11.67	7.70	5.74	12.88	8.37	10.25	10.55	7.15
Totals	99.99	100.00	99.98	100.02	99.98	99.99	100.00	99.99	99.98

APPENDIX 2A. *Numbers of the Total Occupied Male Population of Each Region Located in Each Industrial Category in 1851*

Sector	Scotland	Strathclyde	Dumfries & Galloway	Border	Lothian	Central and Fife	Tayside	Grampian	Highland
1. Agriculture, forestry, fishing	255,614	51,864	22,224	14,693	15,939	17,009	27,612	51,106	55,167
2. Mining, quarrying	53,146	34,185	1,258	295	6,044	8,348	1,343	1,055	618
3. Food, drink, tobacco	43,100	16,766	1,784	1,479	8,151	3,724	4,841	4,304	2,051
4. Coal, petroleum products	—	—	—	—	—	—	—	—	—
5. Chemicals and allied products	4,142	2,303	84	54	753	366	206	277	99
6. Metal manufacture	36,107	18,539	1,171	848	4,629	3,912	2,960	2,733	1,315
7. Mechanical engineering	10,076	5,985	156	221	1,205	739	1,089	540	141
8. Instrument engineering	703	545	87	55	355	124	203	233	101
9. Electrical engineering	—	—	—	—	—	—	—	—	—
10. Shipbuilding, marine engineering	4,395	2,047	81	9	261	223	678	659	437
11. Vehicles	3,183	1,011	128	57	476	267	273	577	394
12. Metal goods not elsewhere specified	5,168	2,175	212	80	1,155	807	386	231	122
13. Textiles	120,436	60,831	2,844	4,055	3,292	17,508	25,970	4,425	1,511
14. Leather, leather goods, furs	4,879	1,568	242	261	1,204	471	532	438	163
15. Clothing, footwear	53,256	20,505	2,732	1,807	7,389	3,950	6,088	6,179	4,606
16. Bricks, pottery, glass, cement etc.	5,089	2,854	189	104	795	573	245	262	67
17. Timber, furniture	19,150	7,535	673	436	3,317	1,350	2,141	2,066	1,632
18. Paper, printing, publishing	8,083	2,699	134	153	3,263	430	528	700	176
19. Other manufactures	1,168	354	1	1	198	13	30	569	2
20. Construction	66,647	23,631	3,818	3,265	9,820	6,175	8,473	6,592	4,873
21. Gas, electricity, water	1,012	475	21	24	211	71	119	71	20
22. Transport, communications	48,396	21,505	1,912	940	7,520	4,149	5,204	4,241	2,925
23. Distributive trades	6,092	2,591	385	172	1,042	410	556	522	414
24. Insurance, banks, business services	637	209	35	15	130	51	100	64	33
25. Professional and scientific services	22,400	6,842	1,113	827	5,595	1,590	2,391	2,397	1,645
26. Miscellaneous services	17,537	5,609	1,045	903	3,278	1,183	2,110	1,821	1,588
27. Public administration and defence	11,607	3,848	423	267	3,095	683	1,096	1,175	1,020
28. Not classified	53,138	22,224	2,944	1,426	6,703	4,267	6,308	4,974	4,292
	856,161	318,700	45,696	32,447	95,820	78,393	101,482	98,211	85,412

APPENDIX 2A. *Numbers of the Total Occupied Male Population of Each Region Located in Each Industrial Category in 1881*

Sector	Scotland	Strathclyde	Dumfries & Galloway	Border	Lothian	Central and Fife	Tayside	Grampian	Highland
1. Agriculture, forestry, fishing	208,502	35,377	16,385	12,014	12,027	13,657	22,565	47,472	49,005
2. Mining, quarrying	82,507	53,980	1,379	229	10,030	12,358	1,410	2,457	664
3. Food, drink, tobacco	60,188	25,809	2,235	1,820	10,363	5,067	6,501	5,775	2,618
4. Coal, petroleum products	—	—	—	—	—	—	—	—	—
5. Chemicals and allied products	8,147	4,076	134	110	2,211	558	383	562	113
6. Metal manufacture	68,218	45,507	1,096	729	5,995	6,177	4,060	3,289	1,365
7. Mechanical engineering	32,912	23,261	287	509	2,720	1,598	3,130	1,183	224
8. Instrument engineering	2,847	1,138	130	88	519	183	291	342	156
9. Electrical engineering	78	38	2	2	21	—	8	5	2
10. Shipbuilding, marine engineering	18,470	14,844	47	22	621	445	1,078	964	449
11. Vehicles	3,641	1,567	142	88	606	222	390	397	229
12. Metal goods not elsewhere specified	7,753	4,222	215	122	1,373	583	564	447	227
13. Textiles	72,045	30,236	1,860	6,319	2,282	8,859	18,521	2,921	1,047
14. Leather, leather goods, furs	6,435	2,845	269	280	1,337	353	690	503	158
15. Clothing, footwear	45,843	19,128	1,986	1,596	6,412	2,962	5,134	5,492	3,133
16. Bricks, pottery, glass, cement etc.	7,041	4,456	94	52	1,211	765	242	171	50
17. Timber, furniture	23,421	10,495	563	418	4,257	1,464	2,225	2,772	1,227
18. Paper, printing, publishing	17,449	6,765	249	381	6,019	946	1,229	1,515	345
19. Other manufactures	3,346	900	22	33	712	768	146	746	19
20. Construction	107,260	44,751	5,164	4,375	17,299	7,840	11,381	9,886	6,564
21. Gas, electricity, water	3,282	1,595	75	74	654	227	372	243	42
22. Transport, communications	85,126	43,752	2,369	1,313	13,394	6,051	8,004	6,380	3,863
23. Distributive trades	7,566	3,285	374	199	912	450	782	798	766
24. Insurance, banks, business services	6,618	2,684	249	174	1,372	449	682	671	337
25. Professional and scientific services	27,959	10,242	1,253	945	5,972	1,948	2,908	2,790	1,901
26. Miscellaneous services	42,074	15,793	2,317	2,062	7,364	2,847	5,038	3,853	2,800
27. Public administration and defence	18,971	7,172	530	406	4,629	1,230	1,600	1,400	2,004
28. Not classified	122,545	62,341	3,617	2,733	16,235	8,710	13,183	9,942	5,784
	1,090,244	476,259	43,043	37,093	136,547	86,717	112,517	112,976	85,092

APPENDIX 2A. *Numbers of the Total Occupied Male Population of Each Region Located in Each Industrial Category in 1911*

Sector	Scotland	Strathclyde	Dumfries & Galloway	Border	Lothian	Central and Fife	Tayside	Grampian	Highland
1. Agriculture, forestry, fishing	195,174	31,962	15,776	11,074	12,001	12,490	21,404	46,779	43,688
2. Mining, quarrying	164,513	86,904	2,244	244	27,299	41,726	1,812	3,856	528
3. Food, drink, tobacco	87,820	40,419	2,542	2,109	15,073	7,692	7,868	8,664	3,453
4. Coal, petroleum products	—	—	—	—	—	—	—	—	—
5. Chemicals and allied products	15,466	7,440	203	139	4,269	1,240	708	1,213	254
6. Metal manufacture	93,345	67,217	822	588	5,953	10,677	3,752	3,016	1,320
7. Mechanical engineering	76,211	58,774	527	367	5,162	3,531	4,664	2,766	420
8. Instrument engineering	3,173	1,529	75	67	602	196	253	328	123
9. Electrical engineering	7,909	4,981	86	77	1,214	619	459	339	134
10. Shipbuilding, marine engineering	50,856	45,314	21	17	1,323	651	1,502	1,771	257
11. Vehicles	10,463	6,685	296	148	986	573	607	801	367
12. Metal goods not elsewhere specified	15,838	10,295	315	158	2,025	1,070	836	813	326
13. Textiles	69,044	27,065	1,555	6,841	2,533	6,268	20,398	3,332	1,052
14. Leather, leather goods, furs	6,257	3,365	185	270	1,077	391	471	400	98
15. Clothing, footwear	37,435	17,655	1,346	1,142	5,137	2,489	3,467	4,163	2,036
16. Bricks, pottery, glass, cement etc.	9,964	6,021	109	24	1,527	1,535	507	192	49
17. Timber, furniture	33,356	15,822	457	417	4,879	2,577	2,591	4,746	1,867
18. Paper, printing, publishing	26,652	10,442	308	400	9,013	2,052	1,805	2,309	323
19. Other manufactures	7,930	2,043	30	60	1,901	2,851	352	650	43
20. Construction	114,706	52,682	4,147	3,313	16,507	12,128	10,419	9,475	6,035
21. Gas, electricity, water	10,264	5,954	167	166	1,443	851	839	722	122
22. Transport, communications	158,498	83,584	3,309	2,114	24,724	12,173	12,359	13,995	6,240
23. Distributive trades	10,365	4,768	322	207	1,325	738	817	1,269	919
24. Insurance, banks, business services	16,034	7,311	448	330	3,133	1,189	1,462	1,562	599
25. Professional and scientific services	41,949	17,388	1,422	1,096	8,884	3,288	3,855	3,736	2,280
26. Miscellaneous services	62,123	25,427	5,000	2,888	9,774	5,334	6,778	4,995	3,927
27. Public administration and defence	42,476	16,080	853	783	8,992	2,473	3,278	2,987	7,030
28. Not classified	105,936	59,112	2,489	1,781	15,136	8,579	7,297	7,721	3,821
	1,473,757	716,239	42,954	36,820	191,892	145,381	120,560	132,600	87,311

APPENDIX 2B. *The Percentage of the Total Occupied Male Population of Each Region Located in Each Industrial Category in 1851*

Sector	Scotland	Strathclyde	Dumfries & Galloway	Border	Lothian	Central and Fife	Tayside	Grampian	Highland
1. Agriculture, forestry, fishing	29.86	16.27	48.63	45.28	16.63	21.70	27.21	52.04	64.59
2. Mining, quarrying	6.21	10.73	2.75	0.91	6.31	10.65	1.32	1.07	0.72
3. Food, drink, tobacco	5.03	5.26	3.90	4.56	8.51	4.75	4.77	4.38	2.40
4. Coal, petroleum products	—	—	—	—	—	—	—	—	—
5. Chemicals and allied products	0.48	0.72	0.18	0.17	0.79	0.47	0.20	0.28	0.12
6. Metal manufacture	4.22	5.82	2.56	2.61	4.83	4.99	2.92	2.78	1.54
7. Mechanical engineering	1.18	1.88	0.34	0.68	1.26	0.94	1.07	0.55	0.17
8. Instrument engineering	0.20	0.17	0.19	0.17	0.37	0.16	0.20	0.24	0.12
9. Electrical engineering	—	—	—	—	—	—	—	—	—
10. Shipbuilding, marine engineering	0.51	0.64	0.18	0.03	0.27	0.28	0.67	0.67	0.51
11. Vehicles	0.37	0.32	0.28	0.18	0.50	0.34	0.27	0.59	0.46
12. Metal goods not elsewhere specified	0.60	0.68	0.46	0.25	1.21	1.03	0.38	0.24	0.14
13. Textiles	14.07	19.09	6.22	12.50	3.43	22.33	25.59	4.51	1.77
14. Leather, leather goods, furs	0.57	0.49	0.53	0.80	1.26	0.60	0.52	0.45	0.19
15. Clothing, footwear	6.22	6.43	5.98	5.57	7.71	5.04	6.00	6.29	5.39
16. Bricks, pottery, glass, cement etc.	0.59	0.90	0.41	0.32	0.83	0.73	0.24	0.27	0.08
17. Timber, furniture	2.24	2.36	1.47	1.34	3.46	1.72	2.11	2.10	1.91
18. Paper, printing, publishing	0.94	0.85	0.29	0.47	3.41	0.55	0.52	0.71	0.21
19. Other manufactures	0.14	0.11	—	—	0.21	0.02	0.03	0.58	—
20. Construction	7.78	7.41	8.36	10.06	10.25	7.88	8.35	6.71	5.71
21. Gas, electricity, water	0.12	0.15	0.05	0.07	0.22	0.09	0.12	0.07	0.02
22. Transport, communications	5.65	6.75	4.18	2.90	7.85	5.29	5.13	4.32	3.42
23. Distributive trades	0.71	0.81	0.84	0.53	1.09	0.52	0.55	0.53	0.48
24. Insurance, banks, business services	0.07	0.07	0.08	0.05	0.14	0.07	0.10	0.07	0.04
25. Professional and scientific services	2.62	2.15	2.44	2.55	5.84	2.03	2.36	2.44	1.93
26. Miscellaneous services	2.05	1.76	2.29	2.78	3.42	1.51	2.08	1.85	1.86
27. Public administration and defence	1.36	1.21	0.93	0.82	3.23	0.87	1.08	1.20	1.19
28. Not classified	6.21	6.97	6.44	4.39	7.00	5.44	6.22	5.06	5.03
	100.00	100.00	99.98	99.99	100.03	100.00	100.01	100.00	100.00

APPENDIX 2B. The Percentage of the Total Occupied Male Population of Each Region Located in Each Industrial Category in 1881

Sector	Scotland	Strathclyde	Dumfries & Galloway	Border	Lothian	Central and Fife	Tayside	Grampian	Highland
1. Agriculture, forestry, fishing	19.12	7.43	38.07	32.39	8.81	15.75	20.05	42.02	57.59
2. Mining, quarrying	7.57	11.33	3.20	0.62	7.35	14.25	1.25	2.17	0.78
3. Food, drink, tobacco	5.52	5.42	5.19	4.91	7.59	5.84	5.78	5.11	3.08
4. Coal, petroleum products	—	—	—	—	—	—	—	—	—
5. Chemicals and allied products	0.75	0.86	0.31	0.30	1.62	0.64	0.34	0.50	0.13
6. Metal manufacture	5.26	9.56	2.55	1.97	4.39	7.12	3.61	2.91	1.60
7. Mechanical engineering	3.02	4.88	0.67	1.37	1.99	1.84	2.78	1.05	0.26
8. Instrument engineering	0.26	0.24	0.30	0.24	0.38	0.21	0.26	0.30	0.18
9. Electrical engineering	0.01	0.01	—	—	0.02	—	0.01	—	—
10. Shipbuilding, marine engineering	1.69	3.12	0.11	0.06	0.45	0.51	0.96	0.85	0.53
11. Vehicles	0.33	0.33	0.33	0.24	0.44	0.26	0.35	0.35	0.27
12. Metal goods not elsewhere specified	0.71	0.89	0.50	0.33	1.01	0.67	0.50	0.40	0.27
13. Textiles	6.61	6.35	4.32	17.04	1.67	10.22	16.46	2.59	1.23
14. Leather, leather goods, furs	0.59	0.60	0.62	0.75	0.93	0.41	0.61	0.45	0.19
15. Clothing, footwear	4.20	4.02	4.61	4.30	4.70	3.42	4.56	4.86	3.68
16. Bricks, pottery, glass, cement etc.	0.65	0.94	0.22	0.14	0.89	0.88	0.22	0.15	0.06
17. Timber, furniture	2.15	2.20	1.31	1.13	3.12	1.69	1.98	2.45	1.44
18. Paper, printing, publishing	1.60	1.42	0.58	1.03	4.41	1.10	1.09	1.34	0.41
19. Other manufactures	0.31	0.19	0.05	0.09	0.52	0.89	0.13	0.66	0.02
20. Construction	9.84	9.40	12.00	11.79	12.67	9.04	10.11	8.75	7.71
21. Gas, electricity, water	0.30	0.33	0.17	0.20	0.48	0.26	0.33	0.22	0.05
22. Transport, communications	7.81	9.19	5.50	3.54	9.81	6.98	7.11	5.65	4.54
23. Distributive trades	0.69	0.69	0.87	0.54	0.67	0.52	0.70	0.71	0.90
24. Insurance, banks, business services	0.61	0.56	0.58	0.47	1.00	0.52	0.61	0.59	0.40
25. Professional and scientific services	2.56	2.15	2.91	2.55	4.38	2.25	2.58	2.47	2.23
26. Miscellaneous services	3.86	3.32	5.38	5.56	5.39	3.28	4.48	3.41	3.30
27. Public administration and defence	1.74	1.51	1.23	1.09	3.39	1.42	1.42	1.24	2.36
28. Not classified	11.24	13.09	8.40	7.37	11.89	10.04	11.72	8.80	6.80
	100.00	100.03	99.98	100.02	100.02	100.01	100.00	100.00	100.01

APPENDIX 2B. *The Percentage of the Total Occupied Male Population of Each Region Located in Each Industrial Category in 1911*

Sector	Scotland	Strathclyde	Dumfries & Galloway	Border	Lothian	Central and Fife	Tayside	Grampian	Highland
1. Agriculture, forestry, fishing	13.24	4.46	36.73	30.08	6.25	8.59	17.75	35.28	50.04
2. Mining, quarrying	11.16	12.13	4.99	0.66	14.23	28.70	1.50	2.91	0.60
3. Food, drink, tobacco	5.96	5.64	5.92	5.73	7.85	5.29	6.53	6.53	3.95
4. Coal, petroleum products	—	—	—	—	—	—	—	—	—
5. Chemicals and allied products	1.05	1.04	0.47	0.38	2.22	0.85	0.59	0.91	0.29
6. Metal manufacture	6.33	9.38	1.91	1.60	3.10	7.34	3.11	2.27	1.51
7. Mechanical engineering	5.17	8.20	1.23	1.00	2.69	2.43	3.87	2.09	0.48
8. Instrument engineering	0.22	0.21	0.17	0.18	0.31	0.13	0.20	0.25	0.14
9. Electrical engineering	0.54	0.70	0.20	0.21	0.63	0.43	0.38	0.26	0.15
10. Shipbuilding, marine engineering	3.45	6.33	0.05	0.05	0.69	0.45	1.25	1.34	0.29
11. Vehicles	0.71	0.93	0.69	0.40	0.51	0.39	0.50	0.60	0.42
12. Metal goods not elsewhere specified	1.07	1.44	0.73	0.43	1.06	0.74	0.70	0.61	0.37
13. Textiles	4.68	3.78	3.62	18.58	1.32	4.31	16.92	2.51	1.20
14. Leather, leather goods, furs	0.42	0.47	0.43	0.73	0.56	0.27	0.39	0.30	0.11
15. Clothing, footwear	2.54	2.46	3.13	3.10	2.68	1.71	2.88	3.14	2.33
16. Bricks, pottery, glass, cement etc.	0.68	0.84	0.25	0.07	0.80	1.06	0.42	0.14	0.06
17. Timber, furniture	2.26	2.21	1.06	1.13	2.54	1.77	2.15	3.58	2.14
18. Paper, printing, publishing	1.81	1.46	0.72	1.09	4.70	1.41	1.50	1.74	0.37
19. Other manufactures	0.54	0.29	0.07	0.16	0.99	1.96	0.29	0.49	0.05
20. Construction	7.78	7.36	9.65	9.00	8.60	8.34	8.64	7.15	6.91
21. Gas, electricity, water	0.70	0.83	0.39	0.45	0.75	0.59	0.70	0.54	0.14
22. Transport, communications	10.75	11.67	7.70	5.74	12.88	8.37	10.25	10.55	7.15
23. Distributive trades	0.70	0.67	0.75	0.56	0.69	0.51	0.68	0.96	1.05
24. Insurance, banks, business services	1.09	1.02	1.04	0.90	1.63	0.82	1.21	1.18	0.69
25. Professional and scientific services	2.85	2.43	3.31	2.98	4.63	2.26	3.20	2.82	2.61
26. Miscellaneous services	4.22	3.55	6.99	7.84	5.09	3.67	5.62	3.77	4.50
27. Public administration and defence	2.88	2.25	1.99	2.13	4.69	1.70	2.72	2.25	8.05
28. Not classified	7.19	8.25	5.79	4.84	7.89	5.90	6.05	5.82	4.38
	99.99	100.00	99.98	100.02	99.98	99.99	100.00	99.99	99.98

APPENDIX 3. *Location Quotients for the Regions by Industrial Category for 1851*

Sector	Scotland	Strathclyde	Dumfries & Galloway	Border	Lothian	Central and Fife	Tayside	Grampian	Highland
1. Agriculture, forestry, fishing	1.00	0.55	1.63	1.52	0.56	0.73	0.91	1.74	2.16
2. Mining, quarrying	1.00	1.73	0.44	0.15	1.02	1.71	0.21	0.17	0.12
3. Food, drink, tobacco	1.00	1.05	0.78	0.91	1.69	0.94	0.95	0.87	0.48
4. Coal, petroleum products	—	—	—	—	—	—	—	—	—
5. Chemicals and allied products	1.00	1.49	0.38	0.34	1.62	0.96	0.42	0.58	0.24
6. Metal manufacture	1.00	1.38	0.61	0.62	1.15	1.18	0.69	0.66	0.36
7. Mechanical engineering	1.00	1.60	0.29	0.58	1.07	0.80	0.91	0.47	0.14
8. Instrument engineering	1.00	0.86	0.96	0.85	1.86	0.79	1.01	1.19	0.59
9. Electrical engineering	—	—	—	—	—	—	—	—	—
10. Shipbuilding, marine engineering	1.00	1.25	0.35	0.05	0.53	0.55	1.30	1.31	1.00
11. Vehicles	1.00	0.85	0.75	0.47	1.34	0.92	0.72	1.58	1.24
12. Metal goods not elsewhere specified	1.00	1.13	0.77	0.41	2.00	1.70	0.63	0.39	0.24
13. Textiles	1.00	1.36	0.44	0.89	0.24	1.59	1.82	0.32	0.13
14. Leather, leather goods, furs	1.00	0.86	0.93	1.41	2.21	1.05	0.92	0.78	0.33
15. Clothing, footwear	1.00	1.03	0.96	0.90	1.24	0.81	0.96	1.01	0.87
16. Bricks, pottery, glass, cement etc.	1.00	1.51	0.70	0.54	1.40	1.23	0.41	0.45	0.13
17. Timber, furniture	1.00	1.06	0.66	0.60	1.55	0.77	0.94	0.94	0.85
18. Paper, printing, publishing	1.00	0.90	0.31	0.50	3.61	0.58	0.55	0.76	0.22
19. Other manufactures	1.00	0.81	0.02	0.02	1.51	0.12	0.22	4.25	0.02
20. Construction	1.00	0.95	1.07	1.29	1.32	1.01	1.07	0.86	0.73
21. Gas, electricity, water	1.00	1.26	0.39	0.63	1.86	0.77	0.99	0.61	0.20
22. Transport, communications	1.00	1.19	0.74	0.51	1.39	0.94	0.91	0.76	0.61
23. Distributive trades	1.00	1.14	1.18	0.74	1.53	0.73	0.77	0.75	0.68
24. Insurance, banks, business services	1.00	0.88	1.03	0.62	1.82	0.87	1.32	0.88	0.52
25. Professional and scientific services	1.00	0.82	0.93	0.97	2.23	0.77	0.90	0.93	0.74
26. Miscellaneous services	1.00	0.86	1.12	1.36	1.67	0.74	1.02	0.91	0.91
27. Public administration and defence	1.00	0.89	0.68	0.61	2.38	0.64	0.80	0.88	0.88
28. Not classified	1.00	1.12	1.04	0.71	1.13	0.88	1.00	0.82	0.81

APPENDIX 3. *Location Quotients for the Regions by Industrial Category for 1911*

Sector	Scotland	Strathclyde	Dumfries & Galloway	Border	Lothian	Central and Fife	Tayside	Grampian	Highland
1. Agriculture, forestry, fishing	1.00	0.34	2.78	2.27	0.47	0.65	1.34	2.66	3.78
2. Mining, quarrying	1.00	1.09	0.45	0.06	1.27	2.57	0.13	0.26	0.05
3. Food, drink, tobacco	1.00	0.95	0.99	0.96	1.32	0.89	1.10	1.10	0.66
4. Coal, petroleum products	—	—	—	—	—	—	—	—	—
5. Chemicals and allied products	1.00	0.99	0.45	0.36	2.12	0.81	0.56	0.87	0.28
6. Metal manufacture	1.00	1.48	0.30	0.25	0.49	1.16	0.49	0.36	0.24
7. Mechanical engineering	1.00	1.59	0.24	0.19	0.52	0.47	0.75	0.40	0.09
8. Instrument engineering	1.00	0.99	0.81	0.84	1.46	0.63	0.97	1.15	0.65
9. Electrical engineering	1.00	1.30	0.37	0.39	1.18	0.79	0.71	0.48	0.29
10. Shipbuilding, marine engineering	1.00	1.84	0.01	0.01	0.20	0.13	0.36	0.39	0.09
11. Vehicles	1.00	1.31	0.97	0.57	0.72	0.56	0.71	0.85	0.59
12. Metal goods not elsewhere specified	1.00	1.34	0.68	0.40	0.98	0.69	0.65	0.57	0.35
13. Textiles	1.00	0.81	0.77	3.96	0.28	0.92	3.61	0.54	0.26
14. Leather, leather goods, furs	1.00	1.11	1.02	1.73	1.32	0.63	0.92	0.71	0.26
15. Clothing, footwear	1.00	0.97	1.24	1.22	1.05	0.67	1.13	1.24	0.92
16. Bricks, pottery, glass, cement etc.	1.00	1.24	0.38	0.10	1.18	1.56	0.62	0.21	0.08
17. Timber, furniture	1.00	0.98	0.47	0.50	1.12	0.78	0.95	1.58	0.95
18. Paper, printing, publishing	1.00	0.81	0.40	0.60	2.60	0.78	0.83	0.96	0.20
19. Other manufactures	1.00	0.53	0.13	0.30	1.84	3.65	0.54	0.91	0.09
20. Construction	1.00	0.95	1.24	1.16	1.11	1.07	1.11	0.92	0.89
21. Gas, electricity, water	1.00	1.19	0.56	0.65	1.08	0.84	1.00	0.78	0.20
22. Transport, communications	1.00	1.09	0.72	0.53	1.20	0.78	0.95	0.98	0.67
23. Distributive trades	1.00	0.95	1.07	0.80	0.98	0.72	0.96	1.36	1.50
24. Insurance, banks, business services	1.00	0.94	0.96	0.82	1.50	0.75	1.11	1.08	0.63
25. Professional and scientific services	1.00	0.85	1.16	1.05	1.63	0.79	1.12	0.99	0.92
26. Miscellaneous services	1.00	0.84	1.66	1.86	1.21	0.87	1.33	0.89	1.07
27. Public administration and defence	1.00	0.78	0.69	0.74	1.63	0.59	0.94	0.78	2.80
28. Not classified	1.00	1.15	0.81	0.67	1.10	0.82	0.84	0.81	0.61

APPENDIX 4. Net Gains (+) and Losses (−) by Region and Industrial Category from 1851 to 1911

Sector	Scotland	Strathclyde	Dumfries & Galloway	Borders	Lothian	Central and Fife	Tayside	Grampian	Highland
1. Agriculture, forestry, fishing	−60,440	−19,902	−6,448	−3,619	−3,938	−4,519	−6,208	−4,327	−11,479
2. Mining, quarrying	+111,367	+52,719	+386	−51	−21,255	−33,378	+469	+2,801	−90
3. Food, drink, tobacco	+44,720	+23,653	+758	+630	+6,922	+3,968	+3,027	+4,360	+1,402
4. Coal, petroleum products	—	—	—		—				—
5. Chemicals and allied products	+11,324	+5,137	+119	+85	+3,516	+874	+502	+936	+155
6. Metal manufacture	+57,238	+48,678	−349	−260	+1,324	+6,765	+792	+283	+5
7. Mechanical engineering	+56,135	+52,789	+371	+146	+3,957	+2,792	+3,575	+2,226	+279
8. Instrument engineering	+1,470	+984	−12	+12	+247	+72	+50	+95	+22
9. Electrical engineering	+7,909	−4,981	+86	+77	+1,214	+619	+459	+339	+134
10. Shipbuilding, marine engineering	+46,461	+43,267	−60	+8	+1,062	+428	+824	+1,112	−180
11. Vehicles	+7,280	−5,674	+168	+91	+510	+306	+334	+224	−27
12. Metal goods not elsewhere specified	+10,670	+8,120	+103	+78	+870	+263	+450	+582	+204
13. Textiles	−51,392	−33,766	−1,289	+2,786	−759	−11,240	−5,572	−1,093	−459
14. Leather, leather goods, furs	+1,378	+1,797	−57	+9	−127	−80	−61	−38	−65
15. Clothing, footwear	−15,821	−2,850	−1,386	−665	−2,252	−1,461	−2,621	−2,016	−2,570
16. Bricks, pottery, glass, cement etc.	+4,875	+3,167	−80	−80	+732	+962	+262	−70	−18
17. Timber, furniture	+14,206	+8,287	−216	−19	+1,562	+1,227	+450	+2,680	+235
18. Paper, printing, publishing	+18,569	+7,743	+174	+247	+5,750	+1,622	+1,277	+1,609	+147
19. Other manufactures	+6,762	+1,689	+29	+59	+1,703	+2,838	+322	+81	+41
20. Construction	+48,059	+29,051	−329	+48	+6,687	+5,953	+1,946	+2,883	+1,162
21. Gas, electricity, water	+9,252	+5,479	+146	+142	+1,232	+780	+720	+651	+102
22. Transport, communications	+110,102	+62,079	+1,397	+1,174	+17,204	+8,024	+7,155	+9,754	+3,315
23. Distributive trades	+4,273	+2,177	−63	+35	+283	+328	+261	+747	+505
24. Insurance, banks, business services	+15,397	+7,102	+413	+315	+3,003	+1,138	+1,362	+1,498	+566
25. Professional and scientific services	+19,549	+10,546	+309	+269	+3,289	+1,698	+1,464	+1,339	+635
26. Miscellaneous services	+44,586	+19,818	+1,955	+1,985	+6,496	+4,151	+4,668	+3,174	+2,339
27. Public administration and defence	+30,869	+12,232	+430	+516	+5,897	+1,790	+2,182	+1,812	+6,010
28. Not classified	+52,798	+36,888	−455	+355	+8,433	+4,312	+989	+2,747	−471
	+617,596	+397,539	−2,742	+4,373	+96,072	+66,988	+19,078	+34,389	+1,899

CHAPTER 7

Women's Spheres

Eleanor Gordon

The period between the early years of industrialisation and the First
World War is littered with images and stereotypes of women: 'Angel in
the house', 'the downtrodden factory worker', 'the hapless Magdalen',
and 'the strident middle-class suffragette'. However, these images of
Victorian womanhood are drawn from the English experience, and
the history of Scottish women has been largely a second-hand one.
This chapter is an attempt to provide a vignette of the lives of
Scottish women in these years by looking at the changing experience
of working- and middle-class women in the areas of employment, the
family, philanthropy, trade unions and political life. The intention is to
establish whether the reality of their lives coincided with any of these
borrowed images, and to examine the extent to which women's lives
were constrained by customs, ideologies and conventions.

Employment

Industrialisation marked the emergence of new social institutions, cultural
formations and ideologies. Of the latter, one of the most important in
terms of the lives of women, was the ideology of domesticity which, in
its Victorian form, stressed the division of the world into the public and
the private sphere, or the division between home and work.

There was little that was new in the association of women with the
domestic sphere. In the pre-industrial period women had combined their
housewifely duties with productive work, either in the home or outside.
The increasing separation of home and work which industrialisation
entailed, and the increasing prosperity of the middle classes, gave rise
to the notion that women's role should be concerned exclusively with
the domestic sphere. The new role of housewife in the working-class

family was remarked upon in 1828 by the author of an article in a Glasgow medical journal:

> In families in which all the members are so far advanced as to be fit for labour, the aggregate amount of their earnings is very considerable and is in general placed at the disposal of the eldest female, whose sole employment consists in making purchases, and attending to household duties.[1]

However, grinding poverty often pushed married working-class women onto the labour market, irrespective of the weight of social convention, and as the century progressed, many middle-class women rebelled against being confined to the domestic sphere. Women's lives were much more complex than the images which pervade the period, and neither Engels's claim that the working-class family had been turned upside-down, with women working in factories, and men tending the home, or the view of women as 'angels in the house', adequately describe the reality.

Many women were drawn into the factories in the early years of industrialisation, and they comprised a substantial section of the labour force. Of 59,314 working in Scottish textiles in 1839, 40,868 were female. However, 43 per cent of the female labour force were under eighteen, and the largest single category of worker was young girls between thirteen and fourteen years of age.[2] It seems to have been more acceptable for young children to work in factories than married women. Although there are no statistics to enable accurate calculation of the number of married women working, evidence suggests that, unless driven out to work by economic necessity, the working-class norm was for wives to remain at home. The manager of the Adelphi cotton-spinning works in Glasgow claimed in 1833 that 'women do not generally work much in factories after they get married', adding that only seven of the women in his works had husbands who were alive, five of whom had no children, and the remaining two had husbands who lived elsewhere.[3] Although female labour predominated in cotton, the major branch of Scottish textiles in the first decades of the century, there is little evidence to substantiate the apocalyptic vision painted by Engels of husbands and wives reversing roles, resulting in men becoming 'unsexed' and losing their masculinity.

Factory employment was by no means the major source of employment for men or women in the first half of the nineteenth century. In 1850, just over one-third of those involved in cotton manufacture were employed in mills and factories, the rest being located in the home or in small workshops.[4] The pattern and location of women's employment is difficult to establish, however, for in addition to the usual problems associated with the census, it is a particularly unreliable indicator of women's work. Changing census classifications reflected the fact that during the course of the century, work was increasingly defined as an activity which was carried on outside the home, for a wage, and which was governed by market relations. Work also tended to be defined as 'regular' activity, implying continuity if not permanency. As many women were engaged in casual and seasonal work, or might only work when their husbands were unemployed or underemployed, it is likely that their work was often omitted from census figures, which related to one day in the year and which were based on a conception of employment defined by a male norm of permanent, full-time work outside the home.

The problem of under-representation was particularly acute for female agricultural labour and married women's work, both of which were intermittent and therefore likely to be excluded from the official calculations. Changes within farming, coupled with growing industrial demand for adult male labour, led to the increasing employment of female labour in agriculture from about the 1830s until the last decades of the nineteenth century. However, as much of the work was seasonal, part-time or casual, it was unlikely to be recorded in census data.[5] The census practice, from 1871, of omitting female relatives of farmers from the statistics, and the tendency to include some classes of farm servant within the 'domestic' category further exacerbated the under-recording of women workers in agriculture.

In 1911 the number of married women working was listed separately for the first time, and recorded as 5 per cent. It is commonly assumed that from about the middle of the nineteenth century married women withdrew from paid work. However, the reports of organisations such as the Social Union, the Charity Organisation Society and the Scottish Council for Women's Trades, which chronicled the conditions of the poor, suggest that the official figure of 5 per cent of married women working was substantially underestimated. These organisations produced voluminous evidence indicating that many working-class wives took work as and when it was available in order to eke out the family income. Dundee Social Union found that in a survey of 3,039 households, approximately half of the wives were working, whereas the census figure for the town was 23.4 per cent.[6] A survey of 660 outworkers by Glasgow's chief sanitary inspector included 300 wives who, it was claimed, consisted 'chiefly of the wives of labourers whose pay is small and whose employment is casual'.[7]

Although the census seriously under-records the extent of women's work, even the official picture substantiates the view that the outstanding feature of women's work throughout the period was not their exclusion from work, but their concentration in certain well-defined areas of work. Women comprised a relatively stable proportion of the labour force from 1841 until 1911, fluctuating between 36 per cent and 29 per cent. However, there was a decline between 1861 and 1871, which was largely due to revised census practices and the decision to omit those wives who worked alongside their husbands in shops, small businesses, farms etc. The decline from 1891 probably reflects the extension of compulsory elementary education, rather than the withdrawal of women from the labour force (Table 1).

Table 1. Women as a Percentage of the Total Labour Force, 1841–1911

Year	1841	1851	1861	1871	1881	1891	1901	1911
Per cent	36.39	36.29	36.81	31.73	31.31	31.30	29.8	28.7

Source: *Census of Great Britain and Scotland, 1841–1911*

Women's work was characterised by low pay and occupational segregation and concentration. However, notions of what constituted women's work were not fixed, but varied over time and place. The factors which determined women's employment pattern were a complex mix of economic, social and ideological factors.

In 1841, domestic service, agriculture, clothing and textiles employed about 90 per cent of the female labour force, although by 1911 the four most important sources of employment accounted for 65 per cent of occupied women. A discernible trend was the widening sphere of women's employment, but this should not be overstated, as, even in 1901, in the four major cities of Glasgow, Edinburgh, Dundee and Aberdeen, the six major categories of women's employment accounted for over 80 per cent of the female labour force.[8]

There were significant variations in the occupational distribution of women workers in the Scottish cities, reflecting their different industrial structures and local economies. For example, in Glasgow throughout the period textiles and clothing were major sources of employment for women, whereas in Edinburgh domestic service dominated. In Aberdeen, textiles were also in the major sector, but the industry here was not confined to one fibre, for the woollen, linen and jute industries all provided employment for women. Dundee's employment base was particularly

36. Nineteenth-century photographers loved taking pictures of women doing their domestic work outdoors. This woman fetching water near Dundee in the 1890s does not look so keen. *Scottish Ethnographic Archive, National Museums of Scotland.*

narrow, jute and linen employing between three-quarters and two-thirds of all working women in the city.

There were also variations in the pattern of married women's work which reflected the nature of local labour markets, local traditions and employer practices. In Dundee, where there were limited opportunities for male employment, married women's work was so commonplace that those women who were not in paid employment were dismissed as lazy, whereas in Paisley, where the major employer in the town disapproved of women 'being taken from their families', the number of married women working was extremely low.[9]

Even in those expanding areas of employment, such as commerce and the professions, the increase in women's employment was limited to particular areas. For example, the increase in commerce is explained almost exclusively by the rise in the number of commercial clerks who constituted approximately 86 per cent of women employed in the commercial sector. In the professions the rise can be attributed to the increase in the number of teachers, sick nurses and midwives. A notable development was the gradual entry of women into the medical profession in the last decade of the nineteenth century, although by 1901 there were still only 60 women doctors practising in Scotland.

Not only was the degree of sex segregation of occupations pronounced, but even within those industries and occupations which employed both men and women, there emerged a sexual division of labour. In textiles there were a few tasks in which both men and women were engaged, such as carpet weaving, cotton spinning and preparing in the Dundee jute industry. However, even within these tasks there was a sexual division of labour; in carpet weaving the men worked on hand-looms, in spinning the men took over the larger mules and the finer counts of yarn, and in the preparing departments of the jute industry men usually performed the heavier work.

In the skilled trades of tailoring, printing and bookbinding, which women began to enter towards the end of the century, there also emerged a sexual division of labour. In tailoring, men monopolised the first-class shops which catered for the 'bespoke trade', with women employed in the finishing processes, such as button-holing. In bookbinding, women's work was confined to 'stitching' and 'folding', and in printing the female compositors' job was restricted to type-setting, with the other processes involved in the trade remaining the preserve of men.[10]

Agriculture and the professions were also beset by sexual divisions of labour. In agriculture in Lowland Scotland women normally undertook hand-weeding and reaping with the sickle. When the heavier scythe was introduced reaping became a male task, and women were confined to gathering the grain. In the north-east Lowlands 'the cultural prescription against women working with horses was absolute'.[11] In the Highlands the women had their specific tasks, principally dairy work and textile work, in addition to their housework. On the crofts, where the men

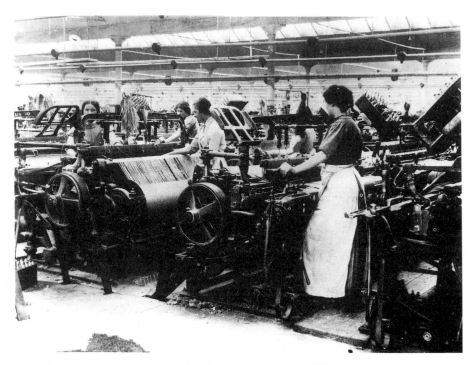

37. Women weavers in a Dundee jute works c.1908. The young women weavers were notorious for their independent ways and 'bold' manner. *Bonar Textiles Ltd., Baxter Archives, Dundee University Library.*

often had to work away from home, the women would take over most of the responsibility for cultivation, but the men performed the heavier work of digging, and cutting and floating the seaweed, before they left, to return in time to do the peat cutting.[12]

Although the cultural norm was for single middle-class women to remain in the home rather than to seek employment, a number of women rebelled against this notion and were anxious to acquire a training for a profession. Women conducted vigorous campaigns to gain entry into certain professions, and they were aided by social changes and developments within particular professions which created wider career opportunities. Developments within medicine, which converted the middle class to the benefits of hospital treatment, contributed to the growth and professionalisation of nursing, whilst the recruitment of women into teaching was boosted by the 1872 Education Act (Scotland), which introduced compulsory elementary education.[13]

In 1851 women comprised 35 per cent of the teaching profession, and by 1911, 70 per cent. There were no social barriers to women entering teaching, in fact it was considered to be a profession ideally suited to their nature. In 1878 senior officials in the Scottish Education Department expressed the view that:

> The education of children should be so conducted as to develop grace and gentleness in their manners and deportment. If they are brought up under the gentler, more natural qualities of female teachers, a better result may be expected to be attained, than if trained entirely by men.[14]

Despite women's increasing presence in the teaching profession, and their increasing standard of qualifications, the highest position a woman could attain was the post of infant mistress in the elementary schools, as men continued to dominate the hierarchies of the profession.

Medicine was a particularly difficult bastion to storm. Even after women were allowed to graduate in medicine, hospitals were reluctant to provide clinical facilities for female students. Women doctors found it easier to obtain posts in hospitals which dealt with women's or children's diseases, or those specialities which male physicians found unprofitable or distasteful. For example, on the subject of diagnosing venereal diseases in women on the Lock wards, one physician wrote that:

> . . . for many other good reasons, he would hand over all the females quarantined to the care of lady doctors. Every one knows that ladies are possessed of keener sensibilities and acuter powers of discrimination than men, and he would guarantee that if this department were entirely handed over to them. . . no case of venereal disease in the female would escape detection for want of delicate diagnostic skill.[15]

The first women doctors to be appointed in Glasgow were taken on by the Samaritan Hospital in 1892. However, general hospitals were slow to open their doors, and Glasgow Western Infirmary set its face against admitting women until the pressures of war forced them to do so in 1943.[16] The hostility of the medical profession to women doctors was based largely on their fear of women as economic competitors in this well-paid and high-status profession. Only a small minority of doctors favoured women's entry, and sometimes this was motivated by self-interest. A contribution to a debate in one of Glasgow's medical societies was particularly revealing:

> Dr Pollock . . . thought medical women would be very useful in obstetric cases, and that men would be relieved of much irksome and poorly paid work.[17]

It seems fair to conclude that the concentration of women in low-status sectors of medicine was more related to the entrenched opposition of the medical profession than the limited ambition of women doctors.

A corollary to the pervasiveness of the sexual division of labour was the notion that a woman's wage should invariably be lower than a man's. The average wage for a woman in Britain at the turn of the century was 42 per cent of the male average, and in textiles, one of the largest areas of women's employment, the annual average wage of a woman was 53 per cent of a man's.[18] One commentator noted that in agriculture, 'At many branches of farm labour, a good girl will do more than an average man, yet she still has to be content with half his wages'.[19] These averages masked considerable variations in women's earnings, and the fact that a few women earned more than some men, but this rarely happened within one industry. The highest paid skilled women in the Edinburgh printing trades earned 20s per week, whereas the lowest paid unskilled men, the warehouse hands, earned 15s to 21s per week.[20] The almost universal dividing line between men's and women's work makes it difficult to make direct comparisons of male and female rates. In the few processes where men and women performed exactly the same tasks, the woman's rate was usually lower than the man's. Margaret Irwin, of the Scottish Council for Women's Trades, commented of the clothing industry that:

> Where the women produce work of the same nature and efficiency as the men and are actually engaged side by side, the rate is much lower than the men.[21]

These lower rates of pay also prevailed in the teaching profession, where the mean annual salary for women between 1872 and 1900 was £62–72 and the corresponding figure for men was £121–143.[22]

The lower pay received by most women was often justified by such statements as 'it takes so much less to keep a woman than a man'. These conventions appear to have been related to the assumption that women were economic dependants rather than providers, and yet the evidence suggests that not only were there substantial numbers of single unsupported women in the population, but that many women were themselves breadwinners with dependants. Although it is difficult to calculate the exact numbers of women who were sole breadwinners, the census recorded that there were 561,745 working women in 1911 who were not dependent on the earnings of a husband. Some of these women would be supplementing the income of a father, or parents, or another relative. This would not be the case, however, for the 12 per cent of the female population who were widows, or the many deserted women. One witness to the Royal Commission on the Poor Laws commented of women's wages in Edinburgh that they were so low that they were 'such wages as they could not possibly live on without the parish help'.[23]

As women were relegated to the status of supplementary earners, whatever the reality of their status, this imposed considerable hardship on those families who had to rely intermittently on the earnings of the wife. The consequences were even more severe for those women who were unsupported — single women, widows, deserted wives, many of whom had dependants.

Some categories of women's work mirrored their domestic tasks and were viewed as extensions of women's cultural roles. Domestic service, work in the clothing industry, nursing and teaching, are the obvious examples of this kind of work. However, not all women's work was of this nature; for example, one of the principal sources of work in the Victorian period was the textile industry, and in the early twentieth century, clerical work, neither of which related to women's domestic role, and which previously had been dominated by men. For this reason, explanations of occupational segregation have developed which focus on the fact that women provided employers with a cheap and unskilled source of labour, and were likely to be recruited to industries in periods of technological innovation or intense competition. Although this approach explains women's work in areas such as tailoring and some branches of textiles and engineering, it is not adequate as a general explanation of women's work, as it ignores the fact that employers made few systematic attempts to introduce women into a range of occupations, despite their obvious advantages as cheap labour.

Trade unions played an important role in maintaining occupational segregation, and printers, tailors, spinners and bookbinders at various times tried to exclude women from their trades.[24] When unsuccessful, they resorted to controlling women's entry into the trade in a way which ensured that they captured the highest-paid work, often with the collusion of employers. There were limitations, however, on the extent to which trade unions could successfully impose their will on employers, particularly in Scotland, where trade unions for much of the period were relatively weak. Whilst trade union sectionalism contributed to the pattern of occupational segregation, it was only one factor of many influencing employment patterns. Local labour markets, wider market conditions and the nature of industrial relations within an industry all influenced the sexual division of labour.

However, any explanation of the pattern of women's employment has to address both economic and ideological factors. Women's status as cheap labour could be used to great effect by employers, although the trade union movement was not constantly faced with attempts by employers to substitute male labour with cheaper female labour. In any case, women's status as cheap labour was itself premissed on ideological assumptions about the role of women which profoundly affected both the pattern of their employment and their experience of employment. The sexual division of labour in the family with its emphasis on women's domestic responsibilities and the ideology of separate sexual spheres strongly influenced women's participation in the labour force. It did not exclude women from paid work, but it dictated the terms of their entry.

The degree of sex segregation of the labour force was particularly pronounced in Scotland, and the percentage of married women working was lower than in England. Both of these phenomena probably reflected the predominance of the heavy industries in the industrial structure which employed mainly male labour, and the fact that there were fewer opportunities for regular waged work for women. Nonetheless, throughout the period, working-class women, married and unmarried, formed a substantial section of the labour force, although the participation of the former often went unrecorded. Towards the end of the nineteenth century there was a widening sphere of employment for single middle-class women, although still of a limited scope. It seems then that it was only for a section of the middle classes that the Victorian ideology of domesticity and 'angel in the house' dovetailed with actual experience.

Family, Marriage and Sexuality

Cultural conventions aside, the family cycle and high fertility rate were important constraints on women's ability to seek paid employment outside the home. It was by no means the case that women with young children did not work, as the frequent references in philanthropic literature to 'irregular work such as baby minding' testify, but the rhythms of the family life cycle often determined when women could seek work.

At the beginning of the period women could expect to marry at about twenty-five years of age. There was a slight upward trend in the average age of marriage in the course of the century to twenty-six by 1911, by which time the fertility rate had also declined. Indeed, one of the most significant developments in this period for women was the decrease in family size which, although evident in all layers of society, seems to have originated among the professional middle class.[25] The crude birth

38. Women winders in a Galashiels woollen mill c.1912. Men controlled the supervisory jobs. In some border towns there were four women to every man. *Courtesy of Dr J. II. Treble.*

rate remained at around 35 per thousand from the mid-1850s, when this figure was first calculated, until the 1870s, at which point fertility began to decline. By 1911 the crude birth rate was down to about 25 per thousand. Although fertility rates were halved between the late 1870s and the late 1920s, the decline was moderate until the turn of the century, and accelerated thereafter.[26] By the end of the century, the average family size of many professional groupings was under four, whereas the average for the population as a whole was 5.82.[27]

The explanation for this decline is uncertain. Conventionally it has been attributed to the introduction and increasing availability of new methods of contraception. However, there also seems to have been more systematic use of traditional techniques which suggests there was more motivation to limit family size.[28] Whatever the precise explanation, clearly the ability to have more control over reproduction must have removed an enormous burden from women who previously had to endure pregnancy after pregnancy. It is important to bear in mind that at this stage smaller family size was only an emerging trend, and that large families were still relatively common, particularly among the working class.

The statistics on marriage and divorce tell us nothing about the quality of the former, or whether marriage was for love, money or social mobility. The low incidence of divorce (only 142 people sued for divorce in Scotland in 1900) was more an indicator of the rigid legal and religious stance that desertion and adultery were the only grounds for divorce, than an index of the fulfilled nature of Victorian marriages. The law governing family relationships was unequivocally patriarchal. Until the Married Women's Property Act of 1877, women ceded rights of property ownership to their husbands, including the right to keep their own unearned income, and custody of children was as a rule given to the husband.

What is clear about day-to-day life within the household is that wives of all social classes, whether or not they were in paid employment, shouldered responsibility for domestic tasks and child-rearing. However, the ideology of domesticity had distinct class connotations, and the domestic ideal was imbued with different values and meanings in the context of working-class and middle-class culture. The image of 'angel in the house' as aspired to by the middle classes, associated woman with household management as well as with the virtues of gentility, manners and etiquette. The meaning of domesticity in the working-class household was more concerned with the acquisition of practical skills, such as cooking, baking, cleaning, sewing, washing, whilst the virtues stressed were cleanliness and thrift.

Training for this role began early in working-class households where children, especially girls, were expected to make a contribution to domestic labour. A stonemason's daughter recalled that the division of labour in her household required that the girls do all the domestic work:

> They [the boys] didn't have to do anything in the house. We used to have to wash out their white gloves and clean their patent shoes to let them get away to the dancing. They were the apple of my mother's eye. Nothing could go wrong with the boys.[29]

The middle-class girl could expect to have a more leisured existence. According to the daughter of a coffee merchant, 'you just played around . . . sewing and fiddling about and meeting your friends and dancing and enjoying yourself . . .' Any tasks which they were expected to perform were related to their prescribed role, such as dusting and flower-arranging.[30] Although middle-class girls were under no pressure to contribute to the family income, there were other constraints imposed

39. Women's waged work often reflected their domestic roles. Even washing was influenced by technology and economies of scale. This is the laundry room at the Poor House, Greenlea in Edinburgh in 1904. *Scottish Ethnographic Archive, National Museums of Scotland.*

upon them. The surfeit of leisure which they enjoyed was closely regulated and supervised. A stockbroker's daughter who was born in 1888 recalled:

> I never went out alone then. You didn't go about alone and never came home alone. My father always came for us if we were at friends' houses in the evening. But of course that was the generation then.[31]

By 1914 there were a number of changes, both legal and social, which improved the position of women within marriage, but they were of a limited nature, and it was not until after the First World War that family limitation, changes in divorce laws, etc., were to have a significant impact on women's lives.

Victorian Scotland has acquired a reputation as a profoundly Calvinist nation wedded to a strict moral code, characterised by guilt, temperance, self-denial and thrift. The Church of Scotland certainly endorsed the traditional Christian doctrine regarding sexual behaviour by condemning antenuptial fornication and adultery as prurient. Nonetheless, the sexual behaviour of the Scottish people did not always conform to Calvinist teaching, and illegitimacy and bridal pregnancies were common occurrences, at least among the working classes, giving Scotland a particularly high proportion of illegitimate births in comparison with the British average.[32] Illegitimacy and prenuptial pregnancy were rare amongst the middle classes, which suggests that it was mainly middle-class women who conformed to the Victorian ideal of chaste womanhood.

Attitudes to sexual intercourse before marriage seemed to be governed as much by local tradition as by the teachings of the church, as a notable feature of Scottish illegitimacy patterns was the wide variations in regional rates. The illegitimacy rate was higher in the countryside than in the towns, but within the rural experience there were also marked variations. The counties of north-east Scotland and the south-west Lowlands had averages of 14–18 per cent of illegitimate births compared to the Scottish average of 9.3 per cent, whilst Orkney and Shetland and Ross and Cromarty were below 6 per cent.

In those areas where both illegitimacy and bridal pregnancies were common, it appears that the woman was not publicly stigmatised or made a social pariah. The Church of Scotland also gave tacit acceptance to the common occurrence of antenuptial conception, when it argued in favour of retaining irregular marriage, that is, a marriage requiring only the consent of freely contracting parties in order to be valid. The reason given was:

> Instead of leaving a woman to dishonour and ruin who has yielded on the faith of a solemn promise of marriage, and enabling her seducer to escape, the law protects the weaker party and gives her the rights of a wife and her children the status of lawful children.[33]

On this question it seems that presbyterianism has gained an ill-deserved reputation for misogyny and adopting a particularly repressive attitude to women.

In stark contrast, the harsh treatment meted out to the working-class women who provided casual or commercial sexual intercourse to middle-class men, whose own moral code prevented them seeking or at least obtaining sexual fulfilment from the chaste and virtuous women of their own class, was clearly a function of the Victorian double standard of morality. These women were the objects of moral opprobrium and relentless efforts by members of the philanthropic middle classes to rehabilitate and reform them. One of the most important organisations in this area were the Scottish Magdalene asylums, which were charities for the moral rehabilitation and training of 'prostitutes', the majority of whom were unemployed factory hands and domestic servants. They were supported by the new and unprecedented powers of the Glasgow Police Act (1866) and the Edinburgh Municipal Police Act (1879) which were designed to suppress brothels and street soliciting, and therefore to drive the poor and desperate woman from the streets.

One historian has commented that in Victorian Scotland breaches in the church's code of sexual morality were evident in all social classes. It appears, however, that it was only the women of the working classes, who provided casual or commercial intercourse for men of all social classes, who still suffered public condemnation.

WOMEN IN PUBLIC LIFE

Marriage, family and the household were not the sole concerns of women, many of whom had a public presence whether by choice or necessity. It was in this sphere that women demonstrated that their circumscribed public role and their subordination as a gender in the home and in the workplace, did not reduce them to silence and submission, or prevent them from asserting their rights and generally imprinting their presence across a range of public arenas.

Industrial Militancy

One of the most enduring images of Victorian women is that of the exploited factory workers whose long hours, poor conditions and low wages sapped their will and strength to improve their lot. This image, however, is not supported by historical evidence. Women have struggled constantly, if not always successfully against their oppression and to alter their material circumstances. The history of women is replete with examples of their contribution and participation in struggles of many kinds, from their role in militia riots, food riots, and the patronage protests of the late eighteenth century, to their role in the Owenite socialist movement and the chartist movement of the 1830s and 1840s.[34] However, the notion of the passive woman worker has remained firmly embedded in the historical literature and in popular consciousness. Yet the evidence suggests that almost from the moment they entered factories and mills, women organised to redress their grievances and advance their claims.[35]

Women were not involved to any great degree in formal trade union organisations, although their membership record is not so dismal when compared with unskilled male workers. As early as 1833 the women

40. The expansion of consumer industries, like the confectionery trade, provided many job opportunities for women. These were working at William Keiller's works in Dundee. *Dundee District Libraries.*

power-loom weavers in Glasgow formed an association 'to enable them by small subscriptions to be supported in making strikes against their employers for higher wages and for other purposes'. One of the most difficult occupations to organise was homework, because of the isolated position of the workers, yet even here there is evidence of women's attempts to organise collectively. In 1866 a meeting of homeworkers was held at New Pitsligo, Aberdeenshire, to discuss the question of prices for knitting, and in 1867 the homeworkers who knitted Ayrshire bonnets held a general meeting to discuss tactics over a threatened reduction.

Women workers' strike record indicates that they were capable of militancy and self-organisation, albeit outside the portals of the trade union movement. Between the 1850s and 1914, women workers in Scotland were involved in over 300 disputes. This figure is based on newspaper reports from 1853 and on the officially compiled statistics which were collected from 1889. Therefore it is by no means an exhaustive list, as both sources are incomplete.

In the period between 1850 and 1890, before there were official records, there were over 100 strikes involving women, most of them in the textile industry, as in this period textiles accounted for 90 per cent of women workers in the manufacturing sector. It is difficult to make general assessments about the pattern of strike activity, given the fragmentary nature of the sources. The strikes tended to be spontaneous and short-lived, although the general trend was punctuated by a number of protracted disputes. The issues involved in the disputes covered the gamut of industrial relations questions. However, the majority of the disputes were about wages. What is clear is that the women did not lack resolve and determination and were often prepared to take action when men either refused or prevaricated. It was observed by one member of the all-male committee organising the agitation over the extension of the meal-time in Dundee in the 1870s that 'the better plan would be to get the fair sex on your side and go to the employers and you will get the money from them'.

Women's strikes contributed in no small measure to the escalation of militancy in the immediate pre-war years, both in numbers and in their general impact. In Kirkcaldy in 1911 women weavers struck in support of nine members of the newly formed union who had been dismissed after a number of demands had been presented to the company. These demands included a 20 per cent wage increase, recognition of the union, and no victimisation. During the course of the dispute fifteen of the strikers were fined for 'disorderly conduct', receiving a tumultuous reception from the Kirkcaldy townsfolk when they returned from their trial. The strike was eventually won by the women, and according to the correspondent in *Forward*, it was their example which inspired other workers in the town to organise and fight for wage increases. It was claimed that since the women weavers' strike, an increase had been sought and granted in every factory in the district. The *Forward* article concluded, 'Public opinion in Kirkcaldy says, "We owe it to our women folk."'

Although women occupied a subordinate position in the labour market, this did not prevent them from organising to protect and improve their wages and conditions. Investigations of working-class women's employment have revealed that whatever ideology was articulated, economic necessity forced many women onto the labour market. And once women were involved in work, they adopted the most expedient methods available to them to protect their wages and conditions, irrespective of whether they challenged contemporary views of them as passive or docile.

Philanthropy

For the women of the leisured classes in the early and mid-Victorian period paid work was neither necessary nor socially acceptable, therefore many of them channelled their not inconsiderable energies into philanthropic and voluntary work. Charitable work was thought to require application, benevolence, piety and self-sacrifice, and therefore was deemed to be ideally tailored to the moral character of the Victorian lady. The membership rolls, the boards and the committees of philanthropic and temperance organisations were crammed with middle-class women jostling to reform the inebriate, uplift the Magdalene and educate the ignorant.

The British Ladies' Society for Promoting the Reformation of Female Prisoners, which was founded in 1835 by Elizabeth Fry, had a number of branches in Scotland. The aim of the society was to seek out and reform women recommended by prisons, Lock hospitals, Magdalene asylums, etc. In addition to reforming 'fallen' women, the Ladies' Societies also believed in pre-emptive action, and directed some of their reforming zeal towards women who were regarded as being in moral danger. Thus the Greenock branch of the Society taught Bible classes at the local paper, cotton, woollen and flax mills.[36]

Charities which were organised by men were usually supported by Ladies' Committees who were depended upon as tutors, home visitors and fund raisers. Such was the case with the Magdalene institutions which were founded in the late eighteenth century for the purpose of reforming women who had been 'led astray from the paths of virtue'. The Edinburgh institution was opened in 1797 and the Glasgow one eighteen years later. A Ladies' Committee of the Edinburgh Magdalene Asylum was formed the year after the asylum opened, and took on a great deal of responsibility in the running of the homes. In Glasgow a Ladies' Committee was not formed until 1861, when an appeal was made to Christian ladies to devote some of their time to the care of the fallen. The Glasgow Institution was encouraged by the response of one hundred ladies volunteering their services.[37]

Women's involvement in philanthropy was not simply a reflection of the restrictions placed on their lives and on their circumscribed public role. It was also a means of extending and redefining their role. For some women, such as Miss Elizabeth Hadwen, it also became a stepping stone into civic life. Miss Hadwen had already chalked up an impressive record of philanthropic endeavour as a visitor at the Prison, a member of the Scottish Women's Trades Council and a member of the First Executive

41. A typical middle-class drawing room in St Andrews in 1889. Note the drapes, tassles, frills, aspidistra and general clutter that was such a feature of the late-Victorian house. Domestic servants made such clutter possible. *St Andrews University Photographic Collection.*

Council of the City of Edinburgh Charity Organisation, before becoming a member of Edinburgh Parish Council in 1898.[38]

Women's involvement in local government has been a forgotten and largely unexplored area, partly because it has been eclipsed by the campaign to obtain the parliamentary franchise. The 1868 Reform Act gave women ratepayers the local vote, which enabled them to vote in elections to the school boards, town councils, poor law boards and, from 1888, to the county councils. Married women who were disenfranchised could still stand for school boards, poor law boards and, from 1894, for parish councils. Most of the women who were active in local government were single, middle class, wealthy, Liberal and committed to improving women's social and political position. They used their positions in local government to advance causes espoused by the Women's Movement. For example, Flora Stevenson, who was elected to the newly formed Edinburgh School Board in 1873, and became the first woman to chair a school board, campaigned vigorously to introduce cookery lessons into board schools. After her death, her contribution to public life was paid tribute by Sir John Gillard who wrote:

> At a time when public ladies were sneered at as masculine, it required no little courage on the part of Miss Stevenson to break down the walls of prejudice which encircled the causes of women's emancipation. Thanks to ladies of this type no more is heard of the unfitness of women for public life.[39]

Women's philanthropic work did not seek to challenge the notion of separate sexual spheres or contemporary conceptions of women's moral nature. However, it did provide them with the opportunity to carve out a public space, and to push back the boundaries of their lives, as well as providing a training in organisational and administrative skills.

Education

Not all women in the higher social strata were satisfied with operating within their socially defined spheres, as seen in campaigns for access to higher education and the suffrage crusade. From the second half of the nineteenth century there developed a Women's Movement which sought to penetrate male preserves from which women had long been excluded. In the words of Lady Frances Balfour: 'In the Women's Movement there were always three great fights going on. First Education, then Medicine, then the Suffrage for Women'.[40]

The campaign to promote higher education for women was conducted chiefly by the various Ladies' Educational Associations which had been formed in the major cities of Scotland from the 1860s. The first LEA was established in Edinburgh in 1868 by women from the Edinburgh Essay Society, a small élite ladies' society.[41] In Glasgow an association was not formed until 1877, and in the same year an Aberdeen LEA was formed. The membership of these associations included substantial numbers of men, who tended to be university lecturers and professors, school-teachers, or 'in the church'.[42] Largely as a result of the campaigns and propaganda of these organisations as well as through individual pioneers, the Scottish universities opened their doors to women in 1892, fifteen years after the University of London, but many years before Oxford and Cambridge. The Universities (Scotland) Act 1889 and its subsequent Ordinance, No. 18, admitted women to instruction and graduation, either in separate classes or alongside men, and in 1893 the first women graduates were capped at Edinburgh University.[43]

42. Each to their allotted task: domestic servants pose at the front door of Major Playfair's house, St Leonards, St Andrews c.1855. *St Andrews University Photographic Collection.*

The campaign to admit women to medical faculties was more protracted and encountered considerable resistance. The most entrenched resistance came from within the medical profession, although it was more widespread than this. In 1870, in Edinburgh, there was a riot at Surgeon's Hall when male students attempted to prevent women from attending an anatomy lecture. Male doctors also opposed the admission of women to the Royal Infirmary, thus preventing them from receiving medical instruction. It was also likely that families would not be so supportive of daughters who wished to study medicine. As one of the leading campaigners for medical education for women noted, Victorian fathers were unlikely to be willing to make the large financial outlay necessary for a lengthy medical training for their daughters.[44]

Although the Universities (Scotland) Act 1889 allowed women to enter medical faculties, their position was by no means equal with male medical students. At Glasgow University the medical faculty denied women professorial teaching and equal facilities for clinical instruction, whilst at Edinburgh medical women were only allowed to become full members of the University in 1916.[45]

Politics

The campaign for votes for women is the most renowned of women's struggles in this period. The dominant image of the suffrage campaign is a montage of dramatic episodes and life-endangering exploits, consisting of women chained to railings, flinging themselves in front of racehorses, and being forcibly fed in prisons. Important as these episodes are to illustrate the courage and commitment of these women, they by no means capture the spirit or the essence of the movement.

The Scottish suffragettes did not embark on a campaign of sabotage or what the *Glasgow Herald* termed 'Scottish Outrages', until 1913, at the tail end of what had been a long and hard fought struggle.[46] Moreover, the Women's Social and Political Union, the militant wing of the suffragettes, which was responsible for most of the spectacular incidents in Scotland, such as the bombing of the Royal Observatory in Edinburgh, did not have a Scottish branch until 1906, and was only formed nationally in 1903. The movement to enfranchise women had a longer history and a more varied pedigree than the Women's Social and Political Union.

Women had been active in the chartist movement of the late 1830s and 1840s, often forming their own lodges. Their struggle, however, was dedicated to achieving universal adult *male* suffrage which they identified as being in their own interests. It was on this basis that Agnes Lennox of the Gorbals Female Universal Suffrage Association urged support for the chartism: 'Sisters! To obtain our rights, we must assist our fathers and brothers to carry the People's Charter'.[47] It is unclear whether the female chartists interpreted the extension of the vote to adult men as a stepping stone towards female suffrage, or whether they subsumed their rights with those of their menfolk. It was not until 1867, with the failure of the amendment to the Reform Bill, which would have given women the vote on the same basis as men, that women organised a vigorous campaign for female suffrage.

The first Scottish Women's Suffrage Society was formed in Edinburgh in 1867, and, unlike the female chartist lodges, the movement was overwhelmingly upper class and middle class, particularly in the early years. Until the turn of the century, the campaign for female suffrage was conducted assiduously, but unspectacularly. The main forms of propaganda were public meetings and petitions to parliament, over two million signatures being collected in Scotland between 1867 and 1876.

The campaign for the vote was part of a wider struggle of women's rights to education, to economic independence, and to work. It has become a truism, however, to say that the vote was not sought as an end in itself. It was argued by suffragists themselves that the vote was not simply about the acquisition of a 'natural right', but was a means to gaining legislative power in order to redress a battery of women's grievances, and to infuse the world of politics with women's civilising influence.

Far from challenging contemporary notions of the female nature, the majority of suffragettes were anxious to display their feminine traits, and to distance themselves from the few 'advanced' women who cut their hair short and adopted a masculine mode of dress. Suffragists were sensitive to charges of being harridans and harpies and took care over their appearance, particularly when appearing in public. Lady Frances Balfour remembered that Mrs Fawcett, a leading suffragist, defended one of their number who had been criticised for her public remarks by observing, 'besides, she looks so nice'.[48]

The notion of women's 'special nature' was shared by most of the different suffrage organisations and used as a means of justifying women's entry into the public sphere. In the early years of the twentieth century they capitalised on current political concerns about the health and welfare of the nation, which focused on the importance of motherhood in improving the quality and quantity of the nation, by arguing that women's expertise in this area justified their participation in the state. They also argued to extend their domestic roles into the public arena, and that women should be responsible for issues such as sanitation and housing which 'were in need of cleaning up which only women could accomplish'.[49]

The only working-class women's organisation formally affiliated to the suffrage movement was the Women's Co-operative Guild, which was the first and most persistent of the socialist and labour organisations to support the extension of the parliamentary franchise to women. As early as 1893 the Guild sent a petition to the government in favour of women's suffrage, and consistently passed resolutions on votes for women at annual conferences.[50] In common with the suffrage movement, the Scottish Co-operative Women's Guild argued that women's involvement in politics and wider social questions would introduce a 'purifying and elevating influence'.

Until 1912, the Labour Party adopted the adult suffrage position, that

43. For many young women shop work offered a 'respectable', but hard occupation. This is the millinery shop of Smith's department store in Stirling c.1890. *Smith Art Gallery, Stirling.*

is, they refused to support the extension of the franchise to women on the same basis as men, arguing that this would only give the vote to propertied women who were unlikely to be sympathetic to the aims of the labour movement. Perhaps for this reason the women of the labour movement were not to the forefront of the campaign for the vote. Nonetheless, there is evidence that working-class women supported the struggle. The Dundee Union of Jute and Flax Workers, which was predominantly female, passed several resolutions in support of women's suffrage, including a resolution condemning the imprisonment of suffragettes who had demonstrated in the House of Commons. The Committee of the Union discussed forging closer links with the WSPU, but opposition from the male members forced the question to lie on the table.[51] The women networkers of Kilbirnie, who were involved in one of the longest strikes of the pre-war years, were reported by the correspondent in *Forward*, the paper of the Independent Labour Party, to be 'Keen suffragists, and for the most part socialists too'.[52]

The movement for female suffrage was spearheaded by women of the upper and middle classes, but there appears to have been widespread support from working-class women who were not formally affiliated. Although the dominant image of the struggle for the vote is a campaign of dramatic exploits, its conduct was on the whole a more sedate affair, characterised by the more conventional political tactics of lobbying, petitions and public meetings.

The higher profile of middle-class women in the campaign for the national franchise, and in local government, did not mean that working-class women were politically dormant. Women had been involved in the political movements of the working class in the 1830s and 1840s, albeit in a supplementary role. When there was a revival in socialist politics in the late nineteenth century, women also played a part. The Independent Labour Party, which in Scotland was the dominant organisation of those forming the Labour Coalition, contained a substantial contingent of women. Indeed it was often these women who initiated the campaigns which were such a prominent feature of local politics in the pre-war and war years.[53] The Women's Labour League, which was effectively the women's section of the Labour Party, was dominated by women of the ILP, and consequently its political ideology was derived from this organisation. These organisations made concerted efforts to foster organisations of local democracy such as ward committees and tenants' defence associations, and emphasised the importance of grass roots involvement and local issues. It also cast the net of its educational activity to include women and children. The ILP stressed the importance of enlisting women to the socialist cause because of their role as moral guardians of children:

> When we win the men for the socialist cause, we do no more than that; when we get the women, we get at the same time all the men and women of the next generation.

Women were urged to take an interest in sanitary and education committees, in housing, the provision of school meals and a whole range of similar issues on the basis that:

> . . . though Woman's place is in the home, she cannot fulfill her duties there unless she looks beyond its four walls, and takes her part in public affairs which affect the home and children closely.

The women of the Co-operative Guild were equally active in political issues, and took an active interest in poor law legislation, municipal and school-board work, labour exchanges and sweated labour. In common with many middle-class feminists, socialist women tended to emphasise the particular contribution they could make to public life because of their role as wives and mothers and the innate qualities of womanhood. However, whereas many middle-class women challenged their exclusion from male spheres of employment, most socialist women sought to

44. Scottish women campaign for political rights at an Edinburgh suffragist demonstration in 1909. *People's Palace, Glasgow Museums.*

realise the ideal of separate sexual spheres by arguing that men should receive a wage which was adequate to support a non-working wife and children.

Conclusion

Women's experience was differentiated by class and region, amongst other factors, and there were many realities to their lives. It is impossible, therefore, to speak of a universal female experience or even a class specific experience of women in this or in any other period. This is not to deny that prevailing customs, ideologies and conventions defined their social role and hedged their lives with restrictions. The ideology of domesticity and the notion of a separate sphere for women clearly constrained their lives. However, women did not passively accept them. Many women endorsed the ideology but used it as a passport into public life; others sought to redefine and extend their roles; and for many women the material reality of their lives forced them to reinterpret the ideology, and in some cases to reject it. Women did not remain in their allotted sphere, and in traversing the divide between the public and the private, they constantly blurred the distinctions between them.

NOTES

I would like to thank the Leverhulme Trust for granting me an award to research this article, and Linda Mahood who read an earlier draft and gave generously of her time and her own research.

1. G. M. Ritchie, 'The Medical Topography of Neilston', *Glasgow Medical Journal* (1828), p. 26. I am grateful to Alan Steele for this reference.

2. *Accounts and Papers*, 1843, lvi, (27).

3. *Factory Inquiry Commission. First Report on the Employment of Children in Factories With Minutes of Evidence and Appendix.* pp. xx, 1833.

4. J. Butt, 'Labour and Industrial Relations in the Scottish Cotton Industry during the Industrial Revolution', in J. Butt and K. Ponting (eds.), *Scottish Textile History* (Aberdeen University Press, 1987).

5. T. M. Devine, 'Women Workers, 1850–1914', in T. M. Devine (ed.), *Farm Servants and Labour in Lowland Scotland* (John Donald, 1984), p. 102.

6. Dundee Social Union, *Report on Housing and Industrial Conditions and the Medical Inspection of School Children* (Dundee, 1905), p. 24.

7. *Royal Commission on the Poor Laws.* Williams and Jones Report. Appendix 0 (1) *PP* (cd 4690) 1909. p. 657.

8. J. Butt, 'The Changing Character of Urban Employment 1901–1981, in George Gordon (ed.), *Perspectives of the Scottish City* (Aberdeen University Press, 1985), p. 215.

9. *Royal Commission on Labour. The Employment of Women* cd 6894 Vol. xxlll, p. 192.

10. Sian Reynolds, *Britannica's Typesetters* (Edinburgh, 1989).

11. Quoted in T. M. Devine op. cit. p. 100.

12. I. F. Grant, *Highland Folk Ways (Routledge and Keegan Paul, 1961)* p. 168.

13. R. Gaffney, 'Women as Doctors and Nurses', in O. Checkland and M. Lamb (eds.), *Health Care as Social History: The Glasgow Case* (Aberdeen, 1982).; H. Corr, 'The Sexual Division of Labour in the Scottish Teaching Profession, 1872–1914' in W. H. Humes and H. M. Paterson (eds.), *Scottish Culture and Scottish Education 1800–1980* (Edinburgh, 1983).

14. Quoted in H. Corr, *op. cit.*, p. 142.

15. L. Mahood, *Prostitution in Scotland* (London) forthcoming.

16. R. Gaffney, 'Women as Doctors and Nurses', in O. Checkland and M. Lamb (eds.) *Health Care as Social History: The Glasgow Case* (Aberdeen, 1982), p. 137.

17. *Ibid.*, p. 135.

18. *Return of the Rates of Wages in the Minor Textile Trades of the United Kingdom.* PP 1890 cd 6161 p. viii.

19. T. M. Devine, *op. cit.* p. 119.

20. *Return of Wages, 1830–1886.* PP 1887 cd 1572 pp. 58, 310.

21. M. Irwin, 'Women's Work in Tailoring and Dressmaking' (Scottish Council for Women's Trades, 1909).

22. H. Corr, *op. cit.* p. 147.

23. *Royal Commission on the Poor Laws and Relief of Distress. Report on Scotland* Appendix vol. vi, Minutes of Evidence 1910 cd 4978 p. 392.

24. E. Gordon, 'The Scottish Trade Union Movement: Class and Gender, 1850–1914', *The Journal of the Scottish Labour History Society*, No. 23, 1988.

25. D. Kemmer, 'Victorian Values and the Fertility Decline: The case of Scotland', *Critical Social Research*, vol. 2, 1986, 1–30..

26. M. Flinn (ed.), *Scottish Population History* (Cambridge, 1977), p. 336.

27. D. Kemmer, *op. cit.*, pp. 13–15.

28. *Ibid., passim.*

29. L. Jamieson, 'Growing Up in Scotland in the 1900s', in Glasgow Women's study Group, *Uncharted Lives. Extracts from Scottish Women's Experiences, 1850–1982* (Glasgow, 1983), p. 27.

30. *Ibid.*, p. 30.

31. *Ibid.*, p. 31.

32. The discussion of illegitimacy is based on T. C. Smout, 'Aspects of Sexual Behaviour in Nineteenth Century Scotland' in Laslett, Oosterveen and Smith (eds.), *Bastardy and its Comparative History* (Edward Arnold, 1980), p. 199.

33. K. M. Boyd, *Scottish Church Attitudes to Sex, Marriage and the Family 1850–1914* (Edinburgh, 1980), p. 540.

34. K. Logue, *Popular Disturbances in Eighteenth Century Scotland*, (Edinburgh, 1979); E. King, *The Scottish Women's Suffrage Movement* (People's Palace Museum, Glasgow, 1978).

35. The following discussion of women and industrial militancy is drawn from E. Gordon *Women and the Labour Movement in Scotland, 1850–1914* (Oxford), forthcoming, Chapter 3.

36. L. Mahood, *op. cit.*

37. *Ibid.*

38. *Royal Commission on the Poor Laws and the Relief of Distress.* Appendix vol. vi, Minutes of Evidence, 1910, cd 4978 p. 689. I am grateful to Anne Crowther for drawing my attention to this reference.

39. H. Corr 'The Schoolgirl's Curriculum and the Ideology of the Home, 1870–1914', in *Uncharted Lives*, p. 78.

40. Lady Francis Balfour, *Ne Obliviscaris*, Volume II (1930) p. 120.

41. S. Hamilton, 'The First Generation of University Women 1869–1930', in G. Donaldson (ed.) *Four Centuries: Edinburgh University Life, 1583–1983* (Edinburgh, 1983).

42. L. R. Moore, 'The Aberdeen Ladies Educational Association, 1877–1883', *Northern Scotland*, 3, 1977–1986, p. 127.

43. S. Hamilton, *op. cit.*, p. 103.

44. W. Alexander, *First Ladies of Medicine* (Wellcome Unit for the History of Medicine, 1987).

45. W. Alexander, *op. cit.*, p. 27; S. Hamilton, *op. cit.*, p. 103.

46. King, *The Scottish Women's Suffrage Movement.*

47. *Ibid.*, p. 9.

48. Lady Francis Balfour, *Ne Obliviscaris*, vol. II.

49. Quoted in L. Moore, 'Feminists and Femininity: A Case Study of the WSPU Propaganda and Local Response at a Scottish By-election', *Women's Studies International Forum*, Vol. 15, No. 6, 1982, p. 678.

50. Scottish Co-operative Women's Guild, Annual Reports, *passim*.

51. Dundee Union of Jute and Flax Workers, Executive Committee Minutes, 25 June 1907.

52. *Forward*, 14 June 1914.

53. The following discussion is based on E. Gordon, *op. cit.*, Chapter 7.

CHAPTER 8

Developments in Leisure

W. Hamish Fraser

That there is no chapter on leisure in the first volume of this History does not mean that people in the eighteenth century did not seek recreation and entertainment at times when they were not working. There was rarely a leisure time that was distinct from the world of work, but leisure was nonetheless important. If even a fraction of the denunciations of 'idleness' are to be believed, opportunities for taking casual time off, either to recover from excesses or to share in family life were seized with alacrity by those who were operating at above mere subsistence level.[1] The well-to-do in town and country devised numerous ways of filling their idle hours with field sports, dancing or convivial gatherings. Indeed, in the eighteenth century Sidney Smith's land of 'Calvin, oat-cakes and sulphur' seems to have been a place where opportunities for recreational activity were on the increase. Public gatherings in the Assembly Rooms were the fashion in polite Edinburgh society from the 1730s and were soon followed in other towns which had the pretensions of a growing bourgeoisie. Men's clubs proliferated and public entertainments became socially acceptable. Edinburgh's first playhouse opened in 1764, though the first Glasgow one in the same year failed to survive the depredations of the mob. Even in Aberdeen 'playhouse amusements' were becoming 'so fashionable, so common, and so much patronised and countenanced by all ranks that few can believe they are in any degree sinful'.[2] In the 1770s dancing became all the rage. Race meetings were spreading. Dumfries, Edinburgh, Kelso, Hamilton, Lamberton, Ayr all had regular meetings by the 1790s.[3]

It is doubtful if there was in the period covered by the first volume that loss of leisure time that has been identified as part of the experience of England. The puritan victory of the Scottish Reformation and the reaffirmation of Calvinist values at various times in the seventeenth century had ensured that many of the holy days had disappeared long before 1760 (though a proliferation of penitential fast days replaced them) and there had been a relentless assault on the 'impiety and profaneness that aboundeth'.[4] It was not entirely successful: popular tendencies towards idleness and sabbath-breaking persisted. Despite denunciation and even legislation, weddings and funerals could still degenerate into days of merry-making and drinking. Dancing to the fiddle or the bagpipe required little excuse, and left Scotland with a legacy of rollicking traditional dances.[5] Fairs and feeing markets were opportunities for the young in particular to enjoy themselves. Even at holy, preaching fairs 'some were fu' o' love divine and some were fu' o' brandy'. Remnants of the traditional holiday calendar clung on. Christmas had been swept away as a popish folly, but much of the bacchanalia had been transferred to Hogmanay and the New Year. After 1752 and the reform of the calendar this, in many places, was moved forward to eleven days later and to what was known as 'Auld Handsel Monday', when gifts and treats were provided and revelry ruled.[6]

As moderation gained ground within the church in the eighteenth century, there was a conscious rejection of the strait-jackets of puritanism. Indeed, Adam Smith suggested that 'public diversions', accomplished 'without scandal or indecency' would provide a useful check on the fanaticism and 'popular frenzies' stirred up by popular religious sects.

Alongside the spread of diversions, however, there was pressure on workers for a more disciplined approach and for the drawing of a clearer distinction between work time and leisure time. The organisation of the market by manufacturers and their agents imposed new regulation on the lives of hand-loom weavers and other outworkers. They disliked the laxity of the putting-out system, in which a rise in demand for labour could result in higher wages, but those in turn could result in less, not more output, as workers opted for more leisure. Master craftsmen worked to eradicate traditional idle time during the day when workers had been free to leave the workshop. Changes in workshop patterns, not to mention the noise of new machinery and larger workforces, left little opportunity for the persistence of older practices such as the reading aloud of newspapers, pamphlets or poems.[7] The new factory owners, with a large investment in expensive machinery, needed regular, uninterrupted work and a continuous supervision of employees and control over the proportions of their work and leisure time.

Outside the workplace there was also pressure on popular recreational pursuits. Well-to-do property owners objected to the rowdyism of unregulated street games. Crowds of people gathering for any purpose were seen as something threatening to public order, to property and to commerce. In 1814 a ranger was appointed to keep ball games off

Glasgow Green and to disperse gatherings of noisy young people. New city police forces saw it as part of their duty to bring orderliness to the streets. Even the right to use Glasgow Green for more organised popular sporting events had been temporarily abolished by 1820.[8] On the other hand, Neil Tranter's work on the First and Second Statistical Accounts suggests that, while the popularity of certain sports and pastimes might have faded between 1790 and 1840, there is little evidence of an overall reduction in sporting activities. The amount of recreational activity in any locality tended to depend on the economic health of the place.[9] It was difficult to keep going any clubs or sporting gatherings when times were difficult, but a variety of games continued to be played.

It is doubtful if the older society was either so relaxed and unregulated as E. P. Thompson suggests for England, or the newer society so disciplined, ordered and regulated as either employers wanted or some historians have suggested. It is also questionable whether exhortation or punitive measures could fundamentally alter attitudes to work or to leisure.

I

The popular pastimes of the early nineteenth century were rumbustious ones. Games had a wild disorder and a tendency to violence. The Border towns had their communal "ba games' between different parts of the town, such as the 'croonies and the doonies', where there was little distinction between players and spectators. Looking back to the 1820s, 'An Old Dundonian' recalled that there was no cricket or football being played. Competitive sports were running races, leaping burns and mock battles of 'Englishmen and Scots'. Cock-fighting, despite pretty general disapproval, was held openly in public halls or in the back courts of public houses; bare-fist fighting was held in open spaces remote from police surveillance. Games that allowed for a display of individual prowess and for gambling were particularly popular. Putting the stone, throwing the hammer and wrestling were the most common in rural areas; quoits retained a persistent fascination in industrial parts, with a spread of quoiting clubs in the 1830s and the accompanying inter-county and international contests between skilled practitioners. Feeing fairs persisted in many towns and villages and attracted town as well as country support, providing opportunities for a variety of competitions. They also could readily turn into 'fechtin fairs' ending in battles between town workers and the ploughmen and horsemen.[10]

That boisterousness continued well into the century to growing criticism from the middle classes and from the more sophisticated urban

45. Quoits, skittles and their variations had a long history in many industrial areas. This game of 'kyles' c.1890 was at a Hamilton weaving factory. The formality of the occasion, the smart dress, the capped umpire and the cup indicates a championship match. *Hamilton District Libraries and Museums.*

dwellers who saw such scenes as evidence of an unwelcome rusticity. The *Falkirk Herald* of 1849 lamented the orgies of the half-yearly feeing market at which it was clear that

> . . . the great and primary business of the day is to get drunk as soon as possible, that there are penny reels in the 'Foley' and its minor satellites, that there are pickpockets from Glasgow and Edinburgh — gingerbread vendors and hucksters, 'sweety' stands from everywhere, wheels of fortune and roundabouts from ditto, penny shows, 'bawbee' peeps, weighing machines, nut-archery, sales of rotten haberdashery, lotteries all prizes no blanks, the unchanged blackguard Pirie and his thimble-rigging gang, and all means and appliances that are found by experience profitable in picking the pockets of simple and intoxicated rustics.

Nonetheless, all such activities proved to be remarkably obdurate, and old brutalities never entirely disappeared. Glasgow got a new cockpit in 1835 with room to accommodate 280 spectators and organised cock-fights were reported in Hawick and in Pollokshaws in the 1860s. A bare-fist fight was recorded in Glasgow in 1889.[12]

Drink was central to much leisure activity, and the public house the focus of much working-class life. It was of significance not just for recreation, and often it acted as a centre for business. In all accounts of eighteenth-century Edinburgh the tavern features as business premises for lawyers and as a literary forum for intellectuals. Hume, Raeburn, Ferguson and other luminaries of late eighteenth-century Edinburgh supped their Younger's ale in Johnnie Dowie's tavern and made their business deals there. The 'Saracen's Head', established in 1755 in Glasgow, performed a similar role. That business role was one that continued through to the 1840s, though becoming less and less respectable. This is not to say that business did not continue to be conducted in pubs long after that date, but it was increasingly the world of illicit business, the betting man, the seller of things that had mysteriously fallen off the back of a cart, the money-lender. For the working man it was a place for getting work. Tramping journeymen could make contact there with their trade society. Employers and those seeking employment could come together. While that became less important for artisans it remained vital for many casual workers. Treating of foremen by dockworkers was a means of buying favour at the dockgates in the daily scramble for work. Into the present century it was common for dock foremen to have links with particular bars where labourers, employed by the hour, could get credit to allow them to hang around until the foremen called them. The paying of wages in pubs continued until the truck legislation of the 1870s. They were a meeting place for associations of various kinds, for early trade unions and friendly societies. Public houses were a focal point of the world of work and non-work.

However, most Scottish pubs in the 1830s were little more than rooms in private houses, and left little space for anything other than drinking. And it was drinking on a grand scale and the purpose of much of it was to get drunk. It was a pattern learned from the gentry. The Edinburgh literati, pouring ale and claret down their throats in astonishing quantities, ended in oblivion under the table. By the late eighteenth century whisky was replacing (or perhaps one should say complementing) stout and porter as the drink of the masses. The combination was lethal and the Scots had discovered a cheap, fast, effective way of getting drunk. No doubt it tasted all the better in the knowledge that it most probably had been smuggled: 'Freedom and whisky gang thegither'. There was also a particular appeal in whisky because of the indifferent quality of Scottish beer. It had long been very poor — 'adulterated, flatulent, stupefying, unwholesome stuff'. Whisky was less easily adulterated and only improved with keeping.[13]

Largely focused on drink, signs of a revival of evangelical fervour against popular patterns of recreation were apparent by the 1830s. Thomas Chalmers and his associates sought to restore, if not the rule, then at least the supervision, of the godly to the wynds of rapidly growing cities. That reformation of morals and manners that had increasingly gained influence among the English middle class was making itself felt in Scotland. The 1820s brought a clampdown on illicit distilling, by a combination of reducing the duty and extending the use of excisemen. In 1828 the Home Drummond Act brought the first licensing of Scottish public houses. A publican now required a certificate from a local licensing authority, and the bar had to close during the hours of divine service.

In 1829, under the influence of New England ideas, John Dunlop of Greenock launched an anti-spirits movement, and it spread, helped by powerful missionary activity by Scots, south of the Border. The new temperance movement, with a total abstinence element coming to the fore in the late 1830s, attracted support from many of the evangelical middle class.

It was all apparently to little avail. By the 1840s Edinburgh's 555 licensed houses were roughly one per 30 families; Glasgow had about the same proportion with 2,300 pubs within the boundary of the parliamentary constituency: one for every 150 inhabitants; Dundee had one pub to every 24 families. There was not that distinction that one had in England after 1830, between beer houses, licensed to sell only beer, and spirit shops: all Scottish public houses were licensed to sell beer *and* spirits. Nor was there a difference between off-licences and on-licences. Grocers' shops could sell drink on the premises and, reputedly, this was the favourite spot for women to have their tipple.

Per capita consumption probably reached its peak in the twenty years after 1830. Nevertheless, there are signs that middle-class drinking was becoming more restrained. It was no longer a breach of hospitality to let one's guests leave the dinner table in a sober state. Wine regained some of its popularity over whisky among the better off. It was not, however, until after 1850 that temperance was really 'respectable' among the Scottish middle class. The onslaught on working-class drinking continued with increased intensity. Licensing authorities, coming under the control of evangelical temperance reformers, tried every means of restraining it. The police played an ever more vigilant role. Legislation, in the shape of the 1853 Forbes Mackenzie Act, brought Sunday closing of pubs, though not of hotels. Again, however, the effect was limited. Consumption fell after 1850, but perhaps largely because more alternatives were available. Gradually, drinking to excess did become less acceptable

46. 'Pitch and toss'. An Edinburgh street scene photographed by A. D. Knoblauch in 1909. *Scottish National Portrait Gallery.*

and the respectable working classes began to distance themselves from the pub.

On the other hand, there was a tolerance of drunkenness in Scotland to a much greater extent than in England. Sympathy, pity and jocularity towards it were much more common than moral disapprobation. Scottish laws on drunkenness were less severe than those of England throughout the nineteenth century. Perhaps, as one English visitor suggested, 'the poets of Scotland have thrown round the drinking habits of their country the witching glamour of their genius'. Excessive drink consumption was closely associated with concepts of manliness. *Rites de passage* at work were all associated with drinking, and there was always something desperately competitive about Scottish drinking: getting drunk, but still standing was the sign of the 'real man'. The attraction of whisky rather than beer was part of that same psyche: the alcoholic strength of beer was always underestimated, while that of whisky was always exaggerated. Scottish pubs, certainly in the second half of the nineteenth century, were almost exclusively male domains, probably more so than in England. One drank with one's workmates near the workplace, not with family and neighbours near one's home.

According to Alexander MacDonald, the miners' leader, no Scottish trade union held a meeting in a public house in the 1850s. On the other hand, for many people the pub retained its central position. Publicans rose to the challenge of temperance by making their premises more beguiling. By the 1850s and 1860s there were bright, flashy, gilded 'gin palaces' intended to lure in the passing trade from the street. They were less places for sitting and eating than standing places with counter service. It reflected the changing, growing city, a 'city of strangers', who needed something less communal, who needed a place where the lone drinker was not ill at ease and where 'perpendicular drinking' was the norm. There was also a courting of the young with singing pubs and 'free and easies', which Elspeth King has recently documented.[14]

Ironically, reformer pressure encouraged unfortunate developments. The closure of pubs facilitated the spread of illegal 'shebeens', for after-hours drinking. Sunday closure brought the round of the bona fide traveller, moving from hotel to hotel. Glasgow drinkers developed a standard Sunday route — to Yoker, by ferry to Renfrew and back into town by way of Govan — a round trip that could take in as much drinking as anyone could require. Reformers did not like public houses with lots of little rooms. There was a persistent belief that all kinds of nefarious activities went on in them. They needed to be brought into the open and to be supervised. Licensing magistrates often suggested structural changes to make bars more open. In fact they may have had the effect of encouraging more drinking. It also contributed to the development of single-class drinking. Sub-division, which seems to have persisted in England, meant that different rooms were occupied by different social groups. In Scotland the middle class, the skilled working class and women moved out and the pub world was left to the less 'respectable' male working class. Indeed, women, who had a place in the early eating and drinking houses in private houses, were increasingly excluded both as drinkers and as barmaids. And once again, the effect was precisely the opposite of what the reformers intended. Aggression and drunkenness became worse, and the cultural linking that associated heavy drinking with manliness was intensified.[15]

II

To an extent, the middle class retreated to the privacy of their homes. Reading was catered for with a growing number of family-centred journals, like *Good Words*, *Chambers's Journal* and the *Sunday Magazine*. There was a fear of unregulated social contacts. What extra-mural activities there were were generally associated with the churches. However, from the 1830s and 1840s among the bourgeoisie there appeared a much more systematic pursuit of leisure, as something quite separate from home and work. Once frowned upon as signs of the innate idleness of the labouring classes or of dissipation among the aristocracy, recreational activities began to attract middle-class attention as a rational, moral way of filling increased leisure time.

Positive pursuit of recreation was a way of keeping the young from boredom and from the dangers of being led into vices by unregulated mingling with other social classes. Educationists and moralists were concerned about young women as well as young men who had 'an abundance of time and nothing to occupy it; plenty of money and little use for it; pleasure without end, but not one definite object of interest and employment'.[16] But it also fitted a religious perception that idleness was sinful, and free time should be used positively and systematically. There was an increasing search for a focus for systematic recreation.

The garden was one possible focus. By the 1840s there were many horticultural societies across the country with annual shows, at first among the professional gardeners of estate owners, but gradually extending to the amateur. Flower and vegetable shows were among the most ubiquitous and persistent of public gatherings. Among games, bowling acquired an early popularity as towns grew. As the number of players multiplied there was pressure for order, regulation and uniformity. In 1848, representatives of 200 bowling clubs met in Glasgow and agreed to systematise the rules. William Mitchell, a Glasgow solicitor who produced the regulations, emphasised the contribution that bowling made to the development of fellowship, and this was to be a recurring theme in much of the early organised recreational activities.[17] In a world of increasing individualism, fellowship and conviviality within a safe, regulated network were important. The early choirs and music societies offered a similar fellowship, made easier from the late 1850s with the spread of tonic sol-fa, and, thanks to technological developments, by dramatic reductions in the price of printed music. Glasgow had a musical association that grew from a group of male glee singers. It gave the first Scottish performance of *The Messiah* in 1843, and the Glasgow Choral Union held its first music festival in 1860. Choral singing had the added attraction of being mixed company: 49 members of the first 176 members of the Choral Union were women. The pieces sung were always morally uplifting ones like *The Messiah* or *Elijah*, though Scottish resistance to church singing beyond unaccompanied psalms may well have hindered the spread of choirs. However, the popularity of music-making did increase in the late Victorian period. Its great strength was that it could be linked to good causes, whether temperance, patriotism, socialism or

Christianity. Amateur dramatic societies had a similar appeal: the one in Falkirk, established in 1852, 'having for its object the improvement of its members in reading and speaking the English language', but popular plays, like dramatisations of Scott's *Heart of Midlothian*, had a clear moral message.[18]

There was also a growing sense of the importance of physical activity, which brought the revival and regulating of some old sports as well as the finding of new ones. Curling had long been popular in the winter months, and continued to be so, gradually moving from a predominantly gentry-dominated sport to a middle-class one. Cricket made its appearance in the 1820s, one of the attractions being that it already had a written code of rules which anyone could learn. There was a Glasgow University Club by the early 1830s. The first Scottish championship between the Perth Cricket Club (probably the oldest) and Glasgow Cricket Club was held in 1834. Rowing became popular in the 1850s.[19]

Muscular Christianity helped give a moral legitimacy to what would formerly have been regarded as frivolities. Improvement could come from games, as the *Glasgow Herald* informed its readers in 1869 on 'The Moral Uses of Croquet':

> For success in croquet the moral qualities demanded are command of temper in the widest use of the word, patience, courage and calmness under momentary defeat, due subordination of means to ends, a habit of sacrificing brilliancy to security: in other words, the repression of vanity and sanguine impulses, and the power of concentration.

Cricket too had been puffed for its moral worth, 'conducive at once to that exercise that strengthens the body, and that habit of prompt action which improves and quickens the mind'. Cricket was 'noble and manly'. Wishaw Cricket Club was formed in 1856 'to draw the young men away from the public houses and other evil devices'.[20] Influenced by Thomas Arnold's ideas from Rugby, middle-class schools began to introduce sports. In Scotland, Hely Hutchison Almond of Loretto was one of the most effective advocates of athleticism, and cricket and rugby began to appear in those places that looked to the English public schools as their model.[21] Indeed, one of the attractions of sports clubs was that, like public schools, they were single-sex — offering exercise, male conviviality and relative 'safeness'. In addition, many were linked to former-pupil clubs and had a significant social value.

The volunteer movement that appeared in the midst of the French invasion fears in 1859 had the attraction of offering a manly, vigorous activity for an obviously sound moral purpose. It proved to be

DUMFRIES & MAXWELLTOWN
Juvenile
TEE TOTAL SOCIETY
Instituted 26th June 1837.
This Honorary Medal awarded
TO THE
Best Speaker and Most
Efficient Member.

Pledge
*I do voluntarily promise
that I will abstain from*
Ale. Porter. Wine. Ardent Spirits
and all Intoxicating Liquors.
*& will not give nor offer them to others,
except as Medicines or in a Religious ordinance,
& that I will discourage all the causes
& practices of Intemperance.*

" Train up a child in the way
he should go and when he is old
he will not depart from it.

*Fac-simile of Medal awarded to Samuel Welsh as the best speaker
and most efficient member.*

47. The temperance movement not only provided moral guidance, but was a focus of leisure activities and self improvement for all ages.

exceptionally popular in Scotland with more than 5 per cent of the male population between 15 and 49 enrolled in it, compared with 2.5 per cent in England and Wales. It was particularly strong in Highland counties, suggesting that a deeply-rooted military tradition and the presence of a high proportion of ex-regular army people might be the explanation. Most of the early corps were solidly middle class and organised on the basis of professional groupings. So Edinburgh had its separate bodies of Advocates, Writers to the Signet, solicitors, accountants, bankers, merchants, university staff and civil servants, while Glasgow had procurators, accountants, bankers and journalists. It had all the requisite requirements for moral recreation, and as such 'received the encouragement of the leading people', as the Lanarkshire adjutant remembered:

> First, because of the fact that healthful employment was found for the young men during their leisure hours; second it was smartening up those who previously had slouched in their gait; and, lastly, by becoming Volunteers they were not only improving and preserving their health, but becoming more valuable members of society.[22]

48. Community, work culture, religion and leisure were tightly bound together for most working-class people. The West Calder picnic, 1912. *Scottish Ethnographical Archive, National Museums of Scotland.*

As with the sports clubs, membership of the volunteers was not just about physical exertion. It was about social duty, social status and social contacts. It was about creating fellowship in a world of privacy and individualism. It was about creating an atmosphere of sociability. The annual dinner was a central part of most clubs' year where men — almost exclusively — sat down together to eat, drink and celebrate conviviality. The Volunteers brought together different social classes in devotion to a single cause, though with uniforms having to be paid for by the volunteer himself, the poor were effectively excluded.

In addition to physical improvement and fellowship, a further justi-fication for recreation was intellectual improvement. From the 1830s and 1840s there was a burgeoning of philosophical societies, statistical societies, mutual improvement societies and scientific societies, reflecting the tremendous sense of the possibilities of change and 'improvement' that was so apparent in the 1830s after the passage of the Reform Act. But they were also seen by some as a useful antidote to the political agitation and divisive tension of the early 1830s. Dalkeith Scientific Association, formed in 1835, helped 'remove nearly all the bitterness which politics had engendered [and] . . . tended to soften the asperities of party'.[23] The ideal in some ways was the Ramblers around Glasgow Club, formed in 1869. It was about exercise and education, with two or three hundred people taking part in the Saturday afternoon outings to explore the flora or the history of an area. But there was also the annual dinner to which none would be invited but 'good fellows'.[24]

Provision for rational leisure also came with libraries, museums and art galleries, generally financed by wealthy benefactors. Such places began to be the necessary symbol of a well-ordered city, and civic pride forced competitive emulation. Dundee got its public library in 1869 with the Albert Institute; its museum and art gallery in 1872. The Glasgow museum opened in the old country house at Kelvingrove in 1870, but within a couple of years there was a call for something better, something 'really worthy of the city'. Since it was aimed at the middle class, a city-centre site was rejected for one near the expanding wealthy suburbs. Paisley had its museum, courtesy of J. & P. Coats, in 1871; Aberdeen its Art Gallery in 1885. Public parks too were part of the new municipal enthusiasm for rational recreation. By 1878 Glasgow had three such parks maintained off the rates in addition to the Green. These were parks, not for promiscuous sport, which could lead to violence and disorder, and to the embarrassment of passing families, but laid out to ensure orderly walking past labelled flowers and shrubs. In rational leisure, disorder was to be avoided and no opportunity for improvement was to be missed.

III

Approaches to leisure among all classes were transformed by two developments: first the steamboat and then the railway train. By the 1820s there was a growing competition among steamboats on both the Firth of Clyde and the Firth of Forth. Fares began to fall rapidly. The *Glasgow Herald* advertised the delights of the 'solitary glens' of the Clyde made accessible by the steamboat. Holiday homes in Wemyss Bay, Rothesay, Gourock, Dunoon and Ardrossan ('becoming the most Fashionable Watering Place on the Coast') with easy access by 'Largs Steamboats', began to be advertised. By the 1840s, Fife trippers could cross to Granton or Newhaven for one penny, and the day of the excursion had arrived.

The rail network laid down in the 1840s extended these developments, and the day outing opened up new worlds. It forced decisions about summer holidays: fast days, before the twice-yearly communions, became trip days, and community business leaders began to get together to agree on holiday breaks. Dunfermline, for example, had its first general holiday in August 1850 and its first Monday holidays in April and October, to replace the now abandoned fast days, in 1885.[25] Initially,

49. The discovery of the countryside by rambling was increasingly popular by mid-century. These ramblers were at Haggs Castle near Glasgow in 1852. *Graham Collection, Mitchell Library, Glasgow.*

excursions were seen as ways of providing rational, educative, healthy recreation for the 'respectable' working class. It was an alternative to the temptations and disorderliness of traditional holiday fairs. Mechanics' Institutes, Temperance Societies, Friendly Societies were among the first to opt for pleasure trips as a 'rational' alternative. The purpose of an early steamer trip for workers of the Caledonian Pottery in Glasgow was made quite explicit — 'to draw the workmen from the riot and dissipation of the town, and to improve their health, and revive their pleasing associations'.[26] In very many cases, excursions were organised by firms for their workers. This had many attractions: it encouraged an identification with the firm; it allowed a display of paternalism and *noblesse oblige* by the employer: 'the excursionists returned in the evening grateful for the kindness of their working and respected employer'.[27] It ensured (in the early years, at any rate), an orderly, structured activity. Works' parties were frequently accompanied by bands that would not just entertain, but would provide the rhythm for a march in procession through the town to the park.

The railways gave opportunities for seaside holiday trips to an even larger number of people than the steamboats. New resorts developed as competing railway companies opened up small resorts. But it created tension as different classes and cultures competed for leisure space. Generally, the middle classes were able to keep a check on developments, and there was nothing in Scotland before the inter-war years comparable to Blackpool, aimed largely at the working class. By the 1870s there was growing dissatisfaction with the day excursion as too crowded and too rushed, and calls for the standardisation of works' holidays to bring odd days together into a single week. From the 1880s, the week-long, but generally unpaid, summer holiday was appearing and was pretty general in industrial towns by the end of the century.

IV

The desire to interest the working class in orderly, rational entertainment was not always fulfilled. There was, as Eileen Yeo has said, 'a formidable recalcitrance in Britain' and 'hard drink, hard sport and hard gambling' persisted.[28] The masses clung to more boisterous activities. Midsummer fairs retained their appeal. Each year at the fair 'moral and enlightened Greenock' was taken over by the 'idle, the drunken and the dissolute'. 'Industry is completely unhinged and dissipation reigns supreme'. While excursion trips could be splendidly orderly ways of regulating the working class at play, they could occasionally be the very opposite and end in riot and disorder.[29] Especially after the Forbes Mackenzie Act they were a godsend for the bona fide traveller. From the 1850s to the 1880s, the steamers were notorious as floating bars, and sabbatarians fought long, often violent, battles against Sunday trippers. There was more than one legal conflict between the rights of local authorities to ban steamers and the freedom of commerce to go when and where it wished. In 1884, the Court of Session ruled firmly against the Kirkcaldy Harbour Commission who, it declared, 'were not entrusted in any way with a superintendence over the spiritual condition of the town'. It was probably significant that many of the places having the highest ratio of licensed houses to people were not cities but Forth ports: in 1898 Anstruther had one pub to every 71 people, Queensferry one to 102, Pittenweem one to 115.[30]

Popular pressure could alter the most didactic of exercises. Thus, Abstainers' Union Saturday night concerts, intended to be morally uplifting and 'improving', began to provide more vigorous, bawdy fare. Inevitably entertainers played to the audience, and the risqué or the socially-barbed song or recitation got the laughs. Legitimate theatre had to face the competition of penny theatres, and working men's libraries and lectures gave way to billiards and beer.[31] However, there were undoubtedly moral and social pressures to which the 'respectable' succumbed, and new attitudes did emerge.

There were also new opportunities for leisure which stimulated demands from the working class. Real incomes rose from the mid-century and especially from the 1870s. Working days were shortened and there was a spread of the Saturday half-holiday, first to the skilled working class and then by the last decade of the century to many of the unskilled. The nature of the work itself was probably changing and becoming less intensive and less physically exhausting. Improvements in diet and in public health contributed to more physical energy. All these developments brought a transformation of popular culture of which leisure was a part. Age-old amusements, often casual, often associated with particular communities and regions, were displaced by national, organised activities and with what Stedman Jones has called the 'culture of consolation'.

There seems little doubt that some of the activities brought in were part of an exercise in social control, in the sense that many of the initiators of activities aimed at the working class had fears of unregulated popular pursuits. Social reform groups were at the forefront of providing alternative leisure activities. Temperance reformers like Michael Connal and William Collins in Glasgow in the 1840s were behind enterprises like the Spoutmouth Young Men's Institute and the Buchanan Institute, to provide sober alternatives to East End lads in Glasgow in the 1840s. William Smith, in a similar mould, formed the Boys Brigade in 1883, to cater for rowdy working-class lads at his North Woodside Mission. A number were coming to the view that entertainments and amusements were 'better fitted to make men sober and moral then teetotal pledges'.[32] On the other hand, it would be wrong to denigrate the genuine humane concern of many of the middle class to find ways of bringing relief to the drudgery that was the lot of so many.

Young idealists among the middle classes saw a need to encourage working men to participate in organised activities. This would be a way of bringing the classes together; it would help bring healthiness to an obviously unhealthy section of the population; it would introduce potential leaders of the working class to the habits of organisation and what was called self-government. The Volunteer Movement was ideal, with its officers, NCOs and other ranks, but there was a subversive tendency to laugh at the pomposity and apparent earnestness of the volunteers. Equally earnest young men, instilled by a sense of duty

50. The esplanade and beach at Saltcoats in Ayrshire, 1905. Trains and steamers carried Glasgow working-class day trippers to the Ayrshire coast. Unlike many of the English popular resorts by this time there are few signs of organised entertainments here, apart from the inevitable donkey ride. *St Andrews University Photographic Collection.*

in church and public school, sought to introduce young working-class men to organised games. They had some success: cricket, rugby football, bowling and rowing all gained in popularity among the skilled working class through the 1860s. Cricket particularly gained in popularity as a working-class sport through the 1860s and the early 1870s. Local newspapers gave extensive reports on matches involving clubs, schools, firms and church groups.[33] But the ideal of social mixing was less readily achieved. Those games that required special pitches necessitated some investment and high dues, thus excluding many. Social attitudes could not be excluded from recreation, and cricket and rugby both increasingly became élitist activities. By the 1880s there were suggestions that even skilled, respectable working men were finding themselves excluded from cricket teams, and in 1895 Stirling County Cricket Club was accused of 'selection policies based on social status not merit'.

Soccer was less of a problem. It could be played almost anywhere, and the quality of the playing surface was not too important. It was soccer, therefore, which more than any other became the working-class game. By 1873 'the beautiful dribbling game was beginning to be appreciated in Glasgow', though the number of clubs was still small compared with those playing Rugby style. The Queen's Park Club had been formed in 1867 by young businessmen, and it affiliated to the English FA, which had recently standardised the rules. The first international against English players was held in 1872. By 1873 there were enough clubs to form a Scottish Football Association and to play for a Scottish Cup. Football was a game that seemed to capture the imagination of the industrial working class. Initially the appeal was in playing. Games were very easy to organise and required no special equipment, though uniforms were popular and most of the early clubs raised money, often by door-to-door collections in their locality, to buy distinctive colours and caps. It soon also became a popular spectator sport. The rules were simple and anyone could become an 'expert'. By the 1880s it had a massive popular following in the west of Scotland, particularly in the heavily industrialised Vale of Leven area. With astonishing speed, what had once been confined to a few public schools now became the enthusiasm of the masses, and Neil Tranter has calculated that, at its peak, one in four of all males aged between 15 and 29 in Central Scotland belonged to a soccer club.

The football season lengthened at the expense of cricket, and there were complaints that the niceties of cricket were no longer appreciated by the Scots.[34] Once permanent pitches were obtained then there was a pressure to enclose them and to charge entry fees. The money earned was used to improve the grounds, but these in turn necessitated more regular gate income. As the competitiveness of the game increased both on the field and for spectators, appearance money and illicit fees began to be paid. As a way of making money, the grounds began to be used for other sporting facilities. So both Clyde and Rangers Football Clubs had cycle tracks in the 1880s; professional race meetings were popular. As a result, the football clubs got caught up in the professional *versus* amateur struggles of other sports. The focus of the bitterest of these struggles was athletics. Starting among university and public school people in the 1860s, athletics gradually attracted wider support in both participation and spectating. As soon as this happened there was a tendency to ginger up the sport with betting and with the awarding of cash prizes. There was nothing new in this. Games had almost always been played for wagers, with the participants getting their share. But, in the righteous atmosphere of the late Victorian period, it attracted disapproval as further evidence of

51. By the end of the century organised sport of all kinds was important. Dress for the occasion had not yet been formalised by the time of this walking race. *Wilson Collection, Dundee District Libraries.*

the fecklesness of the poor, as destructive of thrift, as corrupting and as the negation of that moral and social purpose in which the first earnest promoters of popular activity were interested. In almost all sports there began to develop a struggle between amateurism and professionalism.

Some sports lent themselves more readily than others to professionalism. Pedestrianism, as foot racing was known, had been very popular early in the century. It had always attracted cash prizes and betting, and because of this had always been considered slightly disreputable. Nonetheless, running for prize money was a highly popular spectator sport, a part of most of the Highland Games which began to proliferate from the 1830s and 1840s onwards. The first New Year handicap at the recently opened Powderhall ground in Edinburgh in 1870 attracted 25,000 people and remained one of the most popular venues; 20,000 attended the New Year meeting in 1913.[35]

The debate on professionalism was, on the surface, a conflict of different ideals: the gentleman sportsman in the game for physical and moral worth *versus* the paid and, therefore, dependent and, therefore, corruptible, and therefore, potentially corrupting professional player. But, it was also very firmly about class relationships and it is no coincidence that the issue came to the forefront of debate in the later 1880s and 1890s when class attitudes generally were hardening. The strongest upholders of the cult of amateurism were the products of middle-class private schools. Those children of the new rich were more concerned with asserting and defending their less than secure social status than with building bridges between social classes. They had no great desire to popularise their sports or to encourage plebeian spectators. Because of the distribution of such schools, it produced something of an East–West divide. So the Scottish Amateur Athletic Association split in 1895 essentially between the Edinburgh schools element and the Glasgow, football-club dominated element who were into entertainment for the masses. These sports that remained dominated by exclusive cliques, like cricket, rugby and rowing, failed to acquire a large popular following.[36]

The issue of professionalism began to focus also on football. Professionalism had spread first within the English Football League and was quite strongly resisted in Scotland. But, by the end of the 1870s, Scottish players of talent were heading south to England, where they could receive as much as five pounds for turning out for a match. By 1890 there were 300 Scottish players playing for English teams.[37] It was, therefore, an increasingly irresistible pressure, as audiences increased, to acquire players of quality, and these had to be paid for. In 1887 there were plans for a full-time professional team, which the *Scottish Athletic Journal* referred to as 'another sign of approaching crisis in Scottish football'. As clubs began to invest in new stadia the organisation of the sport was becoming more business-like, and this too added to the pressure for professionalism. The Celtic club was a major force in these moves, although the Parkhead ground was built largely by voluntary labour from the Catholic community. Amateur rules were circumvented by setting up some of the best players as public house licensees. Celtic FC was largely responsible for the establishment of a Scottish League in 1890, a necessary step in a programme of regular games if professionalism was to be a practical possibility. Although the Scottish Football Association resisted long and hard the pressure for professionalism, it had to succumb eventually in 1893 when professionalism was at last legalised in Scottish football.[38]

The sheer numbers attracted to football began to arouse middle-class concern; 20,000 watched the first Hampden international in 1878. When the new Hampden was opened in 1902, 102,000 attended. There were complaints of 'flagrant rowdyism' ('even at classic Hampden') and initial attempts to price 'the rougher sections of the masses' out of the crowds. Swearing seems to have been all-pervasive, and already Rangers Football Club, which moved from Kinning Park to Ibrox in 1887, was particularly notorious. Partisan slogans were making an appearance. When 300

Scotsmen descended on Blackburn for the twentieth international in 1891 'nearly all [were] wearing in their headgear expostulatory tickets with the sage advice "Play up, Scotland"'. Attacks on referees were not unknown. The sheer enthusiasm that it aroused, and the fact that what had been about exercise and manliness was now largely a spectator sport, all brought criticism, but there was no halting its popularity. It was in danger of overwhelming all other sports. Sports that had once had a wide popularity became marginalised.[39] A game like shinty disappeared, except in the Highlands; the once popular cricket plunged into obscurity. Reports on football squeezed out other sports from the popular press. It also became a solidly working-class game. The middle class dropped out as players and spectators as working-class support increased.[40]

Football was, by the 1890s, firmly identified as the British national game, and this in itself was new, contributing to the idea of a national community precisely at the time when much of what created a regional identity was being eroded. On the other hand, it also contributed to maintaining a pattern of local loyalties. Teams were attached to specific local communities, and attachment to the team was also about attachment to the community. One extreme example of it was the sectarian loyalties that emerged around Rangers and Celtic football clubs. No doubt the teams had symbolic importance for their partisans; on the other hand, there were sound commercial reasons why those who ran the clubs had no reason to discourage it.[40]

V

As demand for ways of filling something that was specifically identified as 'leisure' time grew, so did the commercialisation of leisure. What had formerly been run by ad hoc syndicates or voluntary associations began to be encroached on by business interests. Groups of local businessmen took an interest in the commercial possibilities of football from the late 1880s. Their motivation may not have been solely the desire for profits. Nevertheless, there were profits to be made. The Celtic club, founded by the Marist Brother Wilfred in 1887, was taken over by businessmen from the local Irish-Catholic community almost as soon as he left Glasgow, and it at once ceased to be a charitable concern. In 1898 the profits were more than £16,000.[42]

There was more commercial provision too for the middle classes. Tearooms, not to provide basics, but as a place where wives and daughters could pass time, began to appear. By the 1870s Italian Opera was available at the Theatre Royal in Glasgow's Hope Street

52. Lawn tennis coming in the 1880s remained firmly a middle-class sport, largely confined to select private clubs. Sir John Lavery's *The Tennis Party* was set in the Glasgow suburb of Cathcart in 1885. *Aberdeen Art Gallery and Museum.*

and even the 'frontier town' of Coatbridge had a Theatre Royal from 1875 offering 'masterly and artistic and genuine renderings of the most popular plays and legitimate drama'. For the working class the 'free and easy' and the amateur concert party, so popular in the mid-century, became transformed into the commercial music hall. The largest in Glasgow in the 1870s was Rossburgh's *Britannia*. H. E. Moss started at his father's hall in Greenock in the 1860s. He bought an Edinburgh Hall in 1875, and began to buy and build a network in central Scotland. In 1892, catching the mood of the times, he opened his first 'Empire' hall in Edinburgh, and soon linked up with English chains to create the dominating force in the Edwardian music hall — Moss Empires Ltd. New custom-built theatrical palaces of magnificent design proliferated in the years immediately before 1914, and although having their roots in the 'free and easies', the new music halls were radically different. Fixed rows of seats replaced the tables and chairs. They were intended to attract families, not just the young and single; to appeal to middle as well as working class; though, of course, safely socially divided. Drink was often not available, and the full-time professionals, bound by contract, rarely ventured beyond a bland smuttiness in their presentations; while the early halls and the concert parties had reflected local and regional popular cultural perceptions, the new halls permeated a national imagery. It was one that trivialised, distorted and sentimentalised Scotland's self-image in a particularly grotesque manner, with the emergence of 'Tartanry'.[43]

Even as the Halls were peaking in popularity, the germ of a new challenge was beginning to appear with the coming of moving pictures. Moss had a fairly disastrous first showing of the 'cinematographe' at the Edinburgh *Empire* in April 1896, but the new cinematography was taken up enthusiastically by showmen, many of whom had for long been offering magic lantern shows at fairs and in village halls. It was they who from 1896 began to introduce people in most Scottish towns and villages to the new entertainment, initially seen as a novelty to be added to the thrills of the fairground, or as an extra in a variety concert.

Gradually permanent premises were established, some of them primitive in the extreme, in converted shops and factories — often dangerous fire hazards. However, by the end of the first ·decade of the century it was clear that the 'pictures' were here to stay. Local authority safety regulations began to curb the 'penny gaffes'. Business interests saw opportunities to invest in the new industry. More and more purpose-built cinemas began to appear.[44]

VI

At the same time, as many aspects of recreational activity were becoming the focus of money-making business interests, community provision of recreational facilities was also expanding. City fathers became conscious of the need to regulate the growth of their cities, and facilities for recreation were an essential part of that process. As they increasingly saw it as part of their function to bring 'civilisation' to their citizens, so parks, swimming baths, art galleries and branch libraries began to spread. Increased encouragement was given to sport. After decades of trying to keep illicit games out of their parks, the Glasgow town council in the 1890s became a major provider of sporting facilities and a deliberate populariser of sport.[45]

Private local benefactors too were often an essential complement to municipal initiatives. Thus, Edinburgh had its fitting monuments to alcohol in the Usher Hall and the MacEwan Hall, Dundee its Caird Hall and Aberdeen its Cowdray Hall. Thanks to Andrew Carnegie, a deeply entrenched hostility to rate expenditure on public libraries was overcome, and libraries spread throughout Scotland between 1890 and 1914. The provision of open space proliferated. Carnegie gave £500,000 to Dunfermline for Civic improvement, and Pittencrieff Park was central to it, 'to bring into the monotonous lives of the toiling masses more "sweetness and light"'. Cameron Corbett gave Rouken Glen Park to Glasgow in 1906.[46]

Despite commercialisation, the desire for leisure to be linked to self-improvement remained a very strong one. The mantle of evangelicalism passed to secular socialists. The need for leisure to have a purpose, to be participatory, for it to be morally uplifting and perhaps most of all for it to be 'dry', was a persistent theme in the Scottish Labour press. The bicycle, especially once the 'safety' had arrived, fitted with Dunlop pneumatic tyres after 1888, and when prices had fallen sharply, was taken up with enthusiasm. Clarion cyclists could discover the countryside and small towns and combine propaganda work with bonhomie. The sentiments were little different from those of the mid-century. Non-socialists would not 'travel long with Socialists, and receive the Socialist fellowship, without becoming of the cause itself'. Also there was the added attraction that the cycling groups could be sexually mixed: cycling was an activity that became 'respectable' for women. Rambling too was reinvigorated by the new 'health culturalists', and the opportunity to confront private landowners and their gamekeepers on the issue of access to the hills was a challenging one.[47]

There were socialist choirs and glee clubs. Out of the Toynbee House Choir there grew the Glasgow Orpheus, under Hugh Roberton, in 1906. For the young there were Clarion Scouts and ILP Scouts. Socialist sunday schools organised socialist swimming clubs. For women there were the Co-operative Women's Guilds, with an annual Co-operative Festival at New Year, and summer galas and picnics. On Sunday evenings there were 'improving' lectures.[48] This was happening at a time when voluntary church-based activities were facing a crisis. It was proving difficult to find those middle-class patrons and activists who had maintained so many voluntary organisations through fifty years of the century. The working class was looking increasingly to secular organisations to provide their leisure.[49]

It is also often overlooked that a great deal of leisure was taken at home. It is true that single-ends and large families left little room for leisure activities at home, and no doubt drove many out to the public houses. Nonetheless neighbours joined in one another's homes to sing, to dance, to drink and to entertain themselves. For most women any relaxation *had* to be in the home and with the family. Annie S. Swan, herself the provider of many volumes of romantic escapism, recalls her mother disappearing to her room for a whole day, housework abandoned, to read *East Lynne*. As the recent work of William Donaldson has shown, there was a huge market among the Scots-speaking working class that was catered for by papers like *The People's Journal* and its supplement, *The People's Friend*. Donaldson calculates that something like 5,000

53. Bicycle racing quickly became a professional sport, often taking place in football grounds.

full-length Scottish novels were published in the popular press in the years between 1860 and 1900, much of it written by amateurs.[50]

Home music was also not confined to middle-class parlours. By the end of the century, cheap, imported pianos and harmoniums were available, perhaps as much for show as for playing, but, certainly in rural areas, the melodeon, the fiddle and the pipes were all available.[51]

VII

Leisure remained a morally and socially problematic area throughout the nineteenth century, perhaps for Scots even more than for their southern neighbours. There was a deeply entrenched view that the wasting of time was sinful, and that all recreational activities had to have a moral justification. Even the new cinema had to be pushed into this category. The Lord Provost of Glasgow, opening one in 1913, hoped that it would provide only 'healthful and legitimate amusement'. Moral disapproval of much that went on was never far away, whether it was of public houses or of Italian ice-cream parlours, of football crowds or Sunday excursions. There were constant efforts to regulate, to licence, to reform and even to eradicate activities which were perceived as a challenge to middle-class cultural hegemony. The sheer weight of moral disapprobation probably accounted for the violence of some of the alternatives, for there is little doubt that the Scots were bringing a vigour and violence to their recreation. Football crowds were larger and more prone to disorder than those in England. The audiences at the music halls struck terror into English entertainers as artistic judgment was displayed by way of pennies and rivets on the stage. And of course the desperation of alcoholic consumption was in proportion to the level of disapproval of it. The paradoxes of Scottish popular culture fed off one another. Recreational activities also reflected social divisions and the extent to which attempts at class collaboration in the mid-century had given way to deeply entrenched class hostility by the end is more than obvious in the patterns of leisure. The football supporters' club or the pigeon-fanciers' gathering was every bit as exclusive as the suburban tennis club or golf club. There were few activities that effectively bridged the social classes.

NOTES

Thanks are due to Gavin Grant for his assistance in gathering some of the material on which this chapter is based, and to Eric Simpson for drawing my attention to his own publications on recreational activities.

1. See C. A. Whatley 'The Experience of Work' in T. M. Devine and R. M. Mitchison (eds.), *People and Society in Scotland*, vol I, 1760–1830 (Edinburgh, 1988), p. 251.

2. T. C. Smout, *A History of the Scottish People 1560–1830* (1969), p. 238.

3. J. Fairfax-Blakeborough, *A History of Horse Racing in Scotland* (Whitby, 1973); G. S. Emmerson, *A Social History of Scottish Dance* (Montreal, 1972).

4. R. W. Malcolmson, *Popular Recreations in English Society 1700–1850* (Cambridge, 1973); Smout, *History* pp. 230–1.

5. Emmerson, *Scottish Dance*, p. 8.

6. E. J. Simpson, 'Auld Handsel Monday', *Scots Magazine* (June, 1979).

7. N. Murray, *The Scottish Handloom Weavers 1790–1850: A Social History* (Edinburgh, 1978), pp. 172–3; W. H. Fraser, *Conflict and Class: Scottish Workers 1700–1838* (Edinburgh, 1988), pp. 17–38.

8. P. Bilsborough, 'The Development of Sport in Glasgow 1850–1914', unpublished M Litt thesis, University of Stirling, 1983, p. 12.

9. N. L. Tranter, 'Popular Sport and the Industrial Revolution in Scotland: the Evidence of the Statistical Accounts', *International Journal of the History of Sport* 4 (1), May 1987.

10. *Dundee and Dundonians Seventy Years Ago: being Personal Reminiscences of an Old Dundonian* (Dundee, 1892) p. 144; W. Milne, *Reminiscences of an Old Boy* (Forfar, 1901); *Glasgow Herald* 7 June, 26 August, 4 October 1833 (prize fights).

11. *Falkirk Herald* 8 November 1849.

12. *Glasgow Herald* 9 May 1863; E. King, 'Popular Culture in Glasgow' in R. Cage (ed.), *The Working Class in Glasgow 1750–1914* (1987), p. 153.

13. On the Scottish pub the best sources are R. Kenna and A. Mooney, *People's Palaces: Victorian and Edwardian Pubs of Scotland* (1983); D. W. Paton, 'Drink and the Temperance Movement in Nineteenth Century Scotland', unpublished PhD thesis, University of Edinburgh, 1977.

14. King, 'Popular Culture', pp. 159–162; J. J. Dunsimore, *Reminiscences of Glasgow (by an Englishman)* (Glasgow, 1874).

15. The main sources of the preceding paragraphs are *PP* 1898 XXXVII *Report of Royal Commission on Licensing Laws; Glasgow 1858. Shadow's Midnight Scenes and Social Photographs* (reprinted, 1976); P. R. Duis, *The Saloon, Public Drinking in Chicago and Boston 1880–1920* (Urbana, Illinois, 1983). There is substantial pamphlet literature on drink in the Glasgow Pamphlets in the Mitchell Library, Glasgow.

16. *Chambers's Journal of Popular Literature* VII (1857), quoted in Mary S. Hartman, 'Murder for Respectability; the Case of Madeleine Smith', *Victorian Studies XVI* (June, 1973), p. 387. The fate of Madeleine Smith aroused particular concern among the Scottish bourgeoisie about what the young were doing.

17. A. H. Haynes, *The Story of Bowls* (n.d.), pp. 67–8.

18. R. Craig, *A Short History, Glasgow Choral Union 1843–1943* (Glasgow, 1944); *Falkirk Herald* 12 January 1860.

19. D. D. Bone, *Fifty Years Reminiscences of Scottish Cricket* (Glasgow, 1898), p. 17; *Glasgow Herald* 17 June 1833, 27 June 1853.

20. *Glasgow Herald*, 11 July 1831, 17, 21 June 1833; R. Duncan, *Wishaw: Life and Labour in a Lanarkshire Industrial Community 1790–1914* (Stirling, 1980) p. 145.

21. R. D. Anderson, 'Sport and the Scottish Universities 1860–1939', *International Journal of the History of Sport*, 4(2) (September, 1987), p. 178.

22. H. Cunningham, *The Volunteer Force. A Social and Political History* (1975) has many Scottish references.

23. A. Mitchell, *Political and Social Movements in Dalkeith from 1831 to 1882* (Dalkeith, 1882), p. 12.

24. Rules Card of 'Ramblers Around Glasgow' in William Young, Scrapbook, Vol 8, p. 80, Mitchell Library, Glasgow.

25. See *Scottish Athletic Journal*, 28 March 1884 for examples of fast-day excursions. E. Simpson, *The Auld Gray Toun* (Dunfermline), p. 102.

26. *Glasgow Herald* 8 February, 10 May, 14 June, 12 July, 19 August 1833; 24 June, 8 July 1844.

27. *Ibid.*, 1 August 1833, 16 June 1840; 8, 12 July 1844. For a discussion

of the role of such paternalistic activities see P. Joyce, *Work, Society and Politics* (1982).

28. E. and S. Yeo, *Popular Culture and Class Conflict 1890–1914* (Sussex, 1981).

29. *Glasgow Argus*, 10 July 1834; 14, 16, 21 July 1840; *Scotsman*, 26 July 1867 for a trip to Linlithgow that ended in a riot. A discussion on the significance of such disorder can be found in P. Bailey, 'Will the Real Bill Banks Please Stand Up?', *Journal of Social History*, 12 (1979).

30. E. J. Simpson in *Edinburgh Evening News*, 10 September 1981. In 1882 the ban on Sunday drinking was extended to steamers. PP 1898, XXXVII, *Royal Commission on Licensing Laws. Glasgow Herald* 26 June, 29 July, 9 September 1853 (for sabbatarian resistance).

31. R. Bremner, *The Saturday Evening Concerts, a Sin and Snare* (Glasgow, 1857; *Daily Record* 2 March 1903; *Airdrie and Coatbridge Advertiser* September 1863. See also Duncan, *Wishaw*, p. 151; *Autobiography of Mr James Houston, Scottish Comedian* (Glasgow, 1889).

32. C. Brown, *A Social History of Religion in Scotland* (1987), pp. 176–77; J. Springhall, *Sure and Steadfast* (London, 1983).

33. N. L. Tranter, 'The Social and Occupational Structure of Organised Sport in Central Scotland during the Nineteenth Century', *International Journal of the History of Sport*, 4(3) (1987), 310.

34. *Glasgow Herald* 18 March 1873; 2; 23 April 1883; *Scottish Sport*, 21 June 1889; K. McCarra, *Scottish Football: A Pictorial History from 1867 to the Present Day* (Edinburgh, 1984), pp. 7–18.

35. D. A. Jameson, *Powderhall and Pedestrianism: The History of a Famous Sports Enclosure 1870–1943* (Edinburgh, 1943); *Daily Record* 2 January 1903, 3 January 1913.

36. *Scottish Sport*, 24 March 1891 'Professionalism and Betting'.

37. *Scottish Athletic Journal*, 8 December 1882, 15 March 1887; T. Mason, *Association Football and English Society 1863–1915* (Sussex, 1980), p. 80; *Scottish Sport* 2 January 1891.

38. *Scottish Sport* 31 October, 21 November 1890; 5 May 1893.

39. *Scottish Athletic Journal* 12 September 1887; *Scottish Sport* 7 April 1891, 12 July 1892; Mason, *Association Football*, p. 150.

40. Mason, *Association Football*, p. 155.

41. W. Murray, *The Old Firm* (1984). Previously curling had been referred to as the *Scottish* national game.

42. Murray, *Old Firm*, p. 31; W. Vamplew, 'The Economics of a Sports Industry: Scottish Gate-Moray Football 1890–1914', *Economic History Review*, XXV (1982), 566.

43. W. H. Fraser, *The Coming of the Mass Market* (1981), pp. 217–19; J. Clarke and C. Critcher, *The Devil Makes Work. Leisure in Capitalist Society* (1985), p. 67; *Glasgow Herald* 5 April 1909, 'Music Hall and Morals'; W. Freer, *My Life and Memories* (Glasgow, 1929), p. 84.

44. This section is based on J. McBain, *Pictures Past — Scottish Cinemas Remembered* (Edinburgh, 1985).

45. P. Bilsborough, 'Development of Sport in Glasgow', p. 76; H. Mellor, *Leisure and the Changing City, 1870–1914* (1976).

46. *Daily Record* 28 May 1906.

47. *Glasgow Herald* 25 January 1910; *Forward* 4 June 1910; 29 April, 27 May, 19 August 1911; *Scottish Cyclist* 8 May 1895, 'Women in Knickerbockers'; 4 January 1905.

48. *Forward* 10 April 1909; *Daily Record* 2 January 1903: Report on Sixth Scottish Cooperative Festival; Duncan, *Wishaw*, pp. 149–150. The first branch of the Scottish Cooperative Women's Guild was formed in Kinning Park, Glasgow in 1892.

49. For a discussion of the crisis of voluntaryism see S. Yeo, *Religion and Voluntary Organisations in Crisis* (1976); Brown, *Social History of Religion*, Chapter 6.

50. Annie S. Swan, *My Life: An Autobiography* (1934) p. 22; W. Donaldson, *Popular Literature in Victorian Scotland* (Aberdeen, 1986).

51. K. Durland, *Among the Fife Miners* (1904), p. 124.

CHAPTER 9
Poverty, Health and Welfare

M.A. Crowther

Let us look to the closes of Edinburgh, and the wynds of Glasgow, and thoroughly understand the character and habits, the diseases and mortality, of the unemployed poor, unprotected by the law, who gather there from all parts of the country; let us study the *condition* of the aged and disabled poor in all the smaller towns in Scotland; let us listen to the tales of misery which come to us from the remote parts of the Highlands and Islands. . .let us compare these things with the provisions for the poor, not only in England, but in many other Christian countries; and so far from priding ourselves on the *smallness of the sums* which are applied to this purpose in Scotland. . .we must honestly and candidly confess, that our parsimony in this particular is equally injurious to the poor and discreditable to the rich in Scotland.[1]

Thus wrote William Pulteney Alison in 1840, in a widely-read attack on the Scottish Poor Law. As a medical professor in the University of Edinburgh, Alison was renowned for his generosity to the poor, but recognised 'the utter inadequacy of private benevolence'.[2] Alison's words expose the fundamental problems: low levels of relief payments; the plight of the unemployed; attitudes towards immigrants; the relationship between poverty and disease; the special difficulties of the Highlands; the shortcomings of charity; and, underlying all of these, the comparison between English and Scottish treatment of the poor. By 1914 these problems had changed in scale, but had not disappeared.

Alison himself took part in the great national investigation of social conditions in the early Victorian period. Towards the end of 1840, he visited part of central Glasgow between Argyle Street and the Clyde. Accompanying him were Edwin Chadwick and two other leading figures in the public health movement. The investigators were no strangers to life in the slums: the same combination of wretchedness, overcrowding, filth, semi-starvation and disease, could be found in all large centres of population. Nevertheless, they accorded Glasgow a special status, as Chadwick reported:

It might admit of dispute, but, on the whole, it appeared to us that both the structural arrangements and the condition of the population in Glasgow was the worst of any we had seen in any part of Great Britain.[3]

The back courts did not possess even the stinking open drains common in other cities; refuse and excrement piled up in a general midden until the private contractors thought it worth taking away. Other writings of the time reinforced this image:

> I did not believe, until I visited the wynds of Glasgow, that so large an amount of filth, crime, misery, and disease existed on one spot in any civilized country.[4]

It is hard to prove whether Scotland's urban poverty was, in fact, the worst in Britain. Information about incomes is both scanty and misleading, since wage data does not take into account the trade fluctuations and short-time working common in many nineteenth-century occupations. Wages in urban Scotland probably lagged behind England until the later years of the nineteenth century.[5] But Glasgow had a combination of problems which justified Chadwick's impression. It was a centre of the textile trade, in deep depression in the early 1840s; it had many poor Irish immigrants; and its housing stock never kept pace with demand. Even workers in regular employment were more overcrowded and poorly housed than in any other British city, and this persisted well into the twentieth century.

If Scotland had some of the worst slums in Britain, it also contained the worst rural poverty. Conditions in the Western Highlands and Islands were revealed during the potato famine of 1846, when the people were kept alive only by charity and government relief. The Highlanders, in their damp hovels of earth and stone, could barely scratch a living from their overpopulated crofts.

In the early 1840s the government could not ignore the problems of Scotland. Trade depression from 1841 to 1843 threw thousands of Paisley weavers out of work, with no clear entitlement to poor relief. This dangerous situation provoked the government into a remarkable response: it secretly raised private funds and organised their distribution.[6] Peel set up a Royal Commission on the Scottish Poor Law, and it reported in 1844; meanwhile, the disruption of the Church in 1843 threatened to wreck Poor Law finances, since the embattled kirk-sessions were responsible for them. Reform of the Scottish Poor Law, barely considered when the English law was reformed in 1834, could be avoided no longer. The Poor Law (Scotland) Act, passed in 1845, remained in force until 1948.

Unfavourable comparisons with England were the essence of Alison's criticisms of the old Poor Law. Unlike the English, the Scots were not obliged to levy a compulsory rate for the relief of the poor; but the kirk-sessions raised voluntary contributions, supplemented by legacies

54. The group photograph from a Poor House in Ross-shire neatly summarizes the most vulnerable in Scottish Society, the very old and women left on their own with children. *Scottish Ethnographic Archive, National Museums of Scotland.*

and fees from hiring out 'mort cloths' to cover the coffin at funerals.[7] In Alison's view, this led to cruel parsimony; but many did not agree. The influential counterpoise to Alison was the Rev. Thomas Chalmers, much admired for his own work amongst the poor in St. John's parish, Glasgow. Each applicant for relief was treated on his merits, closely scrutinised by responsible neighbours, and, after all possibilities of family support were exhausted, aided from voluntary funds. Chalmers believed that the best system of relief was voluntary mutual aid within the local community: family responsibility and personal independence must be the pillars of a Christian society, founded on religious education. Chalmers's view elevated some of the practical aspects of the old Scottish Poor Law into an ideal vision, but Alison argued that in reality it relieved the rich of responsibility: 'If it were not for the poor, what would become of the poor?'.

The 1845 Act seemed a victory for Alison's principles rather than Chalmers's. While the English Poor Law was reformed to *restrict* relief, especially to the able-bodied poor, Scottish reform was intended to *increase* it. Previously, the Scottish poor had no legal claim to adequate support, and took whatever small and irregular amounts the church collections afforded. From 1845, under the management of new parochial boards, parishes were compelled to raise money to relieve the poor, and could choose to levy compulsory rates: within a few decades, nearly all of them did so, and the cost of poor relief rose. The Act also set up the Board of Supervision in Edinburgh to oversee the work of the parishes.[8] The church no longer controlled poor relief, although in country parishes the kirk-session had a strong influence on the parochial boards. Instead, ratepayers elected the boards through a complicated system of votes which favoured owners of property and excluded most of the poor.[9] Each parish appointed an Inspector of Poor to handle applications for relief and decide what should be offered. Only the larger towns paid a full-time salary for this work, and the obvious course for most parishes was to appoint their schoolmaster as a part-time inspector.

The 1845 Act also encouraged, though indirectly, a more complex institutional treatment of the poor. English parishes, long before the New Poor Law of 1834, had been required to give accommodation to the sick, destitute and unemployed, in workhouses which fulfilled with varying degrees of humanity, the functions of hospitals, asylums, refuges and manufactories. In the larger towns, the workhouses were often sizeable institutions with numerous staff. The Scots parishes, with their more limited finance, could not provide such institutions: the most elaborate, the Town's Hospital in Glasgow, had not been founded under the old Poor Law, but as a charitable venture, and even this was modest in scale compared with the workhouses of Liverpool or Manchester. The Act of 1845 did not force parishes to build poorhouses, but, because it allowed the poor to appeal against 'inadequate' relief, failure to provide suitable accommodation for the helpless and the sick might be defined as a breach of the law.

Yet Chalmers cast a long shadow for many years, especially in the Charity Organisation Societies which developed in several Scottish cities from the 1870s. These societies, like the model COS in England, tried to co-ordinate charitable and Poor Law relief. Chalmers was an acknowledged inspiration for the argument that statutory relief destroyed independence.[10] In 1909 a second Royal Commission on the Poor Laws reported, this time on both England and Scotland. The Majority Report on Scotland, much influenced by the COS, endorsed Chalmers's views in a lengthy passage, but relegated Alison to a footnote in the historical appendix.[11] The history of Scottish poor relief during the nineteenth century was, in many ways, a long battle between Alison's principles of statutory relief, and Chalmers's insistence on voluntary effort.

The 1909 Report included an historical survey which showed clearly that, in spite of compulsory assessments, the Scots were still less generous with poor relief than the English. Comparisons of the official figures also demonstrate this, as shown in Table 1.

Table 1. Comparison of Incidence and Cost of Pauperism in Scotland and England in Five-year Averages[12]

	Paupers per 1,000 population[13]			Annual cost per head of population		
	Scotland	England		Scotland	England	
					(pence)	
1860–64	39.8	47.0	(+18%)	52	71	(+36%)
1865–69	40.0	44.8	(+12%)	56	78	(+39%)
1870–74	35.6	41.6	(+16%)	56	81	(+44%)
1875–79	28.4	30.4	(+7%)	53	73	(+37%)
1880–84	26.0	30.0	(+15%)	53	75	(+41%)
1885–89	24.6	28.4	(+15%)	51	71	(+39%)
1890–95	22.6	25.8	(+14%)	50	73	(+46%)
1895–99	22.6	25.8	(+14%)	53	83	(+56%)
1900–05	22.2	24.2	(+9%)	59	89	(+50%)

The rate of pauperism in England was always higher than in Scotland, but the annual amount which the English contributed per head for the relief of the poor was proportionally much greater, and the gap appeared to be widening at the end of the nineteenth century.

Why were the Scots meaner than the English in their treatment of paupers? A simple explanation might be that Scotland was poorer than England, and could not afford a similar burden of relief. So far, all attempts at a systematic comparison between the national income of the two countries have foundered, but a return of wealth assessed for the property tax in 1843 shows that although the ratio of Scotland's population to England and Wales was 1:6.1, the ratio of taxable property was 1:8.8.[14] The Royal Commission of 1844 pointed out, however, that niggardly relief was not confined to impoverished places like the Highlands. Some of the wealthier towns paid out reluctantly, and Edinburgh was particularly tight-fisted. By the end of the century, the Highlands were being depopulated, and Scotland's industrial wealth was increasing rapidly, but Scottish relief was falling even further behind England.

Lower rates of pauperism in Scotland also suggested greater parsimony rather than less poverty. One possible explanation is that the Scottish 'disablement' rule debarred many of the poor from obtaining relief. The English able-bodied poor were legally entitled to relief in a workhouse if they could not support themselves. In Scotland, the able-bodied had no right to any relief unless disabled from work by illness, or, in the case of women, the need to care for young children.[15] A legal decision of 1852 confirmed that this rule applied to the unemployed. In theory, it should have kept the unemployed off the poor rates: in practice, the Scottish and the English administrations did not greatly differ. In Scotland, as in England, the unemployed might be offered the poorhouse when they applied for relief, or else be classed as 'disabled' by the medical officer. Since unemployment and ill-health often went together, few medical officers were anxious to test an applicant's destitution to the limits of starvation. Large numbers of unemployed during trade depressions made both the English and the Scottish laws unworkable. By the end of the century, both countries had expedients for keeping the unemployed off the Poor Law: local authorities organised charitable relief, or offered temporary employment on municipal works; but in hard cases poor relief or accommodation in the poorhouse was given.[16]

The Scots had proportionally more friendless children on poor relief than the English by the late nineteenth century, partly because of demographic differences, but also because the Scottish towns boarded out the children with country families for a small fee. This system was both economical and much admired, because it kept the children in families rather than in institutions. At best, the children were virtually adopted into a new family; at worst, since inspection was lax, they might be brutally treated and exploited as free labour.

The Royal Commission concluded in 1909 that the crucial difference between English and Scottish pauperism was, taking into account the age structures in both countries, the lower numbers of old people on relief in Scotland. The Majority Report argued that this demonstrated a stronger sense of duty towards parents in Scotland; but it might equally show that the Scots reduced pauperism by increasing the burden on poor families.

The real explanation for Scottish parsimony was a Poor Law which left many of the Scottish poor dependent on small local communities. In 1834, the English parishes, usually in groups of thirty or so, were combined into Poor Law unions; but the 1845 Act did not destroy the parochial administration in Scotland. At that time the Church of Scotland was too powerful a force to be undermined by an English government, but, more importantly, Scotland appeared prudent in its administration of poor relief, and less in need of reform. The Poor Law

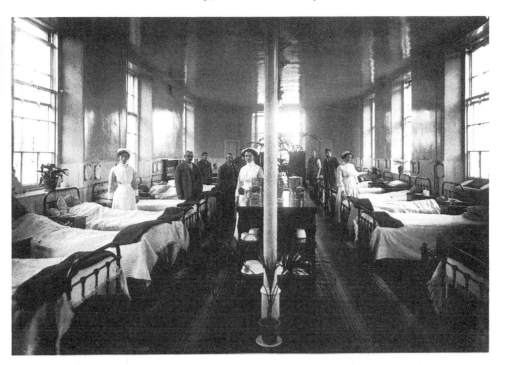

55. Formal and specialized institutions dominated welfare work by the end of the century. The Men's ward at the Greenlea Poor House in Edinburgh, 1904. The whole place bristles with hygienic discipline. *Scottish Ethnographic Archive, National Museums of Scotland.*

Report of 1832 in England was a radical attack on the whole system: its counterpart of 1844 in Scotland was conservative, 'to consider in what way the present law may be made to work most efficiently, without making any very material changes'.[17] One of the main grievances against the old Poor Law in England was its 'abuse' by the able-bodied poor: and the workhouse test was introduced in 1834 to deter them from applying for relief. Unions were big enough to provide sizeable workhouses, but in Scotland this seemed irrelevant, since the able-bodied had no right to relief. The poorhouse was not a central part of the system, but simply a refuge for the sick and helpless. In the English workhouse, all able-bodied paupers were expected to labour in return for their keep: some larger Scottish parishes followed this example, and offered hard labour to 'undeserving' cases; but work was not their central purpose.

The Scottish Poor Law remained in the hands of 886 separate parish administrations, containing less than 15 per cent of the population of

Britain: this should be compared with the 600-odd Poor Law unions of England and Wales. In theory, the Scottish system encouraged close supervision of the poor by parish officials who knew everybody's business. Parishes could combine to share the cost of a poorhouse, and by the end of the century this was common practice in the countryside; but the combined areas were never as populous as English unions, and the poorhouses were small. Only in the cities were large institutions possible, and even here traditional parish boundaries divided the administration, as in the four parishes of Glasgow: Govan and Gorbals united in 1873, but the City and Barony parishes were not merged until 1898.

Small-scale local government also reduced the effectiveness of central control. Central inspection, as recommended by Bentham and Chadwick, was vital to the English system of poor relief; by the turn of the century England had 67 inspectors for its unions, and the Local Government Board complained that this was scarcely adequate. In Scotland, two General Superintendents were appointed in 1856 to carry out all duties of inspection. Their numbers were increased to three, and then to four in the 1880s, even though the Treasury complained of this extravagance. One of them had the duty of visiting every poorhouse in the course of the year; the others were supposed to visit each parish in their district once a year, to inquire into alleged scandals and investigate individual complaints from the poor. They were also instructed to weed out idlers by a careful scrutiny of the local lists.[18] Given the difficulties of transport, inspection of the 886 parishes could hardly be rigorous. The Royal Commission of 1909 found the discrepancy between England and Scotland puzzling. 'Is there any reason for the number of Scottish inspectors being smaller than the number of English and Irish inspectors?' asked William Smart, the Professor of Political Economy at Glasgow. 'Only that Scotland just takes what she can get', replied one of the inspectors. 'The usual neglect since the Union, in fact', commented Smart.[19] The administration in Edinburgh was, in all respects, disproportionately smaller than its London counterpart; the disclosures of the Royal Commission, and pressure from newly appointed Liberal administrators in Scotland, finally resulted in the appointment of more inspectors between 1910 and 1913.[20]

Nevertheless, there was little pressure to consolidate the system. In 1872, the Chairman of the Board of Supervision, W.S. Walker, resisted a modest Parliamentary attempt to merge certain parishes, and praised the existing system:

> The experience of the Board. . .is that the administration of the law is most efficient when the area and population are not so large as to make it beyond the power of one executive body to overlook it, and where all the paupers

are within the knowledge, and under the constant oversight, of one [local] inspector. As a general rule, it may be said that the smaller the area and population the better is the administration of the law, provided that the Parochial Board and the Inspector know their duty, and are anxious to perform it.[21]

Such views prevailed in spite of all changes in local government before 1914. In 1894 the duties of the Board of Supervision were taken over by the new Local Government Board for Scotland, and more democratic parish councils replaced the parochial boards, but the small units remained. The cost of poor relief continued to rise throughout the country in the early years of the twentieth century, and the Royal Commission of 1909 concluded that some urban councils had fallen too much under the influence of an impoverished electorate. They recommended for Scotland and England that poor relief in the towns be handed over to a committee of the town council (this was not done until 1929), but they did not propose radical changes for the Scottish country parishes. In England, they argued, rural unions should be superseded by the county councils, but in Scotland the parochial system should remain, except that institutional care might pass to the counties. As in 1834, English reformers respected the frugality of Scottish parishes where all members of the community were known to one another; in addition, county councillors would have difficulty attending regular meetings in distant county towns.

The Scottish poor looked for aid to a local community where, in theory, their circumstances would be known, their merits weighed and relief carefully dispensed as a supplement to family help and charity. The system was self-enclosed, and the central authority in Edinburgh had few duties except to arbitrate disputes between individuals and their parish. Unlike the central authority for the English Poor Law, which issued a constant stream of instructions and regulations to the unions, the Edinburgh administrators spent most of their time considering appeals against inadequate relief. They tried to persuade the parishes to adopt uniform regulations, but had few powers to enforce them, and lacked the supervision of a large inspectorate. The Local Government Board which took over in 1894 was more dynamic in its attitudes, and employed a medical inspector from 1901, but it had no greater powers over the localities than its predecessor.

The Board of Supervision's role as protector of the poor, by hearing their appeals against inadequate relief (a right unknown in England), is also open to dispute. Appeals fell from around 742 a year in the early 1850s to 49 a year in the early 1900s: very few went to law, since

POOR'S ROLL OF THE PARISH OF ST. QUIVOX, AT THE MONTH OF AUGUST, 1860,

SHOWING THE WEEKLY ALLOWANCE GIVEN TO EACH, THEIR AGES, PLACES OF BIRTH, PRESENT
RESIDENCES, AND REASONS FOR BEING PUT ON THE ROLL.

Name.	Where Born.	Age.	Present Residence.	Weekly Aliment.		How long Received.	Reasons of Receiving Aliment.
Agnew, Widow	Straiton	67	Straiton	1	8	26 years	Paralytic
Armour, James	St. Quivox	64	Whitletts	2	6	15½ years	Bad health
Aitken, Elizabeth	St. Quivox	70	Prestwick	1	3	13 years	Not fit to support herself wholly
Aird, Widow Wm. for her childn.	St. Quivox	36	Dumfries	1	6	4 years	2 children, aged 11 and 4¾ years
Anderson, Widow	Haddington	62	Whitletts	1	6	4 years	Rheumatism and defective vision
Aitkenhead, Mrs	St. Quivox	22	George Street	1	6	2 years	Husband a soldier—2 children, aged 6 [and 2 years
Bell, Ann	St. Quivox	35	Ayr	1	6	26 years	Blind
Brodley, Widow	Ireland	70	Cross Street	1	6	13 years	Debility and impaired vision
Brown, Widow	Maybole	51	Cross Street	1	0	11 years	Defective vision
Brown, Widow	Barony	62	George Street	1	0	10 years	Not able to support herself wholly
Brown, Widow William	Ireland	41	Elba Street	1	0	10 years	2 children, aged 13 and 11 years
Bennet, Mrs Samuel	Ireland	72	George Street	1	6	13 years	Scurvy
Boyd, Robert	St. Quivox	76	Newton-on-Ayr	1	0	8 years	Rheumatism
Boag, Mary	St. Quivox	56	Content Street	1	0	6½ years	A weakly constitution
Boyd, William	St. Quivox	49	Elba Street	3	0	2 years	Bad health—House disponed to Parochial Board
Boyd, James, for his child	Ireland	58	Cross Street	1	6	2 years	Rheumatism
Brown, Widow John	Kilmarnock	44	Content Street	1	6	4 months	Chest disease
Brown, Widow James	St. Quivox	44	Garden Street	1	6	3 months	Chest disease
Bradey, Peter	Ireland	70	Content Street	1	0	3 months	Defective vision
Carnie, Mrs	Maybole	45	Elba Street	1	0	12 years	Defective sight

56. Extract from the Poor's Roll for the Parish of St Quivox, August 1860.
Many Scottish Parishes printed these for public inspection. *Glasgow University
Library*.

parishes usually accepted the Board's recommendation.[22] But the Board
dismissed two-thirds of appeals in the 1850s, and nearly three-quarters
in the 1900s. If the poor ceased to appeal, it was probably because they
expected very little from the system.

Walker's description of the parochial system gives it a certain romantic
gloss, and yet its deficiencies were well known. Scottish demographic
patterns were against it, as the towns steadily expanded and the
depopulation of the Highlands continued. English local authorities
varied greatly in size and population, but not as eccentrically as the
Scottish parishes. The largest parish was Kilmonivaig in Inverness,
covering 267,047 acres: the smallest Anstruther Easter, with 28 acres.
By the turn of the century, Glasgow had a population of over half
a million, compared with the parish of lowest population, Lyne, in
Peeblesshire, with 98 inhabitants. Some parishes were divided between
islands and mainland: the single poorhouse, reached by open boat, was
a form of exile.

With extremes of population went extremes of wealth; the cities could
support not only a range of Poor Law services but charities of every kind.
Smaller towns and the more comfortable rural parishes usually managed
a modest poorhouse, with a few paid staff. In 1850 there were only 21
poorhouses in Scotland, with accommodation for 6,058 paupers. By 1900

there were 65 operational poorhouses, with accommodation for 15,509, but only half that number of inmates.[23] At all times, the Scottish system relied less on indoor relief than the English. Even in 1906, when the numbers in Scottish poorhouses were higher than ever before, the proportion relieved by this means was just under 14 per cent of the whole pauper population, compared with 31.6 per cent on indoor relief in England.[24]

Parishes without poorhouses could pay to board their paupers in a neighbouring poorhouse, but it was much cheaper to give small doles of outdoor relief; hence many country poorhouses were half-empty. The poor also resisted this squalid accommodation, often far from their friends. In the Highlands and Islands, the small combined poorhouses were often so inaccessible to the scattered parishes, that they were used only for very burdensome paupers, especially the insane. From an early period the Board of Supervision followed the English example, and urged parishes to use the poorhouse to discourage certain types of pauper. Poorhouses were originally intended to shelter the sick, insane, handicapped and disabled poor, but the Board asserted:

> It is hurtful in practice to grant relief otherwise than in the poorhouse to the following classes: (1) mothers of illegitimate children, including widows with legitimate families who may fall into immoral habits; (2) deserted wives; (3) persons having grown-up families settled either in this country or abroad; (4) persons having collateral relatives in comfortable circumstances; (5) wives of persons sentenced to terms of imprisonment. . .(6) in general, all persons of idle, immoral or dissipated habits.[25]

Consequently, poorhouses were even more confused in their aim than English workhouses. The larger workhouses attempted (usually unsuccessfully) to separate the helpless from the 'undeserving' classes, but Scottish poorhouses were too small for this. A few towns offered special accommodation for certain groups: Aberdeen, for example, had a set of lodgings where elderly people could live in reasonable comfort and independence, but this was rare. Many rural parishes met their obligation to provide shelter by simply hiring lodgings, and not only children but lunatics were still boarded out with the local population.

Poor relief in Britain was never consistent: it depended on the wealth of the locality and the attitudes of its administration. In 1845, Scottish poor relief showed wide variations, according to the generosity of the kirk-sessions, the legacies enjoyed by the parish and the numbers of poor. After 1845 the inconsistencies remained, both within Scotland and in comparison with England. From the 1870s, larger English workhouses were turning into relatively expensive general hospitals, with trained medical staff and modern equipment. In Scotland, these developments were delayed, and less widespread.

Scottish hospital provision in the nineteenth century revealed immense contrasts, with the munificence of charitable effort set against the low standards of the Poor Law even more sharply than in England. Edinburgh and Glasgow had their great Royal Infirmaries, founded in the eighteenth century, but greatly rebuilt and extended in the Victorian period. Closely connected to internationally renowned medical schools, they were intended only for the poor. They were served by some of the most eminent medical men in Britain, who worked without fee, knowing that the prestige of such appointments would bring them both students and wealthy private patients. Pressure of population led to even greater effort, with new voluntary hospitals such as the Western and Victoria Infirmaries in Glasgow, built in 1874 and 1890 respectively. Aberdeen, with a rather dubious standard of medical education until the university reforms of mid-century, also boasted a substantial infirmary, later expanded to serve its revived medical school. By the end of the nineteenth century, most burghs of any size, from Kelso to Inverness, possessed infirmaries, their solid architecture reflecting the civic pride which supported them.

In both England and Scotland, the Poor Law authorities sent acutely ill patients to the infirmaries for treatment, sometimes over long distances, and made a donation to the infirmary in return. In Scotland, however, the infirmaries continued until relatively late in the century to take in patients who in England would have been consigned to the Poor Law. The charitable infirmaries of England frequently refused to accept as patients the terminally ill, who worsened the hospital's mortality statistics; fever cases, who were dangerous; and the tuberculous, who were likely to take up a bed for a considerable time before they died. As a result, the Poor Law infirmaries in large towns, and sick wards of workhouses, became receptacles for many such cases. In Scotland, where parish authorities even after 1845 rarely provided suitable wards for the sick, the infirmaries continued to take in infectious and thankless cases.

The dominance of the voluntary system, combined with the thrifty habits of parochial boards, delayed the development of Poor Law hospitals in Scotland, and by the end of the century their inadequacy was much criticised. After decades of dirt, overcrowding, untrained staff and general neglect in the hospital sections of the parish poorhouses, Glasgow invested in an elaborate purpose-built system, with Stobhill hospital completed in 1902, followed shortly afterwards by the Western

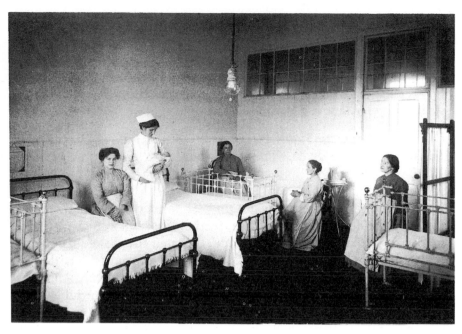

57. The lying-in ward was even more white and starched, although a cautious smile appeared on a few faces. *Scottish Ethnographic Archive, National Museums of Scotland.*

and Eastern District hospitals.[26] Edinburgh and the other cities, although considerably behind Glasgow in expenditure, also began to improve their services, and replaced pauper nurses with trained staff, but most Scottish poorhouses offered only rudimentary medical care. This kept costs lower than in England, and continued the emphasis on the voluntary hospitals, as will be seen.

The parochial system was ill-designed to cope with the worst features of poverty in Scotland, for the remoter Highlands and the city slums strained it to breaking point. The highest rates of pauperism were found in the Highlands and Lanarkshire; the lowest in Perthshire and the Borders. In some Highland parishes, most people were too poor to pay poor rates, and the cost of relief fell on landlords whose own estates were often encumbered with debt. Fear of compulsory assessment for poor relief was one reason for mass evictions, especially after the potato famine of the 1840s.[27] Forcible evictions were then replaced by steady pressure on the Highlanders to emigrate. In the 1880s, against a background of agricultural depression and rioting over the payment of rents and poor rates in Skye, conditions seemed as bad as at any time in the nineteenth century, and a law officer reported:

> There can be no doubt that the mass of the people are very poor, and I am unable to understand how a large portion of the cottar class manage to keep life & soul together. They pay no rent or taxes, they have no land & there is very little if any work for them.[28]

In such conditions, the Poor Law collapsed. Rates could not be collected; relief could not be given. The only source of support was charity, including money, food, and quantities of guano for manure sent by Highland Societies in London.

Although crofting acts gave the poorest farmers security of tenure, and depopulation eased the pressure, further disasters were not avoided. The parish of Barra, a chain of islands, defeated the system completely for several years. Even in the first decade of the twentieth century, its population of 2,545 was amongst the poorest in Scotland, still living in damp stone houses with floors of earth or bare rock sprinkled with sand. The crofters survived by growing potatoes and keeping a few animals, supplementing their incomes by fishing. In 1906 the parish council went bankrupt, and all the councillors resigned, since the entire rental value of the parish was not enough to support its 53 paupers, the parish medical officer and the schools. No-one would serve on the council, and the Local Government Board had to send in one of its own overworked inspectors to enforce payment of rates. This state of affairs continued until 1913. For many people in the north, incomes and living conditions were slowly improving by the end of the nineteenth century, but a persistent problem for the Poor Law was the high proportion of old people left behind as the young emigrated south or across the sea.

The English arrangement of larger Poor Law unions would not have helped the Highlands, where people were few and incomes meagre. Relief was possible only by government action to redistribute resources from wealthier parts of the country, a notion offensive to contemporary principles of political economy. Nevertheless, government was forced to act in the 1880s. Local taxes on agricultural property throughout Britain were lowered to assist farmers faced with the international depression in food prices. The government then had to compensate local authorities for lost agricultural rates. The Highlands received a special grant of £28,000 to subsidise the cost of poor relief: in some parishes this was worth more than half the cost.[29] Government subsidies began to play an increasing part in relieving poverty in remote areas.

Cities, especially Glasgow, had the largest numbers of poor, but also more wealth to provide relief. Urban poverty, as in the rest of Britain, had many causes. Low wages and the irregular demand for labour were the dominant problems, juxtaposed with personal circumstances which few working families could provide against, such as sickness, handicap or injury, widowhood, old age and large numbers of children. The cities experienced particular problems because of rapid immigration and the high incidence of disease: the Scottish Poor Law compounded rather than alleviated these problems.

Scottish urban growth, as in the rest of Britain, depended heavily on immigrants, but the ancient Laws of Settlement bore hardly upon them if they fell into want. A pauper could claim relief only from his place of settlement — usually his place of birth — and could be sent back there if he became destitute anywhere else. The laws were intended to deter strangers from seeking relief, but for centuries the Scottish law was more liberal than the English. From 1672, with a few interruptions, three years of continuous residence allowed an incomer to gain settlement in a parish. In England, the law was extremely complicated, but in practice it enabled employers or parish officers to prevent a poor immigrant from gaining a settlement.

The Law of Settlement led parishes to engage in frequent and expensive lawsuits over complicated cases. Nineteenth-century opinion was divided. Followers of Adam Smith and Malthus deplored the laws on economic grounds for inhibiting labour migration. A Victorian revision of this view argued that the settlement laws allowed 'low grade' (i.e., Irish) immigration, while discouraging honest English countrymen from uprooting themselves. The Chadwick school argued for settlement based simply on place of birth, since they thought the threat of removal encouraged thrift and hard work amongst immigrants. The humanitarian conscience of the Victorians was nevertheless distressed by the sight of paupers being parted from their homes and friends and sent to a long-forgotten place of settlement. The compromise, as time went on, was for incomers to become 'irremovable' after a certain period of residence, and for their parish of origin to send a remittance to their new parish on their behalf. However, as the English law became more liberal, the Scottish law became more severe.

The two laws were closest in the 1840s, when the English law relaxed as the Scottish became tighter. An Act of 1846 made paupers in England 'irremovable' after five years' residence. An 'irremovable' pauper could remain where he was, and his place of settlement would send a remittance. The Union Chargeability Act of 1865 reduced the time of residence to one year, and made the whole union, rather than the single parish,

58. The most prestigious hospitals depended upon voluntary subscription. A nurse collects for Dundee Royal Infirmary. *Dundee District Libraries.*

financially responsible for the poor. In 1876 paupers were permitted permanent settlement if they had lived in a union for three years; this stood until the Law was repealed in 1948.[30]

The Scots became more hostile to strangers. The Poor Law Act of 1845 increased the residence qualification for settlement from three to five years, and this remained until reduced to three years again in 1898. Attempts to reduce it to one year, as for the English 'irremovable' poor, met stolid resistance from MPs and councillors of Scottish cities; they feared the heavy cost of destitute immigrants. Although cities complained of impoverished Highlanders, the Irish aroused deeper feelings of racial and religious hostility. Scottish paupers would usually be allowed to stay if supported by remittance from their place of settlement. The law did not permit remittances for Irish or English poor, who were removed if they became destitute.

Because Scotland was divided into parishes rather than unions, immigrants found it harder to gain a settlement. An Irish family unwise enough to cross parish boundaries while living in Scotland would gain no right to stay, even if they merely moved from one Glasgow parish to another before five years had passed. Itinerant Irish workers, however, also found that the law conveniently provided them with a free passage home. The 1898 Act finally allowed the Irish to gain a settlement if they had lived five years in any part of Scotland (the English law was similarly revised in 1901), but any suggestion of further compromise met passionate resistance. In the late 1840s, nearly 6,000 Irish were sent home annually, most of them 'voluntarily', but by the last decades of the century it was usually less than 300.[31] Harsh laws gave the Irish further reason to huddle in overcrowded ghettos, since without help from their own people they were particularly vulnerable until they gained a settlement.

The final problem to be considered is the relationship between poverty and disease. Alison's argument against inadequate relief grew out of his concern for the health of the working classes. As a doctor, he constantly faced the stubborn combination of poverty and disease, exposed sharply in the cholera epidemic of 1832. About 10,000 of Scotland's inhabitants died, and the mortality rate was considerably higher than in England.[32]

Although Alison and Chadwick walked through the slums of Glasgow together, they came out with different conclusions; as a 'miasmatist', Chadwick believed that the dirt and foul air which caused disease would be vanquished by proper sanitation. Alison was a 'contagionist', believing that disease spread between the infected by some unknown means, possibly 'animalcular life', but, most importantly, that poverty caused its rapid diffusion.[33] Alison and Chadwick did not, in fact, disagree over the need for a sanitary policy, but Alison's first aim was to attack destitution by offering poor relief, including medical treatment. Alison's followers supported the new Scottish Poor Law, but they also blocked the extension to Scotland of the 1848 Public Health Act, which gave some powers of compulsion to a general Board of Health.[34] The Scottish medical establishment was suspicious of control from London, especially because they disagreed with Chadwick's ideas on how disease spread.

The early sanitary reformers also suffered from a lack of statistical information. In Scotland, civil registration of births and deaths began in 1855, 18 years later than England. The English Poor Law unions employed clerks who could also act as registrars; the Scottish parishes had few paid officers, and objected to the expense of employing them.[35] Even after registration (provoked by the disruption of the Kirk), many deaths were uncounted, or the causes of death wrongly stated. Registration of stillborn children was lax, since undertakers did not need a death certificate before burying them. The stillborn had no burial ceremonies, and parents and midwives might agree to save expense by declaring a baby stillborn although it had lived for a short time. Cause of death was not well recorded, especially in areas with few doctors; in 1871, 24 per cent of deaths in Glasgow were uncertified; by 1893 the efforts of the medical officer had reduced this to 3 per cent, but in the county of Inverness, 42 per cent of deaths were still uncertified.[36]

Yet, if the available statistics were to be believed, Scotland was healthier than England. Crude death rates were lower than in England because more Scots during the nineteenth century were country dwellers, and it was the towns which raised the levels of mortality. Scotland shared the national experience of falling rates of adult mortality during the last quarter of the century. This was related to the decline of respiratory diseases, particularly tuberculosis, and may indicate rising living standards; but in Scotland this class of disease was slower to retreat than in England. Cholera and typhus, the epidemic diseases which caused havoc from the 1830s to the 1860s, were slowly driven back by improved sanitation and clean water supplies.

Infantile mortality, the most sensitive social index, showed a different pattern. Again, Scotland seemed healthier than England. Of every thousand babies born in England and Wales in the early 1850s, 150 would die under the age of one year; in Scotland, at the same time, it was 120 per thousand. Against the general trend, infantile mortality did not fall in the later nineteenth century, but actually rose to 129 per thousand in Scotland during the late 1890s — the worst of all the decades of registration.[37] In England, a sharp fall began in the later 1890s and continued until the 1930s; Scotland experienced the same trend, but later. By 1913 the Scottish rate was only slightly better than the English, anticipating the twentieth-century pattern of an infantile mortality rate persistently higher north of the border.

Comparative mortality rates, however, also depend on how boundaries are drawn. Glasgow's infantile mortality in the nineteenth century seemed considerably lower than either Liverpool or Manchester, though the difference was slight by the end of the century. As Liverpool's medical officer complained, the boundaries of his city were drawn around all

59. The committee of the Glasgow Juvenile Delinquency Board in action at Green Street Industrial School 1886. *Strathclyde Regional Archives.*

the worst areas, while the middle class withdrew to neighbouring areas not included in the statistics. Glasgow, by contrast, was an expansive city, including both middle-class and working-class suburbs.[38] For this reason, W. T. Gairdner, Glasgow's first Medical Officer of Health, was anxious to produce small area statistics to show the city's best and worst features. His successor, J. B. Russell, refined the statistics in the 1870s so that mortality could be clearly plotted against changes in population. If Glasgow is seen, not as an artificial 'average', but by comparing its poorest and richest citizens, then the infantile mortality in Glasgow's poorest streets was amongst the worst in the country. As late as 1898:

> In Port-Dundas, Brownfield, Gorbals and Cowcaddens, one infant death occurred in every five born compared with one in eleven born in Langside, Mount Florida and Kelvinside, and one in thirteen born in Hillhead, Pollokshields and Strathbungo.[39]

Russell's own researches showed a clear relation between infantile mortality and overcrowding, particularly in Glasgow's one-room dwellings:

> Of all the children who die in Glasgow before they complete their fifth year, 32 per cent die in houses of one apartment; and not 2 per cent in

houses of five apartments and upwards. There they die, and their little bodies are laid on a table or on the dresser, so as to be somewhat out of the way of their brothers and sisters, who play and sleep and eat in their ghastly company.[40]

Conditions in poor and overcrowded homes led to gastric illnesses fatal to young babies; but the largest proportion died shortly after birth from 'immaturity', probably because their mothers were undernourished and in poor health.

Studies of Scottish mortality emphasise Glasgow because of its drag on the statistics; but other large towns had pockets of disease and their own particular problems. Small towns, with bad water supplies and too careful of the ratepayers' pockets, harboured diseases such as typhoid longer than the cities. Highlanders were generally healthier than town dwellers, but suffered high rates of tuberculosis. On the doomed island of St Kilda so many of the newly born died of tetanus that pregnant women made long journeys in open boats to be delivered elsewhere.

Both Chadwick and Alison believed in a relationship between poverty and disease. Chadwick assumed that disease caused poverty, Alison the reverse: in fact, their positions were not mutually exclusive. Alison's attack on poverty through a reformed Poor Law could not prevent the epidemics caused by inadequate sanitation: Chadwick's sanitary measures reduced epidemic disease, but did not banish tuberculosis or the impoverished environment which slaughtered the children.

Public health policy in Scotland, like Poor Law policy, left a great deal to local decisions. It would be wrong to exaggerate the differences with England, for governments were reluctant to enforce sanitation in any part of the country; but in London the Local Government Act Office, and then the Local Government Board, engaged in constant negotiations with local authorities, and achieved far greater influence than any authority in Edinburgh. Under the Nuisance Removal Act of 1856, the Board of Supervision could act as a central sanitary authority in times of emergency, but it did not gain permanent powers until the 1867 Public Health Act. It could then appoint inspectors and hold special inquiries into local health problems, but this work was left entirely to its three Poor Law inspectors, who had no expertise in public health. Until constrained by the Local Government Act of 1889 to appoint a Medical Officer of Health, the larger towns operated under a series of Police Acts, which allowed them a great deal of discretion in sanitary policy.

Out of the confusing welter of general and local legislation in mid-century, a body of formidable medical officers appeared in Scotland.

They included Russell in Glasgow, Henry Littlejohn in Edinburgh, John McVail in Stirlingshire and Matthew Hay in Aberdeen. They led the battle for cleanliness, drainage, public parks, civic fever hospitals, better housing and collections of statistics for the continual embarrassment of City Fathers.

Glasgow, having the worst problems, was forced into the most expensive solutions. Pure water was pumped from Loch Katrine from 1860, though the Clyde was still the main sewer until 1894, and Glasgow remained, in Russell's words, a 'semi-asphyxiated city' from its coal fires and industrial pollution. The most difficult problem was housing, where public effort, even as vigorous as under Glasgow's City Improvement Trust, could not make up for the deficiencies of the private market; but, given the hectic pace of urbanisation in late nineteenth-century Scotland, the cities may have done well even to mark time in their mortality rates.

Greater success might be claimed for the treatment of the sick. The Scottish Poor Law had never fully accepted this responsibility, and parishes felt no obligation to employ a doctor to treat the poor, as was common in England. Medical reformers like Alison strongly criticised this deficiency, and medical influence on the Board of Supervision was much stronger than in its London counterparts. The Board pressed parishes to appoint district medical officers, even though the 1845 Act did not enforce this except in parishes with a poorhouse. The Board's main weapon from 1849 was its control over the medical relief grant. This amounted to only £10,000 a year at first, but it enabled the Board to subsidise parishes willing to raise a reasonable amount towards the care of the sick poor, and also increased the Board's power. Without the grant, some remote areas would have had no doctor at all, since private patients were too few to support him. A Highland doctor would usually be paid from a number of sources; the Poor Law, a subvention from the local laird, very occasional private fees, payments from the parish council for vaccination and public health duties, and, sometimes, payments from sick clubs in the more populous parishes. By the end of the century, most of the poor in Scotland could expect free treatment from a parish doctor, either in their own homes or in the poorhouse.[41] But, apart from vaccination, bonesetting and pulling teeth, the doctor could probably do little for constitutions enfeebled by poverty.

Treatment of infectious patients was uneasily shared between several groups after 1845. The voluntary hospitals did admit fever patients; but in epidemics parochial boards provided makeshift accommodation. Permanent fever hospitals run by the local councils developed late — Belvidere hospital in Glasgow was not fully operational until 1871.[42]

Free treatment for the tuberculous in county sanitoria was available only after 1911.

If, in the end, the official response to poverty and disease in Scotland seemed mean and dilatory, the survival of the parochial system was the main cause. The burden could not easily be shared across parish boundaries; and central authority was weaker than in England. Consequently, charity had to fill many of the gaps. This was, of course, the Scottish tradition as exemplified by Chalmers and his many successors; it could lead both to charitable effort on a magnificent scale and to great parsimony in local government. The history of Scottish philanthropy shows many notable successes. By the late nineteenth century, the infirmaries were supported not only by middle-class charity, but increasingly from donations by workmen, organised within their workplace, in order to secure admission for their members. Smaller burghs could not match the scale of the great urban infirmaries, or provide specialist hospitals; but most had substantial general hospitals supported by charity, and by the end of the century the cottage hospital movement was beginning to spread in more thinly populated areas.

The hospitals were one of the most visible, expensive and impressive forms of philanthropy, but charities of all kinds proliferated in Scotland — dispensaries, orphanages, district nursing, together with institutions for the handicapped, model lodging houses, ragged schools and homes for fallen women. Charities such as the Strangers' Friend Societies, which gave a night's shelter to the homeless poor, made up the deficiencies of the Poor Law, especially to the immigrants who feared the settlement laws.[43] The financial outlay of Scottish charity has not been estimated, nor is this possible, since so much relied on informal acts by churches and individuals.

A final reflection might be that, from their peculiar circumstances, the Scots were forced to look for assistance from the state long before 1945. Local efforts, because small-scale, were rarely as effective as in England. Again, geography was a crucial factor. From an early stage the government had to subsidise medical care under the Scottish Poor Law, but still failed to secure a reliable medical service in the Highlands. In 1911 an even more radical solution was found in the Highlands and Islands Medical Scheme, which, recognising that health insurance would not provide enough to support a medical service, gave a government grant for the salaries of doctors and nurses in these remote areas. The scheme foreshadowed the National Health Service, but was accepted without demur by both Conservatives and Liberals in Scotland. Similarly, government grants from 1919 were welcomed as a solution to the most intractable housing problems in Britain. Scotland encompassed some of the worst problems of both urban and rural life, and it seemed that only state intervention could finally defeat them. The Scots in the late twentieth century are often criticised for relying too heavily on government services. If there is any truth in this, then the explanation may lie in the excessive burdens placed on small communities in the nineteenth century — burdens which many were happy to hand over to the state.

NOTES

1. W. P. Alison, *Observations on the Management of the Poor In Scotland, and its Effects on the Health of the Great Towns*, second edition (Edinburgh, 1840), p. 66.

2. Archibald Alison, *Some Account of My Life and Writings: an Autobiography* (Edinburgh, 1883), I, p. 458.

3. M. W. Flinn (ed.), *Report on the Sanitary Condition of the Labouring Population of Gt. Britain by Edwin Chadwick 1842* (Edinburgh, 1965), p. 99.

4. For a discussion, see John Butt, 'Housing,' in R. A. Cage (ed.), *The Working Class in Glasgow 1750–1914*, (London, 1987), pp. 41–2.

5. J. H. Treble, *Urban Poverty in Britain* (London, 1979), Chapter 2; E. H. Hunt, *Regional Wage Variations in Britain 1850–1914* (Oxford, 1973); Ian Levitt and Christopher Smout, *The State of the Scottish Working Class in 1843* (Edinburgh, 1979); Cage, *Working Class in Glasgow*, pp. vi–xviii.

6. T. C. Smout, 'The Strange Intervention of Edward Twistleton', in *The Search for Wealth and Stability* (London, 1979), pp. 232–6.

7. For the pre-1845 Poor Law, see Thomas Ferguson, *The Dawn of Scottish Social Welfare* (Edinburgh, 1948), Chapter 8; R. A. Cage, *The Scottish Poor Law, 1745–1845* (Edinburgh, 1981); R. Mitchison, 'The Making of the Old Scottish Poor Law', *Past & Present* 63 (1974).

8. For a general account, see Audrey Paterson, 'The Poor Law in Nineteenth Century Scotland', in Derek Fraser (ed.), *The New Poor Law in the Nineteenth Century* (London, 1976).

9. Robert Peel Lamond, *The Scottish Poor Laws: their History, Policy and Operation*, second edition (Glasgow, 1892), pp. 56–7.

10. Olive Checkland, *Philanthropy in Victorian Scotland: Social Welfare and the Voluntary Principle* (Edinburgh, 1980), p. 298ff.

11. *Royal Commission on the Poor Laws and Relief of Distress. Report on Scotland* (HMSO, 1909 cmd 4922,), pp. 188, 313n.

12. Sources: Karel Williams, *From Pauperism to Poverty* (London, 1981), pp. 158–61; 169–71; *R C 1909 Appendix*, vol vi. (HMSO, 1910 cmd 4978), p. 864. *Nineteenth Annual Report of the Local Government Board for Scotland*, (HMSO, 1914, cmd 7327), p. xvii.

13. The difference between Scottish and English rates of relief may be slightly exaggerated because the English figures were based on the average of paupers counted on 1 July and 1 January, while the Scottish figures were based on a count on 15 May.

14. *Return showing the annual value of Real Property in each Parish. . . (PP* 1844 XXXII), p. 451.

15. For the 'disablement' rule, see Rosalind Mitchison, 'The Poor Law', in T. M. Devine and Rosalind Mitchison (eds.), *People and Society in Scotland*, vol. 1 (Edinburgh, 1988).

16. Ian Levitt, 'The Scottish Poor Law and Unemployment, 1890–1929', in Smout (ed.), *Wealth and Stability*, p. 264ff.

17. *Report from Her Majesty's Commissioners for Inquiring into the Poor Laws in Scotland*, *(PP* 1844 XX), p. xiv.

18. SRO HH 1/916, 25 Feb 1891.

19. *RC 1909 Minutes of Evidence*, vol vi, (HMSO, 1910 cmd 4978), p. 127.

20. Ian Levitt, *Poverty and Welfare in Scotland 1890–1948* (Edinburgh, 1988), p. 51.

21. *Statement by the Chairman of the Board of Supervision respecting the 'Bill for the further amendment and better administration of the laws relating to the relief of the poor in Scotland'* HMSO Feb. 1872, p. 4.

22. *RC 1909 Minutes of Evidence*, vol vi, appendix, p. 855.

23. *Ibid.*, p. 881.

24. *RC 1909* cmd 4922, p. 9; and vol 1 (Majority Report), (HMSO, 1909), p. 34. The English figures are for 1907.

25. *RC 1909* cmd 4922, p. 868.

26. For the Poor Law hospital system, see Rona Gaffney, 'Poor Law Hospitals 1845–1914', in Olive Checkland and Margaret Lamb (eds.), *Health Care as Social History: The Glasgow Case* (Aberdeen, 1982); Gordon Mclachlan (ed.), *Improving the Common Weal: Aspects of Scottish Health Services 1900–1984* (Edinburgh, 1987), p. 42ff.

27. T. C. Smout, *A Century of the Scottish People 1830–1950* (London, 1986), p. 62 ff.

28. HH 1/241.

29. HH 40/235, pp. 4–8.

30. For English law, see M. Rose, 'Settlement, Removal and the New Poor Law', in Fraser (ed.) *New Poor Law*. For the Scottish law, see Lamond, *Scottish Poor Laws*, Chapter 9.

31. Lamond, *Scottish Poor Laws*, pp. 190–1.

32. Michael Flinn (ed.), *Scottish Population History: From the 17th Century to the 1930s* (Cambridge, 1977), p. 370.

33. Alison, *Observations* p. 11, also University College, London, Chadwick Papers 171. For a detailed discussion of contemporary theories, see Margaret Pelling, *Cholera Fever and English Medicine* (Oxford, 1978).

34. Flinn, *Sanitary Condition*, pp. 72–3; B. M. White, 'Scottish Doctors and the English Public Health', in D. Dow (ed.), *The Influence of Scottish Medicine* (Carnforth, 1986), p. 83ff.

35. Flinn, *Scottish Population History*, p. 87.

36. *Reports from the Select Committee on Death Certification* (HMSO, 1893 cmd 373), p. vii.

37. F. B. Smith, *The People's Health 1830–1910* (London, 1979), pp. 65–67.

38. See essays by T. Hart and J. R. Kellett in A. Slaven and D. H. Aldcroft (eds.), *Business, Banking and Urban History, Essays in Honour of S. G. Checkland*, (Edinburgh, 1982).

39. A. K. Chalmers, *The Health of Glasgow 1818–1925* (Glasgow, 1930), p. 193, and also pp. 74–6, 190.

40. James Burn Russell, *Public Health Administration in Glasgow* (Glasgow, 1905), p. 196.

41. For details, see Stephanie Blackden, 'The Board of Supervision and the Scottish Parochial Medical Service', *Medical History* 30 (1986), 145–72.

42. See Stephanie Blackden, 'The Poor Law and Health: a Survey of Parochial Medical Aid in Glasgow, 1845–1900', in Smout, *Wealth and Stability*.

43. For a full account, see Checkland, *Scottish Philanthropy*, especially Chapter 22.

CHAPTER 10
An Exploration into Scottish Education

Helen Corr

One of the most powerful and enduring myths to permeate Scottish society is that Scotland has traditionally enjoyed a more equal and open educational system than England. This assertion is based on the notion that individuals from all social classes had equality of access to an educational ladder running from the parish or burgh school to university. All that was necessary was that the 'lad o' pairts' — the ambitious working-class boy — should have the talent. This 'democratic tradition' had its origins in the parochial schools from at least the eighteenth century. According to Defoe, England was a land 'full of ignorance', while in Scotland 'the poorest people have their children taught and instructed'. It was said that all children, regardless of social background, sat side-by-side in the classroom. The inference drawn was that Scottish society was more democratic and egalitarian than England, and that Scots lacked, as Edwin Muir claimed, the class attitudes of their English counterparts.[1] This chapter examines the validity of the contention that the Scottish educational system was a democratic meritocracy and questions how distinctive the Scottish system was in a European context.

No theory or social history of education can afford to ignore the role of gender in shaping the structure of the educational system. Hence the debate must include issues of sexual equality both in terms of access to education and of conditions of service within the teaching profession. Whether the 'lad o' pairts' was fiction or fact, the discussion is male bounded. The 'lass o' pairts' too, is, sadly, almost entirely neglected in historical research. At least part of this essay, therefore, is exploratory in so far as it aims to provide a framework on many related issues where much more research needs to be done.

Education plays an active and reactive role in shaping the development of modern society and, therefore, it is vital to examine the purposes it was intended to serve in the nineteenth century. This leads to an examination of the role of church and state. How far was education seen as social engineering and how far did the curriculum reflect this? What values did the holders of power see as important to impart to the working and middle classes, and what differences occurred in the experience of the two classes? A final question to consider is the experience of the recipients of education — the pupils.

With the notable exception of Robert Anderson's *Education and Opportunity in Victorian Scotland* there are few books written on the social history of nineteenth-century Scottish education.[2] A considerable literature deals with institutional structures, but how education, or the lack of it, affected the lives of people in an industrialising society is rarely tackled. Teachers form an integral part of the educational structure, but changes over time in relation to recruitment, promotions and pay scales of teachers have received scant attention. The gaps in published material become even more glaring when attempting to read about women's experiences in education. Successive generations of mainly male authors have failed to integrate women alongside men into a mainstream analysis.[3]

The failure to incorporate gender relationships within the framework of a social history is inextricably linked to the way in which Scottish education has been written about during the last hundred years or so. Fortunately, during the last decade or so there have been a number of scholars who have embarked on a critical reappraisal of Scottish identity and the distinctiveness of educational institutions from the universities downwards.[4]

I

One of the most far-reaching changes of the nineteenth century was that public education shifted away from the churches to be placed under the greater control of the state. The crucial turning point came with the passing of the 1872 Education (Scotland) Act. This act brought at least a dozen different types of school under state control. There were the old parochial schools which were traditionally seen as the heart of the system. Here was where the graduate dominie offered education at all levels, with sufficient Latin for the able to reach university. Their quality varied enormously. Some were bad, while others undoubtedly maintained a standard of excellence. In the 1850s and 1860s, thanks to the Dick and Milne Bequests in the North-East and the Cunningham Bequest in Dumfries and Galloway, schools in these area were able to provide a sound classical education, from well-educated teachers, and here the parish system was at its strongest. Elsewhere, isolated parish schools struggled with inadequate facilities and underpaid masters.

Parish schools did not operate in the cities, and instead there were burgh schools, some run by heritors, the rest by town councils. Again, quality varied, but some, like Aberdeen Grammar, Edinburgh's Royal High and the High School of Glasgow provided something like a secondary education.

Since the 1820s there had been numerous efforts to deal with the increasingly obvious gaps in the parochial system. Sessional schools had been developed in the urban areas, assembly schools in the badly-provided Highland areas, where there were also Society for the Propagation of Christian Knowledge schools run by voluntary Christian groups. Elsewhere there were parliamentary funded schools, again the product of limited efforts to supplement an inadequate parish provision.

Since 1843 Free Church schools had begun to proliferate, bringing vastly increased provision; 360 teachers left the Church of Scotland and a Free Church Education Committee at once began raising funds. Figures vary, but by 1865 there were some 570 Free Church Schools. In addition, there were philanthropic schools or industrial schools, generally concerned with giving a vocational training, especially for girls, later developing into reformatories, like the ragged schools associated with Dr Thomas Guthrie in Edinburgh and Sheriff Watson in Aberdeen. Then there were adventure schools, private speculative ventures — 88 identified in Glasgow in 1866. Most reports suggest that many of these were hopelessly inadequate. On the other hand, it has also been suggested that the fact that parents were willing to pay indicates at least some satisfaction with the services provided. For long before the 1860s most pupils were educated outside the parochial system.

There were other privately endowed schools such as the Heriot Trust schools in Edinburgh, financed from property rents, and the Hutcheson's Hospital in Glasgow. Paisley acquired Neilson's in 1852 and Dundee, Morgan Academy in 1861, from private endowment. A few works schools attached to iron works and collieries offered part-time education for working children.[5]

The accessibility of Scottish education was, even in the early nineteenth century, a subject of debate. An 1833 report on Scottish millworkers showed that 96 per cent of them could read and 53 per cent could write, compared with figures of 86 per cent and 43 per cent for England. However, the following year, an evangelical cleric and editor of the *Scottish Guardian*, George Lewis, delivered a devastating attack on complacency

60. Quarter School in Hamilton c.1900. The segregation of sexes began in the school lines. After 1872, elementary education increasingly became the preserve of women teachers. Do the bare feet indicate poverty or were they one of the freedoms of summer? *Hamilton District Libraries and Museums.*

with his book *Scotland: a Half-Educated Nation both in the Quantity and Quality of her Educational Institutions.* Lewis found that only 1 in 12 of the population attended day schools, and that in this Scotland was lagging behind Prussia, France and parts of the United States. Indeed, to pile Pellion upon Ossa, he suggested that there was little to choose between England and Scotland as regards educational provision: 9 per cent attended day schools in England, 9.6 per cent in Scotland.

The Argyll Commission of 1867 was concerned about the lack of adequate provision of schools. It claimed that of 98,767 children of school age in Glasgow only 48,391 were on school rolls. However, it took school age as between the ages of 3 and 15. If only half of that extent is assumed to be more realistic then the school-age population was nearer 50,000. Most children were probably getting some education. This says nothing of quality, which is much more difficult to measure. The Argyll Commission indeed was concerned to emphasise the inadequacy of a great deal of the provision. Often, however, the comments on poor quality teaching in adventure schools perhaps meant little more than that they were not under the control of the Church of Scotland, or that they did not teach Latin. They did not assess whether such schools were providing what paying parents actually wanted. As for levels of literacy, when civil registration of marriages was introduced in 1855, signatures were used as a measure of literacy; 89 per cent of Scottish men could sign their name compared with 70 per cent in England and Wales. For women the figures were 77 and 70 per cent. There were regional variations. In the majority of lowland counties male literacy was over 90 per cent. It was also high in some Highland counties like Argyll, but low in the Western Highlands and Islands due to the difficulties of a scattered population in remote parishes.[6]

Calvinistic influence in education was pervasive, and was exerted through control of denominational schools and in the administration of the teacher training colleges. David Stow, an evangelical elder of Thomas Chalmers's kirk, who, with William Collins, had developed church day-schools in Glasgow in the 1820s, pioneered a teacher-training college in Scotland. Stow and George Lewis, associated in the Glasgow Educational Society, opened the 'normal school' at Dundas Vale in 1836, the first teacher-training college. Its purpose was to ensure that Christian teachers were providing a moral education based on the Bible. This was seen as the way to ensure peace and social stability. As Lewis had written, 'If the nation will not pay for the school-master to prevent crime, it must pay ten fold for the repression of social disorder, and for coercing an unhappy, dissolute and reckless population'. This experiment shortly ran into debt and Stow was forced to seek state aid, thereby losing church autonomy. As a result, the Church and state became entangled in an uneasy and compromising relationship. At the Disruption the Church of Scotland acquired the college and set up another in Edinburgh. Naturally, the Free Church duplicated these, so that by 1850 there were four normal colleges in Scotland.[7]

While denominational religious conflict between the Kirk and the Free Church contributed to an increase in the number of schools and colleges after 1843, it also acted as a barrier to change. There was a widespread recognition that if Scotland were to continue to boast a national system of education then new provision was required, but all attempts at reform of the system between 1843 and 1872 came to grief on the issue of religious instruction and who should control education. Some ten educational bills were brought into Parliament between 1849 and 1862 to try to achieve control and better supervision and inspection of the proliferation of Scottish schools, and to expand provision. All were wrecked on the Scylla and Charybdis of sectarian rivalry. The failure to achieve a specifically Scottish educational measure meant that Scottish regulation was tagged on to English legislation. So Scotland got the Revised Education Code in 1861, which survived until 1885, when grants to schools were firmly related to levels of attendance and to evidence of the elementary provision of the three R's and little else. There was no reward for education beyond the elementary.[8]

The 1872 Act to a large extent continued that pattern of the anglicising of Scottish education, but the Scottish legislation achieved a more unequivocal transfer to public authorities. While in England, voluntary and board schools developed separately, in Scotland all but a tiny fraction of schools were incorporated in the state system. Only Episcopal and Catholic schools remained apart, and continued to be funded by — generally precariously — voluntary subscription. Almost a thousand school boards were created in towns and parishes throughout Scotland, a pattern that survived until 1918. Again, in contrast to England and a reflection of the extent of existing provision, elementary education was made compulsory for all children between the ages of 5 and 13, though with easy exemption in the early years for those who could show evidence of an ability to read, write and do elementary sums.

The new schools boards were in no sense free from church influence since the clergy were always well represented. But the restructuring of Scottish educational institutions involved increasing state control from London. The Scotch Education Department (SED) was created in 1872, but its locus of power and headquarters were in Dover House, London, not in Edinburgh. The administrative links between SED and the English Department were further maintained by the fact that they shared the same president, vice-president and permanent secretary. Until the creation of the Scottish Office in 1885, and Henry Craik's appointment as permanent secretary, the SED lacked any real independence from the English Department.

Because of a franchise that was deliberately geared to property, there was scarcely any working-class representation on urban school boards. Instead they were dominated by the vested interests of the clergy and business. The fact that the meetings were held on a weekday and that there was no payment or expenses for services acted as a further deterrent. For middle-class women, on the other hand, the school board's elections held every three years proved to be of immense symbolic and practical importance as a way of entering political public life. In the absence of the parliamentary vote, they provided the first major political forum for women to be able to participate in local politics and to speak out on issues affecting their sex. In practice however, the number of women was always small. They made almost no progress in rural areas and in cities a maximum of three women was usually elected. Flora Stevenson became the first woman chairman of the Edinburgh board when she was elected in 1900.

The uneven pace of an industrialising and urbanising society was reflected in distinctive religious, cultural and educational divisions. The largest number of schools, pupils and teachers was to be found in Glasgow, but many of those were in the Catholic schools outside the state system. Irish settlement, especially in the wake of the famine, produced an ever-growing demand for Catholic schools and teachers. Nonetheless, by the 1860s, the Catholic clergy could boast that they had overcome the immense difficulties and could offer pupils instruction in the three R's and the Bible. But the community lacked the resources to pay adequate school fees or to raise the necessary funds towards teachers' salaries and school buildings. As a result, by the end of the century, there was a growing crisis in Catholic education.[9] The quality of teaching was variable and inadequate because so many Catholic teachers were unqualified. It was not until 1894 that the first Scottish Catholic Teacher Training College was opened in Bearsden, Glasgow.

In Edinburgh, in contrast, education was dominated by the legal, medical, professional and literary middle classes. A high proportion of pupils attended private, fee-paying schools, many administered by wealthy businessmen belonging to the Edinburgh Merchant Company. There were increasing pressures towards uniformity within the system. Although regional variations were apparent, the inspectorate was an important pressure for centralisation. Inspectors were a remarkably cohesive and influential force, often remaining in their posts for many years, and so imposing a particular perspective. Inspectors provided Henry Craik and John Struthers, who replaced him as permanent secretary in 1904, with invaluable annual reports on the local state of education. Many, like S.S. Laurie and Dr Kerr, did much to propagate the view that in the North-East of Scotland, at least, the meritocratic ladder was still firmly in place as late as 1890. As Kerr commented, 'Out of 150 teachers in Aberdeen, Banff and Moray, at least 130 are Masters of the Arts. You will find that nowhere else in Scotland. . .elsewhere in Scotland you will not find one in fifty'.

61. Flora Stevenson, portrait by Alexander Roche. An end of career formal portrait of the first woman to be a member and then convenor of the Edinburgh School Board. The caring and educational aspects of domesticity were transformed by many determined women into influential public roles. *Scottish National Portrait Gallery.*

The parochial system ended in 1872, although the idealisation of it continued to flourish and to be romanticised by educational writers, inspectors and presbyterian church officials who had reaped the benefits. Recently, Robert Anderson has suggested that the democratic potential of the Scottish educational system would have seemed less remarkable if it had been placed in a European context, especially in relation to the French educational system, rather than contrasting it simply with England. He reached the conclusion that 'the importance of the parochial system was limited to certain regions, that it served the convenience of the rural middle class rather than the direct interests of the poor, and that only a minority of university students came from the parish schools'.[10] Lindy Moore, meanwhile, has explored educational opportunities and gender differences in Scotland. The democratic tradition of education may have encouraged easier access to the higher branches of education, but 'a presbyterian tradition stamped women as second class citizens'.[11] Such a statement may be blunt, but it highlights an aspect of the myth, previously unexplored, of a so-called educational structure based on merit and equality of access.

II

Secondary education was preserved for the middle class. The 1872 Act was concerned almost exclusively with elementary education and, in line with English concepts of different kinds of education for different social classes, the two levels developed separately. Secondary schools were not seen as a stage to follow elementary education. Rather it was hoped that a system of middle-class education would be created without state finance and through the improvement of the endowed grammar schools. In Scotland the difference was that neither schools nor universities had the wealth and spread of charitable endowments that were to be found in England. This was perhaps most noticeable in the private sector for female education. In England, single-sex schools, such as those established by Miss Buss and Miss Beale, mushroomed in the mid-Victorian period. There was no equivalent development in Scotland. The first introduction of this English pattern of girls' education into Scotland was the founding of St Leonard's School in 1877 under the headship of Miss Louisa Lumsden. This was followed by the opening of St George's High School for Girls in Edinburgh in 1888, modelled upon the Girls' Public Day School Company which had started in Manchester in 1872.

Nevertheless, the process of altering the old charity schools was under way in the early 1870s. In Edinburgh, the long-established charitable Merchant Company schools were turned into large fee-paying schools for the middle classes. Despite resistance from the Town Council, George Heriot's Hospital went the same way. Elsewhere, former burgh schools, academies like Montrose and Ayr and the High School of Dundee were designated 'higher class' schools and gave instruction in advanced subjects such as Latin, modern languages and mathematics.

This process was not carried out without conflict and debate. There were two different ideals. For some, secondary education was something that should follow from elementary education for all who wanted to take advantage of it, offering a broadly-based 'useful' education. For others, secondary education was seen essentially as a different kind of education, where a classical culture was passed on that differentiated a small, strictly-limited élite from the rest. The SED encouraged the development of the latter. In 1888 Craik introduced the Scottish Leaving Certificate (SLC) for secondary pupils. It required a level of advanced study that was only available in secondary schools and generally out of reach of most elementary ones. In response to the new certificate, which gave a specific goal to aim for, some school boards began to develop higher-grade schools where children could be taught to SLC level. By the 1890s there were two tiers of secondary education — an upper tier of larger burgh schools, plus the leading endowed schools, providing for the better-off middle classes, and a lower tier of secondary education under the school boards that built on the elementary foundation. But boards found it difficult to develop secondary education because of limited public funds. Rate aid was not allowed and they had to depend on fees and endowments. Class differences in educational opportunity were magnified. The potential for the working classes to receive secondary education broadened after 1892 when all elementary and much secondary education became free and scholarships were more widely available. Typically, the real priority for working-class children was to leave school at the age of 14 (after the 1901 Act raised the leaving age and removed most exemptions) in search of work.

III

For a small nation, the number of universities was impressive. In Aberdeen there were two: Marischal College was in the modern city and catered for the townsmen, while King's College in Old Aberdeen traditionally drew largely on the male population from the rural hinterland. There were also universities in St Andrews, Edinburgh and Glasgow. Technical education could be obtained by working men in day and evening classes at institutions subsidised by the Science and Art Departments. At Glasgow there was 'Anderson's University' which had been founded in 1796, and at Edinburgh the Watt Institution, founded as the Edinburgh School of Arts in 1821. The Scottish universities were considered to be national and public institutions. This was reinforced by the Universities (Scotland) Act in 1858.

An essential strength of the Scottish universities was considered to be that students, coming up at the age of 15 or 16, were offered a liberal, general curriculum with an emphasis on philosophy, rather than a specialised classical or mathematical curriculum under the Oxford and Cambridge system. The Scots, once again, were more in line with countries such as France, as regards the general arts curriculum

62. Not a girl in sight in the chemistry class at Harris Academy, Dundee! Science teaching was gradually introduced in secondary schools by the end of the century. *Dundee District Libraries*.

being taught, than with England. Throughout the nineteenth century the national university system was staunchly defended by the Scots in the face of the English view that state involvement should be minimal. The 1889 Universities (Scotland) Act was a compromise between the two systems. The general curriculum survived, but as an alternative to a new specialised degree. After 1892, the degree became a collection of specialist subjects, requiring a high level of entrance qualification, very different from the philosophical and general education which the Scots had wished to preserve since the early nineteenth century.[12] Then they had been seen as public institutions with a right of access for all who could profit. Then a talented boy could make his way up through the parish or burgh school, and at the age of fifteen could attend university classes and be provided with the option of graduation. The universities therefore did give a genuine semblance of truth to the belief in a meritocratic structure of education, albeit that class differences and inequalities were retained in accordance with occupation and income.

In the 1860s, the Argyll Commission carried out a study of fathers' occupations which showed that the universities were serving a wide range of the professional and skilled sections of the community, but few from the unskilled and poor. Approximately a third of the students came from the professional classes, and the sons of ministers formed 13 per cent of the general sample: the reality was that a minister's son was about a hundred times as likely to go to university as a miner's son. Nonetheless, nearly a quarter of the students at Glasgow University were from the working class, but many of these were adults paying their own way. There were no rigorous entrance standards beyond a knowledge of Latin, though that in itself excluded most from urban elementary schools. Also, many of those from working-class backgrounds did not stay long. Out of 3,122 arts students at Glasgow between 1861 and 1872, 36 per cent stayed for only one session; 17 per cent for two and only 47 per cent for more than two. The commission also somewhat undermined the belief in the centrality of the parish school route to university. More than 60 per cent of students at Edinburgh and Glasgow universities did not come from parish schools but from secondary schools of different kinds. This was slightly less the case in the North-East, but here too the bulk of children who went to university tended to be rural middle class rather than the poor.[13]

IV

The 1892 legislation confirmed the élitist concepts of selective excellence, but it did allow women into the universities for the first time in 1893. This followed a two-pronged attack. During the 1860s, a bitter and protracted struggle was begun by a few female pioneers and a small nucleus of male support to gain admission for women to study medicine. In Edinburgh, Sophia Jex Blake managed to matriculate in 1869, despite a wave of opposition from professors and many students. The controversy culminated in court action and the Surgeon's Hall riot in 1870, when male students hustled and impeded women attending an anatomy lecture. A quieter but no less insistent strand originated with the Edinburgh Association for the University Education of Women, which had its origins in 1868. A series of classes held in parallel with university lectures led in 1874 to the University Certificate in Arts. Like Queen Margaret College in Glasgow, this was the base from which Scottish Universities were to produce many trained and highly educated women teachers in the early years of the twentieth century.[14]

In mid-Victorian Scotland there were two fundamentally conflicting approaches to education. One stressed open access, community and local control, whilst the other stressed restricted access to education and central control. In the latter category were middle-class people consolidating their hold and status over the professions by the restriction of entry, formalisation of qualifications and the establishment of professional associations. Women were seen as especially threatening to occupational and social status, notably by schoolmasters and medical practitioners. This led most male practitioners to tolerate or even encourage the female nursing movement, since there was a demand for labour, whilst vehemently opposing all developments in female education in an already overcrowded profession.[15]

Access to the labour market, and above all, roles within the family and household, were fundamentally influenced by gender. These restrictions and specialisations were supported and reproduced by education. Girls' education provided them with some knowledge of domestic economy, so as to turn out well-trained domestic servants and provide for their future roles as wives and mothers. Domestic service was the single largest source of employment for working-class girls during the Victorian era. A growing interest in domestic training for girls was part of a much wider response to social changes in industrial patterns at the workplace and in family lifestyles.

The family formed a central unit where ideas about class, domestic education and sex segregation in schooling found an important focus. Policy makers feared that the working-class family in towns and cities was falling into a state of physical deterioration through poor housing, disease, bad health and moral decay. Sir James Kay Shuttleworth advocated 'a system of education. . .in which young females of the poor may be instructed in domestic economy'. The gravity of human suffering in working-class homes provoked a crisis of confidence within the middle classes since it was in direct contradiction to the notion of a stable social order. It was thus in a wider context of growing awareness of the social consequences of the industrial revolution that the beginnings of rudimentary and ad hoc learning in domestic education for working-class girls were to be located. In the early and mid-Victorian period it was left to the discretion of the presbytery and voluntary bodies to organise a teacher-training programme in domestic education.

Female entry into normal colleges from the late 1830s onwards was largely due to David Stow, who believed that infant schools should resemble a family. In his view 'no infant school can be perfect. . .without a female hand'. Following the introduction of the 1846 Minute, which instituted the state-financed pupil teacher system, formal distinctions were devised along gender lines in the training college syllabus. Notions of masculine and feminine subjects were constructed in the entrance examination known as the Queen's Scholarship. Girls were expected to answer questions on domestic economy, needlework, French and botany, whereas boys were required to answer questions of mathematics, algebra, physiology, geology, Euclid and Greek. Teaching classics at the colleges was the result of lengthy negotiations with the London-based Privy Council. The successful outcome in favour of the presbytery's wishes provided material support for the belief in maintaining higher intellectual standards for boys in Scotland.

Virtually all males received a grant, but female entrants were required to be self-financed, and were dependent on parental support to subsidise their college education. Females were recruited from the skilled sections of the working classes and from the lower middle classes. Many were daughters of clerks and shopkeepers. Boys, meanwhile, tended to be sons of labourers and farmers.[16] Inspectors who visited the Presbyterian colleges frequently commented that girls tended to be more 'articulate' and 'cultivated' than male students. However, despite their higher social origins, employment in the mainstream sector of education was severely restricted for girls in teaching, especially without a background in classics, whereas in England this was not such a hurdle in gaining employment. Males had different job destinations from females in an educational hierarchy.

Males could confidently expect to teach in mainstream institutions such as parish and public schools, complete with security of tenure. Females found employment in a voluntary network of informal and frequently short-lived schools, such as infant, private, industrial and 'dame' schools. There was a marked difference at a national level in the employment pattern between the sexes in Scotland and England before 1872.

Table 1. *Women as a Percentage of All Schoolteachers in Scotland and England and Wales, 1851–1911*

Year	Scotland Total number of schoolteachers	Female (per cent)	England and Wales Female (per cent)
1851	9,325	35	62
1871	12,192	49	74
1881	13,489	59	73
1891	20,109	64	74
1901	25,414	68	74
1911	26,788	70	73

The census figures (Table 1) probably conceal some of the influence of seasonal demand and informal school networks, but they are enough to show that the feminisation of the teaching profession took place much later in Scotland and took place as a result of the legislation of the early 1870s.

The concept of the Dominie represented a cherished and distinctive part of the educational tradition. This was identified with the 'lad o' pairts', the graduate and the parish schoolmaster. The Scots word 'dominie' derives from the Latin, *dominus*, meaning lord or master. This description conformed to the stereotype of a Scottish dominie. The curriculum was academic and the authoritarian régime enforced by the tawse, a heavy leather strap. The parish schoolmaster was usually equipped to teach Latin, since it was one of the requirements for entry into the universities. The parish school was co-educational, but girls were also frequently educated in separate schools without learning the classics. The census returns of 1851 showed that 5.9 per cent of boys were being taught ancient languages compared with 0.5 per cent of girls. More boys were likely to be learning maths and Greek in Scottish schools than in England. The picture for girls was different; teaching classics was considered by many parents and teachers to be a waste of time, since it could not lead to a career. Rather, employment for girls was seen as an interlude, since the female primary role in life was motherhood. Even so, as a result of the gendering process, employment opportunities were opening up for females, and in 1861 landowners could legally appoint females as sewing mistresses in parochial schools.

The 1872 Act represented a historic turning point in the gender composition of the teaching labour force. Employment opportunities opened up for women teachers in state schools in an unprecedented way. The rule that all children over the age of five should attend school produced a large demand for teachers, especially in the infant sector. Simultaneously, the rhetoric of belief that women, more than men, were 'naturally' more suited to teaching young children was increasingly echoed in the offices of Whitehall. Gordon, Richmond and Hamilton, senior SED officials, expressed the view in 1878 that if children 'are brought under the gentler, more natural qualities of female teachers, a better result may be expected to be attained than if trained entirely by men'.

Economic necessity was another driving force for the changes in educational policies and practices regarding the preferred employment of males. Women were cheaper to employ, willing and plentiful, and school boards, the employers, needed an immediate supply of inexpensive labour. The average salaries of male teachers between 1872 and 1900 varied between £121 and £145 a year, but those of female teachers varied between £62 and £72, albeit that there were many gradations of this, depending on certification and occupational status. Male teachers became scarce, partly with the expansion of white-collar opportunities in banking, the civil service and clerical work, though many male teachers blamed cheaper female labour to explain why they were deserting the profession.

Some eminent church officials, such as Dr Ross from the Glasgow training college, felt that educational standards had dropped and the legacy of the dominie's influence had been eroded. He described 'two evils': firstly, that the churches had to admit more young women to fill the training college vacancies left by the young men, and secondly, that women 'would now have to be employed in the advanced classics with a consequent decline in the numbers taught Latin and maths'.[17]

From the women's point of view, employment in teaching was a mixed blessing. Some of them regarded entry into the profession as a revolutionary movement, and as providing women with a new independence in terms of a career and salary. Many could remember the pre-1872 era, when women performed an important service, but mainly in the religious sector of education. Others deeply resented that they had exactly the same qualifications as men, but were paid much lower wages. Efforts to claim equal pay after 1900 were countered by the male teachers' argument that women were not the main breadwinners in the family and so did not deserve equal pay. Overall, the equal pay movement was much weaker in Scotland as compared with England, where there was an active female lobby in London inside the National Union of Teachers even before 1900.[18]

V

In the late Victorian period, Scottish public schools conformed to one type of organisation — that in which there was a master responsible for the whole and the mistress under him for the teaching of younger children. Big rooms were commonly divided into several classrooms. Public schools were co-educational, but each sex had separate entrances. Pupils' perceptions of teachers varied according to the school, area and community in which they lived. Patrick Dollan, later to become the first Catholic Lord Provost of Glasgow, grew up in the close-knit mining community of Baillieston in the 1890s. His memories of school are fond, and especially of Miss Forster who, in addition to her teaching duties, also acted as musical superintendent for school choirs, gave piano lessons and interviewed parents.

> I am sure Miss Forster and her colleagues must have worked a twelve hour day. . .yet her salary probably did not exceed £100, but I never knew her to complain about her work. . .Very often they used their pocket money to buy books, pencils, pens and rubbers when our parents were hard up. . .She and her mother lived in a small home adjoining the school so she was always at hand when needed.[19]

For other people, the memories of school were less fond. Schools were associated with an authoritarian régime, bullying, the strap, religious indoctrination and cold classrooms. A.S. Neill, a dominie who taught in the Borders village of Gretna Green, was highly critical of rote learning, the belt and the examination system. He reflected on the meaning of education. In his village, the practical reality for boys was leaving school at fourteen and working in the ploughfields, whilst girls entered domestic service or factory work. His pessimistic conclusion was that 'my work is hopeless, for education should aim at bringing a new generation that will be better than the old. The present system is to produce the same kind of man as we see today'.[20]

VI

The early twentieth century saw increased state intervention in the lives of pupils and teachers. Government, especially under the Liberals, made the school a more central agency of reform in terms of improving the physical welfare of the working classes before school-leaving age at fourteen. As a result of the 1908 Education (Scotland) Act, school boards were to provide medical inspection of pupils as well as 'the feeding of necessitous children'. They were given the authority to take action against parents where a pupil was said to be filthy or 'verminous'. The year 1908 also saw the centralisation of Scottish training schools of cookery and household management under the control of the SED. The education of girls in domestic affairs had become a state concern rather than leaving it up to mothers and voluntary agencies, which had been the case in the mid-Victorian era. The 1908 legislation was once again the outcome of a crisis about the family and the nation's health. It had been sparked off in 1899 by the discovery that 8,000 out of 11,000 Army recruits in Manchester were physically unfit to fight in the Boer War to defend the British Empire. High levels of infant mortality and low birth rates were also highlighted. In England, the figure stood at 146 per 1,000 deaths in 1900 and the respective figure in Scotland was 124. In response to these alarming statistics a Scottish Royal Commission was set up in 1902 with 'a view to contributing towards the sources of national strength'. In England, a committee on 'Physical Deterioration' was set up in 1903.

The findings of both reports were comparable, although the Scottish Commission had a stronger bias on the amount of military drill and physical exercises to be undertaken in schools. The school was seen as a vital institution, as pupils would form the next generation of citizens. The commissioners discovered that no statistics existed on the weight and height of children from middle- and working-class backgrounds. Leslie MacKenzie, medical health inspector to the local government, was duly asked to undertake this task, and he selected a sample of 1,300 pupils in Edinburgh and Aberdeen. In both cities, MacKenzie found that pupils in working-class districts were smaller, slighter and less well nourished than pupils from middle-class homes. A correlation was seen to exist between motherhood and nationhood. Anxieties were rife about bad housekeeping and poor diet militating against the improvement of the racial stock. Teachers were increasingly viewed as agents of the state in their capacity as mediators between the home and the school. The introduction of medical inspection into schools created a more direct route for teachers' comments on the standard of physical care of the pupil. James Maxton, the future Labour MP, a teacher at St James's School in Bridgeton, noted that 'in a class of sixty boys and girls of about eleven years old. . .thirty-six out of the sixty could not bring both knees and heels together because of rickety malformations'.[21] Reporting on children walking barefoot to school and checking heads for lice became a standard feature of school inspection. Working-class mothers, because of appalling housing conditions, fought an ongoing battle to keep their children's head free of vermin. Increased state intervention in education brought with it a new degree of bureaucratic officialdom. This took the form of domestic science inspectors, medical officers and school health visitors.

The early twentieth century saw a further shift in the wake of religious influence in education. In 1905 the Presbyterian churches finally relinquished control over the teacher-training colleges in return for large financial compensation from the government. The Catholic church continued to go it alone and retained its religious influence in teacher training. However, the entire organisation of teacher-training was transformed. In the major cities, provincial committees were set up to supervise the training of teachers under the central control of the

SED. Students could undertake concurrent courses at the universities and training centres. From 1906 onwards, educational policy aimed at eliminating all untrained teachers from the profession. By the outbreak of war, the majority of women teachers were certificated and trained. This was a remarkable and unique phenomenon in Britain, since just under half of the teaching force in England and Wales remained untrained in 1914.

VI

An educational ladder based on open access was fallacy for the bulk of the population growing up in 1914. Class differences were maintained in accordance with a hierarchical structure in secondary education and the universities. When the position of women is taken into consideration the Scottish education system was in some respects even more inegalitarian than the English one. Average salaries for women teachers were higher in England, and there were far more promotional opportunities in single sex schools, resulting in female headships. Under the Scottish co-educational system, headships were monopolised by men.

On the other hand, for myths to sustain themselves, they must have an organic life which changes over time and place. As Arthur Miller the playwright once said '. . .A myth in order to exist must be unanswerable. As soon as it becomes fathomable it's discarded'. As recent research suggests, the distinctiveness of Scottish education has been exaggerated, especially if it is viewed in a European context. However, if it is set against a specifically English context then the Scottish system is different. But given that educational policies were largely controlled by the Treasury in Whitehall rather than from the Scottish capital, it is not surprising that the process of anglicising had its roots in the nineteenth century.

NOTES

I should like to express my warm thanks to Hamish Fraser, Lynn Jamieson, Bill Knox, Andrew McPherson and Bob Morris for their most helpful, suggestive comments on an earlier draft of this essay, and to thank Peter Baehn for help with proof reading.

1. E. Muir, 'The Scottish Character', *The Listener*, XIX, 23 June 1938, pp. 1323–5.

2. R. Anderson, *Education and Opportunity in Victorian Scotland* (Oxford, 1983). See also E. G. West. *Education and the Industrial Revolution* (London, 1975).

3. For an attempt to redress this, see H. Corr, 'The Gender Division of Labour in the Scottish Teaching Profession', unpublished PhD thesis, University of Edinburgh, 1984.

4. D. McCrone, S. Kendrick and P. Straw (eds.), 'Representing Scotland: Culture and Nationalism' in *The Making of Scotland: Nation, Culture and Social Change* (Edinburgh, 1989), A. McPherson and C. Raab, *Governing Education: A Sociology of Policy since 1945* (Edinburgh, 1988).

5. For details of the pre-1872 system, see J. Scotland, *The History of Scottish Education*, London, 1969.

6. For a discussion on quality, see E. G. West, *op. cit.* On literacy, see D. Withrington, 'Schooling, Literacy and Society' in *People and Society in Scotland*, vol I (Edinburgh, 1988), pp. 163–88.

7. M. Cruickshank, *A History of the Training of Teachers in Scotland* (London, 1970).

8. J. D. Myers, 'Scottish Nationalism and the Antecedents of the 1872 Education Act', *Scottish Education Studies*, IV, 2, (1972); D. J. Withrington, 'Towards a National System 1867–72', *ibid*; B. Lenman and J. Stocks, 'The Beginnings of State Education in Scotland 1872–85', *ibid*.

9. M. Skinnider, 'Catholic Elementary Education in Glasgow 1818–1918' in T. R. Bone (ed.), *Studies in the History of Scottish Education* (London, 1967).

10. Anderson, *Education and Opportunity*, p. 336.

11. L. Moore, 'Invisible Scholars: Girls Learning Latin and Mathematics in the Elementary Public Schools of Scotland before 1872', *History of Education* 13, 2, (1984), 121–37.

12. Macpherson and Raab, *Governing Education*, pp. 29–50.

13. Anderson, *Education and Opportunity*, pp. 103–161.

14. S. Hamilton, 'The First Generation of University Women' in G. Donaldson (ed.), *Four Centuries: Edinburgh University Life 1583–1983* (Edinburgh, 1983), pp. 99–115.

15. W. Alexander, *First Ladies in Medicine* (Wellcome Institute for the History of Medicine, University of Glasgow, 1987).

16. Cruickshank, *History of the Training of Teachers*, p. 61.

17. For a fuller discussion of all these issues see Corr, 'The Sexual Division of Labour in the Scottish Teaching Profession' in W. Humes and H. Paterson (eds.), *Scottish Culture and Scottish Education, 1800–1980* (Edinburgh, 1983), also J. Fewell and F. Paterson (eds.), *Girls in Their Prime: Scottish Education Revisited* (Edinburgh, 1990).

18. H. Corr, 'Politics of the Sexes in English and Scottish Teachers' Unions 1870–1914', in H. Corr and L. Jamieson (eds.), *Politics of Everyday Life: Continuity and Change in Work and the Family*, (London and New York, 1990).

19. P. J. Dollan, *Autobiography. Recollections of his School Days at St Bridget's School, Baillieston . . .*, pp. 55–6.

20. A. S. Neill, *A Dominie's Log* (1986), p. 12.

21. W. Knox, *James Maxton* (Manchester, 1987), pp. 202.

CHAPTER 11

Religion, Class and Church Growth

Callum G. Brown

I

Since the nineteenth century, it has been received wisdom for British historians and sociologists that industrialisation and urban growth instigated the decline of religion. Social historians who might differ quite fundamentally on other issues have tended to agree on this thesis. Thus, Marxist historians like Edward Thompson and Eric Hobsbawm have generally concurred with anti-Marxist historians like Harold Perkins and Alan Gilbert.[1] Where church growth took place, they generally agree that it was largely confined to the early stages of industrialisation (in Britain, between c.1750 and c.1830) when the new social classes of the bougeoisie and the skilled proletariat found temporary group identity in evangelical religion (like Methodism) before turning thereafter to 'secular' institutions like trade unions.

Historians of Scottish society have usually followed this traditional interpretation. Whilst pointing to evidence of slightly higher levels of church adherence in Scotland than in England, Christopher Smout still stresses the debilitating effects of industrial and urban growth upon religious thought and adherence, and upon the ability of the church to remain the focus of community life. Two supposed dichotomies lie at the root of this approach: a dichotomy between pious rural society and secular urban society, and a dichotomy between the religiously 'respectable' middle classes and the alienated working classes. Smout has argued that 'the eighteenth-century minister, like the laird, personified the community, and when the congregation listened to him it identified him with the parish, a division more meaningful in the rural world than the [urban] division of class'. By 1890, he goes on, 'industrialization and migration had weakened the old idea of the parish community but strengthened that of class. . . . The minister . . . personified nothing but his obvious middle-class background'.[2] This view was put most succinctly, if crudely, by two Scottish ecclesiastical historians, Drummond and Bulloch; speaking of the 1840s, they said: 'The social structure of the industrial areas was a pyramid and its broad base was pagan'.[3]

This traditional 'pessimist' thesis, which sees religious decline emanating in the early (or, at latest, the mid-) nineteenth century, no longer goes unchallenged. Researchers in both England and Wales[4] and in Scotland[5] have started to propose a radically different interpretation which disputes the timing and causes of religious decline. In essence, the 'optimists' deny that religious decline took place during nineteenth-century urbanisation, dispute that the Victorian working classes were alienated from either religion or the churches, and relocate secularisation from the nineteenth to the twentieth century. Contrary to Geoffrey Best's 1971 submission that in studying mid-Victorian religion 'the social historian is driven to rely more completely than usual on his own judgement', new methods of inquiry and detailed research are being brought to bear, and are undermining some very old shibboleths of social and church history. Or, to quote Professor Best more approvingly on this subject: 'Generalisations sink like stones at the touch of fresh research'.[6]

II

The availability from the mid-nineteenth century of statistics of church adherence and practice provides the historian with an idea of long-term religious change. The basic method of measurement is not the absolute numbers of church members or churchgoers, but the *proportion* of the population who fell into those categories. This is particularly important in the period 1830–1914 when there was extreme demographic turbulence. The population of Scotland doubled between 1831 and 1911 (from 2.3 to 4.8 million), and its distribution shifted markedly from rural to urban areas and, in general terms, from the north to west central Scotland. This fracturing of settled patterns of life, work and residence posed enormous religious challenges — not least for migrants — in raising cash and loans to build churches, manses, presbyteries and parsonages in growing districts. Moreover, churches had depended in the past on a more settled social and economic environment, with the parish church nestling amidst the relative stability and tranquillity of rural and village society. The rise of industrialism and larger cities disrupted the traditional place of the kirk.

In volume 1 of this series, it was suggested that despite the emergence before 1830 of dissenting presbyterian churches (notably the Secession and Relief Churches) in which ambitious middle-class and artisan

63. Thomas Chalmers (1780–1847) photographed at the time of the Disruption of the Church of Scotland. This was part of a series taken by Henry Adamson for the massive painting of the Disruption that now hangs in the Assembly Hall of the Free Kirk. Not sure what to read into that tight-lipped face! *Scottish National Portrait Gallery.*

families achieved access to worship and freedom from élite control, the provision of churches fell behind the growth of population during the period 1750–1830; the same occurred in England.[7] By 1841, for example, there were only about 240 church seats per 1,000 population in the Highlands and Hebrides, 401 seats in the North-East (from Shetland to Kincardineshire), whilst in the the Lowlands provision varied considerably from a high of 561 for agricultural Berwickshire to a low of 232 for the rapidly-growing industrial county of Lanarkshire.[8] In the absence of other data, it seems likely that this reflected a decline in active church connection between 1750 and 1840.

When we move into the 1840s, evidence emerges of a reversal of this decline. Church provision improved dramatically, instigated by the most spectacular schism in British ecclesiastical history — the Disruption of 1843 — when nearly half the adherents and over a third of the clergy walked out of the Established Church of Scotland to form the Free Church of Scotland. This unleashed large-scale church building by all denominations over the ensuing four decades, making popular access to worship much easier. Even by 1851, church sittings per 1,000 population had virtually doubled in the Highlands and Hebrides to around 474, and had risen to 592 in the North-East, 701 in Berwickshire and 302 in Lanarkshire. Despite significant Free Church building in urban communities, ratios remained poorer there; in Glasgow (306), Edinburgh and Leith (422), Dundee (449) and Aberdeen (472), though low provision was more often to be found in some smaller towns like Airdrie (327), Arbroath (263), Forfar (366) and Rutherglen (332).

The mid-Victorian improvement in church provision is a key factor to bear in mind when examining levels of church adherence thereafter. In part, it was due to rising standards of living, especially for those in lower-middle- and upper-working-class occupations. Congregations could muster greater members' donations to meet payments on church building loans, and could erect larger churches (with accompanying economies of scale) and mission churches for poorer worshippers. As a consequence, building churches also acted as a 'supply-led' attraction to those who had previously found it difficult to gain access.

The statistical data that become available after mid-century (given in Figure 1) indicate that the Victorian period (though not the Edwardian period) witnessed an increasing degree of popular church adherence. The top line provides an estimate of the total proportion of the population who were connected with a church, either as adult members/adherents or as Sunday-school scholars (of usually 5–15 years of age). Imperfections in the data make it difficult to place too much reliance on the absolute percentage at any given date. However, the figures should be taken as *minimum* ones, for there are many excluded categories of church connection. The value of the top graph line is to show the marked upward *trend* in formal church connection in the second half of the nineteenth century, and the 'levelling-off' that followed at the turn of the century. Despite the tremendous population growth of the nineteenth century, church membership was growing faster — probably more than doubling between 1830 and 1914 — and doing so during the height of industrialisation and urban growth.

Such a conclusion contradicts traditional historiographical analysis.

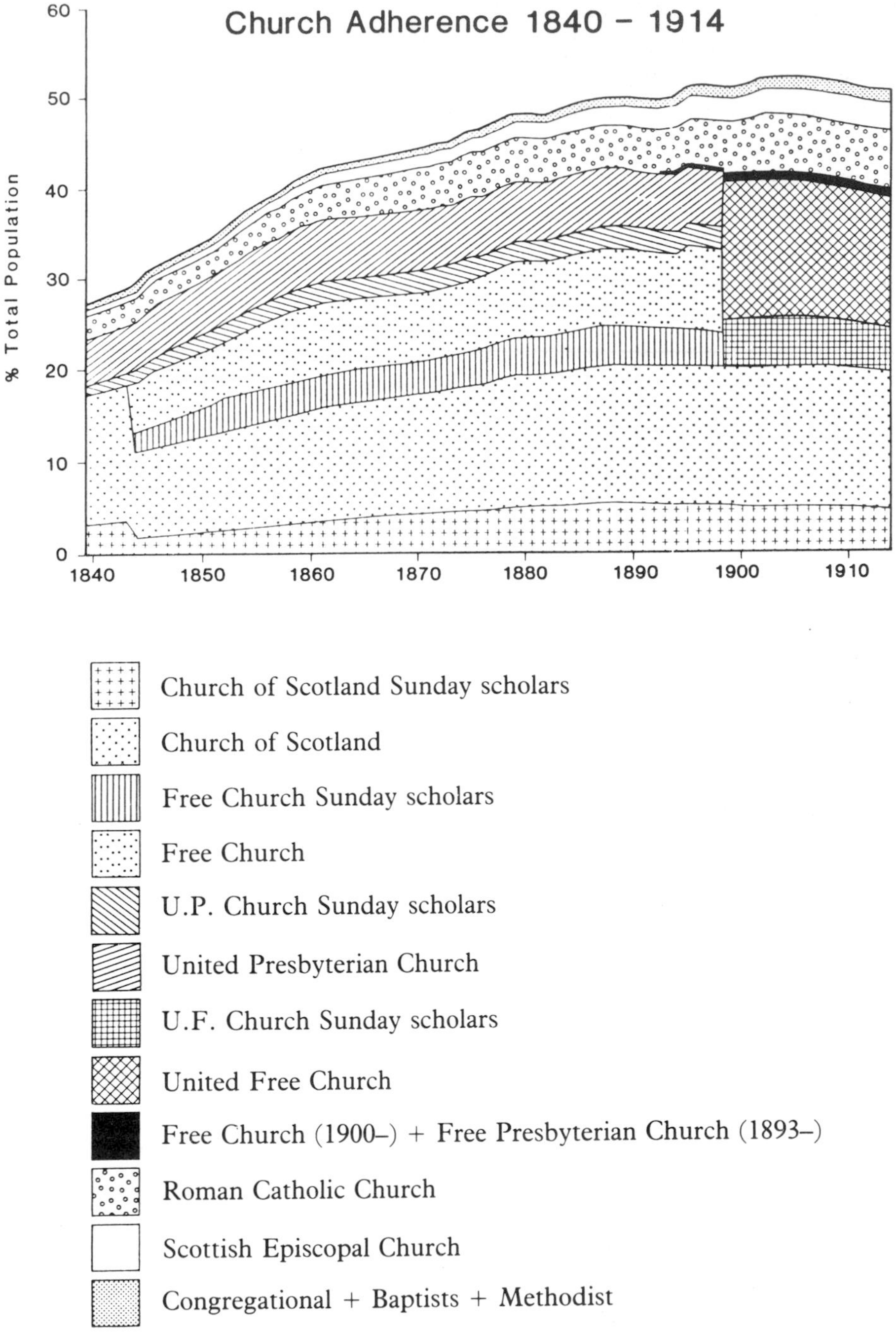
Church Adherence 1840 - 1914
% Total Population
0
10
20
30
40
50
60
1840
1850
1860
1870
1880
1890
1900
1910
Church of Scotland Sunday scholars
Church of Scotland
Free Church Sunday scholars
Free Church
U.P. Church Sunday scholars
United Presbyterian Church
U.F. Church Sunday scholars
United Free Church
Free Church (1900–) + Free Presbyterian Church (1893–)
Roman Catholic Church
Scottish Episcopal Church
Congregational + Baptists + Methodist

Figure 1. See also opposite page.

Gilbert in particular has argued that church growth was largely confined to smaller industrial, or 'proto-industrial', communities in which the qualities of rural religion survived; large cities, he maintains, could not develop the form of community in which religion could thrive amongst all social classes.[9] But recent research disputes this interpretation. A quantitative analysis by the present author of the government's 1851 Religious Census of Great Britain found there to be no statistically significant relationship between levels of church-going and the population size of towns and cities in either Scotland or England and Wales.[10] What did emerge, however, was a statistically significant inverse relationship in Scotland between church-going rate and *rate of growth* of a town's population over the period 1801–51. In short, church-going did not diminish as town size rose; but it *did* diminish when church-building could not keep pace with rapid in-migration to urban areas. Moreover, Hugh McLeod[11] has shown, using the same census, that in total contrast to the position in England and Wales, church-going levels in Scotland in 1851 were *higher* in towns than in rural areas. The reasons for this notable divergence are not fully explained, but may well relate to the relative poverty of Scottish rural society before 1800, and to the resulting low provision of churches.

Figure 1. *Abbreviated technical explanation*
This graph displays the annual estimated membership/active adherence/Sunday-school enrolment of major churches as proportions of the total Scottish population in a stacked-graph format. Considerable manipulation of scant data was required in its construction. For 1870–1914, most data was based on actual church-collected figures, but for 1840–1870 they are derived from sporadic figures and estimates with weighting at 1851 according to denominational alignment revealed by aggregate attendances in the religious census of that year. All gaps, including those between decennial population censuses, were then filled by linear extrapolation. Communicant data of the UP and UF churches were then multiplied by a factor of 1.39 to create a series compatible with Church of Scotland communicants' rolls and Free Church members/adherents. For the year 1841 in the series, estimated Catholic population, the figure 120,000 was substituted for 190,000. That series was then divided by a factor of 1.75 to produce a series of notional mass attenders. Sunday-school data in all cases are based on enrolments. All original church and Sunday-school data are from R. Currie *et al.*, *Churches and Churchgoers: Patterns of Church Growth in the British Isles since 1700* (Oxford, 1977) pp. 128, 132–4, 137 (fns. 7–8), 141–3, 149–50, 153, 154 (fn. 3), 169, 172–3; and *Census of Great Britain, 1851: Religious Worship and Education, Scotland, P.P.*, 1854 lix. Original stacked graph generated by *Supercalc 3*.

In regional terms too, there is little evidence from Scotland that industrial areas had lower levels of church-going than rural areas. Although the highest rates of attendance were generally to be found on the eastern side of Scotland in the mid-nineteenth century, industrial counties and towns did not have lower attendance rates than rural areas; Glasgow, with the lowest church-going rate amongst large towns, was still higher than a quarter of Scottish rural counties. Counties with low attendance rates were mostly rural: Argyllshire, Inverness-shire, West Lothian, and the three south-western counties of Dumfries, Kirkcudbright and Wigtown. Significantly, the high levels of church-going for which the crofting counties of the Highlands and Hebrides were to become famous in the present century did not appear in the 1851 returns — largely because sufficient Free churches had yet to be built.[12]

Scotland, then, experienced a growth of religious adherence until the late nineteenth century. Like Wales, Northern Ireland and Cornwall, the advance of manufacturing and extractive industries does not appear to have adversely affected church connection. And, like England and Wales over the same period, and like the United States between 1880 and 1960, this growth occurred during the very era of rapid urbanisation. The supposed dichotomy between highly religious rural society and irreligious towns is not substantiated from the quantitative evidence

III

An important characteristic which accompanies urbanisation and church growth is *religious pluralisation*, or the multiplication of denominations. In volume I of this series, it was shown that by 1830 somewhere in the region of one-third of the Scottish people were adherents of dissenting churches — predominantly the Secession, Relief, Episcopal and Roman Catholic churches. This extent of dissent was roughly comparable to the situation in England. But the next two decades witnessed major developments in the church structure which raised dissent to dominance. Three events stood out: the Disruption in the Established Church in 1843, which created the Free Church of Scotland; the Irish potato famine of 1845–6 which accelerated migration to Scotland to swell the Catholic Church; and the union in 1847 of the Secession and Relief Churches to create the United Presbyterian (U.P.) Church.[13]

The first of these brought the process of religious pluralisation to its apogee. In ecclesiastical terms, the formation of all the major dissenting presbyterian churches — from the Secession in 1733, the Relief in 1761,

FOR SALE, BY PUBLIC ROUP,

Within CAMPBELL's RED LION HOTEL, King Street, Stirling, on TUESDAY the 8th day of June next, at 12 o'Clock Noon (unless previously sold by private bargain),

1. ALL and Whole that large TENEMENT, fronting the Esplanade of Stirling Castle, presently possessed by Mr William Gaskin, Innkeeper, with a small piece of Bleaching Ground at each end of the House. The House, from its elevated position, commands an extensive and beautiful view. Internally it has good accommodation, and considerable expense has lately been laid out by the present Proprietors in papering, painting and other improvements.

2. Two BUILDING STANCES on the North and South of lot No. 1.

3. All and Haill the First Story or Flat, immediately above the Shop in Broad Street of Stirling sometime possessed by Donald M'Donald, Merchant, and now by William Sinclair, together with three rooms behind the same, which Flat and Rooms are presently possessed by David Pithie and others.

4. The Seat or Pew No. 58, on the ground floor of the East Church of Stirling, presently let to Mr Murray, Clothier.

For farther particulars, apply to ANDREW HUTTON, Writer.

Stirling, 20th May, 1858.

64. Item 4 in this newspaper advertisement shows how Victorian churches were infused with not only the ethos but the reality of *laissez-faire* capitalism. Most church seats were rented out or privately owned, and these rights were bought, bequeathed and (in this case) auctioned like any other property. Note the inclusion of the previous pew-holder's occupation to indicate to bidders the seat's social status. The practice continued in most presbyterian churches until the 1950s (*Stirling Observer*, 20 May 1858. Central Regional Archives).

to the Free in 1843 — had a common origin: opposition to patronage. This system, whereby the Crown, large landowners, universities and town councils selected parish ministers in the Established Church had instigated widespread opposition and secession since the 1730s. But after the Evangelical Party gained control of the Established Church General Assembly for the first time in 1833, it failed, during the so-called 'Ten Years' Conflict' which ensued, to persuade either the courts or government to abolish patronage and withdraw state interference in the Kirk. As a result, just under half of the members and 37 per cent of the ministers dramatically 'went out' on 18 May 1843 to form the Free Church of Scotland.

Although the Disruption was by far the most spectacular church split in British church history, schism was endemic in Scottish Presbyterianism.

In the 1840s alone, a succession of denominations came into being. Indeed, on the very same day as the Free Church was formed, the Evangelical Union (the Morisonians) was created from a split in the Secession Church. Schisms occurred from denominational down to congregational level. In J.M. Barrie's novel *The Little Minister*, a small remnant of Seceders called the Auld Lichts (mostly depressed hand-loom weavers) in the village of Thrums were puzzled one Sabbath when the minister suddenly changed the text for his sermon: 'I hear tell there's saxteen explanations in the Tenements alone', says one worshipper; 'that's a blessing, for if there had just been twa explanations the kirk micht hae split on them'.[14]

Whilst Scottish presbyterianism had a reputation for schism and 'hair splitting', it is important to note that it was a common feature of predominantly Protestant countries; in England and Wales, for example, Methodism had divided into at least nine different churches by the early 1850s. And like Methodism south of the Border, the mid-century witnessed the reversing of the pluralisation process. This can be seen in the rise of church union (or ecumenism, as it is called in the twentieth century). In addition to the formation of the U.P. Church in 1847, most of the remaining Seceders (the 'Auld Lichts') rejoined the Established Church in 1852, and the bulk of the covenanters in the Reformed Presbyterian Church joined the Free Church in 1876. A process of denominational concentration was gathering momentum, perceptible in Figure 1 from the Established Church's increasing proportion of presbyterian adherence after 1860.

Outside presbyterianism, the major development in the church structure was the growth in the Catholic Church. Growth here was almost entirely due to immigration from Ireland, which reached a peak in the 1840s and 1850s, in part sparked by the potato blight of 1845–6. In mid-century, the Church was under-equipped for the flood of mostly poor migrants, and the main chapel building came in the later nineteenth and twentieth centuries. This helps to explain the sustained rise in the Catholic constituency after presbyterian adherence started to fall. However, the most spectacular growth of any of the major denominations was experienced by the smaller Scottish Episcopal Church. After severe decline in the north during the eighteenth and early nineteenth centuries, episcopalianism recruited strongly in the mid-Victorian period amongst the landed classes who were unhappy with developments in presbyterianism, and almost tripled its membership between 1877 and its peak in 1914 through aggressive evangelisation amongst the urban working classes (especially English and Irish immigrants). With smaller denominations like the Baptists and

Congregationalists also growing relatively fast, presbyterian dominance was slipping perceptibly by the turn of the century.

As we can see, the twenty years between 1830 and 1850 constituted an important period of change in the church structure. The explanations of ecclesiastical historians rest on doctrinal issues and the role of leading churchmen like the Rev. Dr Thomas Chalmers, a key figure in the Disruption.[15] However, doctrine and clerical leadership cannot account for changes of such magnitude in organised religion. The social historian must lead the way in examining the powerful grass-roots forces at work in Scottish society.

IV

Underscoring virtually all social-history inquiry into religion during the nineteenth century is the widely-debated issue of class. The greatest consensus amongst historians has emerged in dealing with the religious structure of Highland and Hebridean society. The landowner–crofter split emanating from the previous century only came to rend the Highland Established Church in the midst of the crisis of the 1840s and 1850s; the combination of over-population, the 'Clearances' and potato blight. The Gaels took the 1843 Disruption as the cue for virtually total defection to the Free Church.

As James Hunter, the historian of the crofting community, has said: 'In the Highlands the Disruption was not an ecclesiastical dispute. It was class conflict'.[16] It is hard to overstate the role of the Free Church as a social institution in Highland society, for there was very little else. Attracting between 90 and 95 per cent of church adherents in the North, the social régime of the Free Church marked off the 'godly' crofter-fishers from the 'lukewarm' landowners by strict Sabbath observance, distinctive Gaelic psalm-singing, the ministers' ranting at 'backsliding' through drink, dancing and immorality, and the annual communion seasons, when communicants from several parishes gathered for a week of summer prayer-meetings and open-air services. Though some Free Church ministers in the early years were vigorous in their criticism of landowners and the 'Clearances', the Kirk for the most part seems to have promoted godly dignity and quiet hostility rather than crofter rebellion. Yet, the Free Church association with an 'oppressed' peasantry was to be found in other parts of Scotland. Ian Carter has shown how the Free Church in Aberdeenshire was aligned with the lower orders during the creation of the great 'parks' in mid-century as part of agricultural improvement.[17] The social tensions present in the north-east are evident from the autobiography of Christian Watt, a fisherwoman from Broadsea near Fraserburgh:[18]

> And then the whole world changed. It was not gradual but sudden like lightening. Whole gangs of men came in to reclaim the land, they ploughed bogs and stanks, everywhere was the smell of burning whins. Suddenly huge big parks were marching up the side of Mormand hill, so greedy did they become for land.

By the time of the Disruption, Christian explained that:

> The [Established] Kirk had become an organisation to suppress the working class. Several folk had been evicted from crofts on the side of Benachie. The Aberdeenshire folk banded together right away, – it must stop forthwith. Ministers preached that it was God's will to go if told so, but folk had had enough. If you had no profession you were of no consequence to a minister, save only to fill the kirk on Sundays.

The Disruption turned into social rupture: 'They preached on Broadsea boat shore, the whole natural arena of the braes black with people . . . It was an awful smack in the face to the would-be's [in the Established Church] who were left with nobody to look down on'.

In the Lowlands overall, levels of defection to the Free Church were significantly higher in urban than rural areas. In the city of Edinburgh, for instance, around two-thirds of worshippers fled the Established Church, in Glasgow about half, and in Aberdeen nearly 70 per cent. The Free Church in these parts was undoubtedly of a different character and social composition to the Free Church of the crofting counties. Pioneering research by Allan MacLaren[19] on the Disruption in Aberdeen showed a complex picture of an Established Church eldership, dominated by an old merchant middle-class oligarchy with landed connections and an association with economic protectionism and church patronage. By the 1840s, this oligarchy was thwarting the social and ecclesiastical ambitions of rising 'new' middle classes: commission agents and small entrepreneurs. In ideological terms, these 'insolent social upstarts' were staunch free traders and opponents of church patronage, and led the defection to the Free Church. In spatial terms, the western expansion of Aberdeen's residential area was underway in the 1840s, and the Disruption provided these new middle classes with the opportunity to locate both their houses and their Free churches in suburban areas distinct from the oligarchy's old-town quarters.

Very quickly, however, the upper-middle classes — who could secure loans for church building — asserted their dominance of the Free Church eldership. Peter Hillis[20] has shown this in mid-Victorian Glasgow for both the Establishment (where they made up 81 per cent of elders) and for the dissenters (78 per cent). But a far more contested issue is proletarian religious connection. MacLaren's work stressed the alienation of the working classes from the churches, and especially from the Free Church. He identified elements of the organisation and ideology of the churches as hostile to proletarian church affiliation; the need for fine clothes and pew rents, and kirk-sessions' pre-occupation with offences of sexual immorality. The middle-class nature of the Free Church, he feels, drove out plebians.

However, work by other researchers indicates a very high level of proletarian membership of presbyterian congregations. Indeed, in every published analysis yet undertaken on congregational composition in nineteenth-century Britain, working-class members have been in the majority. In Glasgow during 1845–65, Hillis has shown that 75 per cent of 1,330 Church of Scotland members, and 54 per cent of 2,663 dissenters, were working class. When his data is broken down, it indicates that the majority of working-class church members belonged to skilled occupations: 69 per cent in the Established Church, 80 per cent in dissenting churches. Other smaller-scale research confirms these findings for various periods from the 1770s to the 1960s.[21]

This makes the understanding of working-class religion more complex. On the one hand, investigators like MacLaren and Smout are right in pointing to features of presbyterian church organisation which alienated potential working-class adherents. From the 1810s onwards, middle-class members of congregations objected to attending churches close to disease-ridden 'slum' areas. Two short-term solutions were frequent whitewashing of churches, and the removal of *gratis* and low-priced pews.[22] The more permanent solution, favoured by the 1840s and 1850s, was the relocation of churches in suburban areas, thus impairing church provision in proletarian districts. On the other hand, there is little doubt that very large numbers of the working classes were actively interested in organised religion and attended church. Ethnic and religious minorities tended to retain strong attachment to their churches, especially where there were connections to be maintained with 'the old country', as with Irish and Lithuanian Catholic immigrants, or with a diaspora like the Jews.[23] In part, residential and occupational segregation kept ethnic religious identity alive: the Irish in 'Little Dublins' in many towns and in mining villages, the Lithuanians at Bellshill, and East-European and Russian Jews in the Gorbals district of Glasgow.

Segregation was often reinforced by religion. Irish Catholics found their church a focus of cultural identity, with the bulk of priests by the 1860s

65. Evangelical concern at conditions in the growing cities resulted in a massive extension of home mission activities in the 1860s. *Heatherbank Museum of Social Work.*

coming from Ireland. The church was a refuge in what was frequently a hostile host society. Sectariansim and job-segregation developed in many industries: by the 1850s in the dock, iron and coal industries of Greenock–Port Glasgow, Monklands and West Lothian, and by the 1870s in the shipbuilding industry on the Clyde. Both employers and trade unions were often overtly anti-Catholic, and Protestant working-class hostility was exacerbated when Catholics worked as strike-breakers. Sectarian riots and antagonisms were particularly acute between the 1840s and 1870s in places like Greenock, north Ayrshire, and in the twin communities of Airdrie and Coatbridge, where the first evolved as predominantly Protestant and the second as predominantly Catholic.

Yet, as Gallagher has argued, the level of religious friction in the Scottish workplace was comparatively restrained between 1860 and 1914 because of the growth of skilled occupations in engineering and shipbuilding in which Protestants retained an easy dominance until the end of the period. In the labour market in Liverpool, unskilled Catholics challenged a predominantly unskilled Protestant workforce (giving rise to riotous municipal politics and community strife in the 1890s and 1900s). By contrast, the Protestant — frequently 'Orange' — artisans of industrial Scotland left unskilled Catholics to dominate in labouring and carting. To 'get on' in the social structure before the First World War, many Scottish Catholics resorted to 'getting out' by emigration to America or Australasia.

Catholic segregation was also self-imposed. Aspinwall and McCaffrey have been the most adept at describing the laborious development by Catholic priests of chapel-centred devotional and leisure-time activities — securing a proletarian faith in a presbyterian country from which it had been virtually extinguished three centuries before. In what they call 'the drive to respectability', they show that 'Irish Catholics in Scotland came to be insulated in a cradle-to-grave community' of Catholic Young Men's societies, branches of the League of the Cross and other approved parish organisations. Those writers emphasise that the Catholic Irish were 'in the Scottish Victorian city but hardly of it'. But Walker describes priests encouraging Catholic assimilation to the very economic and social values held by their Protestant 'hosts'. In essence, the social values of industrialised urban society became ubiquitous in religious terms; pew rents, 'Sunday-best' dress, sobriety and self-help were all elements in 'respectability'. However, it is clear that assimilation took place in a manner which sustained identity: for example, whilst Irish language and sport generally lapsed in the Scottish Catholic community, the adoption of 'native' football led to distinctive Irish Catholic clubs like Edinburgh's Hibernian (formed 1875) and Glasgow Celtic (1888).

It is probably fair to conclude that in Scotland, as in other countries (notably the United States), immigrant groups tended to retain a stronger attachment to churches than did indigenous groups. But we should not underestimate Protestant church adherence amongst the Scottish working classes. Popular aspirations were commonly expressed in religious terms — and especially according to long-established presbyterian 'rights' of democratic selection of ministers and congregational self-determination. And the assertion of such rights was most perceptible during the 1830s and the 1840s — a period of considerable economic distress, thwarted political ambition and acute shortage of churches. As a result, religious protest and enthusiasm became, as so often before and sometimes since, a means for expressing grievance and aspiration.

In the early 1830s, Edward Irving, Robert Story and John McLeod Campbell struck a chord amongst tens of thousands who came to hear the gift of 'tongues' and a millenarian gospel of universal atonement preached on the Lower Clyde around Helensburgh and Greenock. The heresy trials which followed in the Established Church sparked the British development of the Catholic Apostolic Church. Transatlantic revivalist influences were very strong in this movement, as they were in others of the decade. Revivals amongst industrial workers, especially after trade depressions, were widely reported in smaller industrial communities: in Lanarkshire colliery villages, Dundee mills, Perth factories and Shotts ironworks. But by far the most affected were the hand-loom weavers, particularly in the most celebrated revival in 1839 at Kilsyth led by the parish minister, William Chalmers Burns. A local man recalled the event:

> The web became nothing to the weaver, nor the forge to the blacksmith, nor his bench to the carpenter, nor his furrow to the ploughman. They forsook all to crowd the churches and the prayer meetings. There were nightly sermons in every church, household meetings for prayer in every street, twos and threes in earnest conversation on every road, and single wrestlers with God in the solitary places of the field and glen. The swearer did not venture an oath nor the drunkard a debauch, nor the thief a theft, nor the deceiver a lie, nor the striker a blow.[24]

Such phenomena were widespread in the 1830s and 1840s. Journals, church conferences and ministerial guidebooks appeared, drawing upon both British and American experiences, to provide advice to clergy faced with spontaneous working-class revivalism. The Baptist, Congregationalist and Methodist churches emerged as focuses in many communities, whilst hostility from some Secession ministers drove many handloom-weavers in the early 1840s to founding Chartist Churches — in which pew-rents were prohibited so that 'all are equally free to enjoy the ordinances of God'. From Chartism and radicalism, too, emerged the total abstinence movement, which remained until the 1850s a highly-suspicious cause for the mainstream churches.[25] The Church of the Latter Day Saints enjoyed considerable success, especially in mining villages, growing from 21 members in 1840 to its all-time peak of 3,300 in 1851. The Evangelical Union (the 'Morisonians') attracted some 7,000 members from the Secession, Congregational, Relief and Established Churches by 1851. And, most importantly of all, the Free Church swept up the Gaelic population almost *en masse*, and in the Lowlands claimed just under a third of all churchgoers, including thousands who had 'sat under' revivalist evangelical ministers like Irving and Burns during the preceding fourteen years.

Economic distress, and the millenarianism and universalist salvation of the preaching, were common features. 'The Saints generally in this country', it was said during the heyday of Mormon recruitment in the late 1840s, 'are well but struggleing [sic] through adverse scenes of Poverty'; two infants blessed by Mormons at Dalry in 1849 were promised that they would 'see Jesus come in his glory and reign with him on earth'.[26]

The Rev. Robert Murray Cheyne, aware of 'cold ministers' amongst his brethren in the Established Church, preached a highly charged revivalism in Dundee in the late 1830s:[27] 'The time is short; eternity is near; yea, the coming of Christ the second time is at hand. Make sure of being one with the Lord Jesus, that you may be glad when you see him'. His diary records a communion prayer meeting:

> The people were brought into a very tender frame. After the blessing, a multitude remained. One was like a person struck through with a dart; she could neither stand nor go. Many were looking on with faces of horror. Others were comforting her in a very kind manner, bidding her look to Christ. Mr. Burns told them of Kilsyth. Still they would not go away. . . . The sobbing soon spread, till many heads were bent down, and the church was filled with sobbing.

The millenarian and universalist preaching of Mormons, Morisonians, Baptists, Methodists and many Presbyterians had enormous appeal to a Scottish working class struggling during the 'hungry forties'.

The maintenance of working-class church-going in the early Victorian period is corroborated from many sources — including the Royal Commission on Religious Instruction which, in the 1830s, found over two-thirds of Established church-goers, and nearly all dissenters, to be working class. These congregations, the Commissioners noted, practised congregational democracy — selecting their own ministers, and setting pew-rents by congregational vote.[28] But the social structure of Victorian congregations was not static. Urban society was characterised by high social and spatial mobility — people rising in occupation and income, and moving to better housing accordingly. This was reflected in church life with congregations tending to rise in the social scale very rapidly, and with frequent rebuilding of churches to ever more expensive and ornate designs. In this way, social divisions could appear within a congregation, when working-class members failed to keep pace with pew-rent increases and with relocation of their church to a distant suburb. The factors promoting working-class alienation never disappeared; they constantly re-emerged as congregations became richer.

By the mid 1850s, the spark of creative energy which had formed new proletarian churches during the previous two decades was to a great extent extinguished. The thirty-odd Chartist Churches had disappeared, the Mormons were in a protracted decline that was to last until the 1960s, and the Free Church lost much of its identification with peasant radical causes. New industries such as shipbuilding, and rising standards of living for (especially) skilled workers, reduced worker radicalism, protest and religious innovation. The leadership of the temperance and total abstinence movements was appropriated to a considerable degree by the middle classes and the churches. The conjunction of the religious individualism of evangelicalism with the economic individualism of *laissez faire* society propelled the social composition of congregations ever upward. At Cambridge Street U.P. Church in Glasgow in the 1860s, the wealthy in the congregation, together with the minister, Rev. Dr John Eadie, built a more salubrious suburban church. A critical scribe chalked on the door of the new church on its opening day:[29]

> This Church is not built for the poor and needy,
> But for the rich and Dr. Eadie.
> The rich may come in and take their seat,
> But the poor must go to Cambridge Street.

As cities and society fractured, so religion fragmented — initially into different churches, but increasingly *within* each denomination. But whilst aspirant middle and working classes desired segregation from the lower working classes, they also desired to hold them within the socially-stabilising grip of organised religion.

V

The Kirk's traditional role in rural communities as the focus of paternalistic social relations could not survive the advent of industrialism and the growth of urban centres. The mere aggregation of the people in cities, coupled with industrial employment, the plurality of churches and the growing chasms between social classes, made this impossible. As Dr Robert Buchanan, a prominent Free Church minister in Glasgow, said in 1850 when seeking support for church and school projects in the slums:

> To the overwhelming majority of our upper classes, the district to which the Wynds belong is a *terra incognita* . . . [Upper-middle-class] Blythswood Hill and [lower-working-class] Bridgegate are not more than a mile apart, and yet practically, they are nearly as far asunder as the antipodes.[30]

Such separation of social classes appeared a direct threat to social order, especially during the years of intermittent working-class violence up to 1848. The apparent conjunction of irreligion with those most given to drunkenness, immorality and proletarian violence created a special function for churches and religious 'agencies' to play. Religious virtues were also the virtues of a well-ordered capitalist society, and their promulgation lay behind nearly every initiative of Victorian social reform. And the principal target were migrants who in mid-century made up over half of the inhabitants of a city like Glasgow.

This was the mission to the working-classes — variously described by Victorian churchmen as the 'lapsed masses', the 'sunken portion' or the 'home heathens'.[31] New evangelical 'agencies' of 'aggressive' proselytising had been developing: starting in the 1780s with Sunday schools, diversifying between 1800 and 1830 into tract distribution, mission schools, city missions, and the Rev. Dr Thomas Chalmers's attempt at St. John's Parish in Glasgow to recreate the parochial visitation system of rural parishes. It was in the 1830s, 1840s and 1850s that this strategy of mini-district evangelising was vastly expanded, spreading to virtually all urban congregations of Protestant dissenting denominations, but especially the Free and U.P. churches. New 'agencies' were developed: city missionaries to visit non-churchgoers in their homes, total abstinence societies, young men's and women's religious societies, Bible institutes and reading rooms, and penny savings banks. From the late 1850s, evangelical denominations, led by the Free and UP churches, encouraged a 'controlled' religious revivalism with great success, culminating in 1873–5 with the work of the Americans, Moody and Sankey, who had a significant impact amongst middle- as well as working-class families in Edinburgh and Glasgow. From the 1870s, the churches became more organised by dividing up cities into mission-districts of around 180 families each in which congregational district visitors carried out monthly visitation. And new agencies continued to appear — including the Boys' Brigade (founded in 1883).

The home-mission enterprise of the mid- and late Victorian era was vast. It is difficult to convey the extent to which the life of church members — Protestant and Catholic — was dominated by voluntary work as Sunday-school teachers, leaders of Protestant Bands of Hope and the Catholic League of the Cross, and conductors of 'mission conversaziones' and 'tea and testimony' evenings. Middle- and upper-working-class recreation was to a considerable extent dominated by the 'respectable' leisure activities of such voluntary religious and temperance work. For their part, working-class homes were bombarded by religious literature and missionaries from a multiplicity of organisations — the local temperance society, congregational district visitors, 'Bible Women', the Salvation Army (from the late 1870s), recruiters for a Mothers' Kitchen Prayer Meeting, or agents of a Medical Mission. There were missions to seamen and railwaymen, shipyard workers and businessmen, as well as evangelistic 'tents' in the major cities for the very poor. Before the advent of the 'secular' sports and commercial leisure revolution in the late 1880s, organised 'respectable' recreation was dominated by religious occasions like Sunday-school excursions and temperance 'walks'; leisure venues were mostly churches or church halls, or else municipal halls where 'sacred concerts' were a staple until the First World War. Even into the 1910s, religious recreation remained prominent for the middle and working classes. Equally, philanthropic endeavour[32] was dominated by religious organisations and ideals. In addition to medical missions, access to hospitals often required a ticket obtained from a minister, priest or evangeliser.

The grip on popular pastimes and ideology was particularly marked with children. In Glasgow in 1890, the number of Protestant Sunday-school scholars accounted for 65 per cent of children aged 5–15 years, and many more were associated with other youth organisations, both Catholic and Protestant. Oral-history testimony from those born at the turn of the century is especially revealing. A woman from Stirling, the daughter of an ornamental cornice maker, recalled before the First World War going with her six brothers and sisters to the Band of Hope on Wednesday nights and to a succession of Sunday schools:

> Well, there was Cowane Centre School and I went to a morning service there, eleven o'clock, a Miss Harvey . . . we just sung hymns and she gave a wee service, and we were oot again the back o' twelve o'clock. And then you had to go home and see ye were all right, your face washed and ready to go to the South Church Sunday School after the church come out at half past twelve . . . [For] going out to the five o'clock Sunday School you got your claes shifted . . . Over in the railway mission, it was a hut that was in Bayne Street. You went there from five o'clock to six o'clock, and that was you finished for the day.[33]

As for adults, Hugh McLeod's examination of socially representative oral-history testimony from all over Britain has shown that Scotland, along with Wales, were the regions with the highest proportion (over 50 per cent) of respondents born between 1872 and 1906 who claimed that both parents were regular churchgoers.[34]

The influence of Victorian evangelicalism extended into the heart of local administration and government.[35] Town councils, schools boards, parochial boards and licensing courts were dominated by clergy and presbyterian elders. They brought to civil administration a religious perspective of 'democratic cities of God' in which municipal tramways, slum-clearance schemes and town waterworks were ingredients in the religious vision of civic pride — just as much as moves (in the absence of national prohibition) to curb the sale of alcohol. In Dundee, Walker

66. The importance of 'Sunday-best' clothes is apparent among the congregation leaving Ogilvie Church, Stobswell, Dundee c.1900. *Dundee District Libraries.*

has shown how the Scottish Prohibition Party developed strong support in the first decade of the twentieth century amongst mill girls, and effected a strong influence upon municipal administration, with followers wearing 'Purity Badges' urging electors to 'Vote as you Pray'.

This is not to say that evangelisation of the working classes was always welcomed. Historians like Smout and MacLaren are right to stress the distance between proselytiser and proselytised, and the hostility that working-class families could feel for the patronising slum-visitor and intrusive kirk-session elder. But until the 1890s, the rejection was not of religious ideas and ideals, but of middle-class attempts to appropriate them. Though religion was undoubtedly used by the élites as a means of social control, it was also important to the development of class consciousness — especially amongst skilled workers.[36] The plain fact is that evangelising did work. Mission 'stations' and churches in working-class districts usually succeeded in evolving to permanent congregations — ultimately self-financing and free from the supervision of a wealthier 'parent' congregation. It was because of this recruitment that church adherence continued to grow until around 1900.

VI

Organised religion reached its peak of social sigificance in the late nineteenth century, from which point decline commenced. In Scotland, as in Britain as a whole, a crisis set in.[37] Membership of most Protestant religious organisations, including churches and voluntary organisations, ceased to grow relative to population; some organisations, like Sunday schools, actually started to lose members and helpers; and religious marriage was forsaken by significant numbers of brides and grooms. At the same time, the large-scale suburbanisation of cities from the 1880s threw many inner-city congregations into insolvency, hastening ecumenical pressures for the reunion of presbyterianism. This gave rise in 1900 to the amalgamation of the Free and UP churches to form the United Free Church. With their membership growth declining rapidly (Figure 1), the dissenters in the United Free immediately entered into negotiations for union with the Church of Scotland — a union achieved in 1929.

Profound forces were behind the crisis for, particularly, evangelical dissent. The rise of 'higher criticism', in which the literal interpretation of the Bible was cast in doubt, shattered presbyterian self-confidence in religious social reform and in mission work. The same consequence arose from the appearance at the turn of the century of state welfarism and of the Labour Movement to challenge the evangelical precepts of self-help, sobriety and personal salvation as the route to social improvement. Christian socialists, especially in the more accommodating Established Church, sought to treat with trades unionists, Fabians and Labour leaders like Keir Hardie; a minister wrote in 1890: 'The fact is that socialism needs to be Christianised, and that Christianity needs to be socialised'.[38] But the progress of Christian-socialist-inspired Social Unions, which between 1890 and 1914 initiated working-class model housing, baby clinics and holidays for slum children, did not for the most part outlive the politicisation of social reform in the 1910s. In that decade of industrial disputes, rent strikes, Red Clydeside and the Great War, the Protestant churches became increasingly foes rather than friends of emergent Labour. They lost control to Labour representatives on many school boards and parish councils, and found their evangelical agenda of moral improvement being overturned by state amelioration of social problems.

One immediate and striking consequence was the quite sudden and dramatic decline of the mission to the working classes. Congregational evangelising associations collapsed and inner-city Sunday schools closed, leaving mission work increasingly in the hands of Protestant anti-Catholic and anti-socialist organisations. With Catholic voters starting from around 1906 to countenance Labour representation, and with declining internal self-confidence, the presbyterian churches and civil establishment started to feel threatened.

But in the crisis of the 'social question' at the turn of the century, there was no sudden working-class rejection of religion or the churches. Submission to evangelising certainly declined. A future Moderator of the Church of Scotland general assembly addressed his brethren in 1893 on the failure of a grand mission event in the east end of Glasgow: 'I am sorry to say that what occurred has made me fear that the gulf which separates class from class in our great centres of industry is wider, and the class feeling deeper, than we had dreamed'.[39] But working-class religion remained more powerful than such comments might suggest. For one thing, Catholic adherence was continuing to grow as the Church strengthened its parish structure. On the Protestant side, historians have yet to show any significant decline in proletarian membership of churches. Moreover, the vast bulk of working-class voluntary organisations which sprang to prominence around 1900 were aligned to religious, temperance or sectarian precepts: notably the 'lodge' organisations of the Good Templars, the Druids, the Rechabites, the Foresters, the Hibernians and the Orange Lodge. In these and other activities, indigenous working-class religious culture survived very strongly until at least the outbreak of the First World War.

Nevertheless, the changes of the 1890–1914 period started a trend that was to accelerate. In the stagnation in church growth, and in the displacement of religious values from the centre stage of social prophecy and improvement, we can perceive the commencement of what was to be a process of the twentieth-century — secularisation.

NOTES

1. E. P. Thompson, *The Making of the English Working Class* (Harmondsworth, 1968); E. Hobsbawm, 'Religion and the Rise of Socialism', *Marxist Perspectives*, 1 (1976); H. Perkins, *The Origins of Modern English Society 1780–1880* (London, 1969); A. D. Gilbert, *Religion and Society in Industrial England: Church, Chapel and Social Change 1740–1914* (London, 1976). See also E. R. Wickham, *Church and People in an Industrial City* (London, 1957), and K. S. Inglis, *Churches and the Working Classes in Victorian England* (London, 1963).

2. T. C. Smout, *A Century of the Scottish People 1830–1950* (London, 1986), pp. 203–4.

3. A. L. Drummond and J. Bulloch, *The Church in Victorian Scotland 1843–1874* (Edinburgh, 1975), pp. 40–1.

4. J. Cox, *The English Churches in a Secular Society: Lambeth, 1870–1930* (Oxford, 1982); T. W. Laqueur, *Religion and Respectability: Sunday Schools and Working Class Culture 1780–1850* (London, 1976); E. T. Davies, *Religion in the Industrial Revolution in South Wales* (Cardiff, 1965).

5. See C. G. Brown, *The Social History of Religion in Scotland since 1730* (London and New York, 1987) which elaborates on issues raised in this chapter and includes an annotated bibliography, Note 10, and the work of Peter Hillis cited in Note 20.

6. G. Best, *Mid-Victorian Britain 1851–1875* (London, 1973), pp. 191, 203.

7. C. G. Brown, 'Religion and Social Change', in T. M. Devine and R. Mitchison (eds.), *People and Society in Scotland, vol. I, 1760–1830* (Edinburgh, 1988), p. 153.

8. The data in this and the following paragraph are calculated from Census of Great Britain, 1851; Religious Worship and Education, Scotland, *P.P.* 1854 lix. General analysis of this census and of church statistics are to be found in C. G. Brown, *The Social History of Religion*, pp. 57–88; and in D. J. Withrington, 'The 1851 Census of Religious Worship and Education, with a Note on Church Accommodation in Mid-nineteenth Century Scotland', *Records of the Scottish Church History Society*, xviii (1973).

9. A. D. Gilbert, *op, cit.*, pp. 113–4.

10. C. G. Brown, 'Did Urbanization Secularize Britain', *Urban History Yearbook*, 1988.

11. H. McLeod, 'Religion', in J. Langton and R. J. Morris (eds.), *Atlas of Industrializing Britain 1780–1914* (London, 1986), p. 212.

12. C. G. Brown, *The Social History of Religion in Scotland*, pp.77–82. A comparison of church-going levels in Scotland and the rest of Britain in 1851 and in 1979–84 is given in C. G. Brown, 'Religion', in R. Pope (ed.), *Atlas of British Social and Economic History* (London, 1988).

13. For developments in church history, on the presbyterian side, A. L. Drummond and J. Bulloch, *op. cit.*, and their *The Church in Late Victorian Scotland 1874–1900* (Edinburgh, 1978); on the Catholic Church, J. E. Handley, *The Irish in Modern Scotland* (Cork, 1947); and D. McRoberts (ed.), *Modern Scottish Catholicism 1878–1978* (Glasgow, 1979), and H. Escott, *A History of Scottish Congregationalism* (Glasgow, 1960), which includes the Evangelical Union.

14. J. M. Barrie, *The Little Minister* (London, 1909), p. 86.

15. See, for example, S. J. Brown, *Thomas Chalmers and the Godly Commonwealth in Scotland* (Oxford, 1982).

16. J. Hunter, *The Making of the Crofting Community* (Edinburgh, 1976), p.

104. Two very useful works on Gaelic religion are C. W. J. Withers, *Gaelic in Scotland 1698–1981* (Edinburgh, 1984), and V. E. Durkacz, *The Decline of the Celtic Languages* (Edinburgh, 1983). A survey of current thinking on the role of the Free Church in crofter resistance is given in E. Richards, *A History of the Highland Clearances*, vol. 2 (London, 1985), pp. 334–41, 357–9.

17. I. Carter, *Farmlife in Northeast Scotland 1840–1914: The Poor Man's Country* (Edinburgh, 1979), and I. Carter, 'To roose the countra fae the caul' morality o' a deid moderatism': William Alexander and *Johnny Gibb of Gushetneuk*', *Northern Scotland*, 2 (1974–5).

18. D. Watt (ed.), *The Christian Watt Papers* (Edinburgh, 1983), pp. 24, 47.

19. A. A. MacLaren, *Religion and Social Class: The Disruption Years in Aberdeen* (London and Boston, 1974); A. A. MacLaren, 'Class Formation and Class Fraction: the Aberdeen Bourgeoisie 1830–1850', in G. Gordon and B. Dicks (eds.), *Scottish Urban History* (Aberdeen, 1983); A. A. MacLaren, 'Presbyterianism and the Working Class in a Mid-nineteenth-century City', *Scottish Historical Review*, 46 (1967).

20. P. Hillis, 'Presbyterianism and Social Class in Mid-nineteenth Century Glasgow: A Study of Nine Churches', *Journal of Ecclesiastical History*, 32 (1981); see also his PhD thesis, same title, University of Glasgow, 1978.

21. This research is summarised in C. G. Brown, *The Social History of Religion in Scotland*, pp. 109–11, 148–51, 218–20.

22. On pewing arrangements, see C. G. Brown, 'The Costs of Pew-renting: Church management, Church-going and Social class in Nineteenth-century Glasgow', *Journal of Ecclesiastical History*, 38 (1987).

23. On Catholic immigrants, see W. M. Walker, 'Irish Immigrants in Scotland: Their Priests, Politics and Parochial Life', *Historical Journal*, xv (1972); R. D. Lobban, 'The Irish Community in Greenock in the Nineteenth Century', *Irish Geography*, 6 (1971); articles by Gallagher on Glasgow and Liverpool, and by Aspinwall and McCaffrey on Edinburgh in R. Swift and S. Gilley (eds.), *The Irish in the Victorian City* (London, 1985); A. B. Campbell, *The Lanarkshire Miners 1775–1874* (Edinburgh, 1979); B. Murray, *The Old Firm: Sectarianism, Sport and Society in Scotland* (Edinburgh, 1984). The Scottish Jewish community awaits systematic social-history treatment.

24. Quoted in J. Hutchison, *Weavers, Miners and the Open Book: A History of Kilsyth* (Cumbernauld, 1986), p. 66. For a general review of revivalism, placing Scotland in a wider context, see R. Carwardine, *Trans-atlantic Revivalism: Popular Evangelicalism in Britain and America, 1790–1865* (Westport, Connecticut, and London, 1978).

25. The major work on Scottish temperance is Daniel Paton's 'Drink and the Temperance Movement in Nineteenth-century Scotland', unpublished PhD thesis, University of Edinburgh, 1977. There is a good summary in D. C. Paton, 'Temperance and the Churches in Scotland 1829–1927', *Scottish Records Association Conference Report*, 7 (March 1987), pp. 22–29. Details of

denominational attitudes and of religious interference in licensing laws are given in C. G. Brown, 'Religion and the Development of an Urban Society: Glasgow 1780–1914', unpublished PhD thesis, University of Glasgow, 1982, vol. 2, pp. 143–82. General discussion of the movement is found in E. King, *Scotland Sober and Free: The Temperance Movement 1829–1979* (Glasgow, 1979), and in T. C. Smout, *op. cit.*, pp. 133–58.

26. F. D. Buchanan, 'The Ebb and Flow of Mormonism in Scotland, 1840–1900'. *Brigham Young University Studies*, 27 (1987), pp. 27–52, at pp. 38, 40.

27. Quoted in A. Bonar, *The Life of Robert Murray McCheyne* (1844). Reprinted London 1960, pp. 150, 155.

28. *Royal Commission on Religious Instruction, Scotland, First Report PP* 1837, xxi, p. 29; Second Report, PP 1837–8, xxxii, p. 17.

29. Quoted in P. Hillis, *op. cit.*, p. 54.

30. R. Buchanan, *The Schoolmaster in the Wynds* (Glasgow, 1850), p. 3.

31. On the extensive evangelical 'agencies' of this period, see P. Hillis, 'Education and Evangelisation: Presbyterian Missions in Mid-nineteenth Century Glasgow', *Scottish Historical Review*, 66 (1988), pp. 46–62; I. A. Muirhead, 'Churchmen and the Problem of Prostitution in Nineteenth-century Scotland', *Records of the Scottish Church History Society*, 18 (1974), pp. 223–43; C. G. Brown, 'The Sunday-school Movement in Scotland, 1780–1914', *Records of the Scottish Church History Society*, 21 (1981), pp. 3–26; C. G. Brown, 'Education' and 'Religion', in J. Hood (ed.), *The History of Clydebank* (Carnforth, 1988), pp. 41–50; S. Mechie, *The Church and Scottish Social Development, 1780–1880* (Oxford, 1960); and J. L. Duthie, 'Philanthropy and Evangelism among Aberdeen Seamen, 1814–1924', *Scottish Historical Review*, lxiii (1984), pp. 155–73.

32. O. Checkland, *Philanthropy in Victorian Scotland* (Edinburgh, 1980).

33. Stirling Women's Oral History Archive, Smith Museum, Stirling, respondent Mrs E.1, transcript p. 6.

34. H. McLeod, 'New Perspectives on Victorian Working-class Religion: The Oral Evidence', *Oral History Journal*, 14 (1986), pp. 31–49, at p. 33.

35. B. Aspinwall, *Portable Utopia: Glasgow and the United States 1820–1920* (Aberdeen, 1984); C. G. Brown, *The Social History of Religion in Scotland*, pp. 196–207; W. M. Walker, *Juteopolis: Dundee and its Textile Workers 1885–1923* (Edinburgh, 1979).

36. R. Q. Gray, *The Labour Aristocracy in Victorian Edinburgh* (Oxford, 1976).

37. On Scotland, see C. G. Brown, *The Social History of Religion* pp. 167–96, and D. J. Withrington, 'The Churches in Scotland c.1870 – c. 1900: Towards a New Social Conscience?', *Records of the Scottish Church History Society*, xix (1977), pp. 155–68. For the crisis in England, see, in addition to Cox (note 4 above), S. Yeo, *Religion and Voluntary Organisations in Crisis* (London, 1976).

38. A. S. Matheson, *The Gospel and Modern Substitutes* (Edinburgh, 1890), p. 184.

39. D. Macleod, *Our Home Mission*, (Edinburgh, 1893), pp. 12–13.

CHAPTER 12

Community and Culture

Christopher Harvie and Graham Walker

> With the advent of the public halls, the motor bicycle, the electric torch and the radio, the life of the Shetlander has changed.[1]

'Modern', secular, collective Scottish society began in the years after World War I, its matrix a combination of public intervention, techological change, and a consciousness of 'community' made acute by the destructive impact of the war and its aftermath. Public intervention expressed itself in the housing improvement and welfare measures which helped give even the unemployed a higher standard of life than many of the employed had enjoyed pre-war – and in the toppling, through increased taxation and shorter opening hours, of a dominant, male-oriented pub-culture. Technology, in the shape of the bus, the cinema, the motor-bike (and sidecar) and the radio opened out life-experience, particularly for the young and for women. Outside the cities the idea of community, expressed in such war-generated institutions as the British Legion and the Scottish Women's Rural Institutes — frequently meeting in a village hall which had itself been built as a war memorial — multiplied facilities for group activity which before the war had been largely confined to the middle classes. Paradoxically, the year 1929, in which one major institution of Scottish rural community — the parish councils set up by the 1895 act — was abolished, also saw the removal of a major hindrance to common action through the amalgamation of the Kirk and the United Free Church.

While we would find it difficult to discover any earlier decade in which change was as rapid as in the 1920s, it is plain that these alterations were not imposed on a society static since the 1850s. Certain groups had established important elements of collective social infrastructure much earlier — notably in mining and railway communities, in some industrial plants with a paternalist management, and in country towns. Some well-informed authorities claim that, at least in country districts, the old order was well and truly subverted in the 1880s, when the bicycle,

336

the school board and the dispensary broke down rural isolation, facilitating voluntary organisation, and granting new social roles to women.[2]

Difficulties arise, however, when we attempt to fit this into a general socio-cultural analysis, and these have not been eased by recent historical writing. Christopher Smout's *A Century of the Scottish People* (1987) is unwontedly weak when confronted with the question of Scottish popular culture (which for Smout seems sometimes to boil down to 'what the Scots did when they weren't drunk'). J. D. Young sees an effervescent and 'rumbustious' working class, potentially high on politics rather than booze, but one which falls silent when confronted with capitalist crisis.[3] Both interpretations seem to fall victim to the subjectivity confessed to by the journalist and nationalist, William Power, writing in 1937 of the period from 1880 to 1914:

> Between an unreal Drumtochty and a too real St Rollox Scotland seemed to have vanished. Probably that was what made me fall so passionately, so obstinately, in love with her. She was my own country, for I seemed to have created Scotland out of books and songs. She was, in a sense, my Galatea. She was the Galatea of many Scots about that time.[4]

Mention of Drumtochty, of course, conjures up the spirit of the Kailyard, and of the 'Unspeakable Scot' of T. W. H. Crosland's polemic of 1902: a country gripped in an artfully-constructed demotic dwam of ploughman poets, little ministers and bonnie briar bushes. The 'too real St Rollox' indicates not only the pollution, human misery and social deformity associated with industrialisation, but the ease with which those interests it promoted could rise to infuential positions in the British élite. The proprietors of the St Rollox Chemical Works, the Tennant family, rose in three generations from sitting on the same school bench as Burns to owning Europe's largest chemical works. One generation more would see a Tennant married to the Prime Minister; the generation after that, with St Rollox works now demolished, would produce Katharine Elliot, the able wife of a collectivist Secretary of State and Stephen Tennant, a homosexual aesthete who kept to his bed for the last thirty years of his life.[5] The stations in Power's quest for his Galatea, though they don't do much to help sociological exactitude, indicate what an alarming range of interpretive trajectories *fin-de-siècle* Scotland offered.

The absence of a central interpretation, however, was critical. There was no straightforward descriptive sociology of the type practised in England by Charles Booth in the 1880s and Seebohm Rowntree in the 1900s — a lapse which seems all the more dramatic when one considers the tradition which produced Sir John Sinclair's two statistical accounts. True, there are a few partial explorations, but these were more than outweighed by a tradition of social intervention which started out from a firmly-held social or religious view, and was reluctant to allow empirically-derived conclusions to distort its purity. The dilemma which had afflicted Thomas Chalmers and Hugh Miller — of reconciling 'science' with evangelical faith — remained, and was held responsible for Scotland's intellectual backwardness in J. M. Robertson's *The Perversion of Scotland* (1885). The Arran-born Robertson, a notable literary critic, sociologist of the school of H. T. Buckle and later Liberal politician, was unsparing in his condemnation of 'the inherent reactionary bias of the ecclesiastical system which has turned back the hands of the social clock':[6]

> Before the Reformation they (the Scots) were vivacious, art-loving, full of healthy life: since then they have become 'Museless', as Mr Ruskin would say; and the darkness cast over their life by clericalism has marked them out as the most fanatical of Protestant peoples, with the nominal exception of the Protestants of Ulster, who are, indeed, mostly of Scottish descent.

> . . . it [the Kirk] taught them to believe its worst incredibilities, and crippled their very faculty of thinking for themselves; but it made hypocrites and fanatics by the thousand.

> Austerity and joyless gloom on the one hand produce their natural corrective in dissolute mirth and defiant licence on the other . . . A moral duality, so to speak, runs through past Scottish life in a way that becomes at times perplexing.

> I could lay my finger at this moment on half-a-dozen small Scotch towns in which, for sheer lack of a theatre or any other recreation, a large proportion of the youths become unintellectual, sottish and dissolute. The more ambitious eagerly flock to the large towns; those left behind have no resource but the tap room.

There is a social analysis here, but it is no more than impressionistic: its issue was to lie in the fiction of George Douglas Brown and John MacDougall Hay rather than in the evolution of any academic discipline.

Robertson's was also, typically enough, a view from exile. It was not until the 1900s that such materialism won acceptance in Scotland, and by then the driving force was Marxism rather than Robertson's Liberalism. In the didactic Marxism of John MacLean's generation, which owed much to American urban radicalism, the Scottish metropolis was seen as a gigantic opportunity rather than as a consequence of Scottish cultural breakdown, while liberal reformism, now represented by Patrick Geddes, applauded the rapidity of Scottish urban development, looking, as Helen Meller has noted, upon the urbanisation of the population as a challenge and great opportunity for cultural development.[7] In his schemes of cultural innovation and education, Geddes (one of the last of the religious Positivists) also incorporated elements of a Marxist analysis. In his 1904 plan for an 'educational park' at Dunfermline he wrote:

> Here, then, is the point: that the feudalism of the palace, the ecclesiasticism of the monastery, viewed from the contemporary economic view of history, which now takes precedence of the common romantic pictures of sword and court, are the two rival ways, temporal and spiritual, of exploiting the miller and his mill. In short, the economic maintenence, and therefore consciously or subconsciously, the policy, of tower and abbey, of medieval Church or State, was very largely in terms of their rival or coadjusted grips upon the corn sack coming to the mill, their dips into the flour sack going out again.[8]

This attitude would later make him presentable to left-wingers like C. M. Grieve and to the Fabians of the inter-war town planning movement (which, oddly enough, got its first chance in Dunfermline, with the garden-city built for naval workers at Rosyth dockyard). But a similar metropolitan vision also prevailed in the political ideas of John Wheatley (most successful and also least nationalist of the Clydesiders) who envisaged a socialist world as consisting of a federation of self-governing city states rather than nations.[9]

The point is that none of these analyses match up to a society which was riven with paradoxes: predominantly urban in population, overwhelmingly rural in land area; deeply class-divided but also devoted to pre-class politics; nationalistic but also intensely regional; Protestant but with a substantial Catholic minority; puritanical but also seemingly alcohol-dependent. Eugen Weber has shown how the three institutions of public education, military service and local communications undermined local identities in France in the same period as that which we are dealing with. At the same time a multi-cultural state was being created in Switzerland, through a carefully engineered constitution, whose identity has proved very resilient in the twentieth century. The difference with Scotland is not the absence of factors and institutions making for change along these lines, but a weak central consciousness of what was going on, at least partly because of the marginality of the country's sociological tradition.

I

This lack of a contemporary analysis confronting the paradoxes of Scotland in the late nineteenth and early twentieth centuries was perhaps the result of the confused picture presented by urban Scotland. In relation to popular culture this sense of confusion and indeterminacy was especially acute. The making of a distinctive urban culture was no straightforward process. For most of the 1850–1914 period, civic pride notwithstanding, it is difficult to view the city as generating a new popular culture outwards. Rather, the process of popular cultural formation seems to have been one of complex interaction between the city, the small town and the countryside.

The idea of the 'Scottish city' is itself problematic. Glasgow, Edinburgh, Aberdeen and Dundee may be safely advanced as the four which qualify for the description, but it is far less evident whether we can make generalisations about them. Indeed, to do so may serve only to obscure the extent to which they were different types of city which happened to be in Scotland. Scottish, of course, also functioned within a British context, and the case for outlining a British urban culture by the late Victorian period, in which Scotland's cities shared, may well be stronger than one which seeks to stress Scottish, as opposed to individual, particularities.

Then there is the problem of class analysis. Scotland has not had the benefit of a Stedman Jones to illuminate the dynamics of working-class culture at this vital historical juncture, or the insights and vivid recollection of urban working-class life provided by someone like Robert Roberts. There have been valuable studies of social segregation in Scottish cities, but not enough to provide us with the empirical evidence necessary to make confident judgements about how this affected cultural life. Conclusions, therefore, must largely be on the level of informed speculation, but before some are drawn it might be helpful to lay down a theoretical framework for future analysis, and to offer some hypotheses to the end of clearing a scholarly path.

Popular culture, it might be argued, should be seen in relation to the city's ecological structure — the 'building blocks' of jobs, housing, transport, communal amenities and so on. We must attempt to show how cultural institutions and leisure pursuits related to environmental variables. It may thus be useful to view Scotland's cities, after the fashion of some American urban historians, as 'opportunity structures' in which spatial arrangements and the opportunities they conferred were all important. The ecological structure of the city can be viewed as exercising an independent effect of its own in accordance with the degree of access to its elements that people variously enjoyed or were denied. Once we know more about such matters as the spatial location of industry in Scotland's cities and its relationship to the residential fabric, and the large topic of the operation of the housing market, we may be in a better position to examine the cultural, as well as the social and economic opportunities which people had access to. Popular cultural activity might be said to have taken most definite shape around work and space; if the physical city is seen as an 'active' entity we may reach a fuller understanding of its relationship with its inhabitants. Studies of culture and community, like everything else in urban history, would seem to stand to benefit from the idea of the city as a 'process' rather than as merely a 'site'.

Thus, we might hypothesise that the scale of a work environment had a lot to do with social opportunities and through them to participation in a range of activities; or that work was the major factor in mobility both within and in and out of the city, and that such mobility shaped a geographical pattern of popular culture; or that as the structure of industry changed, so the opportunities, social and cultural, which it generated, changed accordingly; or that industries which employed a lot of people from one locality thereby induced a greater sense of community coherence which was reflected socially and culturally. The lines of possible future enquiry seem many.

To achieve a clearer understanding of what community meant in our period, how its meaning changed, and how popular culture took shape, we would benefit by applying appropriate organising concepts in our analyses. In this respect some recent work by historical geographers and social anthropologists on 'the city' suggests that the topic could be usefully seen in terms of the 'choices' and 'constraints' which people were faced with. The social anthropologists, in their fusion of such an approach with what they call 'network analysis', provide us with further pointers: by focusing on people's social networks as a means towards understanding their behaviour, we might be able to work out what cultural and leisure activity reveals about social relations, and vice versa. We may also be able to advance a view of what people's social relations offered in the way of cultural choice, and what constraints they imposed, of what cultural choices and constraints were the result of their environment and the space they lived and worked in. Many more theoretical markers could be laid down and an agenda of future research adumbrated.

II

For the present, we have to try to reconstruct the procedures that a Scottish sociology *ought* to have gone through to identify what popular culture accounted for in Scotland. We can, in this case, usefully begin with Patrick Geddes's categories: Place-culture, work-culture and folk-culture.

Place defines the two sections into which this chapter will be divided: the west Scottish conurbation (defined as the counties of Lanark, Dunbarton, Ayr, Stirling and Renfrew) and the rest of the country. The proportion living in the 'West' had grown from less than a quarter in 1801 to almost half of the population in 1901, but to the extent that mass urbanisation was a recent phenomenon, many carried over into their new urban domicile loyalties and habits associated with their earlier Place. This was perhaps most noticeable in the 'exclusive and intensive' community life of the Irish in Scotland. Here an overwhelmingly urban populace was disciplined by its priests as well as by the hostility of the native Scots into retaining an Irish identity which, until a very late date, resisted industrial and class pressures to assimilate. (Yet when it did concede to these, it assimilated to Wheatley's urban, proletarian ideal and not to the small-town politics associated with Free State Ireland or the Scottish nationalism of some of the Catholic intellectuals).[10] This non-urbanism was also present among Scots immigrant groups in the larger cities, whose élites maintained links with their areas of origin, evident in the fairly continuous formation of regional societies, clan societies, and former pupils' groups, or the tendency of this or that church to be linked with a region external to the urban area. It was a highly mobile population: people moved often and moved over short and not so short distances. Moves from Glasgow to Dundee or from Ayr to Glasgow, for example, were quite common, as were frequent moves within, for instance, the east end of Glasgow.

It might be surmised that, for the most part, this high incidence of mobility was related to job and housing opportunities — put crudely, people generally moved where the work was or where they could afford to live — or that they moved around according to the availability of work in their particular trades and skills and the availability of housing. Some of it, however, would undoubtedly have been the result of more personal factors less conducive to historical analysis.

What seems clear is that such a degree of mobility had important implications for popular culture and the nature of 'community' in the Scotland of our period. It is likely that mobility increased the level of cultural interaction between the city and the small town, between urban and rural Scotland within the cities themselves. Certainly the evidence of the popular literature of the time, illuminatingly examined by William Donaldson,[11] suggests that there was neither an urban juggernaut of popular culture boring through the country, nor a self-contained city world from which external influences were excluded. Aberdeen, built up almost entirely by in-migration from its surrounding districts, was probably the best example of a city in Scotland whose popular culture was shaped largely from without. However, even Glasgow and Edinburgh received a substantial cultural input from beyond their boundaries. The *People's Journal*, the most popular Victorian Scottish newspaper, was as popular in the industrialised Lowlands as the more farming-oriented North-East and the West Highlands. Its 'Glasgow and West Scotland' edition sold 205,000 copies a week in 1890, the highest sale of any paper in the region. The paper's staples were serialised fiction in themes which were irregularly, if pertinently, about city life; history which focused on pre-industrial Scotland; folklore which tended to reinforce regional loyalties, particularly to the North-East and the Borders; the use in the published prose and poetry of the vernacular, particularly the rural dialects of the North-East and of Ayrshire; and a form of Liberal politics which grew out of Scotland's rural egalitarian tradition rather more than the challenges of the city.

Other popular newspapers of the period, such as the Glasgow *Weekly Mail*, Edinburgh's *North Briton* and the *Aberdeen Free Press*, used a similar formula to that of the People's *Journal*, and it was not until after the First World War that this type of paper went into decline. The popular press in Victorian Scotland constituted one of the most distinctively Scottish elements of the contemporary popular culture — phenomena such as music-hall, organised sport and gambling and church-oriented activity cannot be viewed solely in a Scottish context — but it was an element which did not encourage an urban distinctiveness. Moreover, it spoke to those many people whose lives in the city were often shadowed by the recent memory of a small-town or rural existence, and to those whose mobility to and from the city perhaps induced an ambiguous sense of identity or a complex set of loyalties regarding Place.

Religion may have functioned as another blending force between Scotland's different environments. Callum Brown has argued persuasively that the Churches, in relation to municipalisation and social reform as well as matters of culture, were of central importance in the urban context, at least until the 1890s. Peter Hillis has revealed evidence of strong working-class membership in mid-nineteenth-century Glasgow parishes, and of the ability of missionary workers to command working-class attention, if only, in many cases, temporarily. What mattered was that these church and missionary society activities, and indeed the whole panoply of temperance organisations, were there, that they could provide a purposeful role or at least a diversion, and that they represented continuity between the city and the small town or the countryside. Moreover, the popularity of church-affiliated organisations like the Boys' Brigade (founded in Glasgow in 1883) ensured that popular culture carried a religious dimension into a more secular age.[12]

In this, the churches were trapped into the strain of imperialist popular culture which took root firmly, if less jingoistically, in late Victorian Scotland. It was, in many ways, a natural offshoot of a romantic militarism which had long been a fixture of Scottish folklore and a symbol of the country's history, as that history was generally taught and written. The popular press of the time abounded with such romantic images of militarism in its serialised fiction as well as its non-fiction content. Again, such a militaristic tradition drew on a mythical, arcadian Scotland of timeless values and qualities; it was presented for urban consumption as something which defied or transcended the influences and forces of industrialisation and urbanisation.

The large degree of mobility may also lead us to look more critically at community culture in city districts. It is not to deny the strength of the colourful street and tenement culture, epitomised in Glasgow's poorest areas, to suggest that there may not have been quite the degree of neighbourhood cohesiveness and the spirit of communal give-and-take as popular myth has it; quite simply, there may have been too little 'residential persistence' to allow such features to spread through an area. In this respect, following once again the social anthropologists, the balance of our analyses should perhaps be shifted, at least tentatively, towards the importance that people in cities attached to 'extra local' relations; these may not necessarily have been less communal and supportive than local ones.

Altering the focus of our analyses in such a way would be to acknowledge that people in cities were being provided with a greater degree of choice, and that it was not always the case that their participation in popular cultural activities somehow complemented a strong sense of community identity. On the contrary, as the provision of a more commercialised and sophisticated range of attractions — from the growth of football as a spectator sport to the cultivation of a 'self-improving' ethos around parks, museums and galleries — increased, it became all the more likely that they would be perceived by many as forms of *escape*, perhaps from community constraints as well as from work and impoverished living conditions. The local pub, of course, had been a refuge from the troubles of work and home from the beginning, but by its very position in the community it could hardly have provided escape in this wider sense.[13]

The period 1850–1914 may have witnessed a growing tendency on the part of city-dwelling Scots of all social classes to redefine their relations to places in accordance with the great increase in choice which they were given. If such a process took place it might account in part for the relatively weak imprint made by an urban class-based culture on the overall Scottish image and profile. City life could make several claims on loyalties. It made it possible to hold different, even conflicting, senses of identity, and it offered transitory relationships as well as intimate ones: its pluralism, in other words, both intensified and diversified the experience of popular cultural participation. This very multi-faceted quality, however, may well have hindered the development of a clearer and stronger value-based alternative to the hegemonic Scottish cultural myths which continued to find such powerful reinforcement in a non-metropolitan context.

Until 1914 the habit — only partly attributable to Scots political archaism — persisted for the politics of the Scottish countryside (notably land reform), to become the pabulum of urban radicalism. Although much has been written on the creation of a Scottish civic consciousness towards the end of the nineteenth century, the peak of this type of interventionism seems to have passed by the late 1900s, helped on its way by the slump of 1906–1908. It was replaced by — what?[14]

Iain Hutchison has suggested that the impact of socialism in the 1900s has usually been overstated, and that of nationalism underrated.[15] There seems logic in this, as the gains of the Scottish socialists, 1906–1914, were limited, and they were anyway deeply permeated with Liberal-nationalist loyalties. Scotland continued strikingly loyal to the Liberal party in both elections of 1910, while the English fell drastically away: a situation not unlike that of the 1980s in that nationalism of a diffuse sort — embodied in the Scottish Exhibition of 1911, for example — was pervasive, while never sharpening itself into a positive political programme. Place was beginning to mean Scotland, but this proposition was still contradicted by civic and local loyalties, and would be rendered even more problematic by the dislocations of the war.

III

If we turn to Work, we are faced with an analogous complexity. Plainly, to abstract culture from work, and isolate it as various types of entertainment, is not only limiting but actively misleading. Only in the most mechanistic examples of 'pin-factory' organisation did commitment to, and fascination with, the work-experience completely disappear (and even such situations, however boring, may have provided other compensations). It is possible to regard work-culture in three ways: First, there were the practices and cultures inherent in learning the techniques of a job, particularly important in an economy where so much of the work-force was (or regarded itself as) skilled. Engineering apprentices would make models in the workshop, and their pride in their skill was something different from their self-esteem as candidate-members of the labour aristocracy. The grandfather of one of the authors trained as an engineer in Wishaw, at Shearer and Pettigrew's, and cherished until he died the small vertical-cylinder steam-engine, brass-and-wood pelton wheel and electric generator he made in his first workshop. Harry McShane, who would have been his contemporary, but whose politics were quite different, spent some time at a factory in Bridgeton while on the run from the police in World War I, taking a derelict donkey engine to bits and putting it back into working order. All unpaid. Such activities do not seem to have been exceptional, when one takes into account the 'public' craft skills associated with painting, signwriting, stonemasonry, engine-driving, and so on. A shepherd in the Borders recollected that he could have gone on to higher education, but 'From the time I could walk I was just daft about sheep', and in the 1940s James Littlejohn recorded the older Westrigg shepherds:

> They do not think of themselves . . . as employees getting a wage by selling a skill to an employer, but hold that shepherds are in the world to look after sheep, which could not survive without shepherds.

In the case of skills more collectively displayed, this consciousness has a bite to it. The Cowlairs fitters who turned out an express engine almost as a shrine to Gladstone would not have done the same for Lord Salisbury, and the skill in handling horses transmitted on the farmtouns by the 'Society of the Horseman's Word' had industrial militancy and diabolism mixed up in it.[16]

This expression of skill was plainly linked to a second factor: the elaboration and ornamentation of the job routine as part of what Ralf Dahrendorf has seen as a British peculiarity — the dominance of work in terms of time though not in terms of intensity. Porters at county stations cultivating gardens, carters grooming their horses, painting and polishing their wagons, bus conductresses (within living memory) performing amazing variations on bus-company uniforms, miners putting hours of additional effort into their rescue services. These are not simply, or even in the first place, to do with obliging employers, but with the workforce's pride in and protection of its own time and space, a notion which can be extended to the numerous Volunteer companies raised in connection with workshops. In pre- 'time and motion' days, we do not in fact know how hard Scottish workers actually worked, but we can imagine that, on the 'one-off' production of non-series goods and in pre-Taylorian days, intensity would vary a lot — with lengthy recuperative spells — from day to day and during the working day. Given the drinking customs recorded by Christopher Smout, Taylorism would have its work cut out before 1914, while, on the other hand, any reader of Robert Tressell will be conscious of the pressure being exerted in the 1900s to speed up, and (as the workers saw it) to skimp work, in trades like building and painting. This may have been less in Scotland, where such trades were comparatively well unionised, and when Taylorist practices were force-fed to Clyde engineers by such innovating employers as William Weir after the outbreak of war, the reaction was hostile. But it was noticeable that this was not deemed unpatriotic, even by a Conservative politician like the former Scottish Secretary, Lord Balfour of Burleigh. It was the workers' legitimate defence of their rights.[17]

There are grounds for seeing a degree of sexual privilege in this: men had a freedom in controlling their work-situation which was not conceded to women, least of all in the industries where they predominated, such as textiles. On the other hand, the fact that women thought less in terms of a lifetime's work (and may, perhaps, have had particularly boring, if undemanding, work to do, from which they could mentally cut themselves off) may have meant that a pre-industrial or oral culture was more likely to survive with them. The Robertson family — tinkers who did seasonal work on north-east farms — proved the great repository of the Scottish ballad tradition. The rhythmic work songs associated with weaving or 'waulking' (fulling) cloth, were conserved by women for directly functional reasons in societies, like the Gaelic-speaking Outer Isles, otherwise deeply hostile to the folk tradition on religious grounds. From what Littlejohn observed in Eskdalemuir, moreover, working-class women seem to have preserved, in their gossip, a wider and more humane range of activity then their menfolk. Common to both were parochial affairs, neighbours and work, but while women could add to this housekeeping, children and the royal family, men could only add sport.[18]

Littlejohn also notes the tendency of women in country districts to be more mobile and to marry above themselves, something probably

owed to this wider culture, and to the increased employment offered by
the Education Act of 1872, which 'feminised' the teaching profession.
Thirty five per cent female in 1851, it was 70 per cent female in 1911,
albeit with women largely confined to primary classes.[19] Even if girls
only went into service, they could 'improve themselves' be acquiring
their mistress's frocks and the smatterings of 'gentility' — although
this may also have produced an element of deference which may help
account for the survival of rural working-class Conservatism in Scotland
until the 1960s.

IV

Folk-culture is obviously more than 'what filled in the remainder of
people's time', but if we start out, experimentally, with this narrow
definition, we have already seen how blurred the line of division
between work and spare time is, although it certainly became starker
as the formal entitlement to 'leisure' increased. Even here, however, a
politicisation process operated. Sabbatarianism, which to a secularist like
Robertson seemed to destroy at least two-thirds of the workers' available
spare time, was defended by Hugh Miller in 1847 in terms which have
the glint of Covenanting fanaticism to them:[20]

> The merry unthinking serfs, who, early in the reign of Charles the First,
> danced on Sabbaths round the maypole, were afterwards the ready tools of
> despotism. The Ironsides, who in the cause of civil and religious freedom
> bore them down, were staunch Sabbatarians.

According to Miller, Sundays were when the Scots got their teeth
into serious matters. To an English sceptic he met in Newcastle, he
retorted:

> Independently altogether of religious considerations, theology has done for
> our people what all your Societies for the Diffusion of Useful Knowledge,
> and all your Penny and Saturday Magazines, will never do for yours: it has
> awakened their intellects, and taught them how to think. The development
> of the popular mind in Scotland is a result of its theology.

Although Miller thought that an injection of secular entertainment or
instruction on the Sabbath would produce 'loquacious *gabbers* . . . Chartists by thousands', it appears that Sabbatarianism, like temperance,
frequently accompanied political militancy: no self-respecting Calvinist
artisan would raise his hat to a Duke caught stravaiging on the Sabbath.
The culture of the Free and United Presbyterian churches, developing

from the 1850s on with halls, choirs, *soirées*, and Sunday Schools, was, as Brown has shown, dominated by the skilled working class. While it is true that much church propaganda was suspicious of, if not hostile to, working-class secular radicalism, the ambiguities starkly visible in the quotes from Miller suggest that the 'free' churches saw their culture as 'alternative' in the same sense as the culture of the German Social Democrats, which after 1870 had to be defended against the hegemony of the state. Or it would have been, had the Church of Scotland been in any sense a hegemonic establishment, which it ceased to be after 1843. The impression that church activities, coupled with Sabbatarianism, convey is a desire to compete with the 'establishment', and also to make use of a patent over-provision of facilities, rather than to control. One imagines that involvement in a range of church-based activities such as choirs, missionary societies and working men's clubs would appeal more to many skilled working men on their day off than either the Chalmersian challenge of wrestling with the devil in the Glasgow slums or losing caste for the sake of a furtive drink in a shebeen.

Moreover, church membership, by implying a certain social status, was a potential reproach to any employer who chose to behave in what his Christian employees regarded as an un-Christian manner. The 'new' town of Clydebank, with 72 per cent church membership in its population of 1870, had an emphatically Christian culture, was dominated by industry — shipbuilding — whose labour relations were notably visceral.[21] When the hard-fought Caledonian railway strike of 1891 reached its climax with a violent riot in Motherwell, a place little less religious in orientation, and the prominent Free Church leader, Robert Rainy, took the side of the strikers, he was mindful of the solidarity a largely Free Church community had shown.[22]

With all this church-based activity, did the distinction in Scotland between the respectable and the rowdy working class sharpen? Bearing in mind that the statistics of alcohol consumption do not start to descend until hit by tax and licensing changes in the 1900s, and the overall sobriety of the Scottish Labour élite; Keir Hardie was a Good Templar, Tom Johnston a member of the Band of Hope. The 'Rowdies' (or, more likely, Hugh MacDiarmid's 'dour drinkers of Scotland') remained more lower-class, and perhaps more concentrated in the growing ports. They were periodically reinforced on the occasions when even the 'respectable' felt the need to let their hair down, but the ingrained habit of heavy drinking in the upper levels of Scottish society seems to have been falling away by the mid-century. Thus wrote Dean Ramsay, who was, I think, a fairly reliable judge. If we accept Robbie Gray's finding that the labour

aristocracy emulated the tastes of their betters, then this suggests that
they, too, tended to dry out.[23]

As the result of such rectitude among labour aristocrats was frequently
an unimaginative conservatism, we seem to be back to J. M. Robertson's
'perplexing dualism', and behind that, to his conviction that Hugh Miller's
attempt to square revealed religion with scientific truth was what killed
him. Yet the definition of religion that the Kirk used during Chalmers's
ascendancy was one which pivoted on the notion that nature was itself
evidence of the beneficence of God's creation, observation of which
would induce a proper awe and obedience in man.[24] It is certainly
implausible that Miller spent every Sunday in church or on his knees,
when he could botanise or geologise — or at least think about botany or
geology — to the glory of God. Such cerebral activity seems characteristic
of many autodidact working men. It is possible that there may have been
a shift *towards* church institutions by such groups, particularly in the
new industrial towns. A comparison of the first two Statistical Accounts
shows a remarkable growth in the number of local libraries in country
districts. In Roxburghshire these grew from two in the 1790s to over
38 in the 1830s, and were accompanied by an expansion in the range
of voluntary societies with literary, historical, or scientific purposes.
Proportionate to their size, the provision of these in the new towns is
nowhere comparable. Motherwell, 'a great and bustling centre of traffic'
with a population of 18,726 in 1891, did not acquire its library until 1904,
and in 1891 the only substantial public building was its Town Hall, built
in 1887.[25] But from the statistics given in the *Ordnance Survey Gazeteer of
Scotland* (1895), we can roughly estimate that if three of the town's eleven
churches provided over 2,500 sittings between them, the total provision
must have added up to enough accommodation for about 40–50 per
cent of the population, or about 60 per cent of those of churchgoing
age.[26] If we extend this to take account of parochial activities — choirs,
sisterhoods, men's clubs, Boys' Brigades, women's guilds, temperance
organisations, etc. — then the religious-based element of what was on
offer in Motherwell overwhelmingly outweighed the secular. Even when
a Conservative Club (1892), a theatre and a music hall moved in during
the 1890s, religion was able to respond with a substantial Young Men's
Christian Association Institute, opened in 1899. One might expect to find
a greater degree of secularism in the bigger cities, where more alternatives
existed, but these still showed larger numbers of the skilled affiliated to
the religious or temperance bodies than to sport or hobby groups.[27] So
religiously-saturated was Scottish literary culture that when in 1900 the
Liberal thread-manufacturer, J. P. Coats, presented a library to every

Scottish board school, he stipulated that it contain no religious work, and appointed an inspector, D. T. Holmes, later a Liberal MP and grandfather of Tony Benn, to see that his requirements were met.[28]

Hugh Cunningham, in *Leisure and the Industrial Revolution*, has argued that a secular popular culture, adapted to industrialisation, gave the consumer what he or she (largely he) wanted, and did not waste much time on didactics or social control. Music and song, the evolution of the pub into the music-hall, and above all the rise of professional football in the 1880s, created a new, and on the whole capitalist, working-class world.[29]

There can be no denying the impact of football, which was so tremendous that it dislodged the Catholic Irish from the Irish nationalist line on team games. Celtic was formed in 1887, initially to raise money for Catholic charities, only four years after the Gaelic Athletic Association put 'British games' under its ban.[30] Within less than a dozen years the professional ethos had triumphed, among Catholic and Protestant alike, and the Scottish footballer had become an export article. Quite why this should be so is not immediately apparent — especially as the laws of supply and demand did not apply to the players, who remained badly paid until the 1950s. But on a local level, amateur teams proliferated. Wishaw (population 8,953 in 1881, 10,385 in 1891) had six teams in the 1880s, twelve in the 1890s. One suspects that the broad streets and back courts of Glasgow tenement areas, the level waste ground around shipyards and engineering works, all played a greater part, before World War I, than public parks or school pitches. Soon (with the Borders, or course, excepted) having a football team was as important to the *amour-propre* of a middle-sized industrial town as having electric light or trams.

It is perhaps possible to see a cultural disjunction between mid- and late-Victorian society. The weekly press, whose rise has been covered by Willie Donaldson, was a powerful amalgam of radical 'improvement' and populism. But by the 1880s, when football, *inter alia*, had brought about the rise of the evening papers, there was a growing division between the religious, the radical and the populist. With a more secular, socially-oriented politics exemplified in the socialist movement, the churches became more institutionalised (even if more sympathetic to social reform) and the popular press tended more to entertainment and escapism.

Supporting football was a function of increased leisure (the Saturday half-holiday), rising real wages and a railway network with the capacity to deal with the crowds involved. The excursion had already become an

accustomed part of working-class life in the 1850s, when thousands of
Scottish artisans were conveyed by train and steamer to the Crystal Palace,
and church and works outings began.[31] By the end of the century skilled
Glasgow workers could expect ten days off in the year at New Year and
the Fair, and although only the better-off could go away for the whole
holiday the excursion had become an efficient and controllable way of
recruiting the strength of the labour force.

The great peaks of excursion traffic could still, however, be fitted into
transport networks which existed to serve the middle and upper classes.
These took the shape of tourists, braving the weather to experience the
land of Scott, to play golf or undergo a cure in a German-style Hydro (a
seemingly perfect method of turning the rigours of the Scottish climate to
advantage) or (if better off) to yacht, or to shoot grouse or deer. The royal
family's discovery of the Highlands in the 1840s and the construction of
Balmoral Castle did not start the trend, but powerfully accelerated it.
The construction of baronial castles and shooting lodges went on apace,
and in fact accelerated when the agricultural depression after 1873 put
an end to the construction of large country houses in England.[32]

The same depression proved a long death-agony for those crofters
who had survived outside the districts covered by the Land Act of
1886, and rationalisation on other farms — transferring production
from arable to pasture — accelerated the drift from the land. The
Highland population fell by 11 per cent between 1841 and 1901, and
while that of the North-East remained static, there was a significant
shift from landward areas to fishing ports or small industrial towns. 'A
giant entered our native place in the night' wrote J. M. Barrie about
what happened to Kirriemuir in the 1870s, when hand-loom weaving
suddenly gave way before steam-powered linen factories.[33] In a much
more brutal way John MacDougal Hay's *Gillespie* (1914) registered the
impact of commercialisation on the Argyllshire fishing industry. By 1900
there were few areas of rural Scotland which were not directly touched
by the revolution wrought by capitalism, in textiles, cash-crop farming,
fishing or tourism. The irony was that Scottish writers, trying to make
sense of, or cope with what was happening, could only grasp for the
images the tourist and entertainment industries offered them.

V

The overwhelming of Scotland by the stereotypes of the Kailyard was
not the result of intellectual incompetence or abdication. The Scottish
fin de siècle intelligentsia was high-powered enough to include Geddes

and Robertson, William Archer, who translated Ibsen, and Thomas Common, who translated Nietzsche, R. B. Cunninghame-Graham, John Davidson and George Douglas Brown. Even those figures who invite being pigeon-holed as the 'Anglo-Scottish men of letters', like Andrew Lang or John Buchan, grow in stature when their work is examined in depth and, with their anthropological concerns, become remarkably 'modern'.[34]

Yet, even when this is done, a disjunction — and a continuing one — remains. Andrew MacPherson has treated it suggestively in his essay 'An Angle on the Geist' when, taking as his subject the ideology of Scottish secondary education, he argues that it has always been posited on the model of the local high school of a smallish Scottish burgh — Kelso, Forfar, Ardrishaig — something which functions fine in the context of its limited *polis*, but is difficult if not impossible to modify in such a way that it can be made to fit the problems of the metropolis of the West.[35]

At the same time, as mentioned at the beginning of this chapter, the ethos of the metropolis was itself injected neat into the bloodstream of Scottish politics in such a way that it discounted the complexities of urban life which were not derived from industrial economics. The plaided Kailyarder co-exists with the rivet-chewing Clydesider, and the ordinary, real Scotsman or more particularly Scotswoman, existing in some built-up-but-not-urban subtopia closer to the phantasmagoria of Alasdair Gray's 'Unthank' than to either myth, derives no benefit from either.

Going on from this, it is possible to see various forces in operation in the 1880s and 1890s which 'fix' the ethos of small-town Scotland with peculiarly indelible results. A paradigm for them can be derived from Germany, where industrial development irrupted in rural areas in the 1870s and 1880s, promising German conservatives the disruptions they had been reading about in Marx's *Kapital*. One means of containing this was state power, and along with the army and the school went Bismarck's system of social security, and agricultural tariffs which preserved the small farms of the peasantry. But added to this, and formally independent of it, was a great revival of peasant clothes and customs and festivals, something which started, not in the most traditional areas, but where industrialisation was making most impact.

Thus, the village of Betzingen, near the cotton-textile centre of Reutlingen, with most of its workers in the mills, became famous in the 1870s for its church parades, with the locals in their *Tracht* (or ceremonial dress); the Catholic Black Forest towns held their *Fasnets* (pre-Lenten Carnivals) on an even greater scale when clock production moved from farm to factory; the Bavarian *Trachtenverein* was set up in 1881 under the patronage of King Ludwig II, only five years after the opening of the Brenner Railway made Munich into one of Europe's major transport interchanges.

All of this amounts to what our colleague, Carola Ehrlich, has called 'synthetic conservatism', the creation of a controllable, and thus partly invented past.[36] This is not, pure and simple, a function of industrialisation, though it needs it, as menace *and* enabler. Other factors are required as well.

Let us conclude with two Scottish examples. The economy of the Shetland Isles was deeply penetrated by capitalist organisation as the nineteenth century progressed, in two main respects: male Shetlanders served in great numbers in the merchant navy, and Shetland was an important station in the annual herring fishing — a highly-capitalised but seasonal enterprise. But both activities had to coexist with the demands of subsistence agriculture in and fishing off bleak treeless islands. By the 1880s the Shetlanders had created a compromise which worked, but required a sophisticated balance. The menfolk served with the merchant service in the winter, while their wives worked in the croft-houses on their knitting; in March was the 'voar' or seed-time; between May and August the peats were cut, but the men could also fish with the herring fleet, and between August and October was the 'hairst' or harvest. The men were therefore needed to plough in February–March, intermittently during the summer, and again in the autumn. The worry was that this delicate structure would not survive, particularly as Shetland seamen could be attracted into the service of the Norwegian merchant marine, already the fourth largest in the world.

So, in the 1880s a somewhat uncouth but genuinely Norse 'yule' custom of rolling blazing tar barrels through the streets of Lerwick was pushed back towards the end of January and reorganised as the Viking ceremonial of 'Up Helly Aa!' in which a wooden longboat was towed through the streets by three hundred torch-bearing Vikings, and then burnt, after which there was house visiting and dancing until the dawn.[37] 'Up Helly Aa!' became, very rapidly, the pivotal date of Shetland life. Not only did it summon the sailor home from the sea *at the right time*, but it provided a peak of experience for the Shetland crofters in the depths of a dark northern winter, and appealed to exiled islanders in Britain and throughout the world.

'Up Helly Aa!' was not unique: the 1880s also saw revivals among the Border Common Ridings and the Highland Games, although the energetic local democracy of the industrial towns of Hawick, Langholm and Selkirk was somewhat different from the mix of Old Etonian chieftains, tourists and Tillicoultry tartans of the latter.

A second example can be dated from 1885 when Lord Rosebery unveiled a monument to Robert Burns on the Embankment in London, after which he was approached by three men, Colin Rae Brown, Provost MacKay of Kilmarnock, and Captain David Sneddon. The result was the foundation of the Burns Federation. Even in the 1850s Burns had acquired an unparalleled presence in Scotland. On 1 December 1858 the *North Briton* anticipated Burns's centenary:

> It is the people alone who can truly keep the birthday of Robert Burns, for they best of all understand him and claim him as one of themselves. Do not then, ye working-men of Edinburgh, give him up to the higher classes of the city.

It could not have been imagined that, from the eight clubs affiliated in 1885, there would be 24 in 1886, 200 in 1911, and 316 by the 1950s. It was, in 1911, the Burns Federation which set in motion the process which organised the Scottish Exhibition in Kelvingrove Park, and as a result secured the Chair of Scottish History at Glasgow University.

Firms created similar ceremonials to foster solidarity — sometimes on a vast scale, like the great excursions from the Springburn railway works. But the structure of any firm was too closely related to the economy to create any real loyalty. Last year's model worker could be this year's choice for redundancy. The local or national appeal was more convincing. In 1914 all these loyalties were to be called on to sustain the war effort; six years later they would be as exhausted as the Scottish economy itself.

NOTES

1. A. T. Cluness, *The Shetland Isles* (1951), p. 168, and see James Littlejohn, *Westrigg: the Sociology of a Cheviot Parish* (1963), p. 72.

2. Elizabeth S. Haldane, *The Scotland of our Fathers* (Glasgow, 1933), pp. 59–60; for the influence of this on the 'Kailyard' literature of the time, see C. Harvie, 'Drumtochty Revisited' in *The Scottish Review*, No. 27, August 1982, pp. 4–10.

3. J. D. Young, *The Rousing of the Scottish Working Class*, (1979), p. 184.

4. William Power, *Should Auld Acquaintance*, (1937), p. 219.

5. See Nancy Crathorne, *Tennant's Stalk*, (1973).

6. J. M. Robertson, *The Perversion of Scotland* (1886), pp. 215.

7. Helen Meller, 'Patrick Geddes: an Analysis of his Theory of Civics, 1880–1904', in *Victorian Studies*, March 1973, p. 298.

8. Patrick Geddes, *City Development* (1904), p. 130; and see T. Wright, *The Religion of Humanity* (Cambridge, 1986), pp. 260–8.

9. I. S. Wood, 'Scottish Labour in the 1920s' in Ian Donnachie, Christopher Harvie and I. S. Wood (eds.), *Forward: the History of Labour in Scotland, 1888–1988* (Edinburgh, 1989), Chapter 2.

10. W. M. Walker, 'Irish Immigrants in Scotland: their Priests, Politics and Community Life' in *The Historical Journal*, XV, 4 (1972), 651.

11. William Donaldson, *Popular Literature in Victorian Scotland: Language Fiction and the Press* (Aberdeen, 1986).

12. C. Brown, *The Social History of Religion in Scotland Since 1730* (1987).

13. See, *inter alia*, Michael Fry, *Patronage and Principle: a Political History of Modern Scotland* (Aberdeen, 1987), pp. 125–6.

14. Bernard Aspinwall, *Portable Utopia: Glasgow and the United States, 1820–1920* (Aberdeen, 1983).

15. Iain Hutchison, *A Political History of Scotland, 1832–1924* (Edinburgh, 1986), pp. 232ff, 245ff.

16. Harry McShane and Anne Smith, *No Mean Fighter*; Andrew Purves, 'A Shepherd Remembers' in the *Scottish Labour History Society Journal (1981)*, pp. 26, 28; James Littlejohn, *Westrigg: the Sociology of a Cheviot Parish* (1963), p. 106; See John Thomas, *The Springburn Story* (Newton Abbott, 1966); Ian Carter, *Farm Life in North-East Scotland: The Poor Man's Country* (Edinburgh, 1979), p. 164.

17. Lady Frances Balfour, *The Life of Lord Balfour of Burleigh*, (Edinburgh, 1918), Appendix 1.

18. Littlejohn, *Westrigg*, p. 194.

19. See above, Chapter 10.

20. Hugh Miller, *First Impressions of England*, (Edinburgh, 1847), pp. 11, 45–47.

21. Callum Brown, *The Social History of Religion*, p. 154; Callum Brown, 'Evangelical Dominance of Leisure', paper given at a conference at Strathclyde University, May 1987.

22. William Knox, *Scottish Labour Leaders, 1919–1939* (Edinburgh, 1983), pp. 26–34; Robert Duncan, 'Eviction, Riot and Resistance: Motherwell and the Scottish Railway Strike, December 1890–January 1891' in *Scottish Labour History Review*, No. 1, Autumn–Winter 1987, pp. 10–12.

23. I. S. Wood, 'Drink, Temperance and the Labour Movement' in *Scottish Labour History Journal*, No. 5, March 1972, p. 30; E. B. Ramsay, *Reminiscences of National Life and Character* (Edinburgh, 1858), Chapter 5; See R. Q. Gray, *The Labour Aristocracy in Victorian Edinburgh* (Oxford, 1976), and W. Knox, *Scottish Labour Leaders, 1919–1939* (Edinburgh, 1983); see above chapters.

24. J. V. Smith, 'Manners, Morals and Mentalities' in W. Humes and A.

Patterson (eds.), *Scottish Culture and Scottish Education* (Edinburgh, 1983), pp. 25–54.

25. See T. Orr, *Historic and Descriptive Sketches of the Joint Burgh of Motherwell and Wishaw*, (Hamilton Advertiser, 1925); and see Robert Duncan, *Wishaw: Life and Labour in a Lanarkshire Industrial Community, 1790–1914*, (Motherwell, 1986), pp. 132ff.

26. *Op.cit.*, Volume V, pp. 74–5.

27. Charity Organisation Society Survey. Edinburgh 1904, quoted in R. Q. Gray, 'Styles of Life: the "Labour Aristocracy" and Class Relations in Later Nineteenth Century Edinburgh' in *International Review of Social History*, Vol. XVIII (1973), 441.

28. D. T. Holmes, *Literary Tours in Scotland* (Paisley, 1909).

29. H. Cunningham, *Leisure and the Industrial Revolution* (1980).

30. Tom Gallagher, *Glasgow: the Uneasy Peace* (Manchester University Press, 1987), pp. 26, 45.

31. See Arthur Rae, 'Visitors to the Great Exhibition', unpublished M Phil thesis, the Open University.

32. See Mark Girouard, *The Victorian Country House*, (Yale, 1979), p. 9.

33. J. M. Barrie, *Margaret Ogilvie*, (1896), p. 169.

34. See, for example, the present writer's 'Second Thoughts of a Scotsman on the Make: Nationalism and Myth in John Buchan', in H. Drescher, (ed.), *Literature and Nationalism in Twentieth Century Scotland* (Frankfurt, 1989).

35. Andrew MacPherson, *art.cit.*, in Humes and Patterson, *op.cit.*, pp. 216–43.

36. Carola Ehrlich, *The Dialectable Duchy: Regionalism in the Novels of Sir Arthur Thomas Quiller-Couch*, unpublished MA thesis, University of Tübingen, 1988.

37. Hance D. Smith, *Shetland Life and Trade* (Edinburgh, 1984), p. 3; Cluness, *op.cit.*, p. 17?

Index